For my father,
Chaim Dym.
Holocaust survivor,
his spirit and spirituality,
his humility and humanity
have guided and inspired me
my entire life.

The Complete Practitioner's Guide to the Bond Market

STEVEN I. DYM

New York   Chicago   San Francisco   Lisbon
London   Madrid   Mexico City   Milan   New Delhi
San Juan   Seoul   Singapore   Sydney   Toronto

1 2 3 4 5 6 7 8 9 0   WFR/WFR   0 1 0 9

ISBN: 9781265913113
MHID: 1265913110

This publication is designed to provide accurate and authoritative information in regard to the subject matter covered. It is sold with the understanding that the publisher is not engaged in rendering legal, accounting, or other professional service. If legal advice or other expert assistance is required, the services of a competent professional person should be sought.

—*From a Declaration of Principles Jointly Adopted*
by a Committee of the American Bar Association
and a Committee of Publishers and Associations

McGraw-Hill books are available at special quantity discounts to use as premiums and sales promotions, or for use in corporate training programs. To contact a representative, please visit the Contact Us pages at www.mhprofessional.com.

CONTENTS

INTRODUCTION

Over the past 20 years I have taught various aspects of the fixed-income markets to well over 10,000 market professionals. My courses can run for weeks, targeting audiences who need broad coverage, beginning with fundamental time value of money concepts and going all the way to incorporating complex derivatives in portfolio management. Other participants require specialized topics, such as callable bonds or interest-rate swaps, and these sessions can last for a day or two. Whatever the structure, my courses were taught in an intuitive, yet rigorous, manner and appealed to those looking to really understand the material, not simply record or memorize it. Invariably, after attending these sessions, participants have asked why I have not produced a book. After many years, I finally acceded, and this is the result.

My purpose in writing this book is to explain how the market works, what the instruments are and how professionals use them. I will also introduce you to much of the jargon of the fixed-income markets. My success in teaching over more than two decades lies, I am told, in my ability to explain esoteric ideas in common, everyday language, without sacrificing correctness. If you like an intuitive approach, this book is for you.

Fixed income does not need to be a dry subject. Stocks may present the allure of a dynamic market, with the potential for rapid wealth creation (and destruction), whereas bonds suggest to most people the unexciting prospect of just earning coupons while worrying about default. Not true. Fixed-income securities are more varied than equities, and they can be quite volatile, thereby presenting the opportunity for significant short-term gains yet at the same time providing a platform for long-term returns, and they allow for a variety of ways to go about investing and trading.

How does this book differ from all other bond books? First, as I mention above, it presents both the basic and the advanced concepts in an intuitive manner, without sacrificing rigor. I want you to understand *why* the market works the way it does, not just accept what you are told about it. Second, I'm not an academic *observer* of the bond market. I'm an insider, a participant in the market. I've been a bond dealer, institutional portfolio manager, and trader (a.k.a. speculator). So this book tells you what the market is really about, not what someone *believes* the market is about. It explains how professional investors and traders actually apply the concepts. I don't present concepts and ask you to apply them. I show you exactly how to do it.

I've included chapters (5 and 6) on the macroeconomy.[1] I believe you won't find this in typical fixed-income books, finance textbooks, or most other books on the capital markets. That's a shame. You can't get a good grasp of the bond market without a decent understanding of the dynamics of the economy. It won't work, as any professional will tell you. My purpose is not to describe the state of the economy, of course—it will be old news and irrelevant by the time you read it. Rather, I'll explain, in a very practical way, what makes the macroeconomy tick. You'll learn cause and effect. You'll understand why a particular event will lead, say, to greater economic activity, and hence to a reaction by the central bank. Then you'll see the effects ripple through the financial markets and affect securities prices. You'll gain insight into the feedback between financial market dynamics and the "real" economy. After you read it a couple of times (still *much* better than reading an economics textbook), you will be able to, on your own, work through the implications of macroeconomic changes and of disturbances to the various sectors of the fixed-income market.

For similar reasons, I've provided a chapter (19) on foreign exchange (FX). Bond investing today is international in scope. Here, as well, I explain the basic economics of FX—and some of the really complex ideas—in a very intuitive way. Only after you appreciate what makes currency exchange rates move can you start to think about incorporating foreign bonds into fixed-income portfolios. You'll not only learn the *how* of FX, but you'll learn the *why*, too. This will give you the basis for understanding the interactions between the forces driving the domestic economy and those affecting international trade and, hence, the country's currency. And once you reach that point, you can take the next step and consider emerging foreign markets, with the special risks they entail, so there is a chapter (20) on emerging market debt as well. Here, too, I give you the economics behind the market so that you'll understand why these economies differ from those of the industrialized countries, and see how—and if—they belong in a fixed income portfolio.[2]

There is a chapter (21) on bond dealers—what they do and how they do it. Most fixed-income books treat this subject cursorily, if they treat it at all. But as an investor, you need to know what's driving the people on the other side of the trade. You also need to know the risk you're taking in trading with them. Further, many of the new products in the market originate from dealers, not their customers. It's all covered here.[3] I teach you about repurchase agreements (repos) in Chapter 22. Dealers, hedge funds, investors—they're all involved with this instrument. Repos are not simply a financing arrangement; the modern bond market rests on repos. I have looked far and wide for a correct treatment of the repo market as it applies to investors. This fruitless search convinced me that I need to fill the gap.

There is also quite a bit on swaps. Interest-rate swaps have become an essential tool for participants in the fixed-income markets. A professional with only a cursory knowledge of swaps must relinquish the title. The swaps chapters (17 and 18) here will "make you whole," to use the language of traders. They explain not only how swaps work—mechanically as well as intuitively—but also how they are actually used in the modern marketplace.

Finally, there is a major chapter (24) on hedge funds. You will find worked-through examples of exactly what these important participants do in the bond market.

A note about notes: When it comes to bonds, technical details abound. I have tried in this book to explain the bond market without resorting to technical or mathematical sophistication. But some are unavoidable. As much as I could, I've relegated them to notes in a section at the end of this book. You should definitely read them. You'll appreciate them, although perhaps not on your first go-round.

PART I

FUNDAMENTAL PRINCIPLES OF BOND STRUCTURE, PRICING, AND INVESTING

1

WHAT IS A BOND?

What is a bond? Let's ask this question another way: what is a bond *not*? A bond is not a stock. Stocks represent ownership in a company. You buy a share of stock and you become an insider. You're entitled to your share of the company's profits (and headaches). If the company makes no profit or collapses, you're not entitled to anything. If the company does really well, so will you.

If you buy the same company's bonds, on the other hand, you're *lending* money to the company. You're an outsider. Indeed, you're not so different from, say, the supplier of leather to a shoe manufacturer. The leather supplier is owed money for the goods delivered to the manufacturer. If the manufacturer doesn't pay, the supplier sues. No money to pay (and no assets to grab in lieu of payment), sorry. It's the same with the bond purchaser. You give the borrower money, and she gives you an IOU, the bond. The IOU represents a promise to pay you moneys in various forms, usually interest plus principal. Should the company do really well, all you get is your interest. If it can't pay the interest (or principal when due), you negotiate, sue, or join the queue in bankruptcy court.

Government Bonds

Consider the bond displayed in the following listing of the characteristics of a security. You give the U.S. Treasury $100 (the price of the bond), and it gives you a piece of paper with its promise on it. It promises to pay $4 every year (we get to the actual frequency later), and $100 at the end of five years. Where does the Treasury get the money to pay you? From tax revenues, hopefully, or by issuing another bond when the money is due.

> Issuer: U.S. Treasury
> Issue: Bond
> Coupon: 4%
> Maturity: 5 years
> Price: $100

Before we think about what a bond is worth and what to do with it, we need to know what it does. You can't think about what anything is worth until you understand what it does. One source of the problems in the markets recently is that investors analyze price, and their vision of future price changes, without their fully understanding what it is they're buying.

Let's stick with Treasury bonds for now. The two most important parameters describing what a bond does are *how much* it pays and *when* it promises to pay it—in bond language: the *coupon* and *maturity*. This particular bond pays 4% for five years. After five years the bond matures, at which time it repays the principal, also known as the bond's "face value." There are other parameters, all important, but secondary to these two. They are:

1. *Frequency.* Does a 4% coupon mean that you receive $4 in the mail (or to your bank account) for every $100 bond you buy? Yes, sort of. If the coupon is designated as "annual," then you'll receive the $4 every yearly anniversary of the issue date. Most U.S. bonds, though, pay *semi*annually. So a 4% coupon really pays 2% of the principal every six months. Sometimes the frequency (also known as *periodicity*) is quarterly, or even monthly (think of mortgages or car loans). In any case, the stated percentage coupon refers to how much you'll get over the *full* year.
2. *Callability.* Some bonds are "callable." This feature gives the borrower the right (but not the obligation) to pay you back your loan prior to the stated maturity. We see in a later chapter (13) that this is a valuable right, valuable enough to require

the borrower to pay the lender a higher interest rate than would have been the case without this feature.

3. *Amortization.* U.S. Treasury bonds pay back all their principal on the maturity date. Some corporate bonds, and almost all home mortgages, require some principal to be paid prior to maturity. The amounts and dates for early repayments are known as the "amortization schedule."

4. *Day counts.* What happens when a coupon date occurs on a weekend or holiday? Interest is not paid until the next business day. But does the lender receive extra interest for those days? In some cases yes, in others (such as U.S. Treasuries) no. And what about the fact that the year has an odd number of days, not divisible by two? Each half of the year has different days from the other half. And months have 30 or 31 (and 28 or 29) days. What happens to interest payments—are they adjusted for these "day effects?" Sometimes yes, sometimes no. These are known as day-count conventions and, unfortunately, they are not uniform.[1]

Because these parameters are less important, market participants will mention just the first two when referring to a Treasury bond. Hence, our bond will be known as a 4% ten-year.[2] Alternatively, professionals may substitute the actual calendar maturity in their description; for example, the 4% of May 2014.

If the bond is not a U.S. Treasury issue, such as an agency or corporate bond (both are explained later), another important parameter is added to the bond's description—the name of the issuer; for example, FNMA (Fannie Mae)5% of 2011 or Dupont Corp 6% of 2018.

Why do governments issue bonds? More generally, why do governments need to borrow? Very simple. They spend more than they earn—a situation described as a deficit.[3] Companies borrow lots of money. Why, then, does corporate debt not have the same stigma as government debt? If a company needs to borrow because the cost of producing its product exceeds the price it receives for selling it, potential lenders would be unwilling to lend (unless it's a start-up that needs to build brand recognition before it can raise prices to an equilibrium level). Why should they? If the company can't produce enough income now to pay the costs of production, how will it have anything left to pay interest on the debt? If, however, the purpose of borrowing is to, say, purchase new equipment in order to expand its production capabilities, then its internal growth should produce income to pay for the debt incurred, and leave a profit for the firm's owners.

The analogy to governments is clear. Governments that borrow to fund, say, infrastructure development, such as roads and sewers, or to build educational institutions look to enhance macroeconomic growth. This growth generates additional tax revenue which is then used to service the debt incurred. On the other hand, governments that borrow because their spending on current consumption exceeds their income have a harder time soliciting funds from lenders, or they pay a higher interest rate.

Be aware that the U.S. Treasury (as well as the U.K. Treasury, Dutch Treasury, etc.) issues bonds even during years the budget is in surplus! Why? Because every year a portion of existing debt matures.[4] Even if the budget were in surplus, the government would need to borrow simply to pay off the principal on maturing debt (unless the surplus is large enough to pay off the maturing debt). Therefore, Treasury bond issuance equals the sum of the period's deficit and that portion of existing bonds that needs to be refinanced.

Benchmarks

"Benchmarks" are found in many markets. Cars and restaurants are good examples. They are what consumers or so-called experts deem to be "best in their class," a standard against which others are measured. Government bonds serve as the benchmarks for fixed-income securities. A five-year government note is the benchmark for all bonds in the five-year maturity area, and a thirty-year government bond serves as the benchmark for the longest maturity bonds. What gives government bonds their benchmark status—what makes them the "best"? Two characteristics, or qualities:

1. *Risk.* Government bonds are not "risk-free." Not by any means. They present a host of risks to investors, just as other bonds do, as we'll see in the following chapters. But they lack one risk that other bonds contain—the risk of default (subject to the

caveats discussed below).[5] Government bonds, therefore, are less risky than all others and in this sense are best in their class.

2. *Liquidity.* Liquidity is not easy to define. A useful way to *describe* the liquidity (as opposed to define it) of a security is by its "bid-ask spread."[6] This is essentially the amount a dealered charges for buying and selling a security. Government bonds tend to have the narrowest bid-ask spreads in their maturity class, hence are the most liquid.

Because government bonds are the least risky and most liquid compared to other fixed-income instruments of similar maturity, they have become the benchmarks for market participants.

What role does a benchmark perform in the bond market? Most importantly, for investors, it is as a quotation device. For example, a 5.6% yield for a ten-year corporate issue would be described as "125 basis points over." This means that, with the benchmark ten-year government bond yielding 4.25%, the corporate bond has a yield in the market of 1.25% (100 basis points = 1%) above the benchmark, or 5.5%. The 125 basis points are also known as the corporate's "spread."

Most governments of large economies issue bonds according to a regular cycle. The U.S. Treasury, for example, has issued three-year, five-year, and ten-year notes quarterly (sometimes more often when funding an outsized deficit is necessary) and thirty-year bonds (known as the "long bond") semiannually. These are more liquid than, say, seven-year notes, a note which has not been issued by the Treasury for quite some time. Liquidity also varies within each maturity sector. For example, there are a number of Treasury bonds with ten-year or near-ten year maturities, since every bond with an original maturity longer than ten years ultimately becomes a "ten-year" bond. Their yields will be close, but rarely equal, to each other. Only one of them is the benchmark for its class. Which one? The one most recently issued by the government. It is typically the most actively traded (greatest trading volume over a given period) among the group; hence it will have the narrowest bid-offer spread. The other bonds in that maturity class may be quoted as a spread (positive or negative) to the benchmark.

Can Government Bonds Default?

Is it possible for government bonds to default? For industrialized countries such as the United States, the answer is highly unlikely, but theoretically possible. Like any other entity, if the central government's revenue is less than its expenses—and it has reached its debt capacity—it will not be able to service existing debt or refinance. But wait a second! Governments are unlike "any other entity." A company, for example, whose earnings are too low to meet its obligations cannot force customers to buy its product. But the government is different. Can't it simply increase taxes in order to raise revenue and pay its debt obligations, thereby avoiding default? Well, no, at least not without constraint, for a couple of reasons. Governments have paying "customers," too. They're called taxpayers, who are represented by members of Congress, who are paid to watch over citizens' pocketbooks. The bigger the piece of that pocketbook the government wants to take, the less likely it is that Congress will approve. Furthermore, the government is aware that raising taxes can be self-defeating. As you will see in the macroeconomics chapter (5), an increase in taxes usually leads to a decrease in consumer spending. This reduces economic activity, which results in lower tax revenue!

The ability of a central government to draw on taxes in order to service its debt depends on the size of the debt, hence its servicing cost, relative to the overall size of the economy, the tax "base." The latter is measured by gross domestic product or GDP (see Chapter 5). Hence, the appropriate measure of government bond default risk is the ratio of government debt to the country's GDP. This ratio is relevant both to mature, industrialized economies, where the possibility of government bond default is usually relegated to the back of investors' minds, and to developing countries, where the risk of government default is arguably a daily phenomenon. It's such an important variable that it's worth a closer look.

The level of outstanding government debt represents the sum of all past government budget deficits (less surpluses). Separate the annual deficit into two components—interest on outstanding debt and the current budget net of interest payments. A little algebra shows that the *change* in the debt-to-GDP ratio equals[7] the current budget deficit as a percentage of GDP, plus the difference between the interest rate the government pays on its bonds and the economy's growth rate.

Now we can understand what makes the debt-to-GDP ratio expand, thus raising questions about the government's ability to service its debt. A budget deficit, of course, adds to the federal debt—the first component above. But even if taxes totally offset expenditures, the ratio will get larger if the economy grows at a slower pace than the interest rate on existing debt—the second component! Furthermore, as the ratio increases, investors become more nervous about the government's finances, which forces an increase in the interest rate, which, in turn, exacerbates the ratio and raises the rate once again![8] Another way to say this is, a federal budget deficit requires the economy to grow at a pace significantly in excess of the interest rate on government debt in order to make a dent in the debt-to-GDP ratio. Otherwise, it just gets worse.

Let's end the section this way. During "normal" times—that is, when the macroeconomy is not in deep recession, government spending not terribly high, and tax revenue not abysmally low—government debt (of major industrialized economies) is viewed by market participants as being default risk-free. Then, the yield on Treasury bonds represents pure "time value of money" considerations, as we view it in this and later chapters. When the debt-to-GDP ratio gets out of hand, Treasury yields equal the risk-fee rate plus a premium for possible default, with the latter rising as a fraction of the total yield according to the size of the ratio.

Agencies

A large and important sector of the bond market is known as "agencies." The U.S. government does not get directly involved much in business (certainly not to the extent that European governments do),[9] but it has decided to "support" certain areas of economic activity. It does this by creating agencies (known also as government-sponsored enterprises or GSEs). These entities (some are corporations; others are simply "entities," because no one knows exactly what their legal structures are) lend funds to the particular sector of the economy they are mandated to support. They get the money to lend by issuing debt securities, known as agency debentures,[10] to investors. The better known agencies are listed below.

Major U.S. Government (Debt-Issuing) Agencies

Farm Credit Bureau
Federal Home Loan Bank Board
Federal Home Loan Mortgage Corporation
Federal National Mortgage Association

Student Loan Marketing Association
Tennessee Valley Authority

These entities are not really *part* of the government; they're related to the government, each in a different, sometimes quite ambiguous way.[11] The Federal National Mortgage Association (FNMA, known as "Fannie Mae") is involved in the mortgage market as both a lender and a guarantor, depending on the program. The Federal Home Loan Mortgage Corporation (FHLMC, or "Freddie Mac") performs similar functions and used to be part of the Federal Home Loan Bank (FHLB) system. FHLB, in turn, oversees savings institutions, and assists them by offering "advances." The Farm Credit Bureau (FCB) is obviously connected to the agriculture sector, providing indirect financing to farmers in a host of ways. The Student Loan Marketing Association (SLMA, or "Sallie Mae") was created to support student lending, and does so by purchasing student loans from originators. The Tennessee Valley Authority (TVA) assists electric utility cooperatives in the Tennessee Valley. Because of their ties to the government, the risk of default by these agencies is believed by investors to be less than that of a U.S. corporation. Hence, their credit spreads tend to be very narrow, certainly less than that of typical corporate bonds with similar parameters.

Corporate Bonds

Corporations borrow lots of money. Most approach banks, which offer them a credit line that can be accessed when they need funds. Large firms can raise long-term funds by issuing bonds. The structure of corporate bonds is similar to that of Treasuries, as presented above, with some special features, described at length in Chapter 9. Because the payments on the bonds are not assured—companies can default—investors demand a higher rate on these bonds than on those issued by the government. The greater the chance of default, and the less investors expect to recover in case of default, the higher the yield. The excess of the yield on a corporate bond over a Treasury bond of similar maturity is known as the "credit spread." Because the fundamental difference between a corporate bond and a government bond is the default risk of the former and this risk results in a yield spread, corporate bonds are usually quoted in the marketplace in terms of their spreads, rather than their outright yields. Asking a dealer, "Hey, where is that new five-year Dupont bond?" will elicit a response such as, "It's at 125," which means its yield is 1.25% above that of the similar Treasury bond, rather than simply 6.30%" (the Treasury bond yields 5.05%).

Companies with "low" risk of default are termed "high grade"; those with substantial risk are known as "high yield." We talk about corporate debt securities and are more precise about the characteristics which cause companies to be classified as "high" or "low" yield in Chapter 9.

Another large component of the bond market is asset-backed securities (ABS). These bonds often get grouped together with corporates because they are (typically) not issued by government entities and therefore present the risk of default. Briefly, ABSs are created in the following way. A legal entity is formed, which buys consumer or corporate loans from banks and/or purchases bonds in the open market. It gets the money to pay for these assets by issuing bonds in its own name. The entity, therefore, owns assets (loans and bonds, and sometimes derivatives) and issues liabilities (collateralized by the assets). This process is known a securitization, a topic we cover to some extent when we get to collateralized debt obligations (CDOs) in Chapter 23.

The Yield Curve

The *yield curve* is simply a chart, plotting bond yields against their remaining maturities at a point in time. See Figure 1.1. It shows that, on the day this "picture" of the bond market was taken, a borrower would have had to pay a 4% interest rate to get funds for one year. It would cost 5% per year to borrow for five years. The fact that the five-year yield exceeds the one-year yield produces an "upward-sloping curve" in the one year to five year region. Notice that the horizontal axis is not complete—not every year is shown. This is because, for some markets, it is common to present only those maturities that have actively traded (i.e., benchmark) securities.

Yield curves can have various shapes—sharply or softly upward sloping, downward sloping, flat (essentially no slope), or some more interesting shapes. The primary determinants of the curve's shape are the state of the economy and market participants' expectations thereof. The yield

FIGURE 1.1 Yield Curve

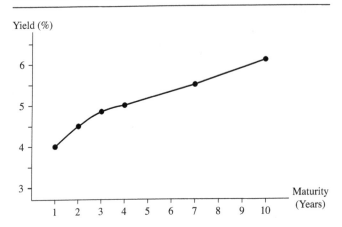

curve for government bonds can look very different from that of corporate bonds.[12] The U.S. yield curve will likely have a different shape from that of Japan. In short, yield curve shapes can vary dramatically; they are affected by the business cycle, they differ by type of bond, and they depend on the currency of the country in which the bonds are issued.

Why do we care about the yield curve? In a simple sense, it presents a quick picture of the state of the bond market at any time. Hence, it provides useful information. But there is a lot more than that. If we examine this information carefully, we'll be able to glean from it what market participants expect to happen to interest rates in the future! No kidding! We explore this in Chapter 8. Relatedly, the yield curve may even suggest investment strategies. We cover this in the chapters (9 and 10) on portfolio management.

A Note on Terminology

Bonds are often termed *fixed-income instruments*. It's pretty obvious why—their regular income in the form of coupons does not change (though the *price* of the bond can change). The terminology has become a bit outdated. A growing proportion of bonds contain coupons whose payments are not fixed. Instead, they "float," or adjust to prevailing market conditions. These are the so-called floating rate notes that we get to later in the book.

2

NONPLAIN VANILLA BONDS

In Chapter 1 we look at "plain vanilla" bonds—bonds with fixed coupons; their principal is paid only at maturity, and so on. We haven't analyzed them yet; we just presented them there. The analysis comes in later chapters. Let's get to know some more interesting bond structures first. These are not prevalent among government securities, but they're quite common among corporate and other nongovernment issuers.

Amortizing Bonds

If a bond is scheduled to pay all of its principal at maturity, it is known as a *bullet bond*.[1] Many bonds have a schedule of partial principal payments to be made prior to their final maturity.[2] Take a look at the bond in Table 2.1.

The bond pays coupons annually. If it were a bullet bond, each of the first nine rows would be the same: coupon of $5, zero principal paid, and remaining principal of $100 at the end of each year. In year 10, besides the $5 coupon, $100 of principal would be paid. Instead, this amortizer follows that pattern only for the first six years of its life, after which the scheduled amortization kicks in. At the end of year 7, $20 of its principal is paid together with the coupon.[3] This leaves $80 in principal outstanding throughout year 8, for which 5% must be paid to the lender, or $4. Another $20 in principal is paid at the end of year 8, further reducing the following year's coupon. In the final year, $40

TABLE 2.1 5% Coupon, 10-year Bond Amortization Schedule: 20% of Principal, Beginning in Year 7

Year	Coupon ($)	Principal ($)	Total Cash Flow ($)	Remaining Principal ($)
1	5	0	5	100
2	5	0	5	100
3	5	0	5	100
4	5	0	5	100
5	5	0	5	100
6	5	0	5	100
7	5	20	25	80
8	4	20	24	60
9	3	20	23	40
10	2	40	42	0

in principal must be paid, since there are no more years available for amortization. Why do companies create such bonds? One reason is that the asset they're purchasing with the funds raised by the bond sale may be expected to produce a revenue stream similar to the amortizing schedule of the bond. A second is that the interest rate paid on the amortizer could well be lower than that of the bullet bond. Since a growing fraction of the principal is repaid earlier, the investor is exposed to less default risk holding the amortizer. That is, should the company default any time after year 7, the potential loss is lower than a bullet bond because the amount subject to default has decreased. Less credit risk means a lower interest rate.

Zero Coupon Bonds

Does "zero coupon bond" sound like an oxymoron? If it has no coupon at all, why use the word "coupon" in its description? No good reason; that's just the way this bond is referred to. Zero coupon bonds pay no interest, only principal at maturity. As such, they are priced at a very deep discount to their face value. If you don't receive any coupons, how are you getting paid for lending money to the issuer? Your payment is in the excess of the principal above the price. Hence, the longer the maturity, the lower the price since you're giving up more coupons.

The U.S. Treasury doesn't issue any zero coupons.[4] Many investors find them attractive, though. We'll see in the chapter (12) on bond risk that, among bonds of the same maturity, those with zero coupons experience the greatest price sensitivity. A speculator anticipating a decline in market yields would want to purchase the bond with the greatest positive price reaction—the zero coupon. Investors who need to lock away assets for the long term—certain types of pension funds are a good example—look to zero coupon bonds as an ideal match to their needs, since their returns are locked in if the zero coupon bond is held to maturity.[5]

Now we have a problem. There are investors who are attracted to bonds with zero coupons, yet the U.S. Treasury shies away from issuing them.[6] Bond dealers solved this problem back in the early 1980s. They bought (and still do) Treasury bonds and "stripped" them! What? Yes, you read right. A dealer buys, say, a 20-year bond with a 6% coupon. The dealer has 41 claims on the U.S. Treasury—$3 every six months for the next 20 years, plus $100 in year 20. She sells each of these claims separately. Each one represents a promise by the U.S. Treasury to pay a fixed amount of money at one particular future date, with no payments until then. Isn't that a zero coupon bond? You bet it is. *Voilà!*

Callable Bonds

A bond is "callable" if the borrower has the right, written into the bond contract at issuance, to pay back the principal before the scheduled maturity date, thus "retire" the bond early. A callable bond is not an amortizing security; an amortizing security has a *required* schedule of early principal repayment. By contrast, calling the bond is a *privilege*; hence, it does not need to be exercised. Consider a ten-year bond with a 6% coupon. It is callable in five years. For the first five years the bond is said to have call "protection"—the issuer may not call it back. Once five years pass, the borrower has a choice: continue servicing the debt or pay it off.

Why would the borrower wish to pay off the bond if it's not due? Because he could borrow the principal for the final five years from a new investor and use that money to pay off the first lender. That only makes sense if the new borrowing rate—five years from now—is below 6%. Assume it's 5.5%. He ends up paying 6% over the first five years, 5.5% over the last five. That's much better than 6% for the entire ten years, which would be the case if the bond were not callable. If, instead, the five-year borrowing rate five years later is 6.5%, he'll just let the original bond run its course. In short, with the callable bond, the borrower will *at most* pay the coupon and may do better if interest rates decline over time. With a noncallable bond, no such option exists. All else the same, therefore, borrowers would prefer callable to noncallable bonds.

What about the investor's perspective? Think about the noncallable bond first. The investor is set to receive 6% for the ten years of the bond's life. If it's callable, she *might* get less. Why? Because, as we just saw, should interest rates drop, say to 5.5%, the borrower will pay back the principal in order to save on the coupon payments. What will she do with the principal received early? Invest in a new bond, right? But it pays only 5.5%, not the 6% she was used to. On the other hand, if rates rise above 6%, the bond won't be called, so she'll get her 6% for the full ten years. But she'd get that with the noncallable, too. So an investor will never do better with a callable bond than a noncallable bond, but might do worse.

Let's put these ideas together. Given a choice, *borrowers* would prefer that a fixed coupon bond be callable. *Investors* would prefer it to be noncallable. The market, therefore, will decide how much a borrower will have to pay an investor in order to induce her to accept the callable bond. The payment is in the form of a higher coupon than an otherwise similar noncallable bond. Hence, we conclude that callable bonds pay a higher interest rate than do noncallables. This excess is known as the call "spread" or call "risk premium," since it compensates the investor for accepting the risk of the bond possibly being called. The investor, of course, must determine whether the compensation is adequate. How does she think about it? She needs to consider the likelihood of interest rates in the future falling below the bond's coupon. The greater that likelihood and the earlier it might occur, the less attractive the callable versus the noncallable, and the greater the risk premium required.

Exercising the call option in order to pay off the existing bond and borrow at a lower interest rate is known as *refinancing*. This is not the only reason firms choose to pay off debt early. As we'll see in the chapter (9) on corporate bonds, borrowers typically make certain promises to lenders. These "covenants" are detailed in the bond "indenture" (a legal document describing, among many things, the relationship between the borrower and lender). For example, one covenant may be that the firm will not sell a particular asset, which bondholders feel is important to keep in the firm as security for their loan. Suppose the firm believes that an attractive investment opportunity exists, and it needs to sell that asset in order to take advantage of this new opportunity? The company would need to convince the bondholders to waive the covenant. This convincing may take the form of paying them a higher coupon rate. If the bond is callable, an alternative would be for the firm to exercise the call option, thereby ridding itself of the constraint imposed by the covenant, even though refinancing may require paying a higher coupon rate going forward.

Step-Up Coupon

Investment bankers (the people who help companies issue bonds[7]) have come up with a plethora of innovations in recent years. One fruitful area in which they have expressed their creativity is new bond structures for "risky" companies. These companies may be newly created or still young, with a novel product or service. Or they might be existing companies refashioned as the result of a merger, or even reorganized following a bankruptcy. What they all have in common is this: Because they are immature entities, lenders perceive their ability to pay their debts (usually rightly so) as more precarious than more mature firms. Hence, lenders demand a higher interest rate for the greater degree of default risk. At the same time, and for the same reason, these firms' earnings are relatively weak, as they need to spend a lot of money in order to get their businesses going, and revenues don't start kicking in until their product becomes accepted in the market. They can still afford to pay the high interest rates. Indeed, the high borrowing cost itself contributes to the firm's heightened default risk. What to do?

Step-up coupon bonds address this dilemma. Suppose, based on its risk factors, the company needs to pay investors a coupon of 8% for a ten-year bond. But it can't afford to pay 8%, at least not during its early years. Instead, it issues a bond with a more affordable 6% coupon-for, say, the first four years. Lenders are compensated for giving up the 2% by receiving a higher 10% coupon for the final six years of the bond's life. The coupon "steps up" from 6% to 10%, providing the company with breathing room during its crucial, formative years. What this bond structure has accomplished is that it allows the company to effectively push off a portion of its interest payment to a future date. This is an example of a "deferred interest" security).[8]

By the way, floating rate notes certainly qualify as "nonplain vanilla bonds." But they are so different—yet so common—that they get chapters (15 and 16) all their own.

3

BOND MATH—WITHOUT THE MATH

It's time to get some of the hard stuff under our belts. Truthfully, though, it's not so hard. People hear "math and they recoil. In fact, at the basic professional user level (as opposed to the "quants"), what market participants refer to as bond math is simply straightforward arithmetic.

Basic Bond Pricing

Let's work with a plain vanilla, 6% coupon bond. It pays $6 for every $100 in principal each year (annual frequency) until it matures in five years. This makes it a five-year bond. We'll assume for now that the bond presents no risk of default, such as a U.S. government bond.[1] That is, the borrower will definitely pay whatever it promises to. But this does not mean that the bond is riskless. No, no! Not by any stretch of the imagination. Pay close attention.

The government sells, or "issues," the bond at par. *Par* means that investors have paid the same price as the face value of the bond. On the bond's "face" it says $100, because that's the principal—the amount the government will return to the investor after five years. You lend the government $100, it promises to give you $6 every year (hence 6%) plus $100 at maturity. Par is short for "parity." Parity, in turn, suggests a sense of evenness, or equivalence, or fairness, if you like. If investors are paying par, this means that, given their perception of the state of the world (including their view of the future) and the savings at their disposal, they are satisfied to receive what the bond promises to pay. They want no less and demand no more than 6% for the money they're lending to the government at this point in time.

Consider the bond "dealers." You can think of these market participants as the storekeepers—the government makes the product and sells it to the stores, and investors go to the stores to make their purchases. Suppose dealers still have some of the bonds left. Very rarely do bonds get sold out immediately, just like dresses or bananas. Some time later, the government borrows again. But this time things have changed in the world, and investors now require 7% for lending to the government. So, the Treasury issues a new five-year bond with an interest rate of 7%, which makes *this* bond par. But the old bond with the 6% coupon is still around, and some of these bonds remain on dealers' shelves. The bond needs to get sold. Investors won't pay 100, or par, for that bond if they can get a new bond at 7% for the same number of years from the same government borrower! So the dealer has to reduce the price of the 6% bond that's still in inventory until it becomes equally attractive to investors as the 7% issue. We have our first crucial result:

> Because the coupon on a bond is fixed on its issuance date, a subsequent increase in market interest rates forces the bond's price to fall. Otherwise, it will not be competitive with new bonds that are carrying the higher rate.

How much must the price fall? There's actually a formula known as the *fundamental bond pricing equation.*

$$\text{Price} = \text{coupon/interest rate} + [(100 - \text{coupon/interest rate})/(1 + \text{interest rate})^{\text{maturity}}]$$

Let's first see what the formula tells us, and then explain the result intuitively.[2] Filling in the numbers with our five-year, 6% coupon bond whose interest rate must be 7% in order to be competitive, we simply calculate $6/.07 + [(\$100 - 6/.07)/(1.07)^5] = \$95.8998$. In other words, the formula says that a bond's price equals two components. The first part is the present value of all the bond's future coupons, assuming that the bond never matures. The second part could be positive or negative and corrects for the fact that the bond does, in fact, mature and pays $100 then.

Now for the intuition: The new price of the 6%, five-year bond is $95.90. Let me try to explain why this happened. If you pay $95.90, you'll receive $6 each year. First, you're getting $6 out of your investment of $95.90, not $100. That's better than 6% (in fact, it's 6.26%). But there's more to it than that. You're not getting your $95 "back" after five years. You're getting $100—an extra $4.10! These two returns—higher regular percentage income, plus extra money at the end—combine to produce what the market refers to as a "yield to maturity" of 7%.[3] Now the old bond is competitive with the new one. But in order to achieve that, it had to drop in price to below par. We call it a "discount" bond.

Over the five years, the bond pays 6/95.90 = 6.26% annually. This calculation is known as the "current yield." Whether or not you hold it for the full five years until maturity is irrelevant. Given its price, it returns 6.26% to the holder every year. You may sell it prior to its maturity for a price greater than or less than $95.90. It all depends on the yield in the market as of the date you sell which you don't know now. But if you hold it until maturity, you will definitely receive $100.

Now let's consider the reverse possibility: new five-year Treasury bonds come with a 5% coupon. Yours, of course, continues to pay its 6%. In this case it's *more* attractive to investors than the new bonds. Investors pay up for it. The price increases. How much? Until it, too, yields 5%. How's that? Its price rises above par, based on the formula, to $104.3295. It is now a "premium" bond. Thus, we can say:

When market yields decline, fixed coupon bonds rise in price because investors are attracted to the higher coupons compared to new bonds.

A purchaser will receive each year 6/104.33 = 5.75%—less than the 6% coupon. Further, that investor will not receive $104.33 at maturity, just $100. It is pulled *down* to par at maturity. The 5.75% current yield plus the loss of 4.33 points over the five years produces a yield to maturity of 5%, the same as the new five-year note.

There you have it. Higher yields in the market for newly issued bonds produce lower prices for existing bonds; lower yields in the market produce higher prices for existing bonds. The intuition should be clear. Since the coupon is fixed, the bond becomes more attractive, hence more expensive, when new bonds are sold with lower coupons. And it becomes less attractive, hence cheaper, when new bonds are sold with higher coupons.

If it's still not intuitive to you, think of dresses. Yes, dresses. When a dress is designed, thousands are produced of the same style. Not every dress is sold; a few remain on the shelf. The season changes. A new style is "in." The old dress is a bit out of style—but not by much, since it's only one season behind. How can it be sold? By reducing its price. By how much? Until the lower price provides adequate compensation to the buyer for the old style. In short, if you can't compete in style, you need to compete in price. Think of the bond's coupon as its style. Once the bond is issued, its coupon is fixed, just like the dress's style. Interest rates in the market go up. A new bond is issued with a coupon reflecting the now higher interest rates in the market, so that it is priced at par. The old bond is stuck with its original coupon. How can it be sold? Only if it is competitive with the new bond carrying the higher coupon—which requires a price below par. It can't compete in coupon, so it must compete in price.

What about the reverse? I guess you can think of a dress ahead of its style (for example, a designer dress), sold at a premium price. The same applies to the bond. If interest rates decline, the bond retains its original high coupon. It becomes very attractive relative to new bonds with now lower coupons. Its price rises until it is equally attractive (on a yield basis) with the new bonds.

Impact of Maturity on Price

You're now ready to move to the next level of bond math, that is, the crucial relationship between a bond's remaining time to maturity and its price.[4] We'll restrict ourselves, at least in this section, to nonamortizing, noncallable bonds. Table 3.1 shows the prices of the five-year, 6% bond at different yields (we're employing the fundamental bond formula of above). Note again the inverse relationship between the bond's yield—the returns that investors demand from the bond—and its price. The table introduces another bond, with the same coupon, but with a 10-year maturity. At a 6% yield, its price is par as well. Does this

TABLE 3.1 Prices of 6% Coupon Bonds

Yield to Maturity	Price of 5-Year Bond	Price of 10-Year Bond
5%	104.3294	107.7217
6%	100	100
7%	95.8998	92.9764

not conflict with the most basic tenet of finance—time value of money—that the further in the future money is to be paid, the lower the value today? Not at all. That is only true if the investor is not compensated for pushing the payments for those extra years into the future. Here, on the other hand, the investor is compensated—with a yearly coupon. And since the coupon equals the yield, the compensation is perfectly adequate. Adequate enough to keep the price at par regardless of how far into the future the bond matures.

What about at a 7% yield? Go back to the five-year bond for a moment. As we learned earlier, when the yield in the market rose to 7% its price had to decline in order to make it competitive with new five-year bonds paying a 7% coupon. Why? Because the 6% coupon was no longer attractive in an environment of 7% interest. The price of that bond had to be pushed down from $100 to approximately $95.90 because for five years the investor would be receiving 6% instead of 7%. Well, the ten-year option is even more unattractive when market yields are at 7%, because for the next *ten* years it will be paying a below-market coupon of 6%. How unattractive? Enough to push its price down to $92.98.

> *Longer maturity bonds experience greater price reactions to market interest-rate changes. This is because their fixed coupons will remain different from market rates for a longer period of time.*

At its new price of $92.98, the 10-year bond's current yield rises to 6.45% (6/92.9764), and the investor gains the difference between $92.9764 and the $100 paid at maturity over the 10 years. Together, these two sources of return produce a yield to maturity of 7%. Conversely, if yields in the market decline to 5%, the table shows that the bond's price jumps to approximately $107.72, much higher than the

$104.33 of the five-year note, since it will be paying an above-market coupon of 6% for ten years, rather than for five. At this high price, the current yield of 5.57% combines with a loss of $7.72 over ten years to produce a yield of 5% to maturity.

So, what have we observed? The negative relationship between yield changes and price reactions is more pronounced for the ten-year bond than for the five-year. In fact, we will allow ourselves this general result: The longer the maturity of a bond, the greater is its price reaction to changes in market yields. An increase in yield has a greater negative effect; a decrease in yield a greater positive effect. Some would rephrase the conclusion this way: the longer the maturity, the greater the risk![5]

Pull-to-Par Effect

Let's look at the numbers in Table 3.1 from another angle. Say you purchase the ten-year bond in a market situation in which the yield is 7%. The price you pay is $92.98. The bond's *current yield* equals 6/92.98, or 6.45%. Current yield represents the investor's earnings from the bond independent of any price change or, alternatively, assuming its price remains constant throughout the holding period. It is different from yield to maturity. Yield to maturity, as we've seen above, reflects *both* the bond's current income plus the pull-to-par effect on the investor's return. (When market participants use the word "yield," they mean yield to maturity.) Consider now a theoretical case: You hold the bond for five years, and the market doesn't change. What do we mean by "the market doesn't change"? The yield to maturity on the sale date is back where it was on the purchase date.[6] That is, only time has passed—the calendar has changed, but nothing else.

What's the bond's price? It's right there in the table—$95.90. Since it's five years later, the bond is now a five-year bond, and the yield by assumption is 7% What is its price five years after that, again assuming unchanged market conditions? Correct, it's $100. (In fact, it would be $100 regardless of market conditions since the bond has matured!) You see, over time, the bond is inching closer to par. What has this done for you, the investor? While you were holding the bond it was paying its current yield of 6.45% (based on your original purchase price). In addition, you were enjoying the pull-to-par. Add the two together and you have the yield to maturity of 7%.

Do the same analysis for the ten-year bond purchased when the yield was 5%. You pay a premium, $107.72, as the table shows. Five years later, assuming unchanged market conditions, the price is $104.33, and five years after that, $100. The pull-to-par is, in this case, a negative factor in your return. You earned 5.57% (6/107.7217) as you carried the bond over that time. Subtract the pull-to-par from that, and you have the 5% yield to maturity.

If the bond was at par when you purchased it and yields remain unchanged, there will be no pull-to-par effect. At maturity, the price is par regardless of yield. This must be true—when the bond is at par, the current yield equals the yield to maturity! In sum:

> *A bond's yield to maturity reflects the sum of the current yield of the bond (also known as its "carry") and its pull-to-par. Both factors are the result of the passage of time—the investor's compensation for giving up money over a period of time, or "time value of money!"*

But what if yields do change and you sell the bond prior to maturity? For example, what if you bought the bond situated in the northeast corner of Table 3.1; that is, you bought a 6% coupon, ten-year bond, when the market demanded only a 5% yield, so you paid $107.7217. Five years later you sell the bond. But its yield has risen to 7%, because that is what investors demanded on five-year bonds then. So its price has fallen to $95.8998—the southwest corner. You didn't necessarily lose money, even though you sold it a lower price, because you earned the bond's coupon while you held it. How do you think about what occurred? Two things happened: the calendar turned and the market shifted. Had the market stayed the same—that is, had the yield remained at 5%—you would have earned the coupon but experienced a negative pull-to-par. Not all the way down to $100, but to $104.3294. That combination would have produced a return of 5%, the yield to maturity at purchase. You can call this the "time factor." But the price actually fell to $95.8998, because market participants demanded a higher yield compared to five years before. This is the "market factor." (In a later chapter we examine more carefully this factor within the context of "attribution analysis," when we consider rate-of-return on investment.) If, instead, you bought the ten-year bond at a 7% yield—the southeast corner—and five years later the yield declined to 6%, the time factor alone would have put the bond in the southwest corner, and the market factor would have bumped it up to par.

Step-Up Coupon Bond: Test Your Understanding

Let's return to one of the more complicated bonds introduced in Chapter 2—one with a step-up coupon. This will help cement your understanding of the basic bond math principles, including the pull-to-par effect. It'll be a bit of a challenge, but worth it.

Suppose a company's risk profile is such that it needs to pay an interest rate of 7% on its bonds. If it were to issue a regular bond at par, its coupon would need to be 7% in order to be priced at $100, as we learned above. This company needs to conserve cash for the next couple of years, so it issues a five-year note with a coupon of 5.75% for the first two years. Of course, if this were the coupon throughout, the bond would be issued at a discount because the yield exceeds the coupon. In order to sell it at par, the company agrees to pay a coupon of 8% for the final three years—it "steps up."[7]

Look at Table 3.2. It examines the bond's price over time, assuming unchanged yields. Let's start in the middle. After the first two years have transpired, the bond becomes a simple fixed 8% coupon issue, with three years to maturity and a yield of 7% by assumption. It is, of course, now at a premium. And, as we saw above, the pull-to-par effect brings the premium down each year until it hits par at maturity. That explains the price path for the last three years. Now consider the issue date. Why is the price par, if the coupon (5.75%) is below the yield (7%) for two years? That's counter to bond math, is it not? No, not here. If this were a simple two-year bond with a 5.75% coupon paying $100 in two years, the 7% yield to maturity would push its price below par. But this bond gives you $102.6243 in two years, not $100! Receiving 5.75% in coupons, plus another 2.6243 on top of the $100 after two years produces a return of 7%. And after the first year the price is higher because one year has already gone by with the coupon below the yield—just like a discount bond rising every year because more and more low coupon years are behind it.

TABLE 3.2 Price Path in Dollars of 5-Year Step-Up Coupon Bond Paying 5.7% First 2 Years, 8%, Thereafter with Constant 7% Yield to Maturity

At Issuance	After 1 Year	After 2 Years	After 3 Years	After 4 Years	At Maturity
100	101.2844	102.6243	101.8080	100.9346	100

Convexity

One more fundamental concepts about bonds—actually, about fixed-income securities in general. Examine the five-year note's price in Table 3.1 as its yield rises. A 1% increase from 5% to 6% causes the price to drop by approximately 4.15%. The next 1% increase in yield, from 6% to 7%, produces only a 4.10% decline in price. Continuing this exercise, you'd find that the next 1% increase in yield pushes the price down to $92.0146, a 4.05% drop. The pattern is pretty clear: Every successive increase in yield results in a *decelerating* path of price declines.[8] Conversely, starting from 7% in the table, a 1% decrease in yield produces a 4.28% increase in price to par. The next 1% yield decrease results in a 4.33% price increase; and the next (not shown), a 4.38% price rise. That's an attractive characteristic—as yields rise, prices fall, but at a decelerating rate; and as yields fall, prices rise, at an accelerating rate!

Look at this another way. Say the market starts off the day with a 6% yield for the bond so that its price is par. It's safe to say that there is an equal probability of yields going up by 1% or down by 1%. As such, you have the same chance of making $4.33 as you do of losing $4.10. That's a pretty good bet! This asymmetric bet in the investor's favor is known as "convexity." The more asymmetric, the more attractive. All else being the same, convex bonds are more valuable than the nonconvex bonds. The ten-year note in Table 3.2 is also convex, but even more so. Starting at par, there is an equal chance of making $7.72 or losing $7.02—a more favorable bet. The more convex a bond is, the more attractive, hence valuable, it is to investors. Further, the greater the chance of yields changing, the more opportunities the investor has to enjoy the convexity. Hence, the value of convexity increases with volatility in the marketplace. This concept of convexity, plus the interaction between convexity and volatility, comes up a number of times in this book.

Callable Bonds—a Deeper Understanding

Earlier we concluded that the longer the remaining maturity of a bond, the more sensitive its price is to a change in yield. We combine this with the notion of convexity to arrive at a deeper understanding of a callable bond.

Recall from Chapter 2 that a callable bond allows the issuer to repay the bond's principal prior to the bond's stated final maturity. Although there are a number of possible reasons to prepay, the most typical is to take advantage of interest rates that are below the bond's coupon and refinance at lower market rates.[9] Suppose a twelve-year bond with a 7% coupon is callable in six years. Let's assume, just for simplicity, that the call provision is such that the issuer gets only one chance to call. Let's further assume that the six-year borrowing rate for this issuer is currently 7%. It is reasonable to say that investors assess the likelihood of the six-year rate falling below 7% in six years as equal to the likelihood of the rate rising above 7%. Thus, there is a 50% chance of the bond being called, hence maturing, in six years, and a 50% chance of it staying the course and maturing in twelve years. We can conclude in a simple fashion that the bond's average expected maturity is nine years (.5 × 6 + .5 × 12). The bond "behaves," therefore, like a nine-year bond. That is, when yields change in the market, its price will rise or fall the way a nine-year, 7% coupon bond would.

Consider now what happens when yields in the marketplace decline, say by a full percent. At 6%, we can no longer say that there is an equal chance of the six-year rate falling below 7% six years from now as the chances of rising above it. Even if nothing changes, the yield is already below the coupon, and the bond will be called. There is certainly a greater likelihood of rates falling below 7% rather than rising above. Since interest rates are already down to 6%, investors, for example, may now assign a 60% probability of the yield being below 7% in six years, hence the bond being called, and 40% above, and the bond not being called. The expected maturity of the bond, therefore, is now 8.4 years (.6 × 6 + .4 × 12), rather than 9 years. This has profound implications. It means that, if yields were to fall again, the price response would be *less* positive, as the bond behaves like one with an 8.4-year maturity, not a 9-year maturity. This is the opposite of the noncallable bond, which, due to its convexity, responds ever more in price when yields drop successively.

What about the reverse—an increase in yield, to 8%? Let's be symmetric and assume that now investors assess the likelihood of rates falling below 7% in six years, hence a call occurring at 40% and above 7%, hence no call, at 60%. This pushes the expected maturity back to 9.6 years. Should yields rise further, this would cause the price of the bond to respond negatively as if it were a 9.6-year bond, rather than as a 9-year, which is worse!

In short, if a bond is callable, a decline in yield shortens the *expected* maturity, thus reducing the beneficial effect of the yield decline on price. A yield increase lengthens the expected maturity, exacerbating the negative effect of the yield increase on price. This is the *opposite* of the dynamics resulting from the convexity of an ordinary, noncallable bond. There the asymmetry works in the investor's favor, as explained earlier. Here, the asymmetry works in the reverse. Indeed, market participants refer to this trait as *negative convexity*. While investors accept a lower yield for a convex bond—they *pay* for the attractive convexity feature; they demand a higher yield for a callable bond—they *require payment* for the negative convexity. This, you see, is simply another way of looking at the additional yield a callable bond must pay—the call "premium" described in Chapter 2.

4

BOND INVESTMENT MANAGEMENT

Let's recap what we know—and what we don't. Given the parameters of a bond—coupon, maturity, and so on—we know what the bond pays. Given what the bond pays, plus knowledge of how much the market requires that it pay—its yield—we can calculate, using the tools of Chapter 3, what the bond is worth, or its price.

How does the market go about deciding how much the bond should yield? The foundations for interest rates are determined by the macroeconomy, explained in the following two chapters (with extensions in Chapter 8, "The Yield Curve," and in Chapter 9 "Corporate Bonds," on the risk premium in corporate bonds: What we need to learn now is what to do with the bond once we know its yield, hence its price. In other words, how do we employ it in a portfolio?

Rate of Return

First we need to make clear what kind of portfolio manager we are dealing with. We're *not* talking about a speculator (you might use the word "trader" as a substitute in this context). By speculator I mean a bond market participant who would purchase a bond solely for the expectation that a price rise is imminent (or who would sell short in anticipation of an imminent price decline). We're also not talking about a bond dealer, whose intention is to hold the bond only temporarily until a buyer is found. Rather, the focus is on an investor. In this context, *investor* refers to a portfolio manager interested in the regular income a bond produces, in addition to any possible price appreciation. As such, this investor has a longer time horizon than the speculator for holding the security.

Let's start by looking at Figure 4.1. In Chapter 1 we discuss how a bond's basic information (we term the basic information "parameters") provides the bond's cash flows. Then in Chapter 3 we use market information, as represented by the bond's yield, combined with the bond's cash flows, to determine its price. The last piece of the triangle is information about the investor. This includes the investor's horizon and his or her expectations about the future.[1] Armed with these three sets of information, we have what we need to determine the attractiveness of a bond and, by extension, what to do with it.

Consider an investor with a one-year horizon. This means that she expects to employ this particular investment strategy for a year. She buys a five-year Treasury note with a 6% coupon, priced at par. Since it's at par, its yield must be 6% as well. So we have information about the investor (one-year horizon), the bond (five-year, 6% coupon), and market situation (6% yield to maturity). Let's summarize these in a timeline, as shown in Figure 4.2. Just for simplicity, let's assume that the coupon is paid annually and that $100 is invested today (time 0). The numbers above each of the succeeding years represent the cash

FIGURE 4.1 Portfolio Management Triangle

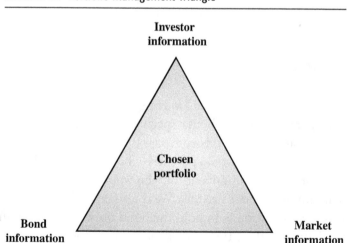

FIGURE 4.2 Timeline

	$6	$6	$6	$6	$106
$100					
0	1	2	3	4	5
	Horizon				Maturity

flows the bond is to pay whomever owns it on that date. Since the horizon occurs prior to the bond's maturity, the bond will need to be sold. What kind of bond will it be then? A Treasury *four*-year, 6% coupon bond. At what price will it be sold? It depends on the yield prevailing then, not now. Here's where the other investor information piece comes into play—her expectations regarding the yield to maturity one year from today. Suppose she expects the yield to remain at 6%. In that case, the bond will be par on the sale date. *And her rate of return will be 6%.* An investor's rate of return (ROR) from a bond measures the total income the bond provides, recognizing all the bond's cash flows over a given period of time relative to what the investor paid for the bond. In this case, an investment of $100, combined with proceeds of $106—$6 in coupon plus $100 from selling the bond at par—in one year produces a rate of return of 6%.[2]

What if the yield of the bond in one year's time is not 6%? What if, instead, interest rates rise in the marketplace, and investors a year from today demand 6.25% of this now four-year note? In that case, the bond's price will be $99.1387 when sold.[3] This makes the proceeds $6 (don't forget the coupon) + $99.1387 = $105.1387, instead of $106, for a rate of return of 5.14%, lower than 6%. If, on the other hand, the bond's yield drops to 5.75% when it's time to sell next year, the price will be $100.8713, producing proceeds of $106.8713 for an ROR of 6.87%.

Let's summarize these crucial points. An investment's rate of return is a function of the bond's earnings, or "proceeds." Proceeds, in turn, depend on the price the bond is sold for at the end of the investor's holding period, or horizon. The higher the bond's yield to maturity on the horizon date, the lower the proceeds, hence the lower the rate of return. The lower the yield, the greater the ROR. Because the ending yield is unknown at the time of the investment, there is risk. All the investor can calculate, therefore is *expected* rate of return. Once the horizon arrives and the bond's yield (price) is realized, the actual rate of return can be calculated and compared to its expected value.

What if the bond is not at par at the time of purchase? Perhaps it is being offered in the secondary market at a yield different from its coupon.[4] Suppose the above bond yields 5.9% on its purchase date, so that its price is above par, at $100.4224. In Figure 4.2, replace the initial $100 with $100.4224. All the other entries are the same; the bond still pays $6 every year and $100 at maturity. As before, the investor's rate of return depends crucially on the bond's price a year from today when it will be liquidated. That price, in turn, depends on the bond's yield to maturity then. Suppose the investor expects the bond to be at par next year—that is, that its yield will increase to 6%. The expected proceeds are $6 from the coupon plus the $100 price. Given an investment of $100.4224, the rate of return is 5.55%[5] less than the original 5.9% yield. Why? Because the bond's yield to maturity rose between the purchase date and the end of the investor's holding period. If, instead, the ending yield declines to 5.8%, the sale price of the bond is $100.6962, producing proceeds of $106.6962 and a rate of return of 6.25%, above the initial 5.9%. Why? Because the bond's yield declined relative to its initial rate before the investor's horizon was reached.

Let's now consider the intermediate case—the bond's yield is at 5.9% at the end of the year, exactly the same as on the investment date. In this case the price of the bond is $100.3473. Why is it lower than the initial price despite unchanged yield to maturity? Because of the pull-to-par effect. Since the bond is at a premium, it must decline toward par as it approaches maturity. What's the ROR? The 6% coupon together with the slight price decline produces an ROR of 5.9%—exactly the same as the yield on the initial investment date! Coincidence? Not at all.

If the yield of the bond when sold equals the yield at purchase, the investor's rate of return will equal that initial yield.

This is a powerful result and very intuitive. It sets a benchmark for buying a bond and for forming expectations surrounding an investor's rate of return. To summarize:

1. All else being the same, the higher the yield to maturity (YTM) of the bond on the purchase date, the greater the rate of return.

2. All else being the same, the lower the YTM of the bond on the purchase date, the lower the rate of return.
3. If the YTM of the bond on the horizon date is the same as the yield of the bond on the purchase date, the rate of return will equal that YTM.
4. If the YTM of the bond on the horizon date exceeds the yield of the bond on the purchase date, the rate of return will be below that initial YTM.
5. If the YTM of the bond on the horizon date is below the yield of the bond on the purchase date, the rate of return will exceed that initial YTM.

Now consider the same investor purchasing a ten-year Treasury note. Let's see the impact a longer maturity has on rate of return. Its coupon is 6.25%, with a yield to maturity of 6.05% for a premium price of $101.4685. Suppose the investor expects its yield to be 6.05% on the horizon date. Its price, therefore, will be $101.3574—it is pulled down toward par.[6] Expected rate of return? You guessed it: the same 6.05%. If, and only if, the bond's yield on the horizon date matches its yield on the investment date, the ROR will equal that yield. Why? The negative pull-to-par effect of the premium offsets part of the 6.25% coupon.

Should the bond's yield to maturity rise to 6.15% on the horizon date, its price falls to $100.6758, producing an ROR of 5.38%. If, instead, its yield declines to 5.95%, its price increases to $102.0450, for an ROR of 6.73%. Just as with the five-year note, a higher YTM on the horizon sale date produces a lower ROR than the initial yield; a lower YTM on the horizon date produces a higher ROR. Table 4.1 summarizes the RORs for the two bonds over the various scenarios. Do you see something dramatic? Both bonds respond the same way to yield movements: higher yield at horizon, lower ROR; lower yield at horizon, higher ROR. But *the degree of response of the ten-year bond—the differences in ROR outcomes when the horizon yield moves away from the initial yield—greatly exceed that of the five-year.* This is a very important conclusion, and it bears repeating. The longer the maturity of a bond, the greater the price change in response to changes in yield to maturity[7] and the greater the impact on rate of return.

A few final points about these fundamental concepts. First, terminology. Our one-year horizon investor, having purchased a five-year note, does not know the price the note will fetch in the market one year

TABLE 4.1 Rates of Return for Different Horizon Yields

	5-Year Note	10-Year Note
Yield 0.10% below initial yield	6.25%	6.73%
Yield equal to initial yield	5.90%	6.05%
Yield 0.10% above initial yield	5.55%	5.38%

from today when it needs to be sold. This means that she faces uncertainty with respect to the proceeds, hence with her rate of return. On the investment date—the date the decision needs to be made—the best she can do is formulate an *expected* rate of return. Her *actual* ROR will depend upon the bond price actually realized at the time of sale. The uncertainty arising from unknown future bond prices which, in turn, is a function of future bond yields, is known as "capital risk."[8] From Table 4.1 it is clear that the ten-year presents more market risk than does the five-year. In Chapter 12 we will establish this as a general principal and quantify it: All else the same, longer-maturity bonds present greater price risk than do shorter maturity instruments.

Second, suppose the investor buys a one-year note instead of a five-year note. Since the note matures on the horizon date, there is no capital risk—it pays $100 regardless of market conditions. If the coupon is 5% and the purchase price is par, the rate of return will be 5%. Suppose the purchase price is different from par, say $99.75, reflecting a 5.26% initial yield to maturity. The ROR is also known with certainty: 5.26%.[9] In short, if the bond's maturity matches the investor's horizon, there is no capital risk.[10]

Third, notice that we focused on only two dates—the investment date and the horizon date. The bond's yields, hence prices, on each of these dates are the crucial parameters determining the investor's expected and actual return for a one-year holding period. The path of the bond's yield between these dates is irrelevant to the rate of return the bond produces (unless the bond pays a coupon in the interim, which is not the case in our examples). Sure, the investor can get nervous watching yield movements in the market, but as long as the bond position is retained, nervousness has no effect on the outcome. On the other hand, the investor may reassess his outlook in response to market conditions prior to the horizon end and sell the bond, with the proceeds held in cash or in a different instrument. We deal with this later.[11]

Current Yield

Another important concept for bond investors is "current yield." Let's return to the 6% coupon five-year note. When purchased at par, the investor receives $6 yearly for every $100 invested, or 6% . Obvious, right? But now consider the second case above, when the bond was purchased at $100.4224 because its yield was 5.9%. In that case, the investor received $6 yearly for the $100.4224 investment, or 6/100.4224 = 5.97%. This is the bond's current yield—the coupon divided by the market price. Clearly, only in the case of the bond price at par will the current yield equal the coupon rate.

Why do we care about current yield? It provides a piece of information important for a class of investors. It measures the regular, ongoing earnings a bond produces relative to the money invested in the bond. If the price of the bond is different from par, it makes sense to measure the coupon's compensation relative to the bond's market price (the cost to the investor), not relative to par. On the other hand, the current yield omits a crucial piece of information—the pull-to-par. Over time, separate from the bond's current yield, the investor is enjoying (for a discount bond) or suffering (for a premium bond) the pull-to-par effect. This *is* captured by the bond's yield to maturity. We conclude that, in a neutral case—one in which the bond's yield to maturity remains intact during the holding period—*the investor's rate of return equals the original yield to maturity which, in turn, equals the initial current yield plus the pull-to-par.*

Consider the five-year, 6% annual coupon bond again. Its initial yield to maturity is 5.9%, for a price of $100.4224 and current yield equal to 5.97%. Assume that after one year the bond is sold—not at the same original yield to maturity, but at the same initial price of $100.4224. What is the investor's rate of return? Not 5.9%, because the ending yield to maturity is not the same as the yield to maturity at the beginning. The ROR equals 5.97%! Let's recap[12]:

1. If a bond is sold at the same yield to maturity as on the purchase date, the investor's rate of return equals that yield to maturity.
2. If a bond is sold at the same price as on the purchase date, the investor's rate of return equals the bond's current yield as of the purchase date.

Longer Horizons

Look at Figure 4.3. It's just like Figure 4.2, but with a few changes. First, it recognizes that a bond's initial price—the investment amount—is not always par. Second, we've changed the investor's horizon to two years. It's still a five-year bond at the outset and will need to be sold on the horizon date. Because the holding period is two years rather than one, the bond on that date will have a three-year remaining maturity rather than two. This has two implications: First, it is, of course, still true that the price on the horizon date depends inversely on the bond's yield on that date, hence presenting capital risk to the investor today. But the degree of risk is lessened, since a three-year note has less of a price response to interest-rate changes than does a four-year note. Second, the coupon to be paid at the end of the first year needs to be reinvested for a year until the horizon date. This is a new factor, which was not relevant in the first example. These two events are depicted with arrows in Figure 4.3.

Let's assume that the bond is purchased at a discount at time 0. Say the initial yield is 6.2%, so that the price is $99.1621. Follow the timeline in Figure 4.3 from left to right. A coupon of $6 is to be paid at the end of the first year. The holding period has not ended. The coupon will, therefore, be reinvested for one year. At what rate? The one-year rate prevalent then. Today, the investor can only form expectations as to what that rate might be. Suppose she expects that rate to be 4.75%. (Why that number? Perhaps because that is the one-year rate today.) If she proves to be right, on the horizon date the investor will be receiving three cash flows:

1. $6 × (1.0475), first coupon plus reinvestment interest
2. $6, second coupon
3. Price of the three-year 6% coupon bond

FIGURE 4.3 Timeline

Price at Purchase	$6 →	$6	← $6	← $6	← $106
0	1	2	3	4	5
	Horizon				Maturity

Suppose the investor expects the three-year yield to maturity in two years to be 5.8%. (Why? That is the three-year rate today, so it seems an innocuous assumption.) That produces a price of $100.5366. Total proceeds on the horizon date, therefore, equal $6.285 + $6 + $100.5366, or $112.8216. Combined with the initial $99.1621 investment, the expected rate of return over the two years solves the equation $99.1621 = $112.8216/(1 + ROR)^2$, for an ROR of 6.67%.

The investor's return of 6.67% stems from a combination of the bond's coupons, including reinvestment of the first coupon, and the selling price, relative to the initial investment. A higher reinvestment rate would produce a greater ROR, all else the same—factor 1 above. A lower reinvestment rate results in a lower ROR. This is obviously known as "reinvestment risk." On the other hand, a higher yield for the three-year bond when it is sold on the horizon date produces a lower price, hence a reduced ROR. Conversely, a lower yield on the horizon date results in a greater ROR. We've characterized this previously as "capital risk." Reread this paragraph, and it will be clear to you that the two risk factors—capital and reinvestment—respond in opposite directions to future interest-rate changes. Note the arrows in Figure 4.3 pointing in opposite directions. Reinvestment brings cash flows from earlier years to later years, when the holding period is over—hence, higher future interest rates add to ROR. Selling the bond brings cash flows from later to earlier years, as the future coupons and principal need to be discounted—higher future rates subtract from ROR.

Suppose interest rates rise across the board after the bond is purchased. Say that the reinvestment rate is 5.75% instead of 4.75% and that the three-year yield in two years, necessary to price the bond when sold, is 6.8% rather than 5.8%. The reinvested first coupon now brings $6.345 to the proceeds on the horizon date, while the bond's sale price falls to $97.8929. The total proceeds equal $6.345 + $6 + $97.8929 = $110.2379, for a rate of return of 5.44%. Quite a drop from 6.67%. Why? Didn't the higher reinvestment rate for the initial coupon offset the price decline of the bond? Sure it did—reinvestment risk and capital risk move in opposite directions. But not entirely. Only $6 of coupon enjoys the 1% higher reinvestment. That's not much. On the other hand, a three-year bond with cash flows of $6, $6, and then $106, are all discounted at the 1% higher rate, thus reducing the price substantially.

We can draw an important inference from this example. Go one step further and assume that the investor's horizon is three, not two, years. And assume that interest rates rise by the same 1% as above. Now, *two* coupons are reinvested at the higher rate. Furthermore, the first coupon is compounded twice at this higher rate. Moreover, the bond that needs to be sold after the *three*-year holding period is up is a two-year, not a three-year, bond. From bond math we know that the price decline of a two-year instrument in response to an increase in yield is well below that of a three-year. Hence, the effect of the increase in interest rates on an investor's return over a three-year horizon is significantly muted. Our conclusion: The longer the holding period, the less deleterious the effect of higher interest rates on rate of return. Of course, the less beneficial a drop in interest rates would be; since there is a shorter remaining maturity, the positive effect on the bond's price when sold is less pronounced. Furthermore, the coupons are reinvested at lower rates.

Rate of Return vis-à-vis Yield to Maturity, Again

The bond the investor purchased in the previous section had an initial yield to maturity of 6.20%. Under the first scenario, with a reinvestment rate of 4.75% and a horizon yield of 5.80%, the investor's ROR was 6.67%. In the second scenario, with rates rising by 1% across the board, the ROR fell to 5.44%.[13] Under what kind of scenario will the ROR equal 6.20%, the same as the bond's yield at purchase? Answer: If the reinvestment rate and the horizon yield both equal 6.20%, the ROR will equal 6.20% as well. Recall a fundamental result near the end of this chapter's first section relevant to an investor with a one-year horizon. "If the YTM of the bond on the horizon date is the same as the yield of the bond on the purchase date, the rate of return will equal that YTM." We need only rephrase it slightly for this two-year horizon case: If the reinvestment rate *and* the horizon YTM are the same as the bond's YTM on the purchase date, the investor's ROR will equal that yield. Indeed, we can say this more generally for any horizon:

> *Over any given investment horizon for a bond, if future coupon reinvestments as well as the yield of the bond when sold prior to maturity*

all equal the bond's initial yield to maturity, the investor's rate of return will equal the bond's initial yield.

Reinvestment rates above the initial yield to maturity of the bond, or a horizon yield below the bond's initial yield, produce an ROR above that initial yield. Reinvestment rates below the initial yield, or a horizon yield above the bond's initial yield, produce an ROR below that yield.

Myth Dispelled

Investors who have just a cursory knowledge of bonds and do not properly understand the concept of rate of return very often subscribe to nonsensical views about investment strategies. Here's one: "I plan to invest for two years. I'll purchase a five-year note, which yields more than a two-year alternative. I know I'll have to sell it after two years at a price unknown to me today. And I know that if yields rise in the interim, my bond will fall in price when I sell it. But my strategy will take care of that. If interest rates do go up, I'll sell my bond and reinvest the money I receive upon the sale at the then higher rates! In the meantime, I've earned the higher yield on the five-year note. I can't lose!"

Let's see how ridiculous this notion really is. And let's see why an investor who does just the opposite—purchases the lower yielding short-term note—will actually do better in the scenario painted above!

Our two-year horizon investor buys a 6.0% coupon five-year note at par, just as in the initial scenario back in the first section. Let's assume that the one-year note yields 4.5%, which the investor chooses to forgo in order to achieve a higher yield. One year later, just as we assumed above, the yield on this now four-year note the investor purchased rises to 6.6%.He sells it for $97.9492, below par because yields have risen. No problem. He takes this money, plus the $6 coupon (total of $103.9492), and buys a newly issued four-year note that yields 6.6%, priced at par. How much of the note can our investor purchase? One with a face value of $103.9492 (which means he can purchase 1.039492 units at par). Let's be magnanimous and assume that interest rates remain stable after this purchase is made so that at the end of the second year, when the investor's horizon is over, the bond is sold at par, providing proceeds of $110.8098 (1.039492 times both principal of $100 plus the coupon of $6.6). Total proceeds of $110.8098 for an investment of 100 over a two-year horizon produces a rate of return of only 5.27%—$100 = $110.8098/(1 + ROR)². Significantly less than 6%! The rise in rates has got to hurt.

What if the investor had held on to the original bond for two years and just reinvested the first coupon in the new four-year bond? After two years, the now three-year, 6.0% coupon bond is sold at a yield of 6.6% (because we assumed that the yield jumps to 6.6% after the first year and remains there), for a price of $98.4138. Including the first $6 coupon reinvested at 6.6%, plus the second $6 coupon paid on the horizon date, the total proceeds are $98.4138 + $6.396 + $6 = $110.8098. Exactly the same as the above strategy! Hence, the RORs are equivalent! Switching to the higher yielding bond didn't accomplish anything, since the capital loss due to the increase in interest rates had to be realized somehow—either by selling the original bond after one year and buying a current coupon bond, or keeping the original bond until the horizon and selling then. Table 4.2 provides a summary of the arithmetic for the two strategies.

How would the investor have fared had he purchased the one-year note, despite its yield of 4.5%? At the end of the year, the note matures.

TABLE 4.2 Proof That Rate of Return Is Equivalent for Two Strategies, Two-Year Horizon

Strategy I	Strategy II
1. Purchase 6%, 5-year coupon bond at par.	1. Purchase 6%, 5-year coupon bond at par.
2. After 1 year, yields rise.	2. After 1 year, yields rise; bond is kept.
3. Bond sold at 6.6% yield for $97.9492.	3. First coupon of $6 received.
4. $97.9492 plus $6 coupon reinvested in new 6.6%, 4-year bond.	4. Original bond retained, first coupon earning 6.6%.
5. After second year, $103.9492 principal returned, plus 6.6%.	5. After second year, bond sold at 6.6% yield for $98.4138.
6. Proceeds = $103.9492 × (1 + .066) = $110.8098.	6. Proceeds = $98.4138 + $6 + ($6 × 1.066) = $110.8098.

Its proceeds of $104.50 are reinvested in the new four-year note, yielding 6.60%. This produces $104.50 × 1.066 = $111.3970 after the second year (remember that we are assuming, for all the strategies, that after interest rates rise, they remain stable at least through the end of the holding period), for a rate of return over the two years of 5.54%, substantially above the 5.27% produced by the five-year note despite its initial higher yield. Why? Because interest rates increased. If interest rates rise, investing in shorter maturity assets turns out to be a better strategy because it allows taking advantage of the subsequent higher rates. Purchasing a longer term asset and then having to sell it, on the other hand, produces a loss, and reinvesting the lower proceeds at the new higher rates accomplishes nothing, as we prove earlier.

PART II

MACROECONOMICS FOR MARKET PROFESSIONALS

5

HOW THE ECONOMY
WORKS

What Is Macroeconomics and Why Does It Matter?

Macroeconomics is the study of the behavior of an overall economy. Unlike *micro*economics, which examines the market for particular goods, specific assets, types of labor, and so on, macro analysis looks at the big picture—the total economic activity of a country, including production, the unemployment rate, inflation, interest rates, and the like. And, crucially, it attempts to understand how the various components of the big picture interact. The tools of microeconomic analysis are portable from good to good and market to market. But when it comes to macroeconomics, you need to be careful when applying concepts that are used to understand the dynamics of an economy such as the United States to, say, a smaller country like Ireland and surely to that of a developing economy, such as that of Indonesia. Of course, there are concepts and analytical techniques generally applicable to most countries. Indeed, the purpose of this chapter is to present these general ideas and show how they can be used to understand the dynamics of *any* macroeconomy. Still, keep in mind that every country needs to be treated as a special case.

Why do fixed-income investors care about the behavior of the macroeconomy? There is almost no decision they'll have to make that doesn't require an understanding of what's happening in the economy and the repercussions on the fixed income markets. Here are a few examples:

- The interaction between movements in the level of economic activity and the central bank's response is the primary determinant of short-term interest rates. Short-term rates, in turn, determine the cost of financing securities holdings as well as serve as a parking place for portfolio cash.
- Longer term interest rates reflect, among other factors, market participants' views concerning the future path of the economy.
- There is a strong link between economic activity and inflation, both current and expected. Bonds contain a premium to compensate investors for inflation.
- The stage of the business cycle is a crucial determinant of corporate profits. This has implications for corporate bond credit spreads as well as the value of any instrument with a credit component, such as credit derivatives.
- The relative levels of interest rates, inflation, and economic growth between two countries are primary ingredients in the exchange rate between the currencies of those countries.
- Volatility is the crucial variable in the prices of many derivatives. Interest rate dynamics and macroeconomic activity, along with politics and market psychology, drive movements in volatility and, therefore, influence decisions concerning whether and how to use derivatives in hedging and otherwise adjusting the risk exposure of a portfolio. Volatility is also a component of the shape of the yield curve and the value of fixed instruments with "convex" characteristics.
- It is impossible to appreciate the special nature of emerging market countries, the stages of their development and the "sovereign risk" they present without a thorough grounding in macroeconomic analysis.

The Big Picture

So you don't want to read an entire chapter on economics? Here are the essentials in one paragraph! But I urge you to work through the chapter anyway.

The level of economic activity, in the short run, is determined by the total of spending on goods and services. Given the country's ability to produce those goods and services—the economy's "potential output"—a gap between actual and potential economic activity will exist at any point in time. This gap is the primary determinant of unemployment and a crucial ingredient in inflation. One of the goals of the central bank is to narrow this gap. The bank's monopoly on ultimate liquidity creation, combined with the economy's need for liquidity—which is a function of the level of economic activity—determines overnight interest rates. Thus, the central bank can influence interest rates, thereby affecting economic activity and closing the gap. How's that? When all else is the same, a wider gap causes the central bank to add liquidity and reduce short-term interest rates in order to stimulate borrowing and, hence, spending on goods and services. Longer-term interest rates are a function of short-term rates plus expectations regarding future rate movements. Business cycles, budget deficits and surpluses, currency values, and commodity prices all influence these expectations.

There it is! One paragraph. Now let's try to understand this all a little better, keeping in mind that our goal is to link the dynamics of the economy to the behavior of fixed-income securities.

What Determines the Country's Level of Economic Activity?

Gross domestic product (GDP) equals a country's total output of goods and services—its level of economic activity. GDP and its components are measured in "real" terms—after adjusting for inflation. This means, essentially, that the quantity of goods and services is measured using prices of a chosen "base" year, as opposed to using current prices, which would constitute "nominal" GDP.[1]

Intermediate transactions are not counted in GDP. A car company paying the manufacturer for the aluminum to be used in an automobile or paying the salary of the assembly line worker is not in the GDP calculations. The price of the car reflects these costs already. So including them separately would amount to counting them twice. Goods and services enter GDP only when they arrive at their final destination (except for inventories—see below).

We know now what GDP is. What drives it? A common and straightforward perspective is that at any time, the level of economic activity is determined by spending for goods and services, termed "aggregate demand." The greater the level of aggregate demand, the more produced to satisfy it and hence the higher GDP. In turn, this means that more of the country's resources are employed to produce that higher level of GDP. Aggregate demand is divided into *sectors*:

- Consumption
- Residential investment
- Business fixed-investment spending
- Government spending
- Inventories
- Foreign trade

Understanding the behavior of aggregate demand sectors helps in understanding—and predicting—the dynamics of GDP and, ultimately, GDP's impact on the financial markets.

Consumption

Consumption refers to spending by households on items that are "consumed," or used up (which excludes the purchase, hence the building, of a home); it accounts for about two-thirds of aggregate demand. In turn, consumption is divided into: (1) durable goods (defined as items with an expected life of at least three years), constituting roughly 15% of consumption and the most cyclically sensitive of its components, (2) nondurable goods—about 30% of consumption, a relatively stable component, and (3) services (i.e., intangibles, such as medical care and entertainment), 55%, and a steadily rising share.

Households spend out of their income. (Some, of course, spend more than their income; i.e., they borrow. But we're looking at the household sector in the aggregate.) The percentage of its (after-tax) income that a household consumes depends upon the state of the labor market (unemployment rate, job availability, opportunity for overtime, wage growth, etc.), home prices (the higher the price of their homes, the less households feel the need to save in order to reach a target wealth level), and the stock market (like housing, a factor in household wealth, but also an indicator of optimism about the economy's future). The

percentage of (after-tax) household income not consumed is, by definition, the *savings rate*.

Residential Investment

Residential investment refers to spending by individuals on housing (the
house itself—not its furnishings, which are part of consumption); it
accounts for only 4% or so of GDP in the United States, but could be
quite volatile because it is sensitive to interest rates (mortgages) and
potential home-buyers' expectations about the state of the labor market
(and expectations are, by their very nature, volatile). Note that only new-
home building is included in GDP, as new homes are *produced*. Buying
an existing home adds nothing to economic activity (except for the real
estate broker's work), unless it elicits spending on furniture, and the like
by the new homeowner, which then shows up in consumption.

Business Fixed-Investment Spending

Business fixed-investment (BFI) spending covers expenditures by firms
on plant and equipment. At the individual firm level, this is known as
capital expenditures ("capx" in market lingo). More than three-quarters
of BFI is for equipment, which includes motor vehicles. Computers and
related equipment have been accounting for the lion's share of BFI
equipment spending in recent years. With consumption and housing
together constituting over 70% of aggregate demand, BFI can be only
a relatively small component of GDP, sometimes reaching as low as
single digits. Yet BFI accounts for a disproportionate share of *changes*
in GDP, so it often bears large responsibility for business cycle fluctuations. BFI's importance lies not only in its outsized cyclicality. Among
the components of aggregate demand, it is the most important factor
in the economy's *future* growth potential since this is where a large part
of the economy's ability to produce comes from (although consumption spending on education and training, and government spending on
infrastructure also enhance future growth.)

Government Spending

Government spending includes federal and state/local government expenditures, the latter representing approximately two-thirds of the total.

Because of political movements to balanced budgets, this component of demand had been shrinking in relative importance in many areas of the world. This has a very important implication: Unlike past situations of recession, government spending can no longer be counted on as the automatic stopgap to replace declines in aggregate demand emanating from other sectors. When government spending is done specifically in order to support (or replace other declines in) aggregate demand—as opposed to spending driven by an actual need for goods or services (e.g., the military)—it is known as fiscal policy. The recession of 2008 and 2009 has changed the calculus. The plethora of government programs demonstrates that simulative fiscal policy has once again been adopted, brought about by the magnitude of the downturn and the precarious nature of the financial system (see Chapter 6). The share of government spending in GDP is set to rise dramatically.

It is important to distinguish between government spending on goods and services and "transfer payments." Transfer payments refer to grants made to individuals, such as aid to families with dependent children, or welfare. While certainly included in any calculations of the government's budget deficit, they are not a component of aggregate demand; they simply transfer spending power from one individual, through taxes, to another. (Social security also involves transfer payments. But it has a special accounting framework.)

Inventories

Inventories—goods produced but unsold—only add to or subtract from GDP when there is a change. An increase in the level of inventories *raises* GDP. Why? Because the additional goods were produced and, therefore, count as output. A decrease in inventories *subtracts* from GDP since it reflects spending from other demand sectors that, instead of resulting in production, was drawn down from stocks. Over a business cycle, inventory additions and subtractions should net out to zero (except for secular shifts in the inventory/sales ratio). Economists examine inventory changes for clues as to the economy's direction. Generally, inventory accumulation, while adding to current GDP, is a precursor to a future decline in production since stocks will have to be drawn down. Conversely, inventory decumulation is positive for future GDP, though negative for current economic output, because businesses ultimately need to restock. For predictive purposes, however, it is necessary to know whether the accumulation was a result of overstocking in anticipation of sales that ultimately disappointed or strong consumer spending that required more goods on shelves and cars in dealer lots. Overstocking points to a reduction in future output; strong consumer spending does not. Note that with the growth of services as a share of GDP, inventories have become relatively less of a factor in explaining the economy's fluctuations.

Foreign Trade

Foreign trade is the final sector. When aggregate demand exceeds what the economy produces, we import more than we export, and vice versa. *Net* exports, the excess of exports over imports, stimulate economic activity just like any of the other aggregate demand sectors. Net exports are a function of relative quality and prices of foreign-produced goods and services compared to domestic goods and services; the level of the home country's aggregate demand compared to that of the country's trading partners, in turn reflecting different stages in their respective business cycles; and currency exchange rates. (Much more on this is found in Chapter 19, which is devoted to foreign trade and exchange rates.)

The Role of Profits

It may seem from this perspective that, with economic activity driven by demand, there is no role for profits in determining production. That does not sound right, and it isn't. Firms produce goods or services (hence employ people and use machines, etc., to do so) in response to aggregate demand for their products only if they earn a profit on what they produce. And the more the demand, the more they will produce (and employ). At times, however, the cost structure of firms (labor, materials, energy, rent, debt service) is such that production means a loss. In that case, more demand will not elicit production, labor input will not be required, and GDP will not grow. In short, corporate profits interact with demand in determining the path of GDP growth.

Potential GDP, the "Output Gap," and Inflation

What an economy *can* produce, as opposed to what it actually does produce, is termed *Potential GDP*, or *potential output*. It also represents the level of output that the economy gravitates to in the long run. The determinants of a country's level of Potential GDP are its:

- Labor force and its experience, education, and training
- Stock of physical capital
- Available natural resources
- Technology and innovation

The difference between potential and actual GDP is described as the *output gap* or *GDP gap*. Potential GDP is important because a primary mandate of the central bank (and possibly other government policy makers as well) is to get the economy's actual GDP as close to its potential as possible, or to narrow the gap. Why? Because the wider the gap, the more unemployment there is—the labor force is not fully utilized or employed.

The federal government as well is interested in closing the gap as much as possible because this reduces unemployment. Were it not for budget constraints, it could do so by increasing government spending. An increase in spending would raise aggregate demand, resulting in a higher level of actual GDP, bringing it closer to potential, and employing more of the country's labor force.

There is a complication, however. The narrower the gap, the greater (ultimately) the inflationary pressure, as is explained below. The central bank, being concerned with inflation, needs to be careful about the impact of its policies on prices, which may force its hand in a way that exacerbates the gap.

Inflation

How does inflation fit into all this? Inflation has three components:

1. *Cyclical.* The position of the economy relative to its potential over the business cycle has historically been correlated with the

inflation rate. This empirical regularity is observed in the United States and most industrialized countries. Typically, as real GDP grows, more labor is needed. For a given labor force, the resultant reduction in unemployment tightens labor markets, forcing wage gains, which usually cause higher prices in goods and services as employers pass on their costs. Furthermore, commodities become more in demand, but since their supply is not immediately forthcoming, their prices must rise. In short, the narrower the GDP gap, the higher the inflation rate, and vice versa.

2. *Embedded.* Inflation can become embedded in an economy if it enters into people's expectations. At that point it becomes self-fulfilling, as labor and commodity contracts turn to be based on *expected* inflation or are indexed to the inflation rate. High inflation leads to expected inflation which leads to actual inflation, and the cycle continues. This source of inflation is extremely difficult to eradicate.

3. *Exogenous.* At times factors from outside the macroeconomic system produce one-off spurts in the price level. An oil price jump is the best example. Whether or not these factors become embedded into the country's price dynamics depends on the frequency of their occurrence and their size, as well as the inflation psychology in the economy. The reverse is possible as well. Commodity prices may be weak in the global marketplace, holding down inflation in the face of a narrow GDP gap.

Why should inflation be a concern? And, by extension, why must the central bank be constrained in working toward its goal of minimizing the gap by its potential inflation implications? A high inflation rate threatens an economy. Business decision making is a function of expected profits. Profits, in turn, depend upon the prices of a firm's output, wages, and other input costs. During inflationary periods, this decision making is corrupted because prices are not in equilibrium. Businesses hesitate to make both production and long-run investment decisions. As explained in Chapter 7, "Inflation-Protected Bonds," interest rates rise as the inflation premium attached to rates increases. Finally, citizens on fixed incomes lose real earnings when inflation accelerates, and they have little recourse. In extreme inflationary situations—and this is more relevant to developing than industrialized economies—citizens can lose confidence in the country's legal tender, thus totally disrupting economic activity.

Employment and Unemployment

The country's unemployment rate measures the percentage of the labor force not working. The labor force is defined as that part of the working-age population either holding a job or looking for one. There should be a close correlation between the size of the GDP gap and the unemployment rate. A higher level of economic activity, as it narrows the gap, reduces the unemployment rate since more of the labor force is employed. A fall in aggregate demand increases the gap as it puts more people out of work.

A low unemployment rate, therefore, reflects tight labor markets, which, in turn, create an environment for rising wages. Conversely, a high unemployment rate will be associated with wages rising less rapidly. When unemployment is at recessionary levels, wages may well decline. Since labor is the largest portion of production costs, wage gains will typically result in price increases, and vice versa. Thus, we have the classical negative relationship between unemployment and inflation.

The relationship is imperfect, for a few reasons:

1. *Hours worked versus jobs.* Employers typically increase hours worked of existing employees rather than add new workers in response to early signs of output growth. Conversely, they will reduce the workweek instead of initiating layoffs when business activity begins to weaken. The unemployment rate, therefore, will show no appreciable change at early cyclical turning points.
2. *Productivity.* If output per labor hour is increasing, firms can grant wage increases and still keep prices under control, since their profit margins will not be significantly eroded by the increase in wages.
3. *Exogenous factors* (as mentioned previously). Soaring oil prices will cause inflation to accelerate despite high unemployment. Conversely, cheap imports of raw materials from developing countries struggling with recessions have, in the past, allowed

low unemployment in the United States to coexist with price stability.

4. *Expectations:* If consumers and workers expect inflation and build that into price and wage decisions, inflation can exist—and even accelerate—in the face of a wide output gap and high unemployment. This is sometimes referred to as "stagflation." The reverse is also possible. As people become convinced that inflation is a thing of the past, unemployment can decline even as inflation decelerates.

The discussion up to now relates to "cyclical" unemployment, that is, unemployment resulting from a decline in demand which leads to layoffs. *Cyclical* is the proper term, because layoffs are closely linked to the business cycle. However, a person can be unemployed by voluntarily leaving a job, perhaps in order to search for a position more closely matching his or her skills. Indeed, this type of unemployment is more prevalent in vibrant, as opposed to stagnant, economies. On the other hand, some people lack skills necessary in the modern job market. Stronger economic activity does them little good. There will always be some of these "structural" (the latter) and "frictional" (the former) kinds of unemployment, which are only loosely related to the business cycle.[2] The labor-market–inflation analysis described above relates primarily to the cyclical portion of unemployment.

Recall that only someone technically in the labor force can potentially be considered unemployed. A person not working but not looking for work is not part of the labor force, hence is not officially "unemployed." At the same time, a person just entering the labor force without a job is considered unemployed, but this is clearly not an indication of a faltering economy. Suppose an increase in aggregate demand results in higher output. If newly created jobs are filled by new entrants into the labor force (immigrants, for example, or recently graduated students) the unemployment rate is unaffected. Conversely, if, after being frustrated in finding a job, a person stops looking, he exits the labor force and is no longer technically unemployed. The relationship between weak economic activity and unemployment, you see, is imperfect.

This lack of perfect correlation between GDP growth and the unemployment rate means that the latter is not a good indicator of the former.[3] On a month-to-month basis, therefore, economists and market participants look more closely at the number of new jobs created in order to get a read on GDP growth (subject to the "hours worked" caveat mentioned earlier). If the number of jobs created during the month exceeds the economy's potential for job creation, then actual GDP is growing faster than potential. All else the same—that is, subject to the exceptions above—this implies a greater degree of wage, hence price, pressure.

Manufacturing versus Services

The notion that spending elicits production (hence employment) holds true whether it is for goods (i.e., manufactured items) or for services. Service producers do not maintain inventory, by definition. A decrease in demand, therefore, will not show up as a buildup of stocks. Rather, employers in the service sector, having hired labor and purchased input in anticipation of demand, will initially find their profits eroding and ultimately respond by reducing the number of employees.

Demand for services is, by nature, more stable than demand for manufactured goods. Thus, although manufacturing accounts for a much smaller portion of the economy, it is responsible for a disproportionate share of the economy's cyclicality. In addition, inflation in the service sector is significantly less responsive to output by that sector.

Summary So Far

Figure 5.1 summarizes basic macroeconomic dynamics. Output, or real GDP, is determined by aggregate demand, the sum of spending on goods and services by the various sectors. (subject to the caveats regarding profits mentioned previously). Given the country's potential output growth, reflecting its labor and its natural and physical resources, a gap may exist. The unemployment rate is related to, and serves as an imperfect proxy for, the gap. The size of the gap is a major determinant of the rate of inflation.

Interest Rates

Figure 5.1 does not yet constitute a complete system. The financial sector is missing. We explore that in the context of macroeconomic dynamics in the next chapter, which highlights the role of the central

FIGURE 5.1 Basic Macroeconomic Dynamics

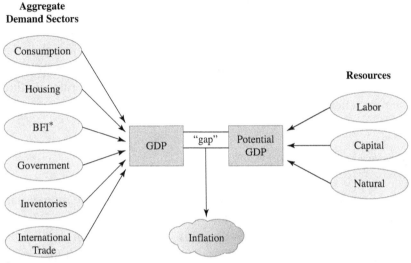

*BFI = Business Fixed-Investment.

bank. But it is extremely worthwhile examining this sector outside the confines of a central bank. Take careful note: interest rates have been around a lot longer than the institutions known today as central banks.[4] So there must be important influences running from the overall economy to interest rates (and back) without a central bank's omnipresence.

Prices for goods and services, if they are set in a free market, equilibrate suppliers' willingness to produce and demanders' desire to consume. The price of an item is simultaneously the cost of and reward for effort incurred in its production. Interest rates equilibrate suppliers' willingness to extend credit and demanders' need for it. Savers are paid to forgo current consumption and lend —they are paid to wait— by borrowers whose own resources are insufficient for current spending needs—they cannot wait.

How does this fit into our macroeconomic framework? When real GDP growth is below potential (and households fear the situation is going to last), with substantial unemployment, people tend to save a greater portion of their income, reflecting their worries about the future.[5] Firms see less profitability in expansion, hence borrow less. Interest rates, therefore, must decline to equilibrate supply and demand. Conversely, when output growth is strong relative to potential, households feel more confident and save less. Businesses become more aggressive and borrow more. Interest rates rise. Furthermore, inflation expectations are added to real interest rates (see Chapter 7). As explained above, inflation tends to accelerate when the GDP gap narrows and decelerate when the gap widens. This magnifies the relationship between the strength of macroeconomic activity and interest rates. In short, even without a central bank, interest rates tend to be procyclical.[6]

Recessions

How do recessions occur?[7] Economists are not really sure, but we can use history as a guide for suggestions. Here are four.

A "classical" recession is one caused by a significant decrease in aggregate demand. This may reflect consumer satiation. Or it may result from households' fear of an imminent recession precipitating an increase in savings, hence a decrease in consumption expenditures (note how perception becomes reality in macroeconomics). Another possibility is that businesses stop spending on equipment, perhaps because of a negative sales outlook or a corporate tax increase, or more familiar to recent history, an oil price jump forcing an increase in imports (explored more fully below). In any case, the result is a drop in domestic aggregate demand, hence a lower output level. The GDP gap widens, and the economy's resources, particularly labor, become unemployed. Although savings have increased in the first two cases, bringing down interest rates, firms are not motivated to borrow. Why expand output capabilities if products are not in high demand?

Companies produce goods or hire labor to produce services *in expectation* of demand for their products. *On a macro level*, the payment for material, energy, and labor that goes into production of goods and services means money in the hands of those workers and suppliers who in turn pay *their* workers. This is money that will be spent, although perhaps not entirely. But each firm *on a micro level* cannot be confident that its particular good or service will be purchased just because it ramps up its production. In short, an environment of uncertainty causes firms to hold off on hiring, purchasing, and producing until they see their own product being demanded. With all firms in the economy waiting this way, on a macro scale there will be no production, and the firms' worries become substantiated.

There may well be latent demand by consumers. Firms, however, may face high costs of production—labor, energy, even debt service—such that producing and selling at the existing price structure entails a loss. Output, hence hiring, stagnates. Unemployment causes a reduction in spending, thereby validating the original decision by the firms.

Companies in the United States rely on credit, as do all major economies, not just for long-term borrowing for plant expansion, equipment purchases, or corporate acquisitions. Day-to-day business operations require bank credit lines, commercial paper programs, and similar short-term liquidity facilities (see Chapter 14 on the money markets for an explanation). Should credit markets "seize up," as happened in 2008–2009, the element of trust, the most basic foundation of financial markets, vanishes (more on this in the following chapter). Producers are willing to produce and buyers are willing to buy, but the flow of credit vanishes, thus preventing transactions from occurring and obstructing economic activity.

Before closing this section, it is worthwhile emphasizing that the point separating expansion from recession is not the same as that separating falling unemployment from rising unemployment. Figure 5.2 summarizes what we've learned in this chapter in this regard. Technically, the zero point of real GDP growth separates recession from expansion. Unemployment, however, does not begin to decline until real GDP begins to increase above its potential rate which, depending upon the country's growth of resources, can be far above zero.[8]

FIGURE 5.2 Summary of Relationship Between Recession/Expansion and Rising/Falling of Unemployment

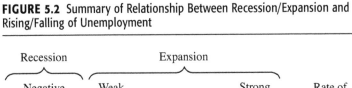

Oil Prices and the Macroeconomy

Oil price fluctuations have played an important role in macroeconomic fluctuations all over the world in recent times. Let's use the tools we've acquired to analyze oil's impact on the U.S. economy.

Demand for oil, in the short run, is relatively price-inelastic. When the price of a good or service increases, buyers typically respond by purchasing less—if possible. The opposite is true when the price decreases. The degree of demand responsiveness to the price change is termed "elasticity." With respect to oil, consumers, businesses, and the transportation sector have a tough time using less oil or switching to alternative energy sources immediately.[9] Homeowners, car drivers, manufacturers, utilities, and so on cannot reduce their consumption of oil substantially. As a result, the higher price simply increases the dollar amount of petroleum imports. The trade deficit jumps, reducing domestic economic activity. In effect, a portion of our GDP is transferred to the oil exporters.

The decline in economic activity pushes up the unemployment rate as the GDP gap widens. Ironically, the drop in GDP will reduce oil demand, since a portion of petroleum consumption depends on the level of economic activity. Indeed, in the short run, it is this "income effect" that will lower oil consumption, as opposed to the "price effect."

Prices are pushed up, directly for petroleum products, of course, and indirectly for others, as oil is an important input to the production process for many goods and services. If labor demands compensation for the higher price level and firms respond by raising output prices, an inflationary spiral may result.

The central bank sees the GDP gap widening. It also worries about inflation becoming embedded in the economy. Depending on the relative degree of each outcome, the Federal Reserve, as we will learn in the next chapter, may respond in opposite directions. If unemployment is more of a worry, it will add liquidity in order to lower interest rates, hopefully stimulate aggregate demand, and narrow the gap. If inflation dominates, the bank will withdraw liquidity, exacerbating the decline in GDP, but likely dampening inflation expectations and hence actual inflation.[10]

If the oil price increase is steep enough and long lasting, the structure of the economy will ultimately adapt. Households will find ways to conserve energy, producers will search for alternative inputs, and innovators will be rewarded for discovering cost efficiencies.[11] Of course, when all is said and done, the economy has to be worse off since one of its main inputs has become scarcer. In other words, potential GDP has declined. Still, the economy's resilience will ultimately show so that the long-term impact will not be as pronounced as that felt initially.

6

THE CENTRAL BANK'S GOALS, TARGETS, AND OPERATIONS

This chapter switches from what economists call the "real" side of the economy—transactions in goods and services, production decisions, and the labor market—to the financial side. Where does "money" fit in, what does the central bank do, and how do the financial markets interact with the real economy? These are the questions we deal with, and they are not easy. Economists are not clear (nor are they in agreement) about the answers. What makes this more difficult is that the analysis is often not intuitive. I'll try my best.

The Financial Sector

Transactions—purchasing goods, hiring labor, and so on—require payment. In a modern economy, this is done via an accepted means of remuneration, such as cash, checks, wire transfer, or credit cards. These means of payment, in the context of macroeconomics, are broadly referred to as "liquidity."[1] The aggregate level of economic activity, as reflected in GDP, determines the number of transactions taking place in the economy. Hence, the level of GDP determines the economy's liquidity needs.

Cash is the *ultimate* form of liquidity in a modern economy. Check payments are ultimately cleared between banks by the banking institutions sending cash—referred to as "reserves" when held at banks—to each other. Credit card transactions, which actually represent borrowing rather than payment, ultimately need to be paid for (typically by check). And wire transfers boil down to interbank transfers of reserves. In short, banks need reserves, or cash, for their day-to-day transactional business. The U. S. Federal Reserve mandates that a minimum amount of reserves be held by commercial banks, known as "reserve requirements." But it should be clear that banks would hold some reserves even without a central bank's imposed minimum. Thus the economy's need for liquidity comprises the nonbank public's cash requirements, plus required and excess reserves of the banking system.

The central bank is the creator, or supplier, of liquidity. The nexus of the bank's creation of and the economy's need for liquidity determines the (short-run) level of interest rates. The next sections describe how.

The Central Bank's Goals and Operations

Before we get into the dynamics of how a central bank's activities affect interest rates, it is necessary to understand the bank's ultimate goals.

All central banks have goals toward which their monetary actions are targeted. These goals are not necessarily compatible, hence trade-offs need to be addressed. The bank must set priorities, which may well depend not only on the state of the macroeconomy, such as, say, the extent of unemployment, but on politics and history as well. The central bank's goals include:

- *"Full" employment of resources.* Recall the definition of the GDP "gap" in the previous chapter. It measures the difference between actual and potential GDP, the latter determined by the economy's resources. This goal, therefore, can be translated as a closing of the gap. Operationally, full employment usually refers to the labor market. The word "full," however, does not necessarily mean zero unemployment. Rather, it is an employment level that removes as much of cyclical unemployment as possible without causing inflation to accelerate.[2]
- *Price stability.* This can mean zero inflation or "low" inflation, depending on the central bank (and on the particular economic environment). In the United States and the United Kingdom,

for example, the central banks seem to be comfortable with the inflation rate in the neighborhood of 2%. They would tolerate higher rates if such were required to climb out of recession.

- *Exchange rate policy.* Currency regimes cover many alternatives— freely floating, calculated intervention and, in the extreme, pegging (all are explained in Chapter 19 on foreign exchange). Exchange rate policy is usually not a priority for the Federal Reserve. It was a priority for many continental European countries prior to the introduction of the euro currency, and remains so for most developing economies (see Chapter 20).
- *Well-functioning financial markets.* The central bank, along with other government agencies, oversees the financial markets and is responsible for their "smooth" functioning.[3] This has taken on sharper meaning recently. The financial market upheaval and resultant dramatic increases in central bank involvement has pushed the U.S. Federal Reserve, the Bank of England, and others into a more direct supervisory role in financial institutions with even more regulatory authority over securities markets. Additionally, in many countries (including the United States), the central bank acts as the fiscal agent for the central government's debt issuance.

Now we're ready to explore how a central bank conducts its operations in order to achieve these goals. We'll use the U.S. Federal Reserve (The Fed) as the working example, although the concepts easily carry over, with some modifications, to other central banks.

The Central Bank's Balance Sheet

Like any bank, the U.S. Federal Reserve has assets and liabilities. Table 6.1 shows a simplified, bare-bones balance sheet. The Fed provides liquidity to the economy—via the banking system—by purchasing assets. It removes liquidity by selling assets. Why is that? Like any balance sheet, assets are matched by liabilities. The Fed's liabilities are the cash held by the public and reserves held by the banking system. That's why a dollar bill has "Federal Reserve Note" inscribed on it, just as a U.S. Treasury note is a liability of the U.S. Treasury. In other

TABLE 6.1 Federal Reserve Balance Sheet

Assets	Liabilities
Loans	
Securities	Cash
Foreign Reserves	
Gold	

words—and this is the key—*the economy's liquidity and the Federal Reserve's liabilities are one and the same.*

The asset side of the balance sheet does not appear unusual. In fact, the asset categories do not seem much different from what you'd see in an ordinary commercial bank's balance sheet. A few comments on the individual asset classes are in order. The Fed lends to financial institutions. Loans to banks are known as "discount window lending," with the discount rate set by the Fed. Loans to dealers, collateralized by government (and other approved) bonds, are made via repurchase agreements (see Chapter 21 on dealers and Chapter 22 on repos), with the interest rate determined in the open market. Foreign reserves are essentially the liabilities of foreign central banks (see Chapter 19). And gold is, well, physical gold (in effect, a global currency). The key to the Fed's influence on the macroeconomy, however, lies in the special nature of its liabilities.

Here are the dynamics. Let's consider the most straightforward operation (albeit not the most common, which we get to later)—a purchase of U.S Treasury bonds.[4] The Fed buys bonds from dealers, just as any other investor does.[5] The Fed pays for its purchase with its own IOU—those green pieces of paper we call money. Where does the money come from? The Fed prints it and "signs" it, just like you would write and sign an IOU when you borrow money from a friend, or a bank for that matter. After selling the bond to the central bank, this particular dealer might well replenish its inventory by purchasing bonds from other dealers or customers, paying for it with the money received from the first transaction. But at the end of the day (literally) there will be at least one dealer or customer holding the new IOU, or cash. That cash will be held at a depository institution, typically a bank. Thus the result of the Fed's action is that there will be one or more banks with more reserves than they had the day before. Cash, or reserves, earn no (or below-market) interest. The banks will search for an outlet for this cash, most likely by lending overnight, since they can't be certain they will not need the reserves for the next day's business. This will push down overnight interest rates. In particular, the *federal funds rate*—the (mostly overnight) interest rate banks charge each other for lending cash, or reserves—will fall, as the banks with excess cash offer the funds to other banks (via a fed funds broker) which may need it.

Let's go a step further. Banks now find that their cost of borrowing—at least from this one source, the federal funds market—is lower. This will feed into interest rates for other financial instruments. Rates on deposits and other money market instruments that banks use for financing are first to react. Since they must compete with the now lower rate on federal funds, their interest rates fall as well. In response, banks will ease their lending terms to customers, though the degree will depend upon their view of the permanence of the Fed policy shift. Then the process continues. Alternative sources of funds to bank customers—such as corporate bonds—need to decline in yield to remain competitive with bank loans. The resultant decrease in the cost of borrowing induces spending by the interest-rate–sensitive aggregate demand sectors discussed in the previous chapter (housing, consumer durables, capital expenditures by firms). GDP finally expands. Indeed, this result was likely the central bank's intention in the first place—to stimulate demand in the face of GDP falling below potential and the accompanying rise in unemployment.

Consider now a liquidity withdrawal by the Fed. This is accomplished by the bank *selling* assets to dealers. The dealer purchasing the bonds from the Fed may sell the bonds to another dealer or customer. Ultimately, though, bonds have left the Fed and entered the marketplace, and they must be paid for. At the end of the day, therefore, one or more banks will have less cash, or reserves, than at the day's start. The resultant search for reserves in the interbank market forces the federal funds rate up. This filters through the financial markets just as in the previous paragraph, but in reverse. Money market rates rise in order to compete with the higher federal funds rate. Bank lending tightens, causing bond yields to rise as well. Aggregate demand ultimately softens, thus weakening GDP growth. If the GDP gap was too tight in the Fed's view, it is now wider, reducing inflationary pressure, which was likely the Fed's goal when it initiated the move.

Central bank open market operations are not always for the purpose effecting a change in interest rates and thereby influencing aggregate demand and the gap. They are often (indeed more likely to be) reactive. Suppose the Fed has chosen a particular target for the federal funds rate which it feels is consistent with a GDP growth rate it deems appropriate for the current stage in the business cycle. One sector of the economy surprisingly increases its spending. Production rises in response. Separate from any effects on the gap and, possibly, inflationary pressure, the increase in economic activity requires more cash, hence more reserves at banks—that is, more liquidity. If the Fed were not to respond by adding liquidity in the manner described above, the interbank rate would rise above the central bank's target. Keeping the rate at its target requires a market operation to add liquidity simply to stay neutral. Similarly, but in opposite direction of course, a surprise decline in economic activity forces the Fed to react by subtracting liquidity in order to hold the federal funds rate steady.

It is important to appreciate the difference between a central bank's *target* and its *goal*. Goals are enumerated above—narrow GDP gap, low unemployment, tame inflation, and sound financial system. These constitute the bank's mandate. They are what the bank was created for. A target is just an intermediate step in meeting the goals. In our example using the Fed, the federal funds rate is the target. If the economy is weak, for example, the Fed reduces its target for the interbank rate. The Fed works to achieve its target by purchasing assets, payment for which adds liquidity, pushing the actual federal funds rate close to the target. If the target rate is not achieved, the Fed adds more liquidity. But the particular target is not important per se; rather the repercussions of the lower target rate on other interest rates and ultimately on lending and aggregate demand are what matters to the Fed. And that is how the bank is judged—not whether it met its targets, but whether it achieved its goals.

Federal Reserve Lending

Federal Reserve purchases and sales of bonds are transacted in the open market with dealers, just as any institutional investor would do. Hence, the term "open market operations." A more common Fed operation involves lending to financial institutions as opposed to outright securities purchases. The usual mechanism for lending is a repurchase agreement (repo).[6] The reason outright sales and purchases in the manner described above are infrequent is that the Fed's involvement in the market typically needs to be temporary.[7] An outright bond sale or purchase will most likely need to be eventually reversed. Repurchase agreements are temporary by nature. The Fed can add liquidity by lending money to bond dealers, taking their securities as collateral (a repo financing transaction from the dealer's perspective). The Fed can remove liquidity by "borrowing" from bond dealers, providing bond collateral (a reverse repo for the dealer). Since the repos unwind at their maturity, an offsetting transaction is unnecessary.

The financial market flow-through dynamics of a repo transaction are very similar to the outright purchase or sale of bonds, although the initial action is different. When the Fed makes a loan to a bond dealer, taking bonds as collateral, the dealer has more cash. The dealer can keep the cash on deposit with its bank (the cash is then labeled reserves). Alternatively, the dealer can buy more bonds from a customer or another dealer. Now *that* dealer has the cash. Or it can lend the cash to another dealer, taking that dealer's bonds as collateral. (In fact, *that* collateral can, in turn, be provided to the Fed to satisfy the original repo.) Whatever the choice, the banking system now has more reserves, ultimately pushing down the federal funds rate in the same manner described above. Should the Fed initiate the reverse action—borrowing money from dealers and providing dealers with bonds as collateral—reserves are drained from the system, causing the interbank interest rate to rise.

The Fed makes direct loans to banks via the "discount window." As a central bank asset, loans add liquidity to the economy. Repayment of the loans subtracts liquidity. The interest rate is known as the "discount rate" and follows the federal funds rate. Unlike repo transactions, which are initiated by the Fed in order to provide a specific amount of liquidity to the market, discount window borrowing is at the behest of banks (with the Fed's approval, of course). The discount window facility was created to provide a sort of liquidity buffer. Without it, should a situation arise causing insufficient reserves in the system for banks to meet requirements, the excess demand can cause an unwanted spike in the federal funds rate.[8] With reserves available to borrow, the federal funds rate still rises, but the rise is capped at the Fed's target. Generally, banks make use of the discount window when they are in a liquidity crunch or when their credit risk is perceived to be poor by other banks and they, therefore, cannot access the federal funds market without paying a penalty rate. Hence, banks have hesitated to take advantage of this funding source for fear of sending the wrong signal concerning their financial health to the market. Therefore, the Fed does not use the discount rate as the primary means of adjusting liquidity and achieving its interest-rate target.[9]

The Central Bank's "Transmission Mechanism"

Although not quite intuitive (especially the part about "money" being the Federal Reserve's liability), at least not on the first reading, all this seems quite logical. The central bank adds liquidity when the economy is weak and subtracts liquidity when it is strong. This affects (short-term) interest rates, a target which the Fed sets in order to manage aggregate demand. Aggregate demand, in turn, determines production, hence employment, allowing the central bank to narrow or widen the gap as it sees fit. Not bad!

The logic is definitively correct. But here's a dose of reality. The path between the central bank's tools—its control of liquidity, or reserves—and macroeconomic activity including inflation (the bank's ultimate goals) is long, circuitous, and uncertain. The name economists give to this path is the "monetary policy transmission mechanism." Consider a country in recession, or one experiencing a weak economy, which has prompted the central bank to add liquidity. Short-term interest rates have fallen to the bank's now lower target. Would this necessarily induce households to increase their spending? Lower borrowing rates—even if substantially lower—are not much of an inducement for an individual facing unemployment or observing others being laid off. On the corporate side, a firm with weak or negative profits does not think about expansionary capital spending, despite very low bond yields. Economists refer to this as the economy having a "low interest-rate elasticity." For us it means that the success of stimulating demand with lower interest rates is far from assured in an economy already in a weak state. On top of this, even if aggregate demand is stimulated, there is a substantial time lag between the reduction in financing rates and the actual spending on goods and services.[10]

The Yield Curve

We have an entire chapter coming up on the yield curve (Chapter 8), a crucial chapter. We need to introduce it partially here because it belongs in any discussion of the "monetary policy transmission mechanism." The yield curve is defined in the first chapter as a graph representing the relationship between maturity and interest rates on bonds. We will see in Chapter 8 that, on the most fundamental level, the yield on a long-term asset reflects short-term interest rates expected over the life of that asset. For example, the three-month interest rate equals the average of overnight rates expected over the next three months. The thirty-year bond yield is the average of the expected next thirty 1-year interest rates. It is clear, therefore, that *expectations* are the crucial variable driving the shape of the yield curve. What drives expectations of future interest rates? We can use our knowledge of the economy's dynamics acquired in the previous chapter (plus borrowing a bit from Chapter 8) to conclude:

- In the near term, interest-rate expectations are driven by market participants' understanding of central bank policy. The bank's policy, in turn, is governed by its view of and goals for the economy.
- Further out on the curve—that is for maturities a couple of years away—credit supply and demand take center stage, which means that the state of the business cycle is the primary determinant of interest rates.
- For longer-term rates, structural factors underlying the economy matter most of all, since business cycle factors tend to balance out. Structural factors include budget deficits/surpluses and the savings rate.
- Market participants' expectations of inflation are an "add-on" to the above "real" factors (see the next chapter).

Here are the implications for monetary policy and the transmission mechanism. The interest rate at any maturity point on the yield curve equals the average of short-term interest rates up until that maturity, as explained earlier. This implies that longer-term rates are affected by all the factors governing expectations for shorter-term rates, *but not conversely*. For example, the 30-year bond yield reflects expectations for near-term monetary policy, the stage of the business cycle plus the budget deficit (plus expected inflation over the next 30 years)—all the factors expected to play out over the next three decades. Because it *averages* those expectations, a change in the overnight federal funds rate cannot have more than a marginal impact on the 30-year rate unless the change is expected to be in effect for a very long time.[11]

So, why does this matter? It's almost obvious. Central banks can set a target for the shortest of interest rates, and, by virtue of their monopoly over ultimate liquidity creation, they can pretty much hit that target. However, longer-term interest rates are a much more important factor in influencing aggregate demand. The yield on corporate bonds is certainly more of a determinant of capital expenditures than is the commercial paper rate. And mortgage interest rates enter the potential homebuyer's cost calculus, not rates on bank certificates of deposit (CDs). But short-term rate movements are not mirrored in long-term rates. This tenuous link between short- and long-term rates—what we now know as the shape of the yield curve—means that the central bank's influence over spending is just as tenuous.[12]

Other Factors Interfering with the Transmission Mechanism

You can see that the central bank's job is not an easy one. Here are some other realities standing between the bank's control over reserves and its influence over the economy:

- *Credit spreads.* Private borrowers—households, firms, financial institutions—pay more than the government does to borrow. This is known as a credit spread, as it compensates the lender for credit risk or risk of default. The Fed may succeed in getting Treasury rates down (or up, as the case may be), but if credit spreads widen (or narrow) substantially, the effort may be for naught. Indeed, credit spreads tend to widen during periods of weak economic activity, just when the central bank wants rates to decline (and they narrow during periods of economic strength, precisely when the bank pushes for rates to rise).[13]

- *Credit rationing.* Credit spreads do not always tell the whole story. Indeed, during periods of financial distress, they provide a quite limited picture of credit availability. Here's an example. Suppose the economy is weak, and Treasury interest rates as a consequence are low, say 4% . Corporate bonds of a particular grade yield 6%. At this 2% spread, there may be more potential borrowers than lenders. Basic economics says that this should cause the spread to rise, discouraging some borrowers and, at the same time, encouraging more lenders, until an equilibrium is reached at a wider spread. Not necessarily. Bonds are not like widgets, cars, bananas, or movies. The wider spread—hence higher interest rate—won't do anything for the lender if the borrower defaults. But here's a more serious departure from widgets, and the like. A lower price for a good or service does not change that good or service; it just makes it more attractive to the potential purchaser. A higher interest rate promised by a borrower *increases the risk of default* (since the firm now has to allocate a greater portion of its earnings to debt service). Lenders, instead of increasing their required rate, or spread, may ration credit as a result. And they may impose other costs upon the borrower, such as more collateral or stricter covenants, in order to reduce their risk exposure.[14] These non-interest-rate factors play an even greater role in household borrowing. Financial institutions don't charge individuals different rates based on their creditworthiness (except for downgrading a mortgage applicant to "subprime"). Downpayment requirements, credit checks, and other devices are used to ration funds. In short, the Fed's ability to influence interest rates may matter little.

- *Liquidity hoarding.* The central bank's injection of reserves, as we've seen above, travels through the banking system on its way to affecting the real economy, the bank's ultimate goal. This liquidity can get off the highway, so to speak, via a number of exits. Banks can keep the reserves on their balance sheet as cash rather than lend it. Or, they can use the cash to pay off deposits.

Either way, they've upgraded their capital base, which banks typically seek to do in a weak economy. Should banks indeed decide to lend out the newly acquired cash, they may well channel it into Treasury securities rather than into the hands of private borrowers who might use the funds to purchase consumer or capital goods.[15]

- *Systemic risk.* If you haven't come across this term, then you've been asleep the past five years. It's been used to describe the fragility of the financial system, to characterize the interdependence of financial institutions, and to warn against "excesses"—excess debt, excess risk, excess derivatives. In short, it's an overused term. Here's what systemic risk means in our context. Lending, investing, financial contracts—they all ultimately rely on trust. Not necessarily trust that the specific entity on the other side of the transaction has the ability and willingness to honor its obligations but rather trust in the financial system—its infrastructure, including the laws that govern the system. After all, a loan, bond, or derivative contract is just a piece of paper! When this trust starts to thin, it quickly evaporates. No one wants to be the last person holding the paper. Clearly, in such an environment, there is little a central bank can directly do, through its management of reserves, to get funds to private borrowers or encourage financial contracts (unless it lends the funds itself!).

The Big Picture

It's time to integrate the past two chapters. A lot has been covered, and a summary with a view of the entire macroeconomic landscape is called for. What follows may, at first, seem like an academic discussion. It's not, because without it, there's a gaping hole in the structure we've built.

We've succeeded in explaining how the interaction between the Federal Reserve's provision of liquidity, reflecting its monetary policy decisions, and the economy's need for liquidity, as governed by the level of GDP, determines interest rates. If this is the case, what role is there for credit factors, such as the government budget deficit, household savings behavior, and the debt dynamics of firms over the business cycle in determining interest rates? They must matter![16]

This is a difficult question. But we can't shy away from it. Here's how to think about all this in a "big picture" way. It might seem from the above analysis that the Fed, and every industrialized country's central bank, has the ability to force the overnight interbank interest rate to any level by adding or subtracting reserves until a target rate is reached. In reality, though, *it cannot do so continuously.* Remember: Interest rates were around way before modern central banking was born. Clearly, there have to be some other fundamental determinants. A central bank cannot push Interest rates away from what they would otherwise be for any protracted length of time. If it forces rates too low for too long, inflation will accelerate until the currency—the central bank's IOU—becomes worthless. If it forces rates too high for too long, people will find ways to economize on the currency, making the currency less necessary, and in the extreme not used at all, vitiating the central bank's source of power.

Where would interest rates be without the central bank's intervention? That is, how do supply and demand for credit—as opposed to supply and demand for *liquidity*—determine rates? During a business cycle upturn, firms tend to demand more capital for expansion purposes, to carry inventory, perform research and development, and so on. Households tend to save a smaller portion of their earnings when the economy is strong. Together these factors cause interest rates to rise as more firms compete for savers' scarcer funds. During an economic contraction, the reverse behavior occurs, resulting in excess fund availability and lower interest rates. Over long periods of time, expansions and contractions tend to balance out, and the economy grows according to its potential.

A government budget deficit will raise interest rates relative to what the business cycle otherwise dictates, as the government competes with businesses for the given pool of savings. This would also result from a noncyclically related lower household savings rate. For example, a deficit may reflect demographic factors such as an aging population or a developing country simply too poor to save. Conversely, interest rates will be lower in the presence of a budget surplus and/or higher savings rates. A budget in balance will be neutral with respect to rates.

To summarize, there is a "natural" level for interest rates—that is, one determined by economic fundamentals, most prominently the business cycle interacting with household savings, and government budget deficits or surpluses—which equilibrates supply and demand for credit. *Notice the absence of the central bank in this rather long sentence.* What is the central bank's role? Because of its monopoly on liquidity creation (and the economy's need for it) the bank can—in the short run—push actual (overnight) rates toward a chosen target, which may differ from the natural rate. Over time, however, the actual rate must approach the natural rate, just as over time actual GDP tends to approach its potential level. What then, is the consequence of the central bank's liquidity creation policy in the long run, if interest rates are set by credit supply and demand and output hovers around potential? The overall price level of goods and services; that is, the inflation rate. In the long run—economists are wont to say—inflation is a monetary phenomenon.[17]

Why would a central bank intervene and cause interest rates to diverge from their natural level? That's where macroeconomics comes in. If GDP is below its potential, with the attendant disruptions to labor markets and household income that this situation brings, there are natural economic forces tending to push GDP back toward its potential. Unemployment of labor should reduce wage demands, making hiring more attractive to employers. Prices of other inputs, such as commodities, should fall, reflecting weak demand and resulting in lower prices for goods and services. This increases demand for products, inspiring producers to hire and produce, raising GDP. The problem is that this process takes time, during which the loss in production and employment, as reflected in the GDP gap, cannot be made up. The central bank, by adding liquidity and forcing rates below the natural rate, can speed up the adjustment process. The converse is true for an inflationary environment, which has its own economic costs. Here, high prices should slow down the economy on its own, which will ultimately release price pressure. The central bank, by removing liquidity, advances the slowdown, which reduces its costs to society.[18]

PART III

INFLATION, YIELD CURVE, AND CREDIT FACTORS IN BONDS

7

INFLATION-PROTECTED BONDS

All bonds protect the investor from inflation. The difference between inflation-protected bonds and ordinary bonds is that the former provide protection from *unexpected* inflation whereas the latter do not. This chapter opens with an explanation of the first sentence above. The rest of the chapter explains the second sentence.

Real versus Nominal Interest Rates

Inflation means an *overall* increase in the price level. Particular goods and services can rise in price because they become scarcer or more expensive to produce than others. This does not mean that their prices have become *inflated*. That would be considered a *real* price change, since their prices have increased *relative* to other goods and services. When *all* goods and services increase in price, that's inflation.[1]

Suppose you're considering lending $100 for a year. You expect inflation to be 2% between now and the end of the year. When the borrower returns $102 to you, you're just breaking even—whatever you could have purchased for your $100 now is expected to cost $102 at the end of the year. So you'll be earning nothing on your loan—you're no better off. Put another way, you're *really* earning 0%. In financial terminology, the stated, or "nominal," interest rate on your loan is 2%, but the "real" interest rate is 0% percent. In order to actually get a return on your money, you need a nominal interest rate greater than 2%.

Another way to say this is that the borrower must pay you 2% *above* the real interest rate. Now think about the market as a whole. Investors have different expectations regarding future inflation—some more, some less, than 2%. But there is only one interest rate stated on a bond. We arrive, therefore, at the following conclusion. Whatever real return investors demand for a particular maturity loan or bond, the nominal interest rate for that maturity must equal that return plus an extra amount for the inflation rate expected by investors as a group over that period. In short:

> *The nominal interest rate for any maturity equals the real interest rate plus the market's expected rate of inflation for that period.*

Real versus Nominal Rate of Return

Suppose that, based on an expected inflation rate of 2%, the interest rate on a one-year loan is 5%, for a "real" rate of 3%. Once the year is over and the loan repaid with interest, the actual inflation rate over the year the loan was outstanding will be known. If the inflation rate turned out to be 2% as expected, the lender earned—in "real" terms—3%, which was the real rate set at the outset, based on the expected inflation rate. If, instead, inflation turned out to be 4%, the real rate of return was 1%, because only 1% was earned over and above the inflation rate. If inflation turned out to be 1%, the real return was 4%. In other words, whereas the "nominal" return is fixed, representing the real interest rate plus the *expected* inflation rate over the period, the real return depends on the actual inflation rate over the investment period. Only when the actual inflation rate turns out as expected will the investment produce the real return anticipated at inception.

Ordinary versus Inflation-Protected Bonds: The Basic Idea

The goal of an inflation-protected bond (IPB) is to provide the investor with a fixed real rate of interest, regardless of the inflation rate that actually occurs over the investment period. The best way to understand

TABLE 7.1 Cash Flows of 5-Year Government Bonds

Year	Ordinary 4% Bond	Inflation-Protected Bond
1	4	1.5 + inflation in Year 1
2	4	1.5 + inflation in Year 2
3	4	1.5 + inflation in Year 3
4	4	1.5 + inflation in Year 4
5	4 + 100	1.5 + inflation in Year 5 + 100

how this novel type of bond accomplishes this is to compare its cash flows to those of an ordinary bond under different inflation scenarios. Table 7.1 compares five-year government bonds. The first is an ordinary fixed-coupon note. The second is a "no-frills" IPB.[2] Both are assumed to pay their coupons annually.

As is normal, coupon payments are made at the end of the payment period, in this case each successive year after the issue date. The ordinary bond pays 4%, or $4 per $100 of face value. What about the IPB? It also makes a fixed payment, in this case 1.5% each year, or $1.5 per $100 face value. Let's assume that the market prices each bond at par on the issue date. Since both bonds are guaranteed by the government and have the same maturity, no one would pay par for the IPB if all it paid were the 1.5% coupon while the ordinary bond pays 4%. It must be providing compensation in some other form. Indeed it does. At the end of the first year, it pays the bondholder whatever the inflation rate was over the preceding year,[3] *on top* of the 1.5%. Say between the bond issue date and the first coupon date, prices of goods and services in the economy rose by an average of 2%. The government sends the bondholder 3.5%—1.5% for the stated coupon plus 2% compensation for the actual inflation rate.

The next coupon works the same way. The government agency charged with estimating inflation calculates the actual inflation rate over the previous year, and the investor receives that rate in addition to the 1.5% coupon. That is, the investor receives 1.5% plus the actual inflation rate between the first coupon payment date and the second. This continues throughout the bond's life—the government is always looking *backward* to get the actual historical inflation rate to add to the bond's stated coupon. That sum multiplies the face value of the debt to produce the coupon. At maturity, there is a final coupon payment of this same sort, plus return of the principal.

When thinking about which bond to invest in, you'll be estimating what inflation is likely to average over the next five years. If you expect inflation to average more than 2.5%, you'll prefer the IPB. If you expect it to average below 2.5%, you'll go with the ordinary bond. If you expect inflation to average 2.5%, you're indifferent. Suppose, in the marketplace, both bonds are priced at par. As such, the market as a whole must believe that there is no advantage of one over the other (otherwise they would fetch different prices). That is, their expected return must be the same.[4] We can conclude that the market's expected inflation rate for the next five years must be 2.5%! This is a very interesting and useful result. When both bonds are priced at par, the difference between the ordinary bond's coupon and the fixed portion of the ITB's coupon reflects market participants' average expected inflation rate. (If the bonds are not at par, the difference in their yields to maturity reflects the market's expected inflation rate.) We have, therefore, a very important implication for investors:

> The choice between an ordinary and inflation-protected bond depends not on the investor's view of inflation increasing or decreasing. It depends on the investor's view of inflation relative to the market's view. (The market's view is given to us by the difference between the yield on an ordinary bond and that of the inflation-protected bond of equal maturity.) If the investor thinks that inflation will be higher than the market believes it will be, then the IPB is the choice. If the investor thinks that inflation will be lower than the market believes it will be, then the ordinary bond is the choice.

The above paragraph involves a forward-looking exercise at the time of purchase. Let's now jump ahead a year and look backward. Suppose during the first year of the two bonds' existence consumer price inflation reaches 3%. The ordinary bond will send you a coupon of 4%. This is the bond's nominal return. But, after inflation, your real return is only 1%. The inflation-protected bond will send you a coupon equal to 4.5%, which is its nominal return. After inflation, that's 1.5%. Now assume that between the first and second year inflation is only 2%. The ordinary bond's coupon is still, of course, 4%, which is its nominal return. The real return it provides is 2%. The IPB's coupon will be 3.5%, its nominal return, but its real return is again 1.5%. Continue this exercise for each of the years. The ordinary bond's nominal return is fixed, but its real return varies according to what the actual inflation rate is each year. Conversely, the inflation-protected bond's nominal return depends on the actual inflation rate. But its real return is fixed. In other words, *the IPB's real return to the investor is unaffected by inflation surprises.* When will their returns (both nominal and real) turn out to be the same? This will occur when inflation turns out to be as expected, in our case 2.5%, as seen from the difference in their coupons.This explains why market participants refer to the IPB as a "real" bond and to the ordinary as a "nominal" bond.

Price Changes and Risk

Let's review some of the basic points of bond price movements from Chapter 3. An ordinary bond's coupon is fixed on the issuance date. The coupon reflects market conditions such as interest rates. Over time, interest rates in the marketplace change. If rates increase, new bonds will carry coupons reflecting current rates, making the existing bond, carrying the old, lower coupon, less attractive. Its price must decline for it to be competitive with the current coupon bonds. Conversely, should interest rates decline, new bonds will carry lower coupons, making the old bond more attractive, thus raising its price.

Now let's combine this with what we learned at the beginning of this chapter. Every interest rate contains two components: a real rate and compensation for expected inflation. When a bond is issued, its coupon reflects the real interest rate in the marketplace as of the issuance date and the market's expectation for inflation over the life of the bond, with those expectations set on the issuance date, based on information available then. Over time, interest rates change. The change reflects movements in real rates, changes in expected inflation, or any combination of the two. This is the crucial idea. If real interest rates rise, due, say, to shifts in the supply and demand for credit as explained in Chapter 6, new bonds will reflect this higher rate, pushing existing bond prices down. Or, if market participants expect inflation to be higher than they were forecast at the time of the bond issuance, new bonds will carry a higher coupon reflecting these revised expectations. This, too, will cause the price of existing ordinary bonds to fall. The opposite is true for a decline in real interest rates or a decline in expected inflation; in those situations prices of existing bonds will rise. In short, whether the source of the change in nominal interest rates is movements in real interest rates *or* shifts in expected inflation, ordinary bond prices will react.

What about the inflation-protected bonds? Remember, the real component of their coupon is fixed as of the issuance date, just like an ordinary bond. Only the extra payment for inflation changes along with actual inflation. If real rates rise in the marketplace, the IPB's price will fall, just as the price of the ordinary bond does in this situation. Why? Since the bond permanently carries the original "real" coupon, which is now low compared to current bonds, its price must fall to be competitive. However, if the market's expectation for inflation increases, the bond will not fall in price, since its coupon payments will rise commensurately. Let's go the other way now. A fall in real interest rates will cause an increase in the IPB's price, since its real coupon is fixed at the old, now relatively high, level. A decline in inflation expectations, on the other hand, will not result in a higher price, as it would for the ordinary bond, since the IPB's coupon will fall commensurately. In short:

> *Inflation-protected bond price movements are insulated from changes in inflation expectations, but not from changes in real interest rates.*

This explains the opening paragraph of this chapter: the *protection* in inflation-*protected* bonds relates to *unexpected* inflation.

U.S. Treasury Inflation-Protected Securities

The U.S. Treasury's version of inflation-protected bonds are known as TIPS—Treasury inflation-protected security. Their structure is somewhat different from that of the simple IPB, but they achieve the same purpose—to protect the holder from unanticipated shifts in inflation, that is, from inflation turning out different from the market's expectations.[5]

Rather than add each year's (or period's) inflation rate to a "real" coupon, the U.S. Treasury's approach is to update the principal according to the actual inflation rate. For example, consider a five-year TIPS. Let's make it simple by assuming that the coupon frequency is annual. Say the "real" coupon is 3%—you'll see soon why the label "real" is appropriate. The bond is issued with a face value of $100, which is the beginning principal. If there is zero inflation throughout the bond's life, you'll receive 3% × $100 = $3 each year, plus $100 at the end of five years. Suppose instead consumer price inflation equals 2% over the first year of the bond's life. At the end of that year, the bond's principal is adjusted to 1.02 × $100 = $102. Your first coupon will, therefore, be 3% × $102 = $3.06. If there is zero inflation for the rest of the bond's life, your coupon stays at $3.06, and you will receive your $102 of principal at maturity. What if there is 2.5% inflation over the second year? Then the $102 principal is adjusted again, to 1.025 × $102 = $104.55. Your second coupon is 3% × $104.55 = $3.1365. The rule, therefore, is that at the end of each year the bond's principal is readjusted based on the past year's inflation rate. The coupon is then calculated based on the inflation-adjusted principal. The final principal payment at maturity thus reflects the *cumulative* inflation rate over the five years.[6]

How TIPS Protect against Unanticipated Inflation

The best way to see how TIPS accomplish what they were created to accomplish is by comparing a TIPS bond with an ordinary, or nominal, bond in the context of an investor's rate of return. A side benefit of this approach will be a dispelling of the notion that TIPS are riskless. They are riskless only with respect to inflation changes, not with respect to real interest-rate changes.

Let's consider the TIPS in the previous section: five-year maturity, 3% coupon (paid annually), issued today at par. We'll compare its performance in hypothetical market situations to an ordinary Treasury five-year note, with a nominal 4.5% coupon, also issued at par. We know that the difference between the two yields—1.5%—represents the market's expected annual inflation rate for the next five years, on average, as of today. The investor has a one-year horizon and will sell each bond at the end of the year. Assume for now that both bonds remain at par on the sale date.[7] The nominal bond produces $104.50 in cash flow at year's end ($100 principal, at unchanged price, plus $4.50 for the coupon). Recalling the methodology of rate of return (ROR) in Chapter 4, the bond's *nominal* ROR is 4.5%. What about its *real* ROR? Assume at first that inflation over the year did turn out to equal 1.5%. The bond's real ROR is 3%—the nominal ROR 4.5% less the actual inflation rate.

What about the TIPS? Since inflation was 1.5%, the bond's principal is adjusted to $101.50. Together with the 3% coupon, the $104.50 proceeds produce a 4.5% nominal ROR and 3% real ROR, equal to those of the ordinary bond.[8] *If inflation turns out as expected by the market, the TIPS and the ordinary bond produce the same rate of return.*

What if inflation turns out to be 2%, greater than expected? The ordinary bond's cash flows are unchanged (again assuming an unchanged price for the bond when sold). Its nominal return is still 4.5%. But its real return is now 4.5% less 2%, or 2.5%. And the TIPS? The principal is adjusted to $102. Adding the coupon, its proceeds of $105 mean that the nominal return is 5% and that its real return is 5% less 2%, or 3%! Regardless of what happens to the inflation rate, the TIPS cash flows adjust, keeping the real return fixed at 3%, the bond's coupon. Of course, were inflation to drop below 1.5%, the nominal bond's real return would exceed 3%, since less would be subtracted from 4.5%. The TIPS, however, will continue to provide the 3% ROR. Only when inflation turns out as expected—1.5%—will the two bonds produce the same nominal and real rates of return. We have our key result: The ordinary bond's nominal return is fixed, hence its real return will be affected by actual inflation over the holding period. The TIPS's nominal return is not fixed—it changes by the amount required to keep its real return fixed. In other words, the TIPS's real ROR is insensitive to shifts in the inflation rate from what was expected. Since this may be a bit confusing—and not understood by many investors—let me restate it, but from a different angle (and see Table 7.2):

- If inflation accelerates, but at the rate the market expected, TIPS and ordinary bonds will *perform equally*. If inflation decelerates, but at the rate expected by the market, TIPS and ordinary bonds *perform equally*.

TABLE 7.2 Effects of Changes in Actual Inflation on Rate of Return (ROR)

	Nominal ROR	Real ROR
Ordinary bond	Fixed	Not fixed
TIPS	Not fixed	Fixed

- If inflation accelerates by more than the market expected, TIPS *outperform* ordinary bonds. If inflation accelerates, but by less than the market expected, TIPS *underperform* ordinary bonds.
- If inflation decelerates by more than the market expected, ordinary bonds *outperform* TIPS. If inflation decelerates, but by less than the market expected, ordinary bonds *underperform* TIPS.[9]

The above analysis assumes that the bonds' yields on the investor's horizon date are the same as on the purchase date. This allows us to concentrate on the inflation effect. Now we need to recognize the possibility that interest rates may move. This will cause the prices of the bonds to change and affect nominal and, perhaps, real rates of return.

Effects of Interest Rate Changes

Let's start with an ordinary bond. Recall that every interest rate contains a real rate plus an expected inflation component. If either of these increases (or decreases), interest rates rise (or fall). Consider the previous case where inflation during the first year climbed from the expected 1.5% rate to an actual 2% rate, which caused the real return of the ordinary bond to decline. If investors now extrapolate this inflation increase to the future, that is, they revise upward their average expected inflation rate for the next four years (the remaining maturity of the bond), the bond's yield will rise. Its price will fall. This is simple bond logic—since the cash flows of an ordinary bond are fixed, they can't keep pace with current market conditions, so their prices must adjust. Not so the TIPS. We already learned that its real return over the holding period remains intact. Further, the upward revision in expected inflation will not cause its price to fall. Investors realize that the higher inflation will simply result in more principal, hence a higher coupon as the coupon rate is paid on the constantly appreciating principal. This will maintain the real return. Hence, the bond will not lose anything by inflation rising in the future, and its price does not fall. Of course it works in the other direction as well. A decline in the market's inflation expectations lowers nominal interest rates, causing ordinary bonds to appreciate. By the same logic, the TIPS's cash flows will be expected to be adjusted downwards, again maintaining its real rate. This will prevent the bond from appreciating. In short, not only are real rates of return from inflation-protected bonds insensitive to inflation shifts, but their prices are as well.

This is not the case for changes in real rates. Remember that the TIPS's *real* coupon is fixed, in our case at 3%. *All* yields have two components—a real interest rate and an expected inflation factor. So, here is simple TIPS logic. Since the *real* cash flows of a TIPS are fixed, they can't keep pace with changing market conditions with respect to *real* interest rates. Their prices must adjust. On the horizon date, real rates for four-year Treasury notes (nominal or otherwise) may well be different from the 3% existing on the investment date. This may be the result of macroeconomic activity strengthening or weakening and investors deciding to change their required compensation for time value of money, or any of the other factors cited in Chapter 6. Furthermore, the note will have rolled down the yield curve by the next year—it will be a four-year rather than a five-year note, with a likely different real yield. In short, because the real coupon on a TIP is fixed, any change in real market interest rates will force the TIPS's price to adjust to the new rate environment, much like a nominal bond must when interest rates change (either because of the real rate or the expected inflation rate changing). So, although TIPS are insensitive to inflation shifts, they are just as sensitive to real interest-rate shifts as their nominal counterparts.[10]

TABLE 7.3 Effects of Changes in Real Interest Rates and Expected Inflation on Bond Prices

	Increase/Decrease in Real Interest Rate	Increase/Decrease in Expected Inflation
Ordinary bond	Lower/higher	Lower/higher
TIPS	Lower/higher	Neutral/neutral

Continuing with our example, if on the horizon date the four-year real interest rate is 3.1% rather than 3%, the TIPS's price (using the bond math of Chapter 3) drops from par to $99.6292.[11] Table 7.3 provides a summary.

Let's conclude this chapter by connecting the last paragraph with one of the main ideas in Chapter 6, concerning central bank behavior. Suppose actual inflation in the economy accelerates, causing people to revise upwards their expectations of future inflation. Tables 7.2 and 7.3 together tell us that TIPS will be unaffected. Indeed, that's the whole point of TIPS. However—and this is a major point, so digest it well— the central bank is likely to respond to this development by raising its target interest rate *by more than the inflation rate*. This means short-term *real* rates rise. To the extent that longer maturity real interest rates follow (which we will see in the next chapter), Table 7.3 tells us that TIPS prices will decline. This is known as the "feedback" effect from inflation to real interest rates.

8

THE YIELD CURVE

Someone suddenly walks up to you and asks, "Tell me what's going on in the bond market right now. You have 15 seconds." You don't need to run away (unless you're in New York City, of course). Just show him or her the yield curve. You don't even need to say anything.

Definition

The yield curve provides the best summary picture of the state of the bond market. It is a graph relating yield, or interest rates,[1] of a representative group of bonds to their remaining maturities. It is rarely a straight line, hence the name yield "curve." Figure 8.1 presents a sample of yield curves.

Market participants identify yield curves by their shapes. Yield curve I is sharply upward sloping, while II is simply upward sloping. Notice that the *level* of yields in II, at least in the early maturities, is above that in I, yet this is not mentioned when contrasting the two shapes. Yield Curve III is downward sloping, also known as a "negative" yield curve. IV is "flat," although it would be unlikely for the slope to be perfectly zero. Finally, Yield Curve V is an example of an unusual shape, known as a "humped" curve.

There really is no single yield curve at any point in time. There will be one for Treasury bonds and another one for corporate bonds. In fact, within the corporate sector, there will be different curves for bonds of different credit risk classes. The curve for Japanese bonds will be different from the curve for U.S. bonds. There is even a yield curve covering derivatives—a swaps curve! Within Treasury bonds, a yield curve can be constructed using only benchmark issues.[2] Or it can cover the gamut of

FIGURE 8.1 Sample Yield Curves

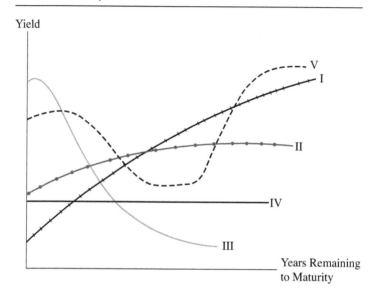

maturities by using all Treasury bonds. Figure 8.2 compares these two methods. The two charts in the figure convey similar information. The chart on the left is a smooth graph, as it contains a continuum of data points—Treasuries of all maturities along with their yields. The chart on the right takes account of only the few most liquid points on the maturity spectrum and splices their yields with sections of straight lines.

Just as yields change constantly, yield curves can change their shapes every day. Of course, the difference between the curve from one day to the next will be small. But over the course of a business cycle, the yield curve's shape will change dramatically. In this chapter our job is to understand what determines the shape of the curve. Crucially, we relate the shape to the market's expectations of the future. Once we understand the determinants of the curve's shape, we'll draw conclusions that we apply in forthcoming chapters.

The Role of Expectations

There are a number of ways to go about examining the relationships among yields on bonds of different maturities. Let's take the perspective of an investor. I believe the approach presented here will give you

FIGURE 8.2 (a) Smooth and (b) Straight-line Plotting of Yield Curves

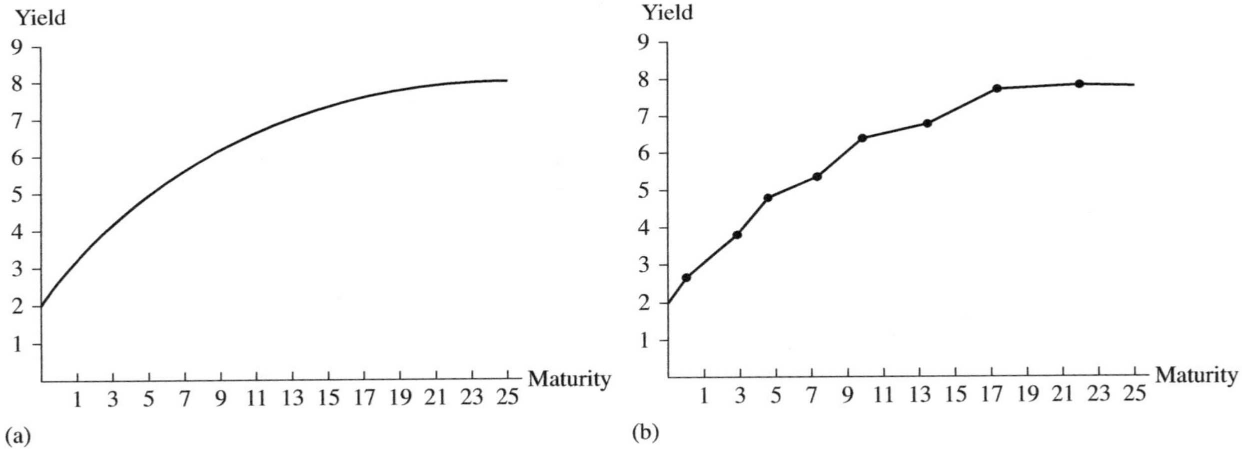

TABLE 8.1 Bond Yields for Various Maturities

1-Year	2-Year	3-Year	4-Year
2%	3%	3.5%	4%

the proper intuition about the yield curve and its implications for bond pricing and investment management.

Look at Table 8.1. It contains just a piece of the yield curve for Treasury bonds at a particular moment. In the situation depicted, the two-year Treasury interest rate exceeds that of the one-year, the three-year exceeds the two-year, and so on. Hence the yield curve, at least in the one- to four-year range, is upward sloping. Why is it so?

Suppose you want to invest for two years; (that is, you have a two-year horizon). If you buy the Treasury's two-year note, you'll earn 3% each year. If you buy the one-year note, you'll get 2% for the first year, and then you'll need to reinvest the money for the second year at a rate unknown as of today. Say you expect the one-year rate next year to be 2% again. You certainly would prefer the two-year note in that case, wouldn't you? In fact, even if you expect the one-year rate next year to be 3% you'd still prefer the two-year note—2% and another 3% is still not as good as 3% twice. On the other hand, if your expectation is 5% for the upcoming one-year rate, then the one-year-at-a-time strategy—known as "rollover"—is preferable. So, here's the obvious conclusion. The choice between the two strategies involves comparing the average of today's one-year rate and the expected one-year rate for next year to today's two-year rate. When will you be indifferent? Only if you expect next year's one-year rate to be 4%, since 2% and 4% average to 3%, the same as the two-year rate available today.[3]

Here's the punch line. Every rational investor with a two-year holding period is looking at the same information and making similar calculations. Those choosing the two-year Treasury with the 3% locked in as opposed to the one-year rollover strategy must believe that the one-year Treasury interest rate next year will be *at most* 4%, or else they'd be acting irrationally. Those choosing the one-year rollover must expect the one-year rate next year to be *at least* 4%, or else *they'd* be acting irrationally. Investors have different expectations. But there is only a single one-year rate in the market right now, and only a single two-year rate right now. These two rates together tell us that the *average expectation* of the entire group of investors must be 4% for the one-year rate next year. How so? Suppose the average expectation is for the rate to be above 4%, say 5%. Then investors on average would be shunning the Treasury two-year note and flocking to the one-year bill. This would cause the price of the two-year to decline and its yield to rise. But the fact is that the two-year is at 4%. So this cannot be the average view. The same logic tells us that the average investor cannot believe the one-year rate next year will be less than 4%, because if he did believe that, investors would be pushing up the price of the two-year and reducing its yield. We must conclude that, based on the observed one- and two-year interest rates, the average expectation of investors is that the one-year Treasury interest rate next year will be 4%.[4]

"Hold on a second," you say to me. "Sounds nice, but didn't you leave out something important? What about risk? Isn't purchasing a two-year Treasury note riskier than purchasing a one-year? Aren't longer-term bonds riskier than shorter-term, as a rule? And, therefore, shouldn't the two-year note yield more than the one-year, independent of market expectations?" No, my friend, not necessarily. Don't accept someone else's "rule" until you've thought it through yourself. This investor has a two-year horizon. If he buys the two-year Treasury note paying 3%, he knows exactly what the total amount of earnings will be at the end of his holding period.[5] But if he buys the one-year Treasury, he has no way of knowing what the second year's interest rate will be. He can form expectations surrounding it, as we have done, but it's *risky*. So there you go. For this particular investor, the one-year note is more risky than the two-year. On the other hand, for an investor with a one-year horizon, the two-year will be more risky, because he will need to sell it after the first year, at a price unknown as of today. In short, we cannot a priori say that a two-year Treasury note is riskier than a one-year.[6] It could go either way. It depends on the particular investor's horizon. And, on an overall market level, it depends on the preponderance of investors with two-year horizons versus those with one-year horizons. The same is true for a ten-year Treasury bond compared to a five-year. Is the ten-year necessarily more risky than the five-year? Not if you have a ten-year horizon. In that case the five-year is quite a bit more risky, since you will be subject to not knowing what the rollover interest rate will be for five years! With the ten-year Treasury, by contrast, you know exactly what you'll be earning. So, again, it depends on the population of ten-year horizon investors relative to five-year horizon investors. You don't like this paragraph? It destroys some preconceived notions? Calm down. We return to this topic later.

We could have gone through this same exercise from a borrower's perspective. If she needs funds for two years and is faced with the choice of locking in 3% for each of the years or borrowing at 2% for the first year and re-borrowing at an unknown rate for the second year she will be indifferent only if she expects the one-year rate next year to be 4%. Work it through yourself, and the conclusion will be that, given these two rates in the market, borrowers *on average* must be expecting the one-year rate next year to be 4%, even though any *individual* borrower can entertain any reasonable expectation.

Let's take one more step. A different investor has a three-year horizon. He can choose a simple three-year Treasury note, locking in 3.5% (Table 8.1) for each of the three years. Or he can invest for one year, reinvest next year for a year, and then again for the third year.[7] The only situation in which he will be indifferent as to which option to choose is one where he expects the average rate of the three-year rollover strategy to be 3.5%. Otherwise, he will choose the one with greater expected return. Applying the same reasoning as above, we can conclude: Whereas each individual investor will choose one strategy over another depending on her or his expectations as to which produces the greater expected return, investors on average, in order for the market to be in equilibrium, must be of the opinion that 3.5% represents the average expected rate for the three-year rollover strategy. Let's use this piece of information. The one-year rate *today* is 2%. That is observed in the market. Based on the observed two-year rate, we concluded earlier that the average expectation of market participants is that the one-year rate *next year* will be 4%. We now additionally conclude that investors' expectation for the one-year rate *in two years* must be 4.5%. Why? Because 3.5%, the observed three-year rate, is the average of 2%, 4%, and 4.5%.

Let's introduce a term. We've been talking about the average of the expectations of market participants for interest rates at some future date. Everyone has his or her own expectations. But there is only one average expectation. We refer to this as the *market expectation,* or simply as the *expected interest rate.*

Now let's recap, employing our new terminology. The two-year interest rate equals the average of the one-year interest rate today and the market's expectation for the one-year rate next year. The three-year interest rate equals the average of the one-year interest rate today, the market's expectation for the one-year rate for next year, and the expectation for the one-year rate the year following. Extending this to any maturity, we can simply say:

> *Any longer-term interest rate represents the average of expected one-year interest rates over that term.*

This is a very crucial idea—for many reasons. First, it connects the interest rates of bonds of various maturities. As we've just concluded, they are not independent. This is, after all, what the yield curve is about. Second, as we'll see below, it links the shape of the yield curve to the economy. Third, it has major implications for an investment manager choosing which point along the yield curve to invest. We cover this in Chapter 11, "Carry, Rolls, Breakevens, and Recovery."

Forward Rates

Market participants use a special terminology when referring to the yield curve. Instead of the "market's expected rate," they'll say "forward rate." Thus the 4% we arrived at above for the one-year rate next year is known as the "one-year forward in one year"; 4.5% is the one-year forward in two years. It's called a forward rate because it refers to an interest rate that applies to a period in the future (forward in time, so to speak). It is worth emphasizing that forward rates are established *today*—not on the future date. The two forward rates of 4% and 4.5% (indeed all forward rates) arose from the actual rates existing in the market today for the bonds in Table 8.1. If we wait a year and observe the actual one-year rate, it may well be different from 4%. Another year later, the actual one-year rate may not be 4.5%. The market's prediction does not necessarily come true. In fact, if the actual rates are consistently above or below the market's expectations as contained in forwards, market participants would be well advised, and they probably will, to reformulate their expectations' formation process. But that does not change the fact that, at any point in time, forward rates reflect the market's expectations given whatever information market participants have at that moment.[8]

Before we go on to use what we just learned in order to explain yield curve shapes, let's apply the above analysis to short-term instruments. Suppose the one-*month* interest rate is 2%, and the two-month rate is 2.5%. The one-month forward rate must be 3% (2.5% is the average of 2% and 3%). Here's another example. In Table 8.1 the one-year Treasury interest rate is 2%. Using our analysis, we can now conclude that the market expects the one-month rate over the next twelve months to average 2%. Finally, if the one-week interest rate is 1.75%, that must be the average of the overnight rates expected by money market participants for the next seven days.[9]

Expectations and Yield Curve Shape

Let's use our newly acquired knowledge to take another look at Table 8.1. With the one-and two-year interest rates at 2% and 3%, respectively, we concluded that the one-year ahead forward rate—the interest rate that the market, as of today, expects to exist one year from today—is 4%. In other words—and this is the key—the two-year rate today, 3%, is above the one-year rate today, 2%, because the market expects interest rates that to go up next year! We also concluded that, given the three-year rate of 3.5% today, the forward rate two years ahead is 4.5%. Hence, the three-year rate today is above the two-year rate today because the market expects rates to rise in two years. You get the idea: *the shape of the yield curve is governed by expectations regarding future interest rates.*

Consider a different market situation. Suppose the one-year interest rate is 4% and the two-year rate is 3%—a negatively sloped yield curve. The one-year ahead forward rate must be 2% (one year at 4% requires the second year at 2% in order to average 3%). The two-year rate today is *lower* than the one-year rate today because the market expects interest rates to *decline* next year. If the one-month rate is 4% and the two-month rate is 3.75%, then the one-month ahead forward

TABLE 8.2 Bond Yields and Forward Rates for 10-Year Period

Year	Bond Yield (%)	Forward Rate (%)
1	2	2
2	3	4
3	3.5	4.5
4	4	5.5
5	4.4	6
6	4.75	6.5
7	5.07	7
8	5.34	7.25
9	5.56	7.25
10	5.68	6.75

rate must be 3.5%, indicating market expectations of an imminent decline in rates.

Table 8.2 extends the yield curve data of Table 8.1 to ten years. The entries in the forward-rate column were derived from those in the bond-yield column in the manner described above. For example, the forward rate for year 2 must be 4%, since the two-year 3% rate averages the one-year 2% bond yield and the 4% forward. So, too, 5.5% must be the forward rate in four years because the 4% four-year bond yield is the average of 2%, 4%, 4.5%, and 5.5%. In short, each maturity yield in the bond yield column is an average of all the rates in the forward rate column up to and including that maturity.

The first thing to notice from Table 8.2 is that in the early years the forward rate shows sharper jumps from year to year than the bond yields do. This is generally true for yield curves and makes sense; as we now realize, longer term yields are averages of short-term rates, and averages of anything don't show as much change as do individual components. Second, until the last couple of years in the table, the steady increase in yields—the positive slope of the yield curve—can be attributed to the rising forward rates. The three-year yield of 3.5%, for example, is above the two-year 3% yield because the market expects the one-year rate in two years (4.5%) to exceed that in one year (4%). The four-year 4% rate exceeds the three-year 3.5% because the market expects another increase in one-year rates, from 4.5% to 5.5%.

You can continue the arithmetic argument yourself. In short, expectations of increasing interest rates result in an upward-sloping yield curve.

There is one surprise, though. The market, in this example, does not expect rates to rise between years 8 and 9 in the future—both forward rates are 7.25%. Yet, the yield curve still shows positive slope in that region. How can that be? Here's why. The eight-year yield—5.34%—is the average of all the one-year rates expected between now and eight years from now. The highest rate among these is the last one—7.25%. So, if another 7.25% is added to the group, it must raise the average, even if it is no larger than the existing highest member of the group of rates. Even more dramatic, the yield curve is positively sloped from year 9 to year 10, despite the market expecting a rate *decline*—the succeeding forward rate, 6.75%, is a half percent lower! Same reason: Although the ten-year forward is below the previous forward, it is still above the nine-year yield, the average of all the forwards.

To summarize, expectations of increasing short-term interest rates *generally* cause the yield curve to have a positive slope; expectations of declining rates impose a negative slope. For longer maturity points on the curve, it is possible to have a positive slope despite expectations of moderate decline in interest rates because of the earlier expectations of increases. The converse is also true.

Incorporating the State of the Economy

We're not done yet. Let's go a step deeper. Since expectations are such a paramount factor in the shape of the yield curve, what lies behind expectations?

In the macroeconomics chapters (5 and 6) we learned of the relationship between interest rates, especially short-term rates, and the state of macroeconomic activity. Stronger economic activity tends to force interest rates up; weaker economic activity pushes rates down.[10] Suppose the economy is in a recession. Recessions, thankfully, don't last forever. If market participants, on average, believe that the economy will rebound next year, then because of the correlation with interest rates, investors and borrowers anticipate an increase in short-term rates compared to their current level. Table 8.2 reflects just such a scenario. The current weak state of the economy has brought short-term interest rates to 2%. Participants, on average, expect an economic rebound next year, bringing along with it a sharp uptick in rates to 4%. Thus, the two-year yield, incorporating the current one-year plus the one-year expected for next year, is above the one-year rate.

Expansions tend to last for longer than a year. As the expansion gathers steam, interest rates rise further. According to the forward rates in Table 8.2, the market expects a more muted increase in rates for the third year, but an increase nonetheless. Hence, the yield curve is upward sloping between years 2 and 3. Market participants realize that economic expansions eventually come to an end, thereby capping the rise in interest rates. The forward rates in the table suggest that expectations are that this will occur eight years into the future.[11]

The reverse reasoning applies to an economy having reached what is believed to be the mature stage of expansion. Just like recessions, expansions don't last forever (although they do tend to last longer than recessions in the United States and other industrialized countries). Once market participants believe that the economy's growth rate has reached a peak, they begin expecting interest rates to decline. Hence, a negatively sloped yield curve reflects *expectations* of decelerating, or possibly declining, economic activity.

Allow me a digression. You have probably heard it said, "A negative yield curve is a leading indicator of recession." Please reread the last sentence of the previous paragraph, carefully. The word "expectations" is crucial. The negative slope in a yield curve merely tells us that market participants foresee a decline in interest rates, which correlates with weakening economic activity. It does *not* tell us that the decline will occur; expectations can be wrong. That's why they're called *expectations,* not prophecies! Furthermore, interest rates tend to decline if the economy decelerates from growing above its potential rate to below its potential rate (please study Chapter 5). In that case the economy is certainly not in recession; it is just growing at a slower rate.[12]

In sum, forward rates are fundamentally reflective of market participants' expectations regarding the future path of interest rates. (Remember, everyone has his or her own unique expectations and will act accordingly. But there is only one *market* expectation representing the average of those of all market participants, which is reflected in forward rates.) Future expected interest rates, in turn, are a function of the stage of the macroeconomic business cycle and the market's expectations regarding its progress.

Inflation and Real Interest Rates

Now that we're on the subject of the macroeconomy and how it affects the shape of the yield curve via its impact on market participants' expectations, it wouldn't be right to ignore inflation. In Chapter 7, "Inflation-Protected Bonds," we learned that every interest rate has two components: a so-called "real" interest rate plus an expected inflation rate, the latter often referred to as the inflation "premium." The sum of these two components is the rate observed, or quoted, for a bond and is known as the nominal rate, or yield. The nominal yield on the Treasury's five-year bond, for example, equals the five-year real interest rate plus the market's expectation for the average annual (compounded) inflation rate over the next five years.

How does this relate to our analysis of the yield curve? The interest rates we've been discussing are the nominal rates. They are the rates typically depicted in yield curves. The five-year rate, as we concluded above, represents the market's expectations as to the average of the one-year rates over the coming five years. Each of these rates, in turn, equals a real rate plus an inflation premium. By extension, therefore, we can reasonably conclude that the five-year nominal rate on the yield curve equals the average of the market's expectations for one-year real interest rates over the next five years plus the average annual inflation rate over the next five years. Pretty easy, huh? This applies to each point on the curve.

> *The nominal interest rate for any maturity equals the sum of: (1) the market's expectations for the average of real interest rates; plus (2) the market's expectations for the average of inflation rates for the term covered by that maturity.*

To see how everything fits together, let's reproduce Table 8.2 but separate the forward rate into its real and expected inflation components, as shown in Table 8.3.

TABLE 8.3 Bond Yields Plus Forward Real Rates and Inflation Rates

Year	Nominal Bond Yield (%)	Nominal Forward Rate (%)	Forward Real Interest Rate (%)	Expected Inflation Rate (%)
1	2	2	1	1
2	3	4	3	1
3	3.5	4.5	3.5	1
4	4	5.5	4	1.5
5	4.4	6	4.5	1.5
6	4.75	6.5	5	1.5
7	5.07	7	5	2
8	5.34	7.25	4.75	2.5
9	5.56	7.25	4.5	2.75
10	5.68	6.75	4.25	2.5

Table 8.3 paints a stylized picture of a weak economy, but one expected to begin its rebound within a year. The third column (nominal forward rate) equals the sum of the last two columns, as just stated. Look at year 1. With economic activity restrained, labor and commodity markets have a great deal of slack, and inflation is quite tame at 1%. The central bank has added liquidity, pushing the nominal one-year rate down to 2%, which means that the real interest rate is 1%.[13] The hope is that the low rates will make borrowing and spending more attractive. Market participants, in this scenario, believe that the policy will work. When economic activity picks up next year, if expectations are borne out, liquidity demands will rise concomitantly, the central bank will be less accommodating, and short-term real rates will increase as shown in the table, from 1% to 3%.[14]

Notice the expected inflation rate column in the table. Even though a pickup in the economy is expected for next year, inflation is not expected to accelerate. True, there is an empirical regularity of inflation rising and falling, more or less, with aggregate economic activity. But it is also generally true that the relationship is lagged. That is, price pressures tend to mount only after the economy has strengthened for a while, not concurrently with the start of the strengthening.

Real interest rates are expected to continue to rise moderately, along with the economy. Three years from now (given our assumptions) inflation is expected to accelerate. Thus, in year 4 the higher expected inflation term will interact with the real forward rate to produce a more sizable 1% jump in the nominal forward rate.

For the following few years, expectations are that both real interest rates and inflation will increase. Real interest rates will rise because the expanding economy becomes more credit demanding; inflation will increase because resources are being used more intensively, thus forcing up their prices. For year 8, market participants foresee a decline in real interest rates, reflecting their view of the expansion coming to an end.[15] Yet they believe that inflation will continue to accelerate, again reflecting its lagged response to the economy's dynamics. This prevents the forward rate from declining. It is not until year 10 that inflation, with a couple of years of economic weakness behind it, is expected to turn. The forward rate then falls. The yield curve, though, remains upward sloping throughout, reflecting the averaging phenomenon analyzed earlier.

Risk and Volatility

Some of you may be thinking to yourselves: "We've taken apart this yield curve topic pretty well. Yet, we haven't heard anything about risk and its influence on the shape of the curve. Doesn't 'everyone' say that long-term bonds are 'riskier' than short-term? And, therefore, that long-term rates must be higher than short-term, reflecting the simple truth that more risk requires more return? Should this basic idea not be incorporated into any discussion of the yield curve?" Yes and no.

This came up earlier. The fundamental conclusion of the analysis in this chapter is that investors' search for the highest expected return (and borrowers' search for lowest expected cost), *given their horizons*, results in long-term interest rates equaling the average of short-term rates over any specific maturity. This appears to leave no room for a risk parameter. But there is one. Suppose an investor has a three-year horizon. A three-year Treasury note yields 4%, and the market's expectations are that the one-year interest rates over the next three years will average 4%. So far, so good. The four-year Treasury note yields 4.25%. If the investor purchases it, she knows she will have to sell it one year before it matures, entailing capital risk. The only way for this strategy to produce the same 4% ROR as the three-year note is if the one-year rate in year 4 *increases* enough so that upon selling the note, the capital loss brings the proceeds down to result in a 4% ROR. Once again, the upward sloping curve (4.25% four-year note compared to the 4% three-year) implies expectations of increasing short-term rates. This is the same argument we use above, but in a different guise. Here's where the argument needs to be amended to reflect risk. Even if the investor does expect rates to rise in year 4, enough to make the expected ROR of that strategy 4%, she would *not* be indifferent to that strategy and purchase a three-year note, The three-year note presents no risk—4% is locked in. The four-year note/sell after three years strategy is only *expected* to earn 4% percent, but is not guaranteed. What if rates rise more than expected after three years, reducing the proceeds upon sale, hence the return? Sure, rates can rise less, or even fall, thus increasing the ROR above 4%. But the investor needs to be paid to accept that risk. How is she paid? By the expected return being above 4%. In sum, in order to induce investors with shorter-term horizons to purchase longer maturity bonds, the bonds must offer yields in excess of the average expected short-term rates over their maturities. Longer-term bonds carry higher yields independent of expectations regarding the path of future interest rates.

Let's summarize what we have so far. Market participants' expectations regarding the future path of short-term interest rates (in turn reflecting their views about the economy's cycle and inflation) are the key ingredient in the shape of the yield curve. But risk matters as well. Investors incur risk when they extend maturity past their holding periods. Since they need to be paid a premium to accept risk, yields on longer-term instruments should be higher than what they would be if they were based solely on expectations. If market expectations were that short-term interest rates were to remain constant, the yield curve would nonetheless be positively sloped, reflecting the term risk premium. There does seem to be a lot of truth to the quotation in this section's opening paragraph after all.

Not so fast. Long-term bonds are *not* necessarily riskier than short-term bonds. You already know this from Chapter 4, and we demonstrated it near the beginning of this chapter. Think about our three-year horizon investor again, facing a 4% yield from a three-year Treasury note. Suppose he expects the one-year interest rate to average 4% over the next three years. Buying a one-year note, rolling the proceeds after one year into another one-year note, then doing it again should produce, according to his expectations, the same 4%. Is he indifferent to this rollover strategy compared to simply buying the three-year note? Certainly not. Even though the *expected* return from both is the same, buying a one-year note and reinvesting the proceeds presents risk. What if rates turn out to be lower than expected? Of course, they may turn out higher as well, but that's the risk. For this investor, a shorter maturity bond is riskier than a longer (three-year) one.[16] A risk-averse investor would require a higher expected return from the rollover strategy, which presents reinvestment risk, than from the three-year note, which presents no risk. This, in turn, suggests that the three-year rate should be *lower* than the average of the one-year rates expected over the next three years. The yield curve should show a negative bias! How can we reconcile this with the seemingly opposite conclusion of the previous paragraph?

Here's how you should think about the yield curve and its relationship to market expectations, investor preferences, risk and, as we explain later, volatility. Without the presence of risk, long-term interest rates would reflect the average of short-term rates expected by market participants over the maturity of the long-term rate. No more, no less. If investor (and borrower) horizons were evenly spread across all maturities, this would be perfectly true. But this is not the case, hence the statement is imperfectly true. If investors were mostly concentrated at the short end of the curve, they would need to be induced to shift to longer-term securities issued by borrowers, since they would be accepting price risk upon sale of the bond when their horizons are reached. The inducement is in the form of a yield above the average expected for short-term rates for that longer term. If investors are concentrated at the long end, they need to be induced to buy shorter maturity bonds, as they would be accepting reinvestment risk. In this case, the inducement is in the form of the expected average short-term rate lying above the long-term rate of the bond they could be buying risklessly. So, whether the yield for long-term rates is above or below the expected average of short-term rates depends on how investors are distributed across maturities. The greater the presence of investors in a particular maturity area, the lower the yield compared to the simple average of short-term rates to that point. The thinner their presence, the higher the yield.[17]

Now it's time to incorporate volatility. Consider a situation in which the balance of investors (and borrowers) is such that there is an excess of lenders in, say, the one- to five-year maturity bracket, and a dearth at the longer end. As explained, longer-term rates must, in this situation, yield more than called for by the average of expectations of future rates over the longer term in order to induce some of the shorter-term investors to accept the risk of longer-term bonds which they will need to sell prior to their maturity. Let's think: Why is there risk? Because expectations aren't always realized. On the sale date of the bond—at the investor's horizon end—interest rates may be higher or lower than expected. The more *volatile* interest rates are, the greater the chance—and the larger the likely movement—of rate changes away from expectations. Hence, the greater the future bond price movements (which are more pronounced for longer-term bonds, as seen in the Chapter 3). Therefore, those investors considering shifting to longer-term bonds despite their shorter-term horizons will demand an even greater premium— in the form of higher yields—the more volatile the environment. In other words, the more volatile interest rates are, the greater the slope of the yield curve in this scenario. In summary:

> *Forward interest rates are not a pure reflection of market expected future rates. There may be a bias resulting from risk, and the bias is exacerbated by volatility.*

Introducing Traders and Speculators

Traders, speculators, and dealers have no horizon in the sense presented above. Consider a hedge fund, for instance. The trader at the fund may anticipate a decline in yields and buy a bond in expectation of its resultant price increase. She has no identifiable holding period; rather, when the price target is reached (or the price goes in the other direction, and she reassesses her view), the bond is sold. It may take an hour, a day, or months. But it will definitely be short term.[18] Speculators on short-term yield changes, hence on price movements, clearly face greater risk from longer maturity instruments, whose prices experience sharper responses to yield changes.[19]

Bond dealers are in a similar position. They maintain inventory to meet potential customer demand. Except for those bonds they may possibly hold for their proprietary trading, their inventory may need to be liquidated at a moment's notice—clearly a very short-term holding period. Bond dealers face more risk, therefore, with longer maturity securities. As compensation, a higher yield than otherwise suggested by expected future short-term rates is necessary.

So, the presence of dealers and speculators in the marketplace imparts a bias toward short-term securities, hence a term yield premium for longer maturity bonds. This helps explain why, historically, the slope of the yield curve has been upward more often than downward.[20]

9

CORPORATE BONDS

Credit Spreads

Most companies get their funds to expand, hold inventory, or make acquisitions internally (known as "retained earnings") or from banks. Large corporations can go to the bond markets. They issue bonds similar to the government bonds we discussed above, but with one big, *big* difference.

What's the difference between a corporate bond and a government bond? The risk of default. You can be confident (I didn't say certain) that Uncle Sam (or Uncle Charles in the United Kingdom, or the Treasuries of the other major industrialized nations) will be able to honor their promises. This is not necessarily so for a private corporation. The possibility that the promised payments will not be made (or made on time) is known as *default,* or credit, risk.[1] It is this risk that causes investors to demand a higher interest rate from corporate than from government borrowers. The difference in rates—as long as we compare bonds of similar maturities—is referred to as the "credit spread."

What determines the size of the credit spread? *It's not the rating agencies.* Credit spreads are determined by the degree of risk investors accept when they purchase corporate bonds and how much they demand as compensation for that risk. (Rating agencies attempt to analyze the risk; they are not responsible for it!) In order to properly understand and appreciate the nature of credit risk and its determinants, we need to spend some time on a company's balance sheet. You'll see it is a very worthwhile, and eye-opening, exercise.

Corporate Balance Sheets

Let me teach you the essentials of a balance sheet in one section of one chapter! A balance sheet has two components: what the company *owns* and what the company *owes*. The former are its assets; the latter, its liabilities. Say you want to manufacture shoes. You have $3,000 of your own (and other partners') money, which is *equity*. You borrow $2,000, half from a bank and half by issuing a bond to investors. These are all liabilities (even your $3,000 is technically classified as a liability, because accountants look at liabilities as *sources* of funds, and your equity certainly qualifies as a source; the assets purchased are the *destination* of the funds).

You take the $5,000 and buy equipment, leather, rubber and other materials to make the shoes. You keep some in a bank account, referred to as cash (it may earn interest). The balance sheet is shown in Table 9.1. Notice that employees are not on the balance sheet—slavery went out with Abe Lincoln.[2]

The firm's *leverage ratio* is $5,000/$3,000 or 1.67:1. Why? Because as the company's owner you have put together a company worth $5,000 (the total value of what the company owns) with only $3,000 of your (and other investors' or co-owners') money. You *leveraged* each equity dollar 1.67 times. Alternatively, for each dollar of investor/owner money, you borrowed an additional $0.67 to build the company. To reflect this way of looking at it, another form of the leverage ratio is the debt-to-equity ratio, here $2,000/$3,000 = $0.67.

Now watch this. Suppose you sell the shoes you manufactured and produce revenue of $10,000 this year. The cost of labor, materials, and electricity add up to $9,000. Say the interest rate on the bank loan is 6% and on the bond, 8%. (Why a higher rate on the bond? It's subordinated

TABLE 9.1 Shoe Manufacturer Balance Sheet

Assets	Liabilities
Equipment: $2,500	Equity: $3,000
Leather: $1,000	Bank Loan: $1,000
Inventory: $1,000	Bond: $1,000
Cash: $500	

to the loan, hence more risky to the lenders—more on this later.) Your interest expense is, therefore, $140(.06 × $1,000 + .08 × $1,000). This leaves you a gross profit of $860 ($10,000 − $9,000 − $140). You pay 40% in taxes, which leaves you with a net profit of $516. You take $400 out of this money, all of which belongs to the equity owners, and send it to them. (This is known as "dividends.") The $116 is retained in the company ("retained earnings") and is part of the equity, since it has been provided by the owners—the equity holders. Now you can clearly see that a company's equity equals the original investment made by the owners plus any subsequent retained earnings.[3] What do you do with these funds? You decide to buy $50 worth more of leather (you had a good year, so you're preparing to manufacture more shoes next year) and put $66 into the company's bank account. The new balance sheet is shown in Table 9.2.

So where's the credit risk in all this? Recall that after paying for labor, materials, and so on the company made $1,000. That money is available to pay interest. So the interest bill is "covered" $1,000/$140 = 7.14 times. This is known as the "coverage ratio." Ratios are a big deal in credit analysis. One of the first things a credit analyst will look at is this coverage ratio. It is simply the amount of money coming into the firm that is available to pay interest on its borrowings relative to the money that needs to go out to pay interest.[4] Why does this number matter so much to lenders? Because the higher the ratio, the more room there is for the company's earnings to decline in the next year and still be able to meet its interest obligations, hence avoid default. You can think of the ratio's 6.14 excess above 1 as the company's cushion. The bigger the cushion, the lower the risk of default and the less bondholders demand for compensation (that is, a narrower credit spread).

Table 9.2 Shoe Manufacturer New Balance Sheet

Assets	Liabilities
Equipment: $2,500	Equity: $3,000 + $116
Leather: $1,000 + $50	Bank Loan: $1,000
Inventory: $1,000	Bond: $1,000
Cash: $500 + $66	

Suppose another firm in the same line of business structures its balance sheet differently. It uses more borrowed money and less equity. Everything else is exactly the same—same amount of equipment, material, etc. Only the liability side is different. The total amount is the same; it just replaces some equity with debt. Perhaps it has only $2,500 of its own funds, and borrows $2,500 through bank loans and bonds. In short, it is more leveraged, 2:1 rather than 1:1. Revenue is the same by assumption. But its coverage ratio is lower because it has more interest expense—its cushion is narrower. The lenders face greater risk of default, and they'd probably demand a higher interest rate as compensation. So here's the result: A higher leverage ratio typically reduces coverage, in turn increasing default risk of bonds.[5]

Now you're ready for one of the most crucial and exciting terms in finance: *volatility*. Consider another firm with a duplicate balance sheet, but in a different business, say, technology. The nature of that business is such that revenue changes from year to year are much more pronounced than for our shoe manufacturer.[6] The leverage and coverage ratios are the same, as we constructed them to be so. Yet you as an investor in the tech company's bonds are more nervous about getting paid. Why? Because there is a greater chance that revenue will decline during the life of your bond to the point where the firm cannot meet its obligations to lenders. The coverage ratio may be well above 1 now, but there is no assurance that it will remain that way for the life of the bond. Of course, you have no assurances from the shoe company either. But the possibility of a substantial decline in revenue to cause default on its debt obligations is more remote. You need a bigger cushion from the tech company to feel as comfortable as you did lending to the shoe company. And if the cushion is not bigger—the ratios are the same—you perceive greater risk and thus demand a higher return. In short, the volatility of the business, as manifested in the firm's earnings, affects credit risk and, therefore, the firm's bond credit spread.

Earnings volatility is influenced by two factors. First, is the industry the firm is in, sometimes known as a "sector." Technology is a more volatile sector than shoes, and a lot more volatile than electricity. The second is the specific firm. Even within a sector, two firms may well have different volatilities, depending on the uniqueness of their product, business model, employee relations, and the like.

The state of investor anxiety, or their tolerance for risk, is another determinant of bond credit spreads. Political developments, the economy's performance, and market turbulence can make investors more or less risk-averse. The same firm may be required to compensate investors with a wider spread at another point in time, despite unchanged balance sheet, credit ratios, and so on simply because investors' appetite for risk has shifted.

Seniority/Subordination

Let's reexamine the company's debt. It borrowed $1,000 via a bank loan, plus $1,000 by issuing a bond. It's very common for these two "classes" of creditors to have different standings on the balance sheet. That is, one may be "senior" to the other. More than likely the bank's claim is senior, which makes the bondholders "junior," or "subordinated" to the bank lenders. Their different standings play out most directly in the event of the company's bankruptcy. Here's how.

Contrary to popular perception, companies in bankruptcy are not worth nothing (an intentional double negative). Firms can have quite a lot of assets—buildings, trucks, inventory, possibly some cash—even as they default on their obligations. Their obligations, or their liabilities, simply exceed the value of their assets. In short, *default* is not *death*. The company may reorganize itself under the aegis of the bankruptcy court. A new company, formed from the leftovers of the original one, will have valuable securities to be distributed to claimants. Or the court may liquidate the firm's remaining assets and pay back what it can to lenders and other creditors.[7] Whether assets are sold or new securities are distributed, the amount bondholders receive is known as the "recovery value." Legally, senior creditors are to receive payment from any assets in bankruptcy prior to junior creditors. Suppose the above firm we created defaults on its obligations. After back wages, taxes, and other prior claims on the firm are paid, assume there is $1,500 worth of assets—maybe a piece of usable equipment—remaining. The senior bank lenders receive $1,000; the subordinated bondholders, $500.

That's not all there is to it. The bankers and bond investors are aware of their different standings. Even when the company is alive and kicking, there is always the possibility of bankruptcy in the future.

Hence, to reflect their different positions in the event of bankruptcy, the bond will pay a higher rate (wider spread) than the bank loan.

Maturity

We know (from Chapter 8, "The Yield Curve") that the relationship between yields and maturities of Treasury bonds depends largely on market participants' expectations regarding the future path of interest rates, plus other factors relating to the volatility of those rates. What about corporate bonds? The yield on a corporate bond equals that of a similar maturity Treasury bond plus a premium for credit risk, as we've seen. What about the relationship between that premium, or spread, and bond maturity?

Why are you receiving a spread for buying a corporate bond? Because you're definitely not going to receive more than the coupon and principal and, unlike a Treasury, possibly less. So your upside is capped, but your downside is theoretically zero. Of course, collateral helps cushion the downside (see the next chapter), and high coverage ratios make you less nervous, but the possibility of your receiving less is why you demand the spread. So anything that increases the possibility of the downside increases the spread. The longer the bond's maturity, very simply, the greater the chance of something bad happening. (It also increases the chance of something good happening, but remember, you don't have much to gain from the upside.) In short, all else the same, credit spreads will increase with maturity.

A representative corporate yield curve is shown in Figure 9.1a, together with a Treasury bond curve. The two curves together show the spread increasing with maturity. Another way to depict the same phenomenon is with the spread curve, shown alongside in Figure 9.1b.

Callable Corporates: Two Spreads in One

The option to call a bond—to pay off its principal prior to its stated maturity—has significant value to an issuer. If a bond is callable, we learned in Chapter 1 that it must pay a call premium to investors in the form of an interest spread on top of an otherwise equivalent noncallable bond. Any

FIGURE 9.1 a. Corporate Yield Curve (C) and Treasury Bond Curve (T); b. Spread Curve (S)

corporate bond has to pay investors more than an otherwise comparable government bond for default risk. Put these two together and you see that a callable corporate bond, of which there are many, must compensate investors for two risks: credit and callability.

There's a problem, though. Suppose you're considering a ten-year corporate bond, callable in five years. It carries a yield of 7.5%, compared to 5% for a five-year Treasury. The extra 2.5% is payment for the two risks you're taking—it is the *sum* of the credit spread and the call spread. As it is presented, you can't tell how much of the 2.5% is for credit risk and how much is for call risk. You need to know. You might be comparing it to a noncallable bond of a different company in the same industry, so you're very interested in how much each is paying for similar risks of default. Or you're thinking about possible interest-rate movements in the future, and hence the likelihood of the bond being called and the risk-return tradeoff you're taking. This is a problem.

Market participants have an approach to this problem, but it's imperfect. They *try* to quantify the value of the call option the company has. Suppose, in the bond we're considering, that the call option is estimated to be worth 1%. Then the rest of the bond's interest-rate spread over the Treasury—1.5%— must be the credit spread. This 1.5% is referred to as the "option-adjusted spread."[8]

Covenants

Stockholders own the company. The company's managers—likely shareholders themselves—are hired by the owners, report to them, and are charged with maximizing the owners' wealth. This, combined with the structure of limited liability corporations in the United States, gives managers an incentive to take risks for the shareholders' benefit. All the upside is theirs, and the downside is limited by their equity investment. Risk can take the form of purchasing assets, or undertaking projects with volatile outcomes, or keeping the business model as is by changing the capital structure of the firm toward more debt and less equity.[9] The more risk undertaken, the worse off the bondholders are because the likelihood of receiving the promised bond payments declines (with no extra compensation should the undertaking be successful). In short, company decisions are made with the shareholders in mind; lenders are a cost of doing business. Bondholders, indeed all creditors, therefore, need a means of reining in managers from taking too much risk with, effectively, bondholders' money. Bond covenants provide one such means.

Simply put, a covenant is a promise made by equity holders to debt holders to limit their risky undertakings. Having the company's managers simply promise not to take too much risk will, of course, not do much. Instead, the promises are phrased in an identifiable way with reference to the company's income statement, balance sheet and/or other corporate parameters. We can group these promises into positive, negative and incurrence covenants:

1. A *positive covenant* requires a bond issuer to *do* something or maintain a certain financial situation (hence, this is sometimes known as a *maintenance covenant*). For example, the firm may be required to keep its coverage ratio to at least 2.5 times interest expense. This limits the firm's capacity to add debt, since it would reduce the coverage ratio (unless, of course, an asset is purchased with the funds acquired through the new debt which produces enough income immediately). Additional debt, all else the same, increases the likelihood of default, which this covenant tries to prevent. Another type of positive covenant compels the issuer to maintain a specific amount of cash (or cashlike instruments) in reserve. A nonmonetary covenant would be one in which bondholders demand regular communication about the progress of a particular business venture in order to ensure that the firm's resources are employed more conservatively than the equity holders would employ them on their own, unfettered by any covenants.

2. A *negative covenant* is a promise by the issuer *not* to do something or not to allow a situation to occur. An example of the former would be a promise by the firm not to sell a specific asset, perhaps a building or a subsidiary. This would be quite understandable if the asset is so important to the firm that selling it changes the nature of the enterprise. Bondholders would rightly argue that the end result would be a company they never intended to lend to! An example of the latter would

be a pledge not to allow the leverage ratio to exceed, say, two times shareholder equity. A more common negative covenant is a *negative pledge clause*. This prevents the firm from pledging—or providing as collateral—existing assets to new lenders when there are existing bondholders who are not secured.

3. *Incurrence covenants* restrict the firm from borrowing new money (i.e., incurring additional debt) or entering into new obligations. Often this agreement is couched within a contingency. For example, if the coverage ratio has reached a certain minimum level and has been maintained for a number of quarters, only then may the firm borrow more funds and raise its leverage to a given level. If the coverage ratio improves further, then permitted leverage may rise commensurately. Another example would be that the company may incur new debt only to expand existing operations, not to acquire other companies.

What if the issuer is looking to undertake a particular activity that will result in a violation of one of the covenants? For example, the board of directors has approved acquiring another firm, to be financed with debt, which will violate the *maximum leverage covenant*. The firm may request a waiver from the bondholders to temporarily relax the covenant until the leverage ratio is brought back down over time. Or it may ask for an amendment to permanently remove the covenant. Why would the bondholders agree? To approve the amendment, they might demand a higher coupon on their bond. If the two sides cannot agree, the firm can get around the restriction simply by purchasing the bonds in the open market (assuming it can somehow get the funds to do so).[10]

There may be some interesting dynamics here. Suppose market participants (aka speculators) become aware of the firm's strategy—either directly, due to the firm having explicitly publicized its intentions, or indirectly discovering that the company entered the market to buy back its bonds. If these participants accumulate enough of a position, they can force the firm to pay a hefty premium to buy the bonds back and thereby remove the covenant constraint. However, if the bond is callable (and past the call waiting period), the firm will just exercise the call option and redeem the bonds so that the maximum price the firm will pay is par (or par plus any premium required to call).[11]

Bond Ratings

A lot goes into establishing the credit risk of a company, as you can now appreciate. We've covered only those factors that apply generally to all firms. Clearly, each borrower has special characteristics—product line, management capabilities and history, customer base, and so on— that need special attention. With so many firms and unique issues surrounding them (to say nothing of the myriad types of bonds—see later in this chapter), it would be nearly impossible for any one investor to perform the proper research. In response to the market's need for such research, credit rating agencies (CRAs) were created.[12] These public (government-overseen) entities examine company financials and business fundamentals, publish periodic credit reports, and summarize their opinions with a series of letter grades. Figure 9.2 displays a grading system.

Treasuries are shown to indicate that they are rated above even the highest corporate grade of AAA. Where does the debt of government

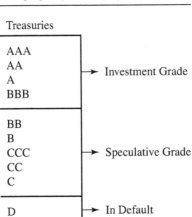

FIGURE 9.2 Representative Credit Rating Agency Grading System

agencies (described in Chapter 1) belong? If the agency is part and parcel of the federal government, its risk is the same as that of Treasuries.[13] If it's not, its "relationship" to the government should place it just below Treasuries, or in the AAA category.[14]

Beyond the Treasury or agency level, default becomes a real possibility. The further down the scale, the greater, in the rating agency's opinion, the probability of default. CRA grades are for the most part consistent with our analysis of credit risk above. For example, given two firms in the same industry (hence similar revenue volatilities), with bonds of similar maturity and seniority level, the firm with the lower grade will likely be more highly leveraged.

There is an official dividing line between firms rated above BB and those rated below BBB. The former are termed "investment grade"; the latter, "speculative grade." There is no *natural* dividing line; one just has to be chosen. Why? Regulations set maximum allocations to speculative grade debt for certain institutional investors.[15]

D is technically not a grade. Firms are not assigned a D following a credit analysis by a CRA. Rather, companies in default are rated D. You might ask, why assign a grade at all? Aren't the bonds of defaulting companies useless? Nope. Companies in default are not *dead*. During the bankruptcy process, the firm may still be functioning and, even if it is not functioning, the company still has assets that need to be allocated to the various claimants, including the debt holders. Hence, debt of defaulted companies trades according to the market's expectations of its "recovery value," as explained earlier.[16]

One important, often misunderstood, point about CRAs: Their job is to analyze and rate *credit* risk. Fixed coupon corporate bonds contain significant interest-rate risk, particularly if their remaining maturities are long. All the analyses regarding interest rate risk for government bonds in Chapters 3 and 4, and the tools forthcoming in Chapters 12 and 13, apply to corporate bonds as well. A company's credit may be stable, indeed improving, yet its bonds may fall in price because of rising overall interest rates, or Treasury yields.[17] But this is not the rating agencies' concern—it is not a credit issue. Furthermore, callable corporate bonds, due to the presence of the embedded call option, respond in price to market volatility (see Chapter 13). Bonds formed out of mortgages contain "prepayment risk." Other structured products created by dealers involve derivatives with their unique brand of risk. Unless driven by credit movements, CRAs generally do not take these factors into account, and make no claim to.

High-Grade versus High-Yield Bonds

The fundamental factors that push companies into the speculative grade region (e.g., volatile cash flow, greater leverage) are the reasons investors demand a wider spread over Treasuries for these firms' bonds than for companies in the investment grade class. Hence, these bonds are also known as "high-yield" bonds. Looked at another way, the inferior credit fundamentals of these firms has resulted in a markedly higher incidence of bankruptcy over time. Higher yields are compensation for investors' losses resulting from bankruptcies. Investment grade bonds are termed "high-grade" bonds.[18] Separate from these fundamental, definitional differences between high-grade and high-yield bonds, other differences between them include:

- *Industry factors.* Speculative grade bonds are more likely to be found in industries that are particularly sensitive to the business cycle. These include manufacturers of durable goods (automobiles come to mind, as opposed to food producers). Luxury service providers, such as casinos, would be found here as well.
- *Market factors.* The size of a speculative grade bond issuance tends to be smaller than its investment grade counterpart. A multi-billion-dollar issue for an investment grade bond has become quite common; it would be unusual for a speculative grade bond. Because of the smaller relative size, high-yield liquidity is inferior to that of high-grade; that is, bid-offer dealer spreads are wider in the speculative grade market. Relatedly, the typical transaction in the high-yield market is of smaller size ($1 to $3 million) than the high-grade market.
- *Bond factors.* A greater variety and number of restrictive covenants are to be found in speculative grade bonds, in order to make investors more comfortable with the credit risk. Similarly, average maturities are lower compared to those for investment-grade bonds. This makes sense since credit spreads

widen with maturity, as we have seen, and this would have a more pronounced effect on a high-yield issuer. A speculative grade borrower requiring more flexibility (fewer and lighter covenants) and longer-term financing would have to pay a very high yield indeed. In some cases, the high yield would reduce the firm's coverage ratio to a point where issuing debt would simply be impractical. To get around this, investment bankers created novel bond types that are specifically targeted to high-yield issuers, a prominent example of which is discussed in the next section.

Payment-in-Kind (PIK) Bonds

Young companies, companies formed from leveraged buyouts,[19] and firms having undergone recapitalizations are likely to be speculative grade. These types of firms are least able to service the coupons of high-yielding debt. As mentioned above, bankers have developed debt instruments, the goal of which is to conserve cash in the early years of new or recapitalized companies. One of these is the payment-in-kind (PIK) bond. It is a member of a class of bonds known as "deferred-interest securities."[20] You'll see why.

Here's an example of a PIK bond. A company issues a $100 million ten-year note with, say, an 8% annual "coupon." At the end of year 1, the company has a choice. It can make an $8 million interest payment, in cash, just like an ordinary bond. Or it can send $8 million in additional bonds to the lenders. These bonds are of the same kind as the original bond; that is, 8% annual coupon and now nine years to maturity. The company faces the same choice at the end of year 2, but now based on $108 million of bonds: pay 8% × $108 million = $8.64 million in cash interest or issue this amount in new bonds in lieu of interest payments. Of course, this choice cannot go on forever because the bonds need to be retired by maturity. Notice that the interest bill grows, and is compounded, year after year. Hence, the label "deferred interest."

Now that we know the bond's mechanics, let's analyze the risk. We do this by comparing this bond to an ordinary 8%, ten-year bond of the same company. At the very beginning of the PIK bond's life, there is some probability of the firm choosing to pay in kind on any or all the coupon dates. Thus, on a probabilistic basis, the company will have the investors' money for a longer period of time than from investors in the ordinary bond. From Chapter 3 we know that this produces a higher degree of interest-rate risk, and from this chapter we know that this means more credit risk.

This result—greater interest rate and greater credit risks—is true of all deferred-interest securities. Let's look more closely at the PIK feature—the company's right to choose the interest payment method— which is what makes this particular deferred-interest bond unique. Suppose at the end of the first year, when the interest payment is due, the company's credit fundamentals deteriorate. Were it to issue a new bond, it would pay a higher interest rate, perhaps 9%, because it now presents more default risk to lenders. The firm would certainly choose to pay its PIK coupon with bonds in this case, even if it had the cash. It is borrowing at 8% from existing bondholders when the market requires 9%. Look at it from the investors' viewpoint. The ordinary bond in the previous paragraph is trading below par, since it pays an 8% coupon when the required yield is 9% (see Chapter 3 for a reminder). This means that although the PIK bondholders are receiving $8 million in *face value* of an 8% coupon bond, they're getting less than $8 million in market value. They'd prefer the cash. But they won't get it.

Suppose the reverse occurs at the end of year 1—the firm's creditworthiness improves. A new bond issued by the firm would yield, say, 7%. The firm will choose the cash alternative in this case. Why borrow at 8% when the market demands only 7%? For the same reason, investors would prefer the bond alternative because an 8% coupon would cause the bond's market value to be above par, hence worth more than $8 million in cash. In sum, investors will receive cash when they'd prefer bonds, and bonds when they'd choose cash.

Investors realize that this choice of paying interest in cash versus a payment-in-kind bond is a valuable one to the issuer and a costly one to them. But there is more to it. For even if the company's credit is unchanged, it can still use the PIK feature to its advantage. The 8% initial yield on the bond equals the Treasury interest rate plus the firm's credit spread, both as of the issue date, as explained earlier in the chapter. If Treasury rates increase, even with the spread intact, the firm gains by paying interest with a PIK 8% bond, since its borrowing rate has risen due to the Treasury rate increase. Investors want the cash, which they won't get. Conversely, if Treasury rates decline, investors would love to be paid with the 8% coupon bond because it would be priced above par. But they won't receive it, since the firm will borrow at the lower rate in the market and give the PIK bondholders cash. Looked at this way, the special feature of a PIK bond is similar to the call option embedded in a callable bond.[21] Therefore, investors need to be compensated for providing this PIK option to the issuer. *The PIK bond will pay a higher yield than will the ordinary 8% coupon bond.*

10

MORE ON CORPORATES: CYCLICALITY, COLLATERAL, AND CONVERTIBLES

Corporate Bonds over the Business Cycle

This is sort of a "big picture" section. It takes what we learned in the macroeconomics chapters (5 and 6), particularly the interactions between the macroeconomy's movements and interest rates, and combines it with our analysis of credit risk and the resultant credit spreads of the previous chapter in order to explain what typically happens to corporate bond yields over various points in the business cycle. Table 10.1 presents a stylized pattern of yields reflecting what we've learned and what we're about to learn. It includes Treasury bonds for two reasons. First, government bonds are essentially without credit risk, so examining their yields over the business cycle allows us to isolate the pure time value of money factor in business cycles.[1] Second, corporate bonds, or "corporates" as they are called, yield the Treasury rate plus a spread, so we need the government bond rate in order to establish corporate bond yields. The interest rates in Table 10.1 are averages across all maturities.

Let's start with the terminology of the first column. They describe the state of macroeconomic activity relative to the country's potential, as defined in Chapter 5. The second row in the first column refers to an

TABLE 10.1 Yields over Various Stages of the Business Cycle

Business Cycle Stage	Treasury Yield	Investment-Grade Corporate Yield	Speculative-Grade Corporate Yield
Weak	3%	5.5%	17%
Potential	6%	7.5%	11%
Strong	9%	10.0%	13%
Stagflation	8%	12.0%	20%

economy operating more or less at its potential.[2] Now look at the Treasury yield column. It serves as the anchor for the rest. Recall that government bond yields, lacking a credit risk factor, contain two components: a base interest rate, known as the "real" rate, plus a premium for the inflation rate expected over the life of the bond. With the economy at potential, we can use a ballpark average real rate of 3%. A midpoint 3% rate for inflation is reasonable as well, since we need to look at longer time periods than just recent experience.[3] The result is a 6% nominal rate. The "weak" row denotes the economy operating below its potential. This is not necessarily a recession (a contracting economy), but recessionary periods are included. Real interest rates are lower in this stage of the cycle, reflecting both weak credit demand and ample liquidity supplied by the central bank. Inflation tends to be more volatile than real interest rates. Thus, this entry assumes a real rate of 2% and inflation of 1%, which sums to 3%. Conversely, the economy operating above potential—the row labeled "strong"—results in higher inflation, say 5%. Credit demand is more robust, which, together with the Federal Reserve holding back on liquidity growth to prevent further inflation, pushes the real rate up to 4%, for a total of 9%. We'll get to the bottom row later.

The investment-grade corporate yield column equals the Treasury yield (real interest rate plus inflation) plus a spread for credit risk. That spread, in turn, reflects (as discussed at length in the last chapter) a host of fundamental factors. These include the makeup of the firm's balance sheet, its industry characteristics, company and management history, investors' degree of risk aversion and, most important to the present discussion, expected earnings. Each individual firm's sensitivity to the stage of the business cycle is unique. However, corporate profits for the

high-grade sector overall are certainly positively related to macroeconomic activity. So let's go back to the "potential"row. A midrange figure for credit spreads, associated with the economy operating near its
potential, is 1.5%, which explains the 7.5% entry. "Weak" economic
activity reduces average corporate profits, raising default risk and hence
default spreads from 1.5% to 2.5%. At the other end, with macroeconomic activity above the country's potential, or "strong," spreads tighten
to 1%, reflecting robust corporate profits. Credit spreads, you see, are
countercyclical; they contract during an economic expansion, and they
expand during an economic contraction. This is a very important point.
Why? Because Treasury interest rates are *procyclical*, as explained previously. Thus the two components of corporate bond yields offset each
other over the dynamics of the business cycle. Looking at the first three
columns of the table, corporate bond yields exhibit less volatility—on
an absolute or a relative basis—than do Treasury yields. Notice further
that the weaker than average corporate earnings add a full percentage
point to average credit spreads (the "potential" row), whereas stronger
than average earnings subtracts 0.50%. Why the lack of symmetry? Simple: The most spreads can fall to is zero, while The upside is limited only
by actual default. To summarize:

- *The yields on investment-grade corporate and government bonds
  exhibit positive correlation over stages of the business cycle.*
- *Investment-grade corporate bond yields are less volatile than their
  Treasury counterpart.*

Now turn to the final column—speculative-grade corporate yield.
Credit spreads for high-yield bonds preserve the cyclical pattern found
in the high-grade column—widening in recessions, tightening in
expansions. But the degree of cyclical sensitivity is so high for the speculative bond sector that it perverts the overall relationship with Treasuries. Here's what I mean. The "high yield" in high-yield bonds is a
result of their very wide spreads over credit-riskless government securities. The wide spreads, in turn, reflect a substantial risk of default, the
result of high leverage ratios in their balance sheets and, compared to
the high-grade sector, more volatile industries (e.g., manufacturing).
The sector's earnings, therefore, are acutely sensitive to changes in aggregate demand in the macroeconomy. This combination of high yield and
greater sensitivity to the business cycle has two major implications for

investment portfolios. Compare high-yield spreads (the fourth column minus the second column of Table 10.1) with high-grade spreads (the third column minus the second column). The high-yield spreads exhibit much greater volatility. Now here's what I meant by the "perverse" relationship. Both spreads are countercyclical, as is clear from the table. But the proportion of a high-yield bond's interest rate resulting from the credit spread component is of an order of magnitude greater than it is for a high-grade bond's interest rate. For example, in the second row, the high-grade spread accounts for one-fifth (1.5/7.5) of the total interest rate, whereas the high-yield spread accounts for nearly one-half (5/11). Any movement in Treasury rates over the business cycle, therefore, is swamped by movements in the high-yield spread. This negates the correlation between Treasury bond and high-yield bond interest rates. Thus, we conclude:

- *Not only do speculative-grade bonds present higher yields than investment-grade bonds, but their credit spreads are more volatile over the economy's business cycle.*[4]
- *Whereas investment-grade bond yields exhibit positive correlation with those of Treasury bonds, the larger role of credit spreads in speculative-grade bonds erases any correlation with Treasury yields.*[5]

There have been few episodes of stagflation in the modern U.S. economy, but they are not forgotten. Stagflation denotes a period of stagnation with inflation. Stagnation describes an economy operating well below its potential with substantial unemployment. It does not qualify as a recession, as economic activity is not contracting, though it may likely follow a period of contraction. Yet, despite the macroeconomic weakness, inflation is relatively high. As explained in the macroeconomics chapters (5 and 6), this is not the typical relationship between the strength of economic activity and price movements. Stagflation can be the result of a period of rising commodity (typically oil) prices and/or inflation expectations that have become embedded in the economy, despite lethargic GDP growth. Stagflation is devastating for corporate bonds.[6] Corporate profits are down because of weak economic activity. Firms are not adding to their capacity, as inflation creates uncertainty as to future demand. This combination of inflation, uncertainty, and economic lethargy causes risk premiums on corporate debt to widen sharply, as shown in the last row of Table 10.1. A sharp eye will notice the qualitative difference between the stagflation row and the others in the table. Using the potential row as the benchmark, observe, as we have before, that in both the weak and strong periods, the Treasury rate and the risk premiums (high-grade and high-yield) move in opposite directions. The dynamics are starkly different under stagflation. Treasury rates increase, due to their inflation component, and, at the same time, spreads widen considerably. Credit spread widening exacerbates corporate yield increases during periods of stagflation.

Collateral

The role of collateral in reducing the credit risk of corporate bonds is intimately linked with the concept of correlation. This is not a well-understood concept. But it is crucial in correctly analyzing the value of a collateralized bond relative to an uncollateralized bond.[7]

Suppose a retail chain has issued bonds, half of them senior, half subordinated. The company owns a major building within which lies its flagship store. The building serves as collateral for the senior debt; hence the debt is "secured." In the event of default, the keys to the building are handed over to these bondholders. The junior, or subordinated, debt is uncollateralized; hence it is a simple debenture.[8] Table 10.2 investigates the four possible scenarios facing the firm, and their implications for the two classes of bondholders.

In Table 10.2, a checkmark (✓) denotes the survival of the business (at least until the bonds mature). An X represents lack of survival, or default. Clearly, the four scenarios exhaust all the possibilities. We make the simplifying, but not unrealistic, assumption that the retail

TABLE 10.2 Possible Scenarios for Retail Chain Bond Issuer

Scenario	Retail Business	Real Estate
1	✓	✓
2	X	✓
3	✓	X
4	X	X

business on its own can pay off both classes of bondholders and that the real estate, if necessary, can be sold to pay off the senior debt. For our purposes, no probabilities need be associated with the possible outcomes. Still, Scenario 1 is (hopefully!) the most likely. If the firm's retail business survives, both the senior and junior debt will be paid in full. The fact that the building has retained its value is certainly a good thing for the firm, but in this situation presents no additional benefit to the bondholders.

If the firm's core retail business falters, and the firm defaults on its debt, the senior secured debt holders will look to the collateral (assuming the firm's other assets have already been deployed to pay off other creditors standing in line before bondholders, such as the government looking to collect any back taxes). In Scenario 2, the building has held its value so the senior debt is paid in full, which was the point of the collateral in the first place. The subordinated debt holders go home empty-handed (the building's market value is only enough to pay off the senior debt).

Scenario 3 represents the reverse, less common situation: The firm's business is doing fine, at least well enough to cover its obligations to bondholders, but the building has lost value. The decline in real estate, in this case, is effectively irrelevant to the bond positions.

Finally, Scenario 4 has the retail business failing and the real estate depreciating to the point where the senior debt holders cannot be repaid in full. This situation is not very likely, but it is quite possible.

The Role of Correlation

Let's step back and take a closer look at the senior, secured bondholders' position. They will only lose under Scenario 4, as they draw their payment from *either* the retail business or the real estate. Looked at another way, they will only lose if both businesses, or assets, fail to cover their claim. Now think about this. What if the real estate and retail business are perfectly negatively correlated? Correlation is a statistical term, but it is easily understood. It measures the degree to which two things—businesses, asset prices, stocks, interest rates, currencies (known as "variables," because they can change)—move together.[9] If they always move in the same direction, they are said to be *perfectly positively correlated.* If they always move in opposite directions, they are *perfectly negatively correlated.* If there is no pattern in their relationship, then their correlation is zero, or simply *uncorrelated.* In financial markets, we hardly ever experience perfect positive or perfect negative correlation, just somewhere in between. Now let's apply this to our company and its debt securities. If the firm's retail business and its real estate were, theoretically, perfectly negatively correlated, then Scenario 4 could never unfold. The senior debt holders could never lose! Said another way, the only possible loss to them is the extent that the building and the firm's business show any degree of correlation, giving Scenario 4 a chance of occurring. Indeed, the more highly correlated, the more risky, as this would increase the chances of Scenario 4 unfolding. You might say, therefore, that the secured debt holders are subject only to *correlation risk.*

Before we consider the other theoretical extreme—the retail business and the real estate perfectly positively correlated—let's look at risk from the subordinated bondholders' perspective. If the company defaults, because the retail business has deteriorated, the junior bondholders will not be looking to the real estate for payment; the building secures the senior debt holders, and that's it. Scenarios 2 and 4 are what these people worry about. In other words, the right-most column in Table 10.2 is irrelevant to the subordinated debt owners. If the two businesses are perfectly negatively correlated, they still stand to lose in Scenario 2. Unlike the secured debt holders, the junior bondholders don't gain from the negative correlation. They are exposed to *outright risk*, not correlation risk.

Now consider the opposite extreme—the firm's retail business is perfectly positively correlated with the value of the building serving as collateral. In this case, only Scenarios 1 and 4 can occur. In Scenario 1, both classes of bondholders are paid; in Scenario 4, neither is paid. Under perfectly positive correlation, there is no added benefit to being senior, or secured. Or, the more positively correlated the collateral is to the core business of the bond issuer, the less valuable the collateral is as an attraction to being senior in the company's capital structure. And the less valuable, in turn, the less it should cost to be senior. They are less willing to give up yield.

> *In bond terminology, the greater the correlation, the narrower the difference in interest rates, or spread, between the senior and junior debt holders.*

Here is a straightforward implication. The more correlated the collateral is with the underlying business of the bond issuer, the less useful it is. Suppose the retail chain provided you with its inventory as collateral. That's the worst! If you're collecting from the collateral, this means that the firm has defaulted—it's not selling much of its goods, or is selling them too cheaply relative to their cost. Well, if the goods are not selling, what good is it to receive them in payment for your bond? The same problem exists with a machine that can be used only to manufacture the one item a borrower produces. If the item is not selling, the equipment to produce it is not worth much. That's why real estate is so often used as collateral. It's rare that the building's value happens to be correlated with the issuer's underlying business.

Now let's alter the structure just a bit. Assume that the retail business can cover only the senior debt. The firm's balance sheet is simple—the sum of the two bonds' face values equals the sum of the (book) values of the core business and real estate. Again, the senior, secured bondholders lose only in Scenario 4. But now the subordinated bondholders will lose in every situation but the first. So, here's the punch line: If the two assets are perfectly negatively correlated, the subordinated debt holders always lose! Said another way, the more negatively correlated the assets are, the greater the risk to them.

This is an admittedly simplistic representation of the interaction between seniority/subordination and default/recovery. But it does clearly explain the crucial role of correlation in credit risk. If you're at the top of the creditor ladder, you don't want to see correlation. As you move toward the bottom (and earn a higher yield for the risk you take), positive correlation hurts you less, and negative correlation hurts you more. Digest this concept; it happens to be a key notion in structured credit products such as collateralized debt obligations (CDOs), which are discussed in Chapter 23.

Convertible Bonds

What are convertible bonds doing in this book, you ask? Aren't they an equity product? Yes, equity investors do own convertible bonds, and rightly so, because these bonds exhibit equitylike characteristics (as we will soon see). Still, these instruments are technically bonds, and they are held by fixed-income investors, so they do belong here.

Convertible bonds are, fundamentally, corporate bonds, with coupons, maturities, covenants, and so on, much like any other corporate bond. But they have one distinguishing feature: They can be exchanged— at the investor's discretion—into a fixed number of shares of the company whose name is on the bond.[10] The fixed number is crucial, because that is what makes the bond convertible. Every bond, convertible or not, can be *exchanged* into stock, simply by selling the bond at its market price and using the proceeds to purchase the stock. What distinguishes the convertible bond is that the investor, if she so chooses, can present the bond to the company to be *converted* into a *fixed* number of shares.

Look at Table 10.3. It compares an ordinary bond of a company to a convertible bond issued by the same company with the same maturity, coupon, and seniority. We assume at first that both bonds are at par and that their prices do not change as the stock price does.

According to the terms of this particular convertible bond, it may be exchanged, at the owner's discretion, into three shares of stock. This is known as the "conversion ratio." When the price of the stock is $20 per share, selling the nonconvertible bond at par and using the proceeds (ignoring transactions costs) produces five shares. So will selling the convertible. At a share price of $20, it would make no sense for the convertible bondholder to exercise the conversion option, because that would produce three shares. If the stock rises to $25, four shares can be obtained by selling either bond and purchasing shares. Again, converting makes no sense. At a price of $33.33, selling or converting each results in three shares. At this share price, therefore, the convertible

TABLE 10.3 Ordinary Bond Compared with Convertible Bond

Shares Acquired through Ordinary Bond	Share Price	Shares Acquired through Convertible Bond
5	$20	5
4	$25	4
3	$33.33	3
2.5	$40	3
2	$50	3

owner is indifferent to selling or converting in order to acquire shares by giving up the bond.

What about at a price of $40 per share? Clearly, converting is the more attractive option for the convertible bondholder because it results in three shares. The ordinary bondholder has no such option. He must sell the bond and can afford only 2.5 shares per bond. At a share price of $50 the difference is even more pronounced—three for the convertible versus two for the ordinary. In short, when the share price is above $33.33, the convertible is preferable to the ordinary. When the stock is trading at $33.33 or below, the convertible is no worse than the ordinary. Given that both bonds have the same coupon, maturity and seniority, the convertible is more attractive—it must be worth more. Said another way, to have the same price as the ordinary bond, the convertible must pay a lower coupon. Either way, the convertible's yield is below that of the nonconvertible's yield. The difference in yield is what investors pay to enjoy the potential conversion feature.

Sensitivity to Stock Price

We now know that, all else the same, a convertible bond should be worth more than an otherwise similar nonconvertible bond. Let's examine the effects of different market situations on this relative value. When the stock's price is $50, the convertible is worth quite a bit more. All the holder needs to do is convert right now and have a stock portfolio worth $150 (3 × $50), compared to the $100 face value of the nonconvertible bond. This $150 is known as the "conversion value"— the value of the holdings upon conversion. The convertible is worth *at least* its conversion value. At $40/share it is still worth more (conversion value = $120) than the nonconvertible, but not as much as at $50. What about at $33.33? Converting won't do anything, since it produces the same $100. So does this mean the convertible has no extra value when the stock is at this price?

Not at all. When the stock is at $33.33, it could go up or down. If it goes up, then the conversion feature has value. For example, even a small stock price move to $35 results in a conversion value of $105, above the bond price. And if it goes down, there is no loss, since the conversion feature need not be exercised. So, as long as there is any probability of the stock price rising, the convertible bond is worth more than the nonconvertible.

Now consider a per share price of $25. Again there is no value in converting now. In fact, it would be pretty stupid—just *buy* three shares and pay $75 rather than give up $100. In order for there to be any extra value in the conversion feature, the stock price has to have a decent chance to go above $33.33. Certainly possible, but less likely than when it was already at $33.33. So there *is* value in the bond being convertible, but not as much as when the stock is trading at $33.33. And at $20/share, there is less of a chance for it to jump above $33.33, so there is even less extra value. In short, the convertible is always worth more than the nonconvertible. But the extra value depends on the stock price. The higher the stock price, the greater the extra value of the convertible. In other words, as the stock price rises, the price of the convertible rises along with it (though not necessarily to the same degree).

We've proved that a convertible bond's price is correlated with the price of the stock that the bond is convertible into. That explains why a convertible may be considered an equity product despite being technically a bond. An investor can buy the convertible, earn the coupons, and enjoy the appreciation in the bond price as the stock price rises. Of course, a decline in the stock price makes the conversion feature less valuable, hence the convertible correlates on the way down as well.[11]

Volatility, Callability

As just explained, an increase in the stock price will bring the convertible's price up along with it, but not to the same degree. A decline in the stock hurts the convertible. But don't lose sight of the convertible's "floor." The convertible is still a bond, so if the stock declines to the extent that the conversion value is below the value of the convertible as a pure bond (e.g., at a stock price of 25 the conversion value is 75, but the convertible's *bond value* remains 100 by assumption), the investor still has the bond. In other words, the benefit of the conversion option is one-sided: As the stock rises, the investor gains from the conversion value rising; as the stock falls, the investor is cushioned by the bond value. Hence, *the more volatile the stock, the more valuable the convertible* because the value of stock movements is asymmetric in the investor's favor.[12]

Many, if not most, convertible bonds are callable. Callable bonds give the issuer the right to redeem the bonds prior to their stated maturity.[13] This is a valuable right, as the issuer can refinance the bonds at a lower yield, if interest rates decline, but choose to keep the bond intact if rates rise. This right is even more valuable when the bond is convertible.[14] Exercising the call option not only removes a bond with a high coupon from the hands of investors (if that is the reason for the call), but it also takes away their conversion option! An increase in the price of the stock, or an increase in volatility of the stock price, has less of a positive impact on the convertible, as the benefit is mitigated by the presence of the call feature.[15]

PART IV

ANALYTICAL TOOLS AND TECHNIQUES

11

CARRY, ROLLS, BREAKEVENS, AND RECOVERY

Carry, rolls, breakevens, and recovery don't sound like bond investment terms, do they? Ah, but they are. All very useful, important everyday concepts and strategies, which we'll explore right now.

Riding the Yield Curve

Consider the yield curve described by the data in Table 11.1. It is a relatively common, upward sloping curve. Why upward sloping? A variety of explanations are possible (all from Chapter 8): expectations of accelerating economic activity, possible inflation expectations, investors on average requiring a premium to extend maturity in the face of volatility. Remember that you individually may agree or disagree with the market's expectations concerning future interest rates and inflation, and you may have a different appetite for risk and require a higher or lower degree of compensation for assuming it. But there is only one yield curve that all investors face, which reflects the *market's* expectations and risk tolerance.

Suppose you have a one-year horizon. You could purchase the one-year note and receive 4% with zero interest-rate risk. But the ten-year note paying 7% looks very appealing; it pays 3% more in yield. Sure, you're aware that what matters to you is the overall rate of return,

TABLE 11.1 Upward Sloping Yield Curve

O/N: 3%; 1-year: 4%; 3-year: 4.5%; 5-year: 5.5%; 9-year: 6.8%; 10-year: 7%

and the bond's yield today is just one aspect of the ROR. And you well know that another crucial factor is the capital risk involved—after one year, when your holding period is over, you'll have to sell the bond at a yield (hence price) reflective of the financial environment *then*, which is uncertain as of now. This risk is pretty serious. If yields rise significantly between now and then, you may end up with a rate of return below 4%, and possibly even a negative ROR.[1] Still, if the ten-year note's yield stays at 7%, you'll earn 7% in return, which looks pretty good compared to 4%. But that's a big if.

Here's an interesting thought process. "I don't want to be judgmental about forecasting yields for next year. As such, wouldn't a nonjudgmental forecast be that yields will be where they are today? Isn't the burden of proof upon anyone who forecasts *changes* in yields? A neutral forecast is for yields to be *unchanged*. Okay, makes sense. But wait a second! My ten-year bond will be a nine-year bond next year! So, a neutral, nonjudgmental forecast for its yield *next* year—when I'll have to sell it—is that it will be the same as this year's *nine*-year yield, not ten-year. And that's 6.8%, lower than the current ten-year yield of 7% by virtue of the positive slope of the yield curve. That's great! If yields just stay where they are today, I'll have a nice capital gain on my investment because my bond's yield will fall."

That's right. If the structure of bond yields next year, when this investor's holding period is over, stays where it is today, the rate of return will be quite high. For example, suppose the ten-year note considered for purchase has a 7% annual coupon. This makes its purchase price par. According to the yield curve, next year this bond will yield 6.8% for a price of $101.3142.[2] Recognizing the coupon, the rate of return equals 8.31%, which exceeds any point on the yield curve! What's interesting about this strategy is that, at least superficially, it does not rely on a forecast of yields declining in the marketplace in order to produce this sizable expected return. It relies only on the yield curve remaining as is, known as a "static" curve assumption. The extra return—above the 7% yield of the bond when purchased—arises from the simple fact that the passage of time changes the yield of a bond, even if the market stays the same, because the bond becomes a different bond.

Let's change the scenario. Instead of the nine-year yielding 6.8% at the inception of the investment strategy, it yields 6.7%. Then, again assuming that the yield curve is static, the bond will drop by 30 basis points in yield by the end of the year—from 7% to 6.7%—for an even greater price appreciation, and a higher rate of return, 8.98%. Similarly, if the ten-year begins with a 7.1% yield and the nine-year is at 6.8%, then the ROR is 9.08% if the yield curve is static. If it begins at 7.2%, the ROR is 9.73%. You see the pattern: the wider the difference in yield between the nine- and ten-year bonds at the investment's inception, the greater the return assuming that yields remain in their position to the end of the holding period. In bond language, *the steeper the slope of the yield curve, the greater the return.* For this reason, the strategy is known as "riding the yield curve." As time passes, the remaining maturity of the bond declines, causing it to move to the left on the curve's time axis. But as it moves left, it travels down the yield curve. The more distance it covers during the one year of traveling, the steeper the slope of the curve and the larger the decline in yield; hence the greater the increase in price and resulting rate of return.

Rolls

How does the term "roll" arise in connection with a yield curve riding strategy? Imagine a bond mutual fund manager. The fund is advertised as investing exclusively in ten-year U.S. Treasury notes. A new ten-year note is issued by the Treasury every three months. On each of these dates, the previously issued note—and the one owned by the fund at this point—has a nine and three-quarter years remaining maturity. To be consistent with the fund's portrayal, the fund manager needs to sell this older note and use the proceeds (as well as any additional money placed into the fund) to purchase the new, true ten-year note. Thus, every three months the manager is said to be "rolling over" the portfolio, or "rolling out of" the old and "rolling into" the new ten-year note. In the strategy above, with the investor facing a one-year horizon, the originally purchased ten-year note will actually have gone through four rolls by the time the horizon is reached. Since the yield curve is negatively sloped in our example, each roll produces a successively higher price for the bond (assuming, of course, that the curve is static).[3]

Attribution

Let's take another example and make it more general. Suppose the bond at the 10-year point of the curve has a 6.75% coupon (assumed, in this chapter, to be paid annually). The curve is as given in Table 11.1. At a yield of 7%, the bond's price is $98.2441 for a current yield of 6.87%. Remember, a bond's current yield represents the annualized return assuming a constant price (6.75/$98.2441). This is also known as the "carry" because this is what you earn by simply "carrying" the bond in your portfolio. One year goes by with the yield curve remaining intact. The bond is now a nine-year, yielding 6.8 percent, for a price of $99.6714. Including the 6.75 coupon, the rate of return (recognizing that the purchase was below par) is 8.32%.[4] Let's analyze this:

- Had the bond's price stayed the same ($98.2441), the rate of return would have equaled 6.87%, which is the current yield.
- Because the bond was purchased at a discount, we know that the price cannot stay the same—it is pulled to par over time. *Had the yield remained at 7 percent*, the price would have been $98.3712, producing a return of 7%, an extra 13 basis points.
- But the yield did not stay the same. Rolling down the curve changed the bond into a nine-year, yielding 6.8%. This yield drop of 0.2% is responsible for the additional 1.32% in rate of return.

We have succeeded in identifying the factors producing the 8.32% ROR. Table 11.2 summarizes our findings, *attributing* shares of the ROR to the three factors.

Now let's see what happens if the yield curve is *not* static. Suppose that at the end of the year, instead of the bond yielding 6.8%, events in the market have caused the yield to increase to, say, 7.15%. Its price is $97.4106. The bond has rolled down the yield curve,

TABLE 11.2 Attribution Analysis 1

6.75%, 10-year bond, 1-year horizon; static
yield curve

Carry	6.87%
Pull-to-par	0.13%
Roll-down	1.32%
ROR	8.32%

becoming a nine-year bond. But the curve is not the same as it was a year ago. Interest rates have risen, resulting in an ROR of only 6.03%. Had the market not changed, the ROR would have been 8.32%, as calculated above. But the market *did* change, resulting in a subtraction of 2.29% from the total return. If we were to perform an attribution analysis for this strategy's ROR as we did in Table 11.2 for the previously discussed case, we would still have the carry, pull-to-par, and roll-down factors exactly as listed there. Why? Because this is what *would have* happened had the yield curve remained intact. But it did not. The market experienced a change. In other words, the *market factor* is responsible for the difference between the 8.32% ROR from the yield curve ride and the actual 6.03%.

We're not finished yet. Let's delve deeper into what caused the nine-year yield to change from 6.8% to 7.15% between the beginning and end of the investor's holding period. Let's take the one-year rate as our anchor. You'll see what this means shortly. Suppose that after starting at 4% when this strategy was put into place, the one-year interest rate declined marginally by the end of the year, to 3.95%. If all the yields across the entire maturity spectrum would have fallen by the same five basis points, we would have described this event as a *parallel shift* in the yield curve. But, in fact, this did not happen. The point on the curve we're interested in—nine years—experienced a 0.35% *increase* in yield (from 6.8% in Table 11.2). The slope between the one-year anchor and the nine-year point steepened by 40 basis points (bps) [(7.15 − 3.95) at the end compared to (6.8 − 4.0) at the beginning]. So, we'll perform the following calculations. Had only a parallel 0.05% shift in the yield curve occurred, as determined by examining what happened to the one-year anchor, the nine-year yield would have declined to 6.75%. This *would have* made the price par, and the ROR 8.66%,

TABLE 11.3 Attribution Analysis 2

6.75% 10-yr bond; 1-year horizon; yield curve
at inception as in Table 11.1, yields at horizon:
1-year = 3.95%; 9-year = 7.15%

Carry	6.87%
Pull-to-par	0.13%
Roll-down	1.32%
Market:	
Shift	0.34%
Slope	−2.63%
ROR	6.03%

34 bps higher than the ROR produced by a static curve. But the curve did *not* shift in parallel. The nine-year yield rose by 35 bps to 7.15% even as the one-year declined by 5 bps. So, what caused the ROR to be 6.03% and not 8.66%? The 40 bps increase in slope. Now we have a full factor attribution analysis, summarized in Table 11.3.[5]

The Fallacy

Part of this seems too good to be true. Ignore for a moment any market shift, since this could go either way, and focus on the roll-down factor. If the yield curve is upward sloping, then as bonds age, we know they roll down the curve, picking up price appreciation on top of any coupon the bond pays. The more steeply sloped, the better. More important, the strategy doesn't require heroic assumptions about the future. On the contrary, it assumes that the current situation will remain as is; that is, that the yield curve will retain its shape while the strategy is in place. The lesson appears quite simple: If you have a short-term horizon, don't be satisfied with the pitifully low yields facing you on the short end of the curve. If the curve is upward sloping, extend maturity, pick up yield (carry), and enjoy the roll-down as well!

Yes, it *is* sort of too good to be true. The above paragraph ignores the central tenet of yield curve analysis (emphasized in Chapter 8): The shape of the curve reflects, fundamentally, market expectations of future interest rates. If the yield curve is upward sloping, this is an indication that the market expects higher interest rates in the future.[6]

This changes everything! The very fact that the yield curve produces a downward ride tells us that next year, when the horizon is over and the bond will be sold as a nine-year in our example, interest rates will be higher than they are today. How much higher? Well, if not for the risk and other nonexpectational factors behind the shape of the curve (see Chapter 8), the curve tells us that the nine-year yield will increase by just enough next year to negate the positive effect of the roll-down![7] A static yield curve is a tenuous assumption. Sorry. You can't get something for nothing in the marketplace.

Take heart, though. This does not mean that there is nothing to yield curve rides. Commercial banks make a good living partly on an assumption similar to that of a static yield curve. They borrow in the money markets and make loans for longer maturities, earning the spread—the static yield curve spread—between the rate on the loans and the rate on their deposit liabilities.[8] So here's the way to think about all this. The yield curve reflects the consensus of *market participants'* expectations—in our case of positive slope that interest rates will be higher in the future. You, as an individual, may be of the opinion that the curve *will* be static and you will, therefore, earn a nice ROR due to the roll-down. Furthermore, supply and demand for credit may be such that the market rewards those investors who take capital risk by extending maturity beyond their horizons (see also the "Risk and Volatility" section of Chapter 8). To the extent that this holds, the yield curve is not entirely driven by expectations, which leaves room for roll-down. What you need to take away is that riding the yield does not rest on an innocuous assumption. On the contrary, the investor undertaking this strategy believes that the future path of interest rates will differ from market expectations as reflected in the curve and is willing to accept the risk—and is paid to do so—of being wrong.

Corporate Bonds

Corporate bonds, or corporates, present a risk of default. As such, they must compensate investors, and they do so by providing a yield in excess of a government bond of similar maturity. That extra yield is termed the corporate's "credit spread." Table 11.4 presents two yield curves—one for Treasury bonds and one for corporates. Notice that the

TABLE 11.4 Yield Curves

Treasury:	1-year, 3%; 3-year, 3.25%; 5-year, 4.25%; 9-year, 5.4%; 10-year, 5.55%
Corporate:	1-year, 4%; 3-year, 4.50%; 5-year, 5.50%; 9-year, 6.8%; 10-year, 7.00%

latter curve is a copy of that described in Table 11.1. Notice also that the credit spread widens with maturity. The extra yield of the one-year corporate obligation above the one-year Treasury is 1%; whereas it rises to 1.25% for the three-year. This is a quite typical phenomenon in the marketplace.[9] Suppose you purchase the ten-year, 7% corporate bond and hold it for a year. Suppose further that the yield of the bond remains at 7% at the end of the year. We know from simple bond math that if the bond's yield at the end of the holding period is the same as it was on the purchase date, the investor's rate of return equals that yield. Ignoring for now the yield curve shape, hence the roll-down, the rate of return of 7% is entirely attributable to the yield, or the carry. The new element here is *credit risk*. Had the investor purchased a credit-riskless Treasury bond of equal maturity, he or she would have earned 5.55% in carry. Hence, of the 7% earned by holding the corporate, we attribute 5.55% to the risk-free rate (or pure "time value of money") and 1.45% to credit risk.

Suppose the coupon on the corporate bond is 6.75%. At a yield to maturity of 7%, its price is $98.2441, for a current yield (its carry) of 6.87%. Now let's break it apart. Of this 6.87%, 5.55% represents the riskless Treasury yield, which the corporate must pay at a minimum. On top of this, it pays a premium for credit risk. If yields are unchanged at the end of the one-year horizon, the corporate's rate of return is the same 7%, with the attribution as shown in Table 11.5.

TABLE 11.5 Attribution Analysis 3
6.75%, 10-year corporate bond; one-year horizon; yield curves at inception as in Table 11.4; yields at horizon unchanged

Carry:	
Risk-free	5.5%
Credit	1.32%
Pull-to-par	0.13%
ROR	7.0%

Now let's see if we can combine all the above into the most general case, allowing the corporate bond yield to change on the horizon date, as we did for the bond summarized in Table 11.3, but recognizing credit spreads and credit spread shifts. The top of Table 11.6 summarizes the starting and ending sets of yields.

The bond began as a ten-year, with a yield to maturity of 7%. One year later, the 6.75% coupon is earned, and the bond—now a nine-year—is sold at a yield to maturity of 7.15% (price of $97.4106). This produced a rate of return equal to 6.03%, just as before. Many things happened during the one-year holding period that contributed to this ROR. (Table 11.6 presents this attribution analysis in summary form. The numbers don't add perfectly to 6.03% because of rounding.)

- *Risk-free rate.* The bond must pay at least the yield on Treasuries of the same maturity, or 5.55%. Furthermore, of this 5.55%, 3% might be termed "pure time value of money," or the one-year Treasury rate plus 2.55% for the Treasury yield curve—the extra yield that a ten-year Treasury pays over a one-year.

TABLE 11.6 Attribution Analysis 4

6.75%, 10-year corporate bond, 1-year horizon; corporate and Treasury yield curves at inception as in Table 11.4. Yields at horizon: Treasury, 1-year 3.05%; 9-year 5.58%; corporate: 1-year 3.95%, 9-year 7.15%

Carry:	
Risk-free	5.55%, of which:
Time value of money	3.00%
Yield curve	2.55%
Credit risk	1.45%, of which:
Pure credit	1.00%
Credit yield curve	0.45%
Roll-down:	
Treasury curve roll	0.99%
Spread curve roll	0.33%
Market shifts:	
Rate level	−0.33%
Risk-free slope	−0.85%
Base credit spread	0.66%
Credit spread slope	−1.75%
ROR	6.05%

- *Credit risk.* As a corporate, the bond must compensate for credit risk. Its credit spread on the investment date was 1.45%. Of this, 1% represents the spread of the one-year corporate over Treasuries (we might term this "pure credit risk"), with 0.45% the extra spread resulting from the fact that the investor is assuming ten years of credit risk, not one year. Note that since we are working with yields to maturity, the carry and pull-to-par are already included.

- *Roll-down.* The spread between the nine- and ten-year corporate yield at the outset was 20 basis points. Had this continued to be the case on the horizon date, the bond rolling down from a ten-year to a nine-year maturity would have added 1.32% in return (had the bond continued yielding 7% as a nine-year, its price would have been $98.3712; but the nine-year yield on the investment date was actually 6.8%, which results in a price of $99.6714, or 1.32% higher). Of these 20 bps, the Treasury spread between the nine-and ten-year (5.55% yield down to 5.4%) accounts for 15 bps, three-quarters of the 1.32% gain. The corporate credit spread (1.45% spread to 1.4%) accounts for 5 bps, or one-quarter.

- *Change in rate level.* The one-year Treasury rose by 5 basis points between the beginning and end of the holding period. Had this been the only change, it would have subtracted 0.33% from the ROR (because the price would have been $99.3443 rather than $99.6714).

- *Shift in Treasury slope.* On the investment date, the spread between one- and nine-year Treasury instruments was 2.4%. On the horizon date the spread widened to 2.53%. This subtracted another 85 basis points from return (because a 6.98% yield produces a $98.5002 price).

- *Change in base credit spread.* On the investment date, the one-year corporate yielded 1% more than the corresponding Treasury. On the horizon date, that credit spread narrowed to 0.9%. This added 66 basis points to the ROR (a 6.88% yield means a $99.1487 price rather than $98.5002).

- *Shift in slope of credit spread.* Finally, while the corporate curve on the investment date showed a 2.8% spread between the one- and nine-year points compared to the Treasury curve's 2.4%, on the horizon dates the curve spreads were 3.2% and 2.53%, respectively. This relative widening of 27 basis points (a 0.4% difference in slope became 0.67%) erased 1.75% in returns.

Breakeven Analysis

Let's return to the situation portrayed in Table 11.1 and not think about credit risk for now. Remember, we're dealing with an investor who has a one-year horizon. She could easily have purchased the one-year Treasury instrument and earned 4% with no risk—no market risk because the instrument matures on her horizon date, and no reinvestment risk as we have assumed for simplicity that the coupon is paid at the end of the year. (We incorporate the coupons later.) Say she buys the ten-year note at par; that is, its coupon is 7%, equal to the yield to maturity. She asks a very reasonable question: How much can the price drop by her horizon date and still produce a 4% rate of return? Reasonable because she could have earned 4% with no risk at all. So how much room is there in the price to *break even* with 4%? This is a simple bond math question. We use the same ROR calculation we've employed here and throughout Chapter 4, but instead of solving for the ROR, we *impose* a 4% ROR and calculate the implied price that would produce it.[10] The answer in this case is simple. Since the coupon is 7%, the price can fall to $97, which provides proceeds of $97 + $7 = $104, or a 4% return on the $100 invested.

Suppose the bond was not at par when it was purchased. Say it carried a 6.75% coupon which, at a 7% yield, makes its price $98.2441. On the one-year horizon date, the price may now drop down to $95.4239, and the ROR hits the break-even 4%.[11] Another way to say this is, as long as the horizon price is above $95.4239, the ten-year note will outperform the riskless one-year note, which pays 4%. We learned in Chapter 4 that the higher the yield on the investment date, all else the same, the greater the rate of return. Therefore, the higher the starting yield, the lower the break-even price to achieve a target ROR.

Consider now an investor with a two-year horizon, purchasing the same bond and, for comparison, also requires a 4% rate of return. As we learned in Chapter 4, for a longer than one-year horizon, the investor must consider the reinvestment rate on any coupons paid during the holding period. Just for simplicity, assume that the 6.75% coupon can be invested at 7% over the second year. The bond's price can drop all the way to 92.2883 after two years and still generate the required 4% return.[12] Why? Because for two years the bond paid 3% more than necessary (7% yield compared to 4% required). *The greater the initial yield and the higher the reinvestment rate, the more the price can drop on the horizon date and maintain a given rate of return.*

Default and Recovery

Corporate bonds pay a higher rate than do Treasuries. We've incorporated this into the analysis above, and elaborated on the reasons for it in Chapter 9. Briefly, nongovernment borrowers present the risk of default. Upon default, the investor will receive at most, and very likely much less than, the stated principal of the bond. Because of this possibility, investors demand a higher yield while the bond is alive.

The amount bondholders receive following bankruptcy is known as the bond's "recovery value." We came across this measure in Chapter 9 in our discussion of bond seniority and subordination. The percentage recovered depends upon, among other factors, the firm's leverage at the time of default, bankruptcy costs, and where the bond stands in the company's capital hierarchy. Suppose the 6.75% coupon bond, purchased at a yield of 7% (price $98.2441) considered in the previous section is a corporate. Assume, as we did above, that the coupon payments are reinvested at 7%. The bond defaults after two years, and the recovery rate is 90%. Since the second coupon is not paid until the end of the year, it is subject to the bankruptcy parameters as well. Hence, the proceeds equal the initial coupon, reinvested, plus the currency value: $6.75 \times 1.07 + .9 \times [$100 + 6.75] = $103.2975, for a rate of return over the two years, given the $98.2441 investment, of 2.54%.[13]

Let's approach this calculation "inside-out." Assume now that the investor has held the bond for four years and reinvested all the coupons at the bond's initial yield, 7%. It is the fourth year, and the firm is tottering. Say a four-year Treasury bond had yielded 6% when the investor made the purchase. He or she could have earned a 6% rate of return over five years without any worries (except for reinvestment risk, which applies equally to the corporate and the Treasury). If the firm were to default now, at the end of the fourth year, what must the recovery rate be in order to achieve a 6 percent ROR? Applying the standard ROR formula, that required recovery rate is 94.44%.[14] In other words, the recovery value would need to be 94.44% to *break even* with a riskless Treasury instrument. If the default doesn't occur until the end of the fifth year, the breakeven recovery rate is 93.12%. *The longer the bond is held—the longer the amount of time the firm survives—the lower the necessary recovery value to achieve a breakeven rate of return.*

12

MEASURING AND MANAGING INTEREST-RATE RISK

Some Preliminaries

You're looking for an easy definition of risk. You don't want to hear "ifs" and "buts," and you want one that applies to all situations for all investors. I'm sorry, I don't have one. And neither does anyone else. But what I *can* do is provide you with an *approach* to understanding the concept of risk in a way that is helpful to you as an investor and consistent across securities.

Suppose you purchase a five-year U.S. Treasury note, speculating that its price will rise by the end of the day. You're at risk. Why? Because if the price goes down, you'll lose money. So one way to describe risk, at least in this situation, is uncertainty concerning the price of an owned asset. Now, instead of a five-year note, suppose you purchased a three-month Treasury bill for a day. Same problem. You don't know the price you'll sell it at when the trading day is over. The problem may be the same, but the *degree* of risk is lower for the bill, as you'll soon see.

Consider now an investor who has money set aside to meet an expense coming due in three months. We might refer to her as a "cash manager." Looking to earn interest on the idle funds, she buys the same Treasury bill as the speculator above. Does she have the same risk? She bought the same security, didn't she? Same security, yes; but same risk, no. Since she has no intention of selling it prior to its maturity, she has no risk. She knows now exactly how much the T-bill will pay in three months. Risk, you see, is not completely objective. *Two investors, holding the same instrument, face different risks.* We need, therefore, to supplement our description of risk. Risk reflects the *uncertainty of an asset's value when it must be liquidated.* The last few words—"must be liquidated"—depend on the investor. For the cash manager, the three-month bill poses no risk at all since it matures at the end of her holding period. For the speculator, at the end of the day it's still a three-month bill. But what if our cash manager buys a five-year note? That's certainly risky. When her anticipated three-month investment period is over, she'll need to sell. But not a five-year Treasury note— rather, a four and three-quarter year Treasury note, which has a different risk profile from the five-year note. Our speculator, on the other hand, is ready to sell at any moment, if need be, or to hold onto the security if so decided. The risk he faces is that of a five-year note or three-month bill—what the securities are *now*, not later.

We have established that risk depends on the expected holding period of the investor. Once that holding period is completed, the security must be sold (unless it matures), and it is subject to price uncertainty. The analysis that follows focuses on that date—the date the bond must be liquidated. This allows us to abstract from the subjectivity of risk. Regardless of who the investor is—hedge fund, cash manager, speculator, insurance company—our concern is the possible price movements of the bond on the horizon date. If a speculator, for example, with an overnight holding period buys a ten-year note, the risk is the possible price movements in the ten-year note. If a longer-term investor—say, one with a one-year holding period—purchases the same bond, the risk is the possible price change on a nine-year note. We won't need to associate the security whose risk we're analyzing with any specific investor or investor type.

One more point before proceeding. The risk we're concerned with here is that of interest-rate changes and what they do to bond prices. There are other risks, of course, and they come up throughout this book— credit risk, equity risk, currency risk, and so on. Exchange rate movements are dealt with in Chapter 19. Equities are not the subject of this book, at least not directly. The effect of stock price movements on convertible bonds is examined in Chapter 10. Equity prices are directly related to corporate profits, which affect corporate bonds. The interactions between profits and the credit risk of corporate bonds are handled in Chapters 9 and 10. Our focus in this chapter is on pure interest-rate risk.

Interest-Rate Risk

Look closely at Table 12.1. All three of the securities are Treasury bonds with 4% semiannual coupons, but they have different maturities. We'll stick with Treasuries so that we do not need to deal with credit risk.

Let's make a number of important observations. For each bond, the higher the yield to maturity, the lower the price. We've seen this many times before (see Chapter 3 for a refresher). The fixed coupon of the bonds means that the market becomes more and more disappointed with it as new bonds entering the market present higher coupons. Conversely, if new bonds in the marketplace have lower coupons, investors become more enamored of existing bonds. Observe how this reaction of price to changing yields is more pronounced for longer maturity instruments. We've encountered this previously as well, and attributed it to the fact that investors' disappointment with bond coupons below that which are available in new bonds is sharper the longer the bond is "stuck" with the low coupon. (And their enjoyment of the higher than market coupons is greater the longer they get to keep them.) A 1% increase in yield from 4% to 5% causes the two-year note to drop 1.88% below par. The same yield increase forces a 4.38% decline in the five-year's price and leads to a 7.79% reduction in the ten-year. Let's look at these numbers more closely. The 1.88% price decrease in the two-year is sensible. The 1% yield increase "hurts" for each of the two years of the note's remaining life—two times 1% is 2%, which

TABLE 12.1 4% Semiannual Coupon Treasury Securities, Prices ($) at Various Yields

Yield	1-Yr. Maturity	5-Yr. Maturity	10-Yr. Maturity
3%	101.9272	104.6111	108.5843
4%	100	100	100
5%	98.1190	95.6240	92.2054

approximates 1.88%. This reasoning should result in the five-year's price declining 2.5 times as much as the two-year. Yet it doesn't—the ratio of 4.38 to 1.88 is 2.33. Further, the ten-year note declines only 1.77 times (7.79/4.38) as much as the five-year, not twice as much. *Price sensitivity to interest-rate changes does increase with maturity, but not linearly.* Why not? We'll soon see. And solving this puzzle will also explain why the two-year in fact declines by 1.88% and not a full 2%.[1]

Table 12.2 looks at price sensitivity from a different angle: the effect of the coupon.

The bonds presented all have five-year maturities, so you would expect the effect of yield changes on their prices to be pretty similar. In fact they're not. The middle coupon column (4%) reproduces that of the previous figure. The first column is a "zero coupon" five-year security. A 1% increase in yield to maturity for the zero does, in fact, produce a nearly 5% decline in price, which makes sense (1% for each of the five years remaining to maturity). The existence of a coupon, though, apparently changes everything. Consider the 4% coupon note. An increase in yield from 3% to 4% causes only a 4.611% price decline. The next 1% yield increase has a negative 4.38% effect. Now consider the 8% five-year coupon. The first 1% yield increase results in only a 4.32% price decrease; the next one pushes the price down by 4.28%. So we've observed the following:

- The existence of coupons on a bond destroys the linear relationship between maturity and price sensitivity (or risk). For example, a ten-year note does not display twice the price sensitivity to the same interest rate change as a five-year note does, despite having twice the length of time to maturity.
- Given bonds of the same maturity, the greater the coupon, the less the price sensitivity.

TABLE 12.2 Five-Year Treasury Securities, Prices ($) at Various Yields

Yield	0% Coupon	4% Coupon	8% Coupon
3%	86.1667	104.6111	123.0555
4%	82.0348	100	117.9652
5%	78.1198	95.6240	113.1281

These observations have major implications for bond investors. Suppose you're a speculator, and you expect interest rates to decline. You want longer maturity bonds since, as every bond guy knows, they will experience greater price increases in response to your expectation of yield decline. Not so fast. That's true only if they have the same coupon. If two bonds have the same coupon, then you want the longer maturity. If they have the same maturity, the above demonstrates that you want the lower coupon. What if one bond has a longer maturity and the other a lower coupon? The same dilemma exists if an investor expects interest rates to rise. Since you want to lose less money as bond prices fall in response, you want lower maturity and a higher coupon. Again, what if one bond has the shorter maturity and the other the higher coupon? There is a solution, as we'll see soon. First, let's try to understand the problem: Why do coupons matter?

Importance of the Coupon

Clearly, the coupon is important for the bond's price. That goes without saying. If two bonds are otherwise equivalent (same maturity, issuer, seniority, etc), but one has a higher coupon, its price will be higher. How much higher? Basic bond math (Chapter 3) teaches us: high enough to force its yield to maturity to equal that of the other bond. So, in terms of the bond's *yield*—buying it and holding it until maturity—you'll do just as well with both bonds, despite their different coupons.

Our concern here is with the coupon's importance as an ingredient in the bond's price *change*, not price *level*. Here's the intuition you need. You already know that the longer the maturity of a bond, the more its price will react when yields change. This is a direct extension of the "time value of money" concept. Interest rates are the compensation for time. The longer the time for the bond to remain outstanding, the more the change in interest rates matters. Here's another way to look at the same thing. A dollar to be paid in five years is *discounted* to the present by the annual interest rate, or yield, five times. A dollar to be paid in two years is discounted only two times. An increase in the rate of discount—the interest rate—affects the five-year two and a half times as much as it does the two-year.

Now compare the five-year zero coupon bond (we'll call it "Z") in Table 12.2 to the 4% coupon bond ("F"). All of Z's money is to be paid in five years. But some of F's money arrives earlier, doesn't it? The semiannual coupon payment of $2 in half a year's time, another $2 in one year, $2 in a year and a half, and so on until $102 is paid at the end of five years. Thus, looking at *all* of F's cash flows—coupons as well as principal—you see that the *average waiting time* is less than that of Z's cash flows. A purchase of Z means that you wait five years. A purchase of F means that you wait six months for $2, one year for the next $2, and so on until $100 plus the final $2 at the end of five years. Well, if the average waiting time until payments is lower for F than for Z, then the effect of a change in interest rates—the *payment for waiting time*—should be less on F's price than on Z's price. And indeed it is—about 4.5% for F compared to 5% for Z when interest rates change by 1%. Why are the two effects close (4.5% is not that far from 5%)? Because the cash flows that F pays earlier than Z—the coupons—are not that large compared to the principal. But they clearly do matter.

What about the 8% coupon bond, the final column in Table 12.2? It has a five-year maturity as well. But its high coupon means that you receive relatively more of its cash flows earlier compared to the other two bonds—it has a much shorter average waiting time. Hence, its price will be the least responsive of the three bonds to interest-rate movements (approximately a 4.2% price change for a 1% yield change, compared to 4.9% and 4.5% for the other two). We conclude, therefore, that bond coupons, by shortening the average waiting time for a bond's cash flows, reduce the bond's price sensitivity to interest-rate changes.

Duration

A bond's "duration" is simply a formal measure of its average waiting time. It is an important and extremely useful measure for bond professionals. The longer the duration—the longer the average waiting time for a bond's promised cash flows—the more sensitive (more risky) the bond's price to shifts in market interest rates. This is simply a restatement of the conclusion in the last paragraph, but in bond language. Here's a simple illustration. Consider a two-year amortizing bond (defined in Chapter 1). Let's ignore the coupon (and the bond's yield) at first, and assume this simplest amortization schedule: Given a face value, or principal, of $100, it pays $50 at the end of the first year and $50 at the end of the second. What's your average waiting time (AWT)? 1.5 years—halfway between one and two years (50/100 × 1 year + 50/100 × 2 years). Now apply this idea to coupons. Consider a two-year, annual 10% coupon bullet bond. It pays $10 after one year, $10 plus $100 after two. Its AWT is (10/120 × 1 year + 110/120 × 2 years) = 1.92 years.[2] Close to 2, but not quite 2. The bond matures in two years, but it pays some cash prior, hence its AWT is less than 2.

If you understand AWT, then you understand duration, because a bond's duration is just a modification of AWT. And the modification is eminently sensible. It simply recognizes that when calculating AWT, the cash flows in the averaging process cannot all be treated the same. In the previous example, the first $10 coupon arrives a year earlier than the second. So it is worth more. It also arrives earlier than the principal. In short, we need to recognize the time value of money.

> *Duration measures the average waiting time for all the cash flows promised by a bond, where the cash flows are discounted, recognizing the time value of money.*[3]

Unlike AWT, duration will be affected by movements in yield (hence price). When interest rates change, the waiting time in years is, of course, unaffected. But because duration utilizes the discounted value of the cash flows, which *do* respond to interest-rate movements, the measure will change.[4]

Table 12.3 presents the duration measures for the bonds in Table 12.1.

In each case duration is shorter than maturity because it recognizes the time until coupons are paid, not only principal. Duration increases

TABLE 12.3 Duration of Bonds Differing by Maturity

Maturity	Coupon	Yield	Price	Duration
1 year	4%	4%	100	0.9886
5 years	4%	4%	100	4.5811
10 years	4%	4%	100	8.3392

with maturity, but that is not surprising. What is interesting is that the increase slows down—the duration of the five-year note is about six months shorter than five years, whereas the duration of the ten-year note is one and three-quarter years less than ten. This observation has major implications for risk. We delve into this later, but it's worth mentioning now. The key ingredient in interest-rate risk is duration, not maturity. A ten-year note is twice as long in maturity as a five-year note, but significantly less than twice as long in duration (8.3392/4.5811 = 1.82, not 2.)

How does the coupon quantitatively affect duration? Table 12.4 shows the duration measures for the bonds in Table 12.2.

These bonds are all of five-year maturities, allowing us to concentrate on the coupon factor. The first thing to notice is that the duration of the zero coupon bond is the same as its maturity. This is no surprise. In fact, if its duration would be anything else, it would call into question the definition! A zero coupon bond has only one cash flow—the last. The average waiting time (either on a present value or absolute value basis) is, of course, its maturity. This is an important point to remember for the risk discussion coming up later.

Once a coupon is added to the bond, duration declines. A 4% coupon, bringing the bond to par, pushes the duration down to 4.58 years. Doubling the coupon to 8% raises the price, of course, as the bond pays more cash flows. More to the point, the duration declines further, by about three and a half months. Why? A larger percentage of the bond's payments are scheduled to arrive earlier.

So there we have it. Duration is the measure we're looking for. Whereas maturity is one-dimensional, duration is multidimensional, taking into account both maturity and coupon. In fact, duration is more inclusive than that. It also reflects the yield to maturity of the bond plus its callability and amortization schedule, if any.[5] Given a set of bonds with different characteristics—maturities, coupons, yields, call options,—the

TABLE 12.4 Duration of Bonds Differing by Coupon

Maturity	Coupon	Yield	Price ($)	Duration
5 years	0%	4%	82.0348	5.0000
5 years	4%	4%	100	4.5811
5 years	8%	4%	117.9652	4.2898

one with the longest duration is the most price sensitive to interest-rate changes; the one with the shortest duration is the least sensitive.

Quantifying Interest-Rate Sensitivity and Risk

Duration is a great tool. As we've seen, with a single number, it ranks bonds with respect to their price sensitivities to interest-rate changes. But it's more than that. It actually quantifies the sensitivity and thereby has become one of the most, if not the most, useful measures in fixed-income management and analysis.

Let's go back to first principles for a minute. Consider a security that pays $100 in one year, nothing earlier than that, nothing later. (We've called that a zero coupon bond.) If it begins the trading day at a yield of 4%, its price is $96.1169.[6] Were the yield to rise by 1% to 5%, its price would fall to $95.1814, approximately a 1% decline. Why 1%? Since the security's payment is coming in one year, the increase in yield of 1% subtracts 1% from the price. Now consider a security making the same single payment, but in two years. An increase in its yield from 4% to 5% pushes the price down from $92.3845 to $90.5951, nearly a 2% decline. Why 2%? Because the 1% increase in yield is *per year*—so it subtracts 1% twice from the present value. If the yield increases by 0.50% its price falls by approximately 1%—0.50% for each of the two years until the money is paid. Now it is no longer a mystery why the five-year zero coupon bond in Table 12.2 declines by almost 5% when its yield increases by 1%—1% for each of the years until the money is paid.[7]

If the five-year bond were to pay a coupon, we would not be able to use the same reasoning. The investor is not waiting five years for the money. Rather, some money is paid in one year, some in two, and so on. How long is the investor waiting? On average, 4.5811 years—that's the duration of time until the average (present value) dollar is paid. Therefore, an increase in yield of 1% causes the price to fall by approximately 4.58%. That's it![8]

The duration of a bond, being a measure of average time until a bond's (present value) cash flows, provides a close approximation of the effect of a change in yield on the bond's price. In particular, a 1% change in yield causes an approximate percentage change in price equal to the bond's duration.

Dollar Duration

We've used the word "approximate." A five-year zero coupon bond has a duration of five years. A 1% change in yield causes an *approximate* 5% change in price. A five-year 4% coupon par bond has a duration of 4.58 years. A 1% percent yield change causes an *approximate* 4.58% price change. To make it exact, we need to divide the duration measure by 1 plus the bond's yield (or 1 plus the bond's semiannual yield, if the coupon is paid semiannually).[9] This is known as the bond's "*modified duration.*" The five-year, par 4% semiannual coupon note's modified duration is $4.5811/1.02 = 4.4913$ years. Going forward we employ modified duration in place of the definitional duration and omit the adjective "modified."

Duration supplies us with the *percentage* change in a bond's price resulting from a change in yield. To get the dollar price change, simply multiply the percentage change by the bond's dollar price.[10] "Dollar-duration" equals the bond's duration multiplied by the bond's price. Table 12.5 presents the dollar-durations of bonds with various coupons and maturities.

What is the intuitive meaning of dollar duration? Its units are neither years nor dollars. It is years multiplied by dollars! What the heck is that?!! It is a very useful measure of risk. We agree that the longer the

TABLE 12.5 Duration and Related Measures of Risk (4% Yield to Maturity; Modified Duration)

Maturity (Yrs.)	Coupon (%)	Price ($)	Duration (Yrs.)	Dollar-Duration
1	4	100	0.9692	96.9200
5	0	82.0348	4.9020	402.1314
5	4	100	4.4913	449.1275
5	8	117.9652	4.2057	496.1246
10	0	67.2971	9.8039	659.7758
10	4	100	8.1757	817.5686

duration of a bond, the more sensitive its price is to a change in yield. But if its price is very low, that sensitivity doesn't amount to much because it can't change much. The bonds shown in Table 12.5 rise monotonically with respect to dollar duration, but not with respect to duration by itself. The ten-year zero coupon bond has the longest duration. But its price is far from $100. Therefore, it has less dollar duration. The 4% ten-year bond has a significantly lower duration than the zero by virtue of its coupon. But the holder of the bond has more money invested in it; hence it presents greater risk—more dollar duration. The ten-year zero is exactly twice as long in duration years as the five-year zero. But its risk, as reflected in duration dollars, is only 64% greater. In other words, market participants would say the one-year note has 96.92 dollars of risk in it; the five-year note presents 496.12 dollars of risk, 5.12 times as much as the one-year.[11]

We now can easily calculate the effect of a 1 basis point change in yield—referred to fondly as one "tick"—on the price of a bond. It's simply *the bond's dollar duration multiplied by .0001* (since 1 basis point is one hundredth of a percent, and 1% is one-hundredth of one, which would be the entire dollar-duration). This oft used measure is known as the "dv01 (dollar value, or discounted value, of 1 bp) and is shown in Table 12.6 for the bonds displayed in Table 12.5.[12] In other words (and in a very famous bond math equation):

$$\Delta P = dv01 \times \Delta bps$$

The change(Δ) in price of a bond equals the bond's dv01 multiplied by the change in its yield, given in basis points.

TABLE 12.6 Duration and Dv01 of Bonds (4% Yield to Maturity)

Maturity (Yrs.)	Coupon (%)	Price ($)	Duration (Yrs.)	Dv01
1	4	100	0.9692	.0096
5	0	82.0348	4.9020	.0402
5	4	100	4.4913	.0449
5	8	117.9652	4.2057	.0496
10	0	67.2971	9.8039	.0660
10	4	100	8.1757	.0818

How is dv01 applied by investment managers? Straightforwardly. Suppose an investor expects the Federal Reserve to raise its overnight rate by 0.25% and that all bonds will respond (in yield change) equally. The investor's portfolio, consisting of some of the bonds in Table 12.6, and the anticipated impact of the central bank's action, are shown in Table 12.7.

Consider the one-year note, of which $50 million is held. Its dv01 implies that the price moves by .0096 per $100 market value for each basis point. Therefore, a 25 basis point move results in a price move of $25 \times .0096 \times \$50,000,000/100 = \$120,000$. Similarly, the calculation for the $100 million face value five-year zero coupon bond is $25 \times .0402 \times \$100,000,000/100 = \$1,005,000$. (Note that the bond's price being different from par is already recognized in the dv01.) After doing the calculation for the other two bonds in the portfolio, the total portfolio exposure to a 25 basis point yield movement is now a simple matter of adding the numbers in the final column, or $2,299,750. A 25 basis point change in interest rates across the curve will produce a $2,299,750 change in the portfolio's value.

The yield curve shape rarely stays perfectly constant. That is, when interest rates change, the change is not equal across all maturities. Still, a parallel shift in the curve is a good starting point for assessing the risk of a bond, or a bond portfolio as just performed. Let's adjust the scenario. Suppose that the portfolio manager, anticipating the 25 basis point increase in the federal funds rate, expects the one-year rate to rise by the same amount. Because longer-term rates reflect expectations of the future, not just the present, the manager believes that the central bank's rate hike will dissipate as maturities lengthen: 15 basis points for the five-year; 5 basis points for the ten-year. In that case, the portfolio's

TABLE 12.7 Impact of Yield Change on Bonds via Dv01

Maturity (Yrs.)	Coupon (%)	Price ($)	Dv01	Face Amount Held ($ mm)	$ Impact of 25 Bps
1	4	100	.0096	50	120,000
5	0	82.038	.0402	100	1,005,000
5	4	100	.0449	50	561,250
10	4	100	.0818	30	613,500

value will decline by 25 × 0.0096 × \$50,000,000/100 + 15 × [0.0402 × \$100,000,000/100 + 0.0449 × \$50,000,000/100] + 5 × 0.0818 × \$30,000,000/100 = \$1,182,450. Duration, you see, has no predictive value. You supply the rate change; duration gives you the price reaction.

Hedge Ratios

Another popular, and important, use of duration is in hedging interest-rate risk. Suppose an investor owns \$10 million of the five-year, 4% note in Table 12.7. He intends to hold the note for the long term, but is concerned about price deterioration in the near term, perhaps fearing the above-mentioned 25 basis point rate increase by the central bank. What to do? Sell short the ten-year. For the present, you can simply think of a "short" position as the opposite of owning the bond.[13] If you are short a bond and its price falls (rises), you earn (lose) the change in price. Why sell the ten-year short if you own the five-year? If interest rates rise and cause the price of the five-year to drop, hence resulting in a loss, the rise in rates will also cause the ten-year to fall in price, thus producing a profit when it is repurchased to cover the short. How many of the ten-year notes to sell? Here's where duration comes in. The investor should sell \$5.4890 million of the ten-year note, or 0.5489 for every one five-year. Why that number? It is equal to the ratio of the dv01s: 0.0449/0.0818. If you think about it, it is quite intuitive. For the same change in yield, the ten-year is 0.0818/0.0449 = 1.8218 times as price sensitive as the five-year, since price sensitivity is measured by dv01. So, to offset the effect of a change in yield on the price of one five-year note, less than one ten-year needs to be shorted. The ratio of the dv01s, therefore, is known as the "hedge ratio." In our example, the investor would sell \$10 million × 0.5489 = \$5.489 million face value of the ten-year note against the \$10 million of the five-year that it hedges.

Here is an important caveat. People hear the word "hedge" and they think "riskless." Not true. Generally, a hedge removes the risk of the *overall* market but leaves other risks uncovered. Our example is a good illustration. Suppose the yield on the five-year note increases by 25 basis points. The investor incurs a loss of 25 × 0.0449 × \$10,000,000/100 = \$112,250. Further assume that the ten-year note's yield rises by the same 25 bps. Its price falls, but as the investor is short

$5.489 million, the *gain* is 25 × 0.0818 × $5,489,000/100 = the same $112,250. Notice that the numbers match (hence cancel each other) only because the yield change incurred by both bonds are equal. But they don't have to be equal; the yield curve can change its shape. The hedge works only for a parallel shift in the yield curve. What if the yield change on the ten-year is less than that of a five-year? The gain on the hedge is less than the loss on the original bond. Of course, the yield increase on the ten-year might exceed that on the five-year, and the hedge may produce more profit than the loss incurred. Since we can't predict with any accuracy how, and if, the yield curve will shift, the hedge is imperfect. This is known as "basis risk."

How about using the five-year zero coupon bond to hedge the five-year 4% bond that the investor owns? As they are both on the same point of the yield curve, would that not remove the basis risk? Very good point. However, the five-year zero coupon bond is much less liquid than the ten-year note. The latter is the benchmark issue for the ten-year sector (as the five-year 4% is for the five-year sector). This means (see Chapter 21) that the five-year zero coupon bond has a significantly wider bid-offer spread. Hence, selling it short and then buying it back once the hedging period is over may entail significant cost.[14]

Hedging Corporate Bonds

Fixed-rate corporate bonds (as opposed to floating-rate notes) pay the Treasury interest rate plus a spread for credit risk. Changes in Treasury yields, therefore, evoke price changes in corporate bonds just as they do in Treasuries. Given the corporate's coupon, maturity and yield, we calculate its duration exactly as we do for a Treasury bond. Multiply the duration by its price, and you have its dollar duration. And multiply that by 0.0001, you have its dv01. Nothing new here. Interestingly, given a corporate bond and a Treasury bond of equal maturity, the higher coupon of the corporate reduces its duration and hence lowers the degree of interest rate risk! But less interest-rate risk does not translate into less *total* risk. Be careful. The corporate contains credit risk, which the government bond does not.[15] Let's examine the implications.

Hedging the interest rate risk of a corporate bond follows the same procedure as above. Suppose an investor owns a five-year corporate and is worried about a rise in market interest rates. She can short the five-year Treasury benchmark security. How many Treasuries should she short for each corporate owned? The ratio of their respective dv01s, just as above. Note, however, that only the pure interest-rate risk of the corporate is hedged. For example, suppose that the Treasury yields 4%, and the corporate yields 5.5%. If both change in yield by, say, 25 basis points, the price decline in the corporate will be offset by the gain in the Treasury short position, as the price decrease of the latter produces income via the short. If the corporate's yield instead rises by 30 basis points, because its credit spread relative to Treasuries widened (by 5 basis points), the additional price decline brought about by the extra 5 basis points will not have been offset. In other words, shorting Treasuries hedges the pure interest-rate risk of a corporate, not its spread risk. Spread risk, then, is another example of basis risk.[16]

13

CONVEXITY, VOLATILITY, AND CALLABILITY

This is an interesting, and perhaps more challenging, chapter. It pulls together the fundamental ideas and measures of bond yield and return, plus those of risk from the previous chapter, and weaves into them the notion of nonlinearity in fixed-income products. This is a crucial notion. We've seen it a few times before; for example, in the discussion of convexity. Now we do it justice.

Revisiting Convexity

Let's start with a plain vanilla bond, maturing in five years with a 4.5% (semiannual) coupon. Our concern in this chapter is with interest-rate movements and their ramifications, so we'll work only with bonds that lack default risk. The second column in Table 13.1 shows the bond's prices at various yields to maturity. We deal with the other two bonds displayed in the table later.

Suppose that the bond begins the day at par. There are a couple of ways to see the nonlinearity of the price-yield relationship. A 50 basis point increase in yield forces a price decline of 2.1880%. A second yield increase of equal size produces a smaller, 2.1797% drop in price. Now go in the other direction. A 50 bp decline in yield from 4.5% cause the bond's price to rise by 2.2456%. The next 50 bp drop in yield produces

TABLE 13.1 Nonlinear Effects of Yield Changes on Bond Prices

Yield	5-Year Maturity, 4.5% Coupon		10-Year Maturity, 4.5% Coupon		8.16-Year Maturity, 0% Coupon	
	Price ($)	Percentage Price Change	Price ($)	Percentage Price Change	Price ($)	Percentage Price Change
3.5%	104.5506	2.2544%	108.3764	4.1201%	75.3474	4.0852%
4.0%	102.2456	2.2456%	104.0879	4.0879%	72.3902	4.0750%
4.5%	100	0	100	0	69.5558	0
5.0%	97.8120	−2.1880%	96.1027	−3.8973%	66.8389	−3.9060%
5.5%	95.6800	−2.1797%	92.3864	−3.8670%	64.2344	−3.8967%

a better, 2.2544% increase in price. As yields increase, price declines decelerate. As yields decrease, price increases accelerate. Clearly, this asymmetry of the price response is to the investor's advantage.

Another way to look at the asymmetry is as follows. From a starting point of 4.5%, it is safe to say that there is an equal chance of yields rising by 0.50% and falling by 0.50%. The former causes a price drop of 2.1880%; the latter, a price improvement of 2.2456%. Thus, the investor has an equal chance of losing $2.1880 per $100 invested and of making not $2.1880, but $2.2456! This is an unfair bet, but the unfairness is favorable to the investor.[1] This asymmetry, found in all fixed-coupon instruments, was termed "convexity" back in Chapter 3. Convexity is a desirable feature of a bond—the chances of a specific positive price change exceeds the chances of the same negative price change. It exists simply because a bond's price cannot drop below zero. Yields can rise to any heights, but eventually the resulting price decline becomes negligible. These ideas are important enough and complex enough to warrant repetition:

> *Fixed income instruments display convexity. Convexity describes the asymmetrical price responses to changes in a bond's yield to maturity. The positive price impact of a yield decrease is greater than the negative price impact of the same yield increase.*

The difference between 2.2456% and 2.1880% may not appear to be large (although in institutional $10 million bond sizes it amounts to thousands of dollars). Let's see what happens if we allow a full 1% yield "shock" to the bond on either side of the starting 4.5% yield. The top and bottom rows of Table 13.1 tell us that the trade-off is a gain of 4.5506 (per $100 face value of the bond) versus a loss of 4.3200 (per $100). The asymmetry is larger, the greater the change in yield. Figure 13.1 shows this quite clearly.[2] Begin at 4.5% and a price of par. An increase in yield to maturity—moving left to right on the horizontal axis—always causes the bond's price to decline. But because the price can never *cross* the axis, each successive yield increase must bring with it ever-declining price decreases. Now go the other way. Every yield decrease from 4.5%—moving right to left—pushes the bond's price upward. Here the upward movements accelerate.

FIGURE 13.1 Price-yield Relationship for Fixed Coupon Bond

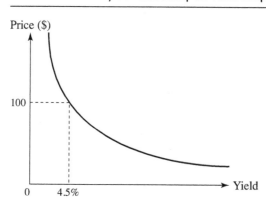

How do investors approach convexity? Consider two bonds, the second more convex than the first, but otherwise equivalent. The second is more attractive. Why? An increase in market yields causes the prices of both to decline equally (due to their initial equivalence), but continuing increases in yield have less of a negative impact on the second. A decline in market yields results in the same price increase for both, but further yield declines have a more positive effect on the second. Since investors prefer the second, they will bid up its price relative to the first. A higher price, of course, means a lower yield. We have arrived at an important result:

> *Investors prefer convex bonds. Investors pay for convexity by accepting lower yields.*

Here's another way to look at convexity. Bonds provide income, known as "yield." Given the bond's coupon, a lower price provides greater yield; a higher price provides lower yield. Bonds also provide convexity—a cushion to the impact of price declines as yields rise and an acceleration of price increases as yields decline. Convexity is paid for by a higher price. Hence, there is a trade-off between yield and convexity. Investors face a choice. From a group of otherwise similar bonds, the investor can choose those with greater convexity, but they will need to give up income. Or, they can choose more income, but accept less convexity. How should investors go about making this choice?

Convexity and Volatility

As observed earlier in Table 13.1, when the five-year note starts at par, a 1% yield increase causes an approximate 4.32% fall in price, while an equal yield decrease produces a 4.55% rise in price. The difference between the two changes—the asymmetry, if you will—is markedly higher than the difference when we allow only a 0.50% movement on either side of 4.5%. It is an even better bet for the investor! What have we learned? The greater the movement from the starting yield, the greater the benefit to the investor from the bond's convexity. Volatility measures the sizes (and associated probabilities) of potential yield movements. Hence, the more volatile interest rates are, the more desirable convexity is. Lower yields, as explained above, are the payment for this convexity. We conclude the following:

> *The more volatile the interest-rate environment, the greater the benefit of convexity. Since investors pay for convexity by accepting lower yields, an increase in volatility causes yields to fall, all else being the same. And, they will fall more depending on how convex a bond is.*

Maturity and Convexity

Let's shift to the next two columns in Table 13.1, where the subject bond has a ten-year maturity. It has the same 4.5% coupon as the five-year note and begins life in the middle row at par. A change in yield provokes a greater price response from this bond than from the five-year bond examined above. We've seen this many times and explain it in Chapter 12: Since the two bonds share the same coupon, the longer maturity creates a higher duration and greater price sensitivity. But the ten-year bond is also more convex. You can see this in the "price" column for the ten-year bond, where the price increase accelerates as the yield declines. The rate of acceleration exceeds that of the five-year note. Similarly, as yields rise for the ten-year, the rate of price decrease decelerates, and the deceleration is greater than it is for the five-year. Look at this in another way. Starting at par, there is an equal chance of there being a 50 basis point yield decrease as there is a 50 basis point yield increase. For the ten-year bond, the price gain from the yield decrease is 4.0879%, while the price loss from the yield increase is only 3.8973%. This is a superior asymmetric trade-off compared to that of the five-year bond (the ten-year's ratio 4.0879/3.8973 is greater than the five-year's ratio 2.2456/2.1880). And the relative asymmetry is greater still if we consider 1% changes—the outer rows of Table 13.1—rather than 0.50% changes. We conclude that the longer the maturity of a bond, all else the same, the greater the convexity.[3]

But why? What makes longer maturity bonds more convex? We just need to repeat the answer to the more basic question—what makes bonds convex?—and you'll probably see the reason yourself. The negative relationship between yield and price for fixed coupon bonds cannot be linear. Since a bond's price cannot be negative—you wouldn't lend someone money and then pay him or her interest!—a higher and higher yield must have an ever-decreasing negative effect on price. Now let's consider the five- and ten-year notes in Table 13.1. They both start at par, with the same yield. Way back in Chapter 3 we learned intuitively why an increase in yield would force the ten-year to decline in price more than the five-year. Every 1% increase in yield subtracts roughly 1% in price *for each year remaining*. The first increase in yield, therefore, causes the ten-year to fall more than the five-year. Hence, the ten-year is already closer to zero! It has less room to decrease in reaction to the *next* increase in yield. Now think about that next 1% yield increase for both bonds. Again, the ten-year must fall relatively more than the five-year (because of its longer maturity). Both will fall less than the preceding change. But the ten-year's deceleration must be greater since it has less room before hitting the floor of zero. There you have it!

Here's another implication of this analysis, one that we make use of later. Just as every increase in yield reduces the distance between the bond's price and zero, which forces the next yield increase to have less of an effect, so, too, does every increase in maturity cause the price response to a higher yield to be greater, also narrowing the gap toward zero. In other words, convexity accelerates with maturity.[4] That's a bit complicated to digest, so here's an example. Take the five-year bond above. If we were to replace it with a six-year issue, the convexity would increase by amount X. If we were to replace it instead with a four-year, convexity would decrease by amount Y. But X is bigger than Y. That's it. So, by selling the five-year at par and taking $50 of the proceeds to purchase, say, a four-year note and $50 to purchase a six-year, we have increased the convexity even though the average maturity is intact.[5]

Duration Again

Duration, as we saw in the previous chapter, measures the length of time an investor waits for the average (on a present value basis) dollar to be paid by a bond. As such, it provides a measure of risk, since it quantifies the price reaction of a bond to a change in its yield. Duration is not good or bad. It is simply a measure of waiting time, hence a measure of price responsiveness. Convexity, on the other hand, is unambiguously good. And, therefore, it comes with a cost, namely a lower yield. But convexity and duration are profoundly linked.

Consider the ten-year note in Table 13.1. At par, it has a duration of 8.1580 years.[6] Its *modified* duration is 7.9785 and, as we know from Chapter 12, modified duration quantifies a bond's price response to changes in its yield to maturity. Unless explicitly noted, we'll work with modified duration.[7] A 1% drop in yield will produce, approximately, a 7.98% increase in price. Allow the yield to decline by 0.50%. As the table shows, the exact price is now $104.0879. Its duration has also risen to 8.0447 years.[8] A 1% yield decline *from this point* will produce an approximate 8.04% increase in price, greater than the increase from the previous starting point. Why do declines in yield produce ever-larger price increases? You see it yourself because duration rises every time yields drop. Let's go in the other direction. From its beginning price of par, the 7.98-year duration implies that a 1% increase in yield should cause the price to decline by approximately 7.98%. Suppose the yield increases by 0.50%. The new price, according to Table 13.1, is exactly $96.1027. But the bond's duration is now 7.9144 years, *lower* than it was at the start. This means that the *next* 1% increase in yield will cause an approximate 7.91% decline in price, less than that from the original point. Thus, increases in yield produce ever smaller price decreases. Why? Because duration declines every time yields rise. We might say, therefore, that a bond's convexity is reflected in how duration changes with the bond's yield:

> *Convexity is an attractive characteristic of bonds. A decrease in yield causes prices to rise. How much it rises depends on the bond's duration. Once the yield declines, duration is greater. Thus, the next yield decrease produces an even larger price increase. An increase in yield causes prices*

to fall, the degree of which depends on duration. Once yields increase, duration is lower. Thus, the next yield increase causes less of a price decrease. This nonconstancy of duration is due to convexity.

Now consider the five-year note shown in Table 13.1. At par, it has a modified duration of 4.4320 years. A 1% change in its yield, therefore, will produce, approximately, a 4.43% change in its price. After a 0.50% yield decline, the duration is 4.4444 years. Not much of an increase, but an increase nonetheless. Following a 0.50% increase in yield, duration falls to 4.4150 years, again a small shift. As we observed with the ten-year note, the five-year's duration rises when yields fall and declines when yields rise. However, the movement in duration is slight—the five-year is less convex than the ten-year.

Back to Dv01

Chapter 12 explains the intimate relationship between a bond's duration and its dv01 (dollar value of 1 basis point). Both are measures of price sensitivity to yield changes, or interest-rate risk. Duration is a percentage change measure; dv01 is a dollar change measure. Hence, we can restate everything in the section above in dv01 terms. In particular, *the convexity of fixed-coupon bonds describes the phenomenon that its dv01 rises as its yield declines and that its dv01 declines as its yield rises.*

Zero Coupon Bonds

We already know that the ordinary duration of a zero coupon bond is the same as its maturity. Since there is only one cash flow—the principal—the "average" waiting time is exactly the time until that cash flow is paid. Here's an interesting exercise. Consider a zero coupon bond with maturity, hence duration, equal to the duration of our ten-year note above, or 8.1580 years. This is shown in the final two columns in Table 13.1 The zero begins with the same yield as the ten-year note, hence shares the same initial modified duration, 7.9785 years as well. Its price, of course, is well below par, reflecting its 0% coupon. A 0.50% decline in yield results in a 4.0750% increase in price—close to, but less than, that of its counterpart 4.5% coupon ten-year bond *of the same duration.* The next 0.50% decline in yield produces an even greater percentage price increase. But, as the figure shows, the rate of acceleration is not as positive as that of the ten-year. Why? Because, as both their yields decline, the zero coupon bond's modified duration does not increase to the degree of the 4.5% coupon bond. Similar, but opposite, results apply on the way down: despite beginning with equal durations, the zero coupon bond falls in price more than the 4.5% coupon does, and the rate of deceleration for the subsequent price decline is less as well. Again, the zero's duration does not decline as fast as that of the coupon bond.

Table 13.2 shows how the durations of the ten-year coupon bond and of its counterpart zero bond respond to movements in yield. In short, the zero coupon bond is less convex. Although this is just one example, the result generalizes.

> *Among bonds of similar duration, those with the highest coupons will have the greatest convexities. Zero coupon bonds, therefore, will have the lowest.*

Interesting result. But does it matter much? For fixed-income portfolio managers, quite a bit, as the next section shows. It also explains the reason that this result holds and why, in fact, it is just a special case of a broader concept.

TABLE 13.2 Duration Changes in Response to Yield Movements

Yield	Duration of 10-year maturity, 4.5% coupon bond	Duration of 8.16-year maturity, 0% coupon bond
3.5%	8.0983	8.0104
4.0%	8.0447	7.9988
4.5%	7.9785	7.9785
5.0%	7.9144	7.9529
5.5%	7.8551	7.9368

Barbells

Let's put some color into this convexity topic! Assume that the ten-year yield to maturity has risen to 5.25%, with the five-year yield intact at 4.5%. The slope of the yield curve, in other words, has gone from flat to positive. In addition, the yield on a seven-year bond is 4.8%. Table 13.3 displays the data, along with prices and durations of bonds for each maturity.[9]

An investor is interested in purchasing the seven-year note. The yield is adequate and, more important for this investor, the duration, as a measure of price sensitivity to yield changes—that is, interest-rate risk—fits his or her parameters. The problem is that the note is not liquid. The U.S. Treasury has not issued seven-year maturity bonds in a while, so this is an old ten-year note—three years old, to be exact. With a resultant wide bid-asked spread, the investor's rate of return will be reduced due to transactions costs.[10]

In Chapter 12 we measure the interest-rate risk of a portfolio of bonds as the sum of the dv01s of the respective components of the portfolio. Duration measures interest-rate risk as well, but in percentage, or relative, terms as opposed to the absolute terms of the dv01 measure. *The duration of a portfolio of bonds equals the (weighted) average of the durations of the component bonds.* If that's the case, why don't we construct the following two-bond portfolio to have the same duration as the seven-year note the investor is interested in:[11]

- 1   five-year note
- 0.6311 ten-year note

From Table 13.3, the total portfolio is worth:

$$1 \times \$100 + 0.6311 \times \$94.2225 = \$159.4638.$$

TABLE 13.3 Yield Curve with Bond Prices and Durations

Maturity	Coupon	Yield	Price ($)	Duration
5 years	4.50%	4.50%	100	4.4320
7 years	6.00%	4.85%	106.7573	5.7191
10 years	4.50%	5.25%	94.2225	7.8836

The five-year note represents $100/159.4638 = 62.71\%$ of the portfolio, with the ten-year note representing the other $0.6311 \times \$94.2225/\$159.4638 = 37.29\%$. Hence, the portfolio's duration is: $0.6271 \times 4.4320 + 0.3729 \times 7.8836 = 5.7191$, the same as that of the seven-year.

We have constructed a portfolio of bonds to match the duration of a single bond—the seven-year note. Our duration-matching portfolio consists of two bonds, whose maturity surrounds that of the "target" bond. This is known as a "barbell."[12]

What has the barbell accomplished? It has given the investor the duration—hence, interest-rate risk exposure—he or she had sought from the seven-year note. (We get to the yield soon.) In addition, the bonds in the barbell, being benchmark issues, are more liquid than the seven-year note. Actually, that's not the main reason; I just used that argument for motivation. *The barbell is more convex than the single bond.* That is the key fundamental reason for the barbell's superiority. Let's prove it and then try to understand why.

By construction, the barbell and the seven-year note begin with the same duration. The first group of three columns in Table 13.4 repeats what we already know about the five-year note. The second group applies to the ten-year, the yield of which begins at 5.25%, requiring a new set of calculations, as presented. The third group is for the barbell and is simply the weighted average of the first two (initially weighted 62.71% and 37.29%, respectively, as suggested above). The final group refers to the seven-year note the investor was interested in initially.

The middle row is the starting point, hence the entry in the yield change column is 0. Let's concentrate on the barbell and seven-year column groups, as the others are just building blocks for the barbell entries. Notice that both begin with the same duration—that, of course, is the point of the barbell. As we allow yields to decline, first by 0.50% and then by 1%, the prices of both the seven-year note and the barbell increase, and both exhibit accelerating price increases. Both are convex. But the barbell accelerates faster.[13] Conversely, as yields rise, both exhibit decelerating price decreases. Once again, both are convex. But the barbell decelerates more. Look at how their respective durations change. Both durations increase as yields fall; both decrease as yields rise. But the barbell's duration changes are more pronounced. *The barbell*

TABLE 13.4 Convexity Comparison: Barbell versus Bullet

Yield Change	Five-Year Maturity, 4.5% Coupon, 4.5% Initial Yield			Ten-Year Maturity, 4.5% Coupon, 5.25% Initial Yield		
	Price ($)	Percentage Price Change	Duration	Price ($)	Percentage Price Change	Duration
-1.0%	104.5506	2.2544%	4.4649	102.0195	4.0716%	8.0092
-0.5%	102.2456	2.2456%	4.4444	98.0281	4.0390%	7.9468
0	100	0	4.4320	94.2225	0	7.8836
0.5%	97.8120	-2.1880%	4.4150	90.5932	-3.8518%	7.8206
1.0%	95.6800	-2.1797%	4.4020	87.1314	-3.8213%	7.7568

Yield Change	Barbell, 1 Five-Year, 0.6311 Ten-Year			Seven-Year Maturity, 6% Coupon, 4.85% Yield		
	Price ($)	Percentage Price Change	Duration	Price ($)	Percentage Price Change	Duration
-1.0%	168.9351	2.9395%	5.8157	113.0832	2.9285%	5.7873
-0.5%	164.1111	2.9143%	5.7647	109.8657	2.9117%	5.7546
0	159.4638	0	5.7191	106.7573	0	5.7191
0.5%	154.9854	-2.8084%	5.6713	103.7539	-2.8133%	5.6889
1.0%	150.6686	-2.7853%	5.6264	100.8516	-2.79735	5.6560

is more convex than the seven-year note, despite sharing the same initial duration.

More convexity is better. We've seen that before. It provides a greater price cushion when bond prices fall in response to increases in yield. And it allows greater participation in price increases when yields decline. We also concluded earlier that investors pay for more convexity by accepting a lower yield. If this is the case, shouldn't the bullet yield less than the seven-year note, being more convex yet having the same duration? Indeed it does: The weighted average yield of its component bonds is 62.71% × 4.25% + 37.29% × 5.25% = 4.62%, less than the 4.85% yield of the seven-year note. Perfect.

> *Investors pay for the extra convexity in barbells by accepting a lower yield.*

In an earlier section we concluded that convexity becomes more desirable when market participants expect greater volatility. The combination of a price cushion on the way down and participation on the way up has a higher value when there is a greater chance for prices to move up or down. Investors, therefore, pay more for convexity (that is, accept a lower yield) in more volatile market environments. Now we understand the trade-off between a barbell and a single bond of matching duration. Investors who want more downside protection along with their upside participation—a type of insurance, if you will, against volatility—will pay for the protection offered by the more convex barbell via a lower yield. Investors who are more willing to accept the effects of volatility and are not willing to pay for protection will take the single bond and gain the higher yield.

The remaining question is why. Why should a barbell be more convex than a single bond? Actually, the answer was already given above; it just needs to be applied here. Convexity, as we have seen, accelerates with maturity. A ten-year bond is more convex than a five-year; and a twenty-year is more convex than a ten-year. But the increase in convexity from ten to twenty is much greater than twice the increase from five to ten. Now let's examine our situation. Start with the seven-year note. The convexity gained by shifting some weight to the ten-year note exceeds the convexity lost by shifting the offsetting weight to the five-year note in order to keep duration intact. When the seven-year is totally replaced by the five- and ten-year notes, there is, therefore, a net increase in convexity. That's the answer. This also now explains why the zero coupon bond in Figure 13.2 is less convex than the ten-year note, despite having the same duration. The zero coupon bond has a maturity of 8.16 years, less than 10 years. The ten-year note contains a multiple of cash flows—principal at the end of 10 years, and coupons dispersed throughout. The ten-year note has the same duration as the 8.16-year zero because the durations of principal in year 10 plus the coupons in years 9 and 10 are offset by the durations of the coupons in the first 8 years. Start with the 8.16 year zero. As weights are shifted to the cash flows longer than 8.16 years, more convexity is added than the convexity lost by shifting offsetting weights to the cash flows earlier than 8.16 years. This, you see, is very similar to the argument for the barbell relative to the single seven-year. We can say this all in one sentence: Bonds are more convex than zero coupon bonds with the same duration because of the dispersion of their cash flows; zeros have, by definition, a single cash flow. Or:

> *The greater the dispersion of a security's cash flows, the greater its convexity.*

Barbells contain more dispersed cash flows than do single bonds. The principal payments of the five- and ten-year notes are on either side of that of the seven-year note (with the coupons providing further dispersion). That's why market participants refer to single bonds, as compared to barbells, as "bullets." Recall from Chapter 1 that a bullet is a bond with no amortization—its principal is repaid only at maturity. A barbell, on the other hand, has two principal repayments. More dispersion, hence more convexity.

Callable Bonds

We've examined callable bonds a number of times in this book. In Chapter 2 we describe their structure, their appeal to borrowers, and their risk to investors. In Chapter 9 we consider them as an item on the menu for corporate issuers. We are now ready to more carefully examine the determinants of the call spread—the extra yield a callable bond pays over that on a similar, but noncallable, issue. We consider it with respect to convexity and relate it to volatility. This will be fun.

As is generally the case, and as we've done a number of times in this book, a good way to investigate a special feature of a security is by comparing it to a security alike in all other ways except in that special feature. So examine Table 13.5, which shows prices for three bonds, all with an 8% coupon. We'll assume that the yield curve is flat and that the market begins at an 8% yield.[14] This simplification allows us to concentrate on the call feature and not be sidetracked by the shape of the curve. The five- and ten-year noncallable bonds are easy. A 1% increase in their yields to maturity produces the price declines as presented, using the bond math we've grown to love. What about the callable bond? How can we price the bond without knowing whether it will be called or not, hence without knowing the maturity? The regular bond pricing formula won't work.

Here's what we'll do.[15] Begin by simplifying the borrower's call option: The company has one opportunity—call the bond at the end of five years or leave it until maturity. We need to think *today* what that decision in five years is likely to be. Table 13.6 helps. (We'll be moving back and forth between Tables 13.5 and 13.6.) Just as in Table 13.4, we start the dynamics with yields at 8%, the middle row in both figures. Under our assumption of a flat yield curve—in particular, that the five- and ten-year interest rates are equal—it is reasonable to state that the market (expectations by who determines the shape of the yield curve— remember Chapter 8) believes there is an equal probability of the five-year interest rate in five years being either above or below 8%. Below 8%, the bond will be called; above (or equal to) 8%, it will not be called and, as a result, remains outstanding until its maturity another five years later. Thus the *average expected maturity* for this bond is 7.5 years (.5 × 5 + .5 × 10), shown in the middle row of Table 13.6. Since the coupon equals the yield, the price is par for this "7.5-year" bond, shown as such in the entry for the callable price column in Table 13.5.

Let's investigate the bonds' reactions to a 1% increase in the market's required yield. The five- and ten-year noncallables fall by about 4% and 6.5%, respectively, reflecting their durations (4.05 for the five-year, 6.79 for the ten-year), as seen in Table 13.5. With an expected maturity of 7.5 years, the callable bond should react to the yield increase

TABLE 13.5 Effects of Yield Changes on Bond Prices (8% Coupon): Callable versus Noncallable

Yield	Five-Year Maturity, Noncallable		Ten-Year Maturity, Callable in Five Years		Ten-Year Maturity, Noncallable	
	Price ($)	Percentage Price Change	Price ($)	Percentage Price Change	Price ($)	Percentage Price Change
4%	117.9652	4.2757%	118.7734	3.9398%	132.7029	7.5530%
5%	113.1281	4.2365%	114.2713	3.2868%	123.3837	7.4046%
6%	108.5302	4.1971%	110.6350	4.6107%	114.8775	7.2558%
7%	104.1583	4.1583%	105.7587	5.7587%	107.1062	7.1062%
8%	100	0	100	0	100	0
9%	96.0436	−3.9564%	94.6307	−5.3693%	93.4960	−6.5040%
10%	92.2782	−3.9204%	88.7259	−6.2398%	87.5378	−6.3727%
11%	88.6936	−3.8846%	82.5885	−6.9172%	82.0744	−6.2412%
12%	85.2798	−3.8490%	77.3674	−6.3218%	77.0602	−6.1094%

TABLE 13.6 Expected Maturity Analysis for Callable Bond

Today's Yield	Probability of Yield below 8% in Five Years	Probability of Yield above 8% in Five Years	Expected Maturity
5%	.95	.05	5.25
6%	.90	.10	5.50
7%	.70	.30	6.50
8%	.50	.50	7.50
9%	.30	.70	8.50
10%	.10	.90	9.50
11%	.05	.95	9.75

as would an 8% coupon, 7.5-year bond. Its price falls to $94.6307—a 5.4% decline, which is between that of the five- and ten-year notes. Its duration is 5.60 years.

Here's where it gets exciting, so hang onto your hat. Now that interest rates are 1% higher (remember—we're still assuming a flat yield curve), investors need to reassess the likelihood of the bond being called in five years. Since yields have already reached 9% for this group of bonds, there is no longer a 50-50 chance of yields being below 8% in five years. The odds have shifted markedly to rates above 8%, say 70-30. As such, Table 13.6 shows that the new expected maturity of the callable bond is 8.5 years (.3 × 5 + .7 × 10). Let's think about the *next* 1% increase in interest rates. Look back at Table 13.5. Both the five- and ten-year noncallable bonds decline in price somewhat less than they did in the previous decline. We know this already—they display convexity. Their durations are lower at the higher yield—3.96 and 6.50, respectively. What about the callable? Using the new 8.5-year expected maturity, a 1% yield increase causes its price to fall to $88.7259, a 6.24% decline. Its price decline is steeper than before! Why? Because the market now believes it is a longer maturity bond. Indeed, at a 9% yield, its duration has *risen* to 5.71 (from 5.60 at the 8% yield). This is exactly what investors do *not* want. They prefer duration—price reaction—to decelerate as rates rise, not accelerate.

At a yield of 10%, the market once again reassesses its outlook for the bond being called. As Table 13.6 shows, the market now believes that there is only a 1 in 10 chance of interest rates ending up below 8% in five years, hence the bond being called, given that rates are at 10% currently. This produces a 9.5-year expected maturity. Should the yield at this point increase by another percent, Table 13.6 shows that the callable's price declines by 6.92%, an accelerating price decrease once again because it has become an even longer maturity bond compared to the deceleration experienced by the noncallable bonds.

Let's see what happens in the other direction—a decline in interest rates. We begin again at a yield of 8% with all the bonds at par. The callable's expected maturity is 7.5 years, as above. A 1% decline in yield causes a 4.16% and 7.11% increase in price for the five- and ten-year issues, respectively, in line with their starting durations. The callable rises by 5.76%, between the two noncallables, as it should be, given its expected maturity (7.5 years, 5.64-year expected duration) between the two of theirs. But at the new lower 7% yield, the probability of the bond being called in five years is greater—70% instead of 5%, resulting in a 6.5-year expected maturity rather than 7.5 (Table 13.6). Thus the next 1% drop in rates produces less of a price increase—only 4.61%. As is seen in Table 13.5 the noncallables, by contrast, display accelerating rates of price increase. Their durations rise as yields fall; by contrast, the callable's duration has decreased (to 5.12 years). With interest rates now at 6%, the callable's expected maturity falls further, to 5.5 years, as the likelihood of it being called in five years has jumped to 90%. A 1% decline in yield, therefore, results in only a 3.29% price increase, a further deceleration, disappointing the investor. The five- and ten-year bonds, on the other hand, accelerate in price healthily, to the investor's satisfaction.

A summary is in order at this point. As yields rise, bond prices fall. As yields decline, prices rise. This is true of both callable and noncallable bonds. But noncallables display another characteristic, which is attractive to fixed-income investors. Each successive yield decrease produces successively greater percentage price increases. And each successive yield increase results in successively smaller price decreases. This is what convexity is all about. Callable bonds seem to behave perversely. As yields decline, the resulting price increases are progressively smaller and smaller. As yields rise, resulting price drops are progressively larger. Market participants refer to this trait as "negative convexity."[16] We know that investors value convexity, and pay for it by accepting a lower yield.

Investors, therefore, must *be paid* to accept negative convexity. Their payment is in the form of a higher yield, which we know as the call spread.

Callability and Volatility

We've observed a number of times the crucial relationship between convexity and volatility. A bond's convexity is valuable to investors only when there is market volatility. The greater the chance of interest-rate changes, the more opportunities there are to utilize the price cushion on the way down and take advantage of the participation on the way up. Investors pay, by way of lower-yielding bonds, to gain convexity; they demand payment, through higher yields, to accept negative convexity. Hence, just as investors pay more for convexity during volatile periods, they demand more payment for negative convexity during volatile times. In other words:

> *The call spread—the extra yield a callable bond must pay relative to an otherwise similar noncallable bond—widens when interest rates become more volatile and narrows when interest rates become less volatile.*

As an outgrowth of our investigation into the negative convexity of callable bonds, we've learned two more things about them. A ten-year bond, callable in five years, displays less interest-rate risk than a ten-year noncallable bond. Why? The possibility of call gives the callable an *expected* maturity of less than ten years (and a duration below that of a ten-year noncallable). At the same time, the callable bond contains much more volatility risk—and in the other direction—than its noncallable counterpart.

Here's a major implication of the result above. Suppose you own a callable bond and expect market volatility to increase. The bond will decline in value—even as interest rates are unchanged—should your expectations be realized. Here are some steps you could take:

- *Sell the bond.* If you expect interest rates to rise along with the increase in volatility, put the money into cash (that is, money market instruments) or floating rate notes. If you expect rates to be steady or decline, buy a noncallable bond of similar duration.

- *Sell the bond and use the proceeds to purchase a barbell, the duration of which matches that of the callable.* You'll give up yield because you'll lose the call spread. Further, the barbell has an even lower yield than a noncallable bullet, as we learned above. However, the value of the barbell will rise should your expectations be born out, since the barbell's positive convexity becomes more valuable when volatility increases.

- *Keep the callable bond, but purchase call options on bonds.* Although spending money on the calls reduces yield, options offset the negative convexity in the callable.[17]

- *Replace the callable bond with a "putable" bond.* Or retain the callable, and instead sell a bullet bond from your portfolio and use the proceeds to buy a putable bond. A putable bond gives the investor the right to sell the bond back to the issuer and demand par. The put option embedded in the bond works in the opposite direction to the call option embedded in the callable bond. It is very positively convex. Hence, the investor must give up substantial yield. For the same reason, it will rise in price should volatility increase.[18]

One last thing. Let's look at the two outer (top and bottom) rows in Table 13.6 and their implications for the outer lines in Table 13.5. At an 11% yield, the likelihood of the bond being called in five years is 5%. This is not much lower than the 10% the market assessed when the yield was 10%. It *can't* be much lower, since there is little room left until 0%. This produces an expected maturity of 9.75 years. Now let's see what happens to the set of bond prices at the next 1% yield increase. Table 13-5 shows that they all decelerate—even the callable does! Let's go in the other direction. At a 5% yield, the market assesses the probability of being called at 95%, again not much different from the probability at a 6% yield, producing a 5.25-year expected maturity. Again because there is little room left until 100%. A 1% decrease in yield at this point causes an acceleration of price increases for *all* the bonds in Table 13.5! Why does this happen? The answer is intuitive. As yields get further away form the bond's coupon, the uncertainty regarding the borrower's call decision decreases. In our example, at about 5%, the bond will almost certainly be called. The callable bond behaves, therefore, almost

FIGURE 13.2 Price-yield Relation for Callable Bond

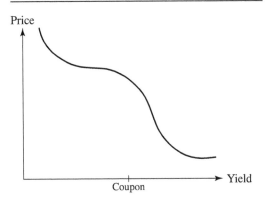

like a noncallable five-year note. At about 10%, it almost certainly will not be called. The bond behaves almost like a noncallable ten-year note. At these relatively extreme points, therefore, the bond's natural positive convexity overrides the negative convexity of the call feature.

This behavior is summarized in Figure 13.2, which shows a callable bond's negative convexity contained in the region close to the bond's coupon.

PART V

LIBOR-BASED SECURITIES
AND DERIVATIVES

14

MONEY MARKET INSTRUMENTS

Technically, a money market instrument refers to a security with an original maturity of less than a year. Money market instruments usually don't pay coupons. Instead, you get your interest along with the principal at maturity.

Why are they called "money market" instruments? Because investors use them as money substitutes. Suppose a cash manager at a company has a few days until payrolls are due to be paid. Rather than letting the funds sit idly in a checking account, the manager will purchase these short-term instruments which pay some interest. Investing in longer-term instruments is not advisable. Should market interest rates rise during those days, we know from Chapter 3 that bond prices will decline, and the decline is greater the longer the maturity. Because of their ultra-short maturities, money market instruments will hardly be affected by these rate movements. "Money" does not change in "price," either; hence the name.

Treasury Bills

Treasury bills (T-bills) are the prime example of a money market instrument. The U.S. Treasury issues bills with one-, three-, and six-month maturities on a weekly basis.[1] You lend the Treasury money, and it returns your principal with interest on the maturity date, nothing in-between. Lenders face no credit risk with T-bills. And, because of their short maturity, their prices don't react much to changes in market interest rates. Investors who buy these securities, therefore, desire as little price risk as possible. They may need their money in a short period of time and are looking only for a parking place. Or they are looking to reduce the risk of their overall portfolio by allocating some portion of their funds to government-backed money market instruments.

Treasury bills (as well as agency and commercial paper—see below) are issued at a discount. That is, they don't pay interest explicitly. All you get is the principal—or face value—at maturity. Why would you buy it? Because you pay less than the face value. Your interest is the difference between what you pay and what you receive at maturity. For example, if you pay $99 for a three-month T-bill, you will earn 4.05% on an annualized basis.[2]

Agency Paper

U.S. government agencies access the money markets. A number of them issue paper similar to Treasury bills—less than one year maturity and issued at a discount from face value. Agencies sell these *discount notes* for the same reason the U.S. Treasury does—to bridge a short-term gap between receipts and expenses. Investors buy them as an alternative to T-bills, to earn the slightly higher rate due to the note's modest credit risk. Chapter 1 lists and briefly describes the activities of the major U.S. agencies.

Bank Deposits

Banks issue lots of money market instruments. It's their modus operandi. You know what these are—they're called "deposits." Banks issue many types of deposits, pay interest on them (except for demand deposits), and use the money to make loans, hoping that the interest on the loans, net of any defaults, is more than enough to cover the costs of the deposits. Their profit, therefore, is a function of the differential, or spread, between the interest rate on their liabilities—deposits—and that on their assets—loans. Those bank deposits referred to in the context of money market instruments are those sold to institutional investors in multimillion dollar denominations, as opposed to the retail deposits at local branch banks.[3] Institutional-size bank deposits come in various maturities, sometimes as short as overnight. They may also come with a host of "bells and whistles" (known in our language as "embedded options"), such as caps and floors.[4]

What Is This Thing Called LIBOR?!

The world's largest banks borrow and lend among themselves in all major currencies, around the clock. They must be involved so because their customers do business in all currencies, and different markets have different operating hours. A customer may need a loan or must access its credit line. If the bank's funds from existing deposits are fully allocated, it may look to borrow the sum from another bank. On the other side, a bank may have received deposit money and does not foresee immediate loan demand. The "interbank market" facilitates movement of these excess funds from the second bank to the first. The U.S. "onshore" interbank market for transactions which settle the same day is known as federal funds. We discuss these at length in Chapters 5 and 6 in the context of central bank monetary policy and the macroeconomy. "Offshore" U.S. dollar denominated deposits are known as "eurodollar" deposits. Technically, a U.S. dollar deposit in any bank outside the United States would be termed a eurodollar deposit, even if not in Europe. Much, but not all, *interbank* eurodollar activity takes place in London. At 11 a.m., London time, thought to be the time of day when the market is very liquid, a number of the largest participants in the market are polled. They are asked the rate at which they are prepared to lend ("offer") funds to each other. An average is calculated and published as the "London interbank offered rate" or the well-known "LIBOR." There is a LIBOR for all the major international currencies, each rate reflecting financial conditions in that particular country (hence, currency) or region. And, for each currency, there is a different LIBOR for a wide set of maturities; for example, one week, two weeks, one month, two months, etc.[5]

The term *eurodollars* can be misleading. So, bear two things in mind. First, the dollars are not necessarily in Europe. The market *began* in Europe; "euro" today simply denotes offshore (same for euroyen, eurosterling, etc.) Second, this is not a *currency*—it is a *deposit*. Don't confuse it with the euro common currency (as in Chapter 19 and the euro versus dollar *exchange rate* which, unfortunately, is also termed "eurodollar!"[6]

LIBOR for any currency is important for a number of reasons:

- As a short-term interbank deposit rate, it reflects the particular central bank's policy stance, the robustness of macroeconomic activity and associated inflation pressures, and their interrelationships.
- The spread between LIBOR and the rate on short-term government borrowing (T-bills) indicates market participants' perception of the overall health of the banking system.
- LIBOR is an essential ingredient in determining the interest rate on floating-rate notes (covered in Chapters 15 and 16) and in the cash flows paid to counterparties in interest-rate swap contracts (Chapters 17 and 18) and other derivatives.

Commercial Paper

Firms can borrow short term from their banks. But banks need to earn an interest rate on their lending above the rate on their deposits. By going directly to short-term lenders and avoiding banks, firms can reduce the cost of their borrowing. Commercial paper, very short-maturity corporate IOUs, is one such vehicle. Bonds sold to the public need to be "registered" with the Securities and Exchange Commission (SEC).[7] Among the exemptions the SEC allows to this rule is one that permits firms to sell unregistered paper in the open market as long as its maturity is less than nine months. Once a commercial program is in place, firms can issue with little delay, affording them a significant liquidity source. The paper typically is uncollateralized. Because of the lack of registration (and collateral), commercial paper issuers are dominated by large, well-known firms. Many companies have come to rely on this instrument for long-term funding. That is, they regularly "roll over" the paper at maturity; i.e., they issue new paper to refinance maturing securities. To allay investors' fears that the firm will not be able to roll over the paper, commercial paper issuers will negotiate a "line of credit" with a bank to accompany the paper issuance program. The line of credit calls on the bank to extend funds to the firm to pay off maturing paper should the firm be denied funds for new paper issuance.

It is important to appreciate that this line of credit is no more than a liquidity facility. It is *not* a credit guarantee. The line can be drawn upon only if the firm's credit has not deteriorated significantly. (The line where "significant" is crossed may not always be explicit in the bank-company agreement.) That is, if the firm is locked out of the commercial paper market when investors shy away because there has been a material change within the firm causing it to be considered too risky to be granted credit, the credit line disappears. When, then, is the line operative? When investors exit from the commercial paper market due to "liquidity" events in the market at large. Perhaps a macroeconomic event has occurred that has caused a "flight to quality," and investors want nothing to do with any credit risky paper. In that case, the firm can draw on its line of credit, pay off the maturing paper with the bank funds, and repay the bank when the paper market returns to normal.[8]

Commercial paper issuers pay a modest annual fee to the bank for the line of credit. The fee is paid for the *unused* line. Suppose the firm has a $1 billion credit line backing its commercial paper program. It might pay 0.50% per year on the billion dollars for the right to draw upon it. If conditions require drawing down, say $200 million, the firm will pay its normal borrowing rate to the bank for the $200 million, and then 0.50% on the remaining $800 million of the credit line.

Asset-Backed Commercial Paper

Banks are always looking for ways to economize on the use of their balance sheets. The "traditional" model of banking has the institution issuing deposits and using the funds to make loans and, secondarily, to purchase securities. Hopefully, the interest and other earnings on these assets exceed the cost of servicing the liabilities (mostly interest). This is known as the bank's interest "spread," or "margin." Figure 14.1 presents an alternative business model.

Here's how the model works. A conduit (also known as a special purpose vehicle, or SPV) is established. It is a legal entity whose sole purpose is to stand between the bank and investors. Like any physical conduit, it is a conveyor. It simultaneously conveys funds from investors

FIGURE 14.1 Alternative Business Model

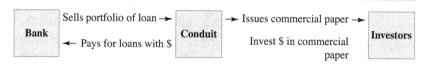

to the bank and the economic exposure of the loans from the bank to investors. The process starts when the bank sells a portion of its loans to the conduit. Bingo! The bank's balance sheet is reduced, since it can use the money to pay off depositors (or to make new loans, which then are sold to the SPV, and the process continues). The conduit gets the funds to pay for the loans by issuing commercial paper to money market investors. Note that the commercial paper is not backed by any company producing cars, selling clothes, operating hospitals, and the like. The only backing is the loans that the conduit owns. Hence, investors have purchased *asset-backed commercial paper* (ABCP if you will).

It's important to understand that the bank no longer has any credit exposure to the loans sold; that was the entire point of the transaction from the bank's perspective. Any default is a loss to investors. If this were not the case—if there were any recourse back to the bank in event of default—the loans would not be removed from the bank's balance sheet. At the same time, though, the selling bank (also known as "originating" bank, since it made the loans in the first place) provides a line of credit to the conduit for its commercial paper program, for which it receives a fee, as explained above. But this is a liquidity provision, not a credit provision.

Figure 14.2 depicts the periodic cash flows between the parties after the loans have been sold and the commercial paper issued.

FIGURE 14.2 Cash Flows among Parties to Asset-Backed Commercial Paper

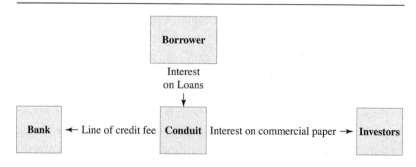

Included in the figure is the borrower's position, making its regular interest payments on the loan to the conduit.

Step back from the structure's details and consider the big picture. The removal of the loans from the bank's balance sheet and their sale to the conduit has resulted in a shift away from the traditional banking model. Instead of depositors funding loans, bond market (commercial paper) investors have become the ultimate suppliers of capital.

Other Money Market Instruments

Other money market instruments include:

- *Banker's acceptances.* Banker's acceptances (BAs) usually are born from international trade. An importer may not be able to pay for the goods until they are sold, and the exporter is unwilling to extend credit. The importer draws up a *draft* (an IOU) payable to the exporter, so that the exporter is prepared to ship the goods. The draft is a promise to pay a specific sum at a future date. If the importer's bank accepts responsibility to pay, then the draft—known as a banker's acceptance—reflects the credit of the bank, not the importer. The exporter can hold onto the BA, or sell it in the open market at a discount to its face value, much like Treasury bills and commercial paper.
- *Trade credit.* Firms borrow from each other in the normal course of business. A manufacturer will ship clothing to a retailer and ask to be paid, say, within 30 days, after which interest begins to accrue on the money owed. Known as trade credit, this is simply an IOU between two businesses "trading" with each other. This loan by the manufacturer is normally not sellable—it is not a "security." But it is a source of funds for the retailer. (It becomes a security, to be sold in the open market at a discount from its face value, in the event of default by the retailer.)
- *Repurchase agreements.* We delve into repurchase agreements more deeply in Chapter 22. For now, it's sufficient to point out that dealers (and other market participants, such as hedge funds) borrow lots of money in order to finance their inventory before

it is sold. A preferred mechanism to do so is a repurchase agreement (repo). Simply put, a repo is a short-term loan, typically overnight (hence qualifying as a money market instrument), collateralized by high-quality fixed-income instruments.[9]

Money Market Yield Curve

The above instruments will carry different interest rates based on their unique structures and on the creditworthiness of the issuer. Furthermore, within each class of instrument, there will be a series of interest rates based on remaining maturity. For example, three-month LIBOR will have a different yield from one-month LIBOR, and one-month commercial paper will not yield the same as overnight paper. This pattern of interest rates according to their remaining maturities is known as the money market yield curve. Yield curves are discussed extensively in Chapter 8. As explained there, the shape of the curve is primarily a function of investors' expectations of future interest rates, in this case money market rates.

15

FLOATING-RATE NOTES

Floating-rate notes (FRNs) don't have a long history in the United States. They found their place in the portfolios of fixed-income investors back in the late 1970s/early 1980s, when interest rates were high and, more relevant to FRNs extremely volatile. You'll soon see why volatility would attract certain bond investors to floating rate instruments.

Description

In many ways, a floating-rate note is just like any other bond. A company borrows money and promises to pay the coupon plus (possibly amortizing) principal. Here is a list of the most important parameters of a typical FRN:

Company XYZ
ten-year maturity
LIBOR + 1%
Reset quarterly

Company XYZ wishes to borrow for ten years. Rather than issue a plain vanilla fixed-coupon security, it decides to issue a bond whose coupon changes regularly according to market conditions. Suppose the issue date is April 15. On that date, three-month U.S. dollar LIBOR is set at 4%. The upcoming coupon—to be paid July 15—will be 4% + 1% = 5%, but divided by 4 since it is paid after three months. (Just like plain bonds, the coupon of an FRN is quoted annually.)

What will the coupon payment be on October 15? We won't know until July 15. On that day, besides a coupon being paid, a new LIBOR is established for the *next* coupon. Whatever that will be, 1% is added to it (the total divided by 4), and is paid by the firm to the bondholder on October 15. And so on, until the final coupon is established nine and a quarter years later on January 15 for payment on April 15. On that date the principal is paid as well.

A floating-rate note's coupon has (at least) two components. The first is the "reference rate," also known as "the index (or base) rate," which is the part that "floats." In the examples that follow, the index is LIBOR, the most typical for corporate FRNs.[1] The second component is the "spread," the amount added to the reference rate in order to calculate the full coupon. The spread is determined when the floater is issued and is typically fixed for the life of the note. It reflects the credit risk of the issuer. The creditworthiness of an FRN issuer, hence the size of the spread, is governed by the same factors that determine the spread of a fixed-coupon corporate bond (see Chapter 9). The less creditworthy the issuer is, the greater the spread as compensation to the investor for accepting the risk of default. Note that the constancy of the spread over the FRN's life means that the FRN's coupon is not entirely floating. This has major implications, as we will see later in this chapter.

Attractiveness as Investment

Ignore the floating-rate note's spread for a moment. That is, let's assume that the floater under discussion pays exactly LIBOR (known as "LIBOR flat"), because default risk is essentially absent.[2] Three months from today, referred to as the "repricing date," if interest rates rise in the market, the new coupon would be higher, reflecting the changed market conditions. Were this a fixed-coupon bond, the coupon would obviously remain where it was on the issue date. Hence FRNs are attractive to investors since they adapt to market conditions.

Conversely, if interest rates decline on the repricing date, the FRN's coupon is set lower. A fixed-coupon bond would retain its original coupon. In short, FRNs are suitable for investors comfortable with receiving current interest rates or for those expecting rising rates.[3]

Let's look at this in another way, from the perspective of price. Recall the price dynamics of fixed-coupon bonds from Chapter 3. If yields rise in the market, the bond will have to fall in price since its coupon is now relatively less attractive. If the bond can't be competitive in coupon, it must be competitive in price. Its price will decline until its yield matches that of current coupon bonds. Conversely, a decline in market interest rates makes this bond more attractive because its coupon is now relatively high compared to current coupon bonds. The price rises, until the bond's yield drops to match that in the market. In short, fixed-coupon bonds exhibit price volatility precisely because their coupons are *fixed*.

Now consider the floater. If interest rates increase, the note will pay a higher coupon next period (reflecting the new LIBOR setting). The note does not lose its attractiveness relative to new securities in the market. If interest rates decline, the note will pay a lower coupon. It does not become more attractive, either. In short, the fact that an FRN's coupon continually (on coupon reset dates) adjusts to market conditions means that its price need not adjust. It's always competitive in coupon, so it need not be competitive in price. Here's another way to say the same thing: Floating-rate notes exhibit considerably less price volatility than do fixed-coupon bonds.[4]

Caveat

Is reduced price volatility necessarily a good thing? It *is* a good thing if you're buying the bond for its coupon. In that case, any price change at the end of your investment horizon presents risk. But what if you're a market timer and wish to express a view on the direction of interest-rate changes? Market timers (aka speculators) attempt to anticipate changes in bond yields and position portfolios accordingly. They will buy bonds if they expect yields to decline, and they will profit by selling the bonds at a higher price should their expectations be realized. They will lose money if yields increase, causing bonds to fall in price. Conversely, if they expect yields to increase, they will short-sell bonds, in order to profit from their expected resultant price declines. They will lose if yields decline, causing the bond to rise in price. Based on their degree of confidence in their expectations, they will choose longer or shorter maturity bonds through which to express their interest-rate views. Only fixed-coupon bonds are useful in this regard, as their prices react to yield changes in the manner described. A floating rate note won't do the trick; expected interest rate changes will not be manifested in price movements.

The Floater's Spread

As mentioned above, the FRN's spread reflects the credit risk of the issuer as perceived by investors as of the security's issue date. The greater the risk of default, the more the firm needs to pay to borrow, as reflected in the size of the spread. All the factors examined in Chapter 9—leverage, volatility, maturity, seniority—apply to FRNs. The greater the leverage ratio, the more volatile the industry; the longer the maturity and the lower the security in the firm's capital structure, the higher the credit risk and the credit spread. Once issued, the spread is established and fixed until the note matures. In this respect, the FRN is similar to a fixed-coupon bond. This has profound implications.

Consider the FRN presented earlier. The 1% spread over LIBOR was agreed to by the firm and investors on the issue date of the security, reflecting the firm's risk parameters and investors' view of them. Suppose a year after the issue date the firm experiences an unexpected decline in sales, and the market believes it not to be temporary. The risk of default is now greater than it was when the FRN was issued. Were the firm to issue a nine-year floating-rate note today, with LIBOR as the reference rate, it would have to pay a wider spread over LIBOR, say 2%, to compensate investors for the now higher credit risk. Yet the FRN's spread remains 1%, fixed by the terms of the bond. The only way to convince investors to purchase this note today would be to lower the price. The price would need to drop by enough to make the LIBOR + 1% coupon competitive with an FRN of the same issuer priced at par but with a LIBOR + 2% coupon.

`Notice the similarity with the price dynamics of a fixed-coupon bond in Chapter 3. There, with the entire coupon fixed for the bond's life, an increase in market yields makes the bond unattractive at its original price. The price needs to drop by enough to make investors indifferent between that bond and a new par bond from the same issuer but with a coupon equal to the new required yield. Recall that the yield on a corporate bond equals the sum of a base interest rate—the yield on a Treasury bond of equal maturity—plus the company's credit spread. Hence, an increase in either component (or both) would force down the price of the bond. The price of the company's FRN, however, responds only to changes in the spread.

Let's go in the other direction. Suppose the firm's creditworthiness improves during the life of the FRN so that the market requires a spread of, say, only 0.50% on a new floater of this issuer. Then the FRN under discussion would rise in price, since it would be maintaining its 1% spread even as the market is content with 0.50%. By contrast, the company's fixed coupon bond would appreciate if *either* (or both) the base Treasury rate or spread contracts. Table 15.1 summarizes these conclusions.[5]

Consider now a floater of the same issuer, but with a longer maturity, say 20 years. It comes to market at par paying a spread of 1.5%. Why 1.5%, whereas the ten-year floater pays a spread of just 1%? As we saw in Chapter 9, "Corporate Bonds," credit risk increases with maturity. Longer maturity floaters, therefore, require wider spreads, if all else remains the same. Assume that after a year the company's earnings decline, causing investors to reconsider the firm's ability to honor its obligations. The market now requires a 2.5% spread. With the stated spread stuck at 1.5%, the FRN's price needs to drop to make investors comfortable with holding it, just as we conclude above. But the price of the 20-year FRN will fall further than the price of the ten-year issue. The logic here is the same as we employed in thinking about price dynamics for fixed-coupon bonds. It's one thing for investors to hold onto a ten-year bond paying 1% in interest spread less than bonds paying current market level spreads for that issuer. It's quite another for

TABLE 15.1 Effects of Interest Rate Changes on Bond Prices

Type of Change	Fixed Coupon Bond	Floating Rate Note
Increase in base rate	Decline	Stable
Increase in spread	Decline	Decline
Decrease in base rate	Rise	Stable
Decrease in spread	Rise	Rise

them to agree to hold a bond deficient in spread by 1% for *20* years. Its price must drop relatively more to induce investors. The same is true for the other direction. If the firm's earnings increase enough to convince investors that it warrants a narrower credit spread, the floater's price will appreciate since the stated spread is fixed for life. The longer the FRN's maturity, the more attractive the existing wide spread, and the more its price will rise. In sum, with respect to changes in the market's required spread, FRNs behave just like fixed-coupon bonds behave with respect to their yields—the longer the maturity, the more price responsive they are.

Before ending this section, it's only fair to point out that there is actually another source of price variability for floating-rate notes, separate from the fixed nature of the spread. Consider a floater whose coupon is reset quarterly, as in our example. On the repricing date, three-month LIBOR is observed, and the upcoming coupon is established. For the next three months, variations in market interest rates will not be reflected in the coupon. The investor needs to wait until the next repricing date for the coupon to reset in order to reflect market conditions. Hence, if short-term interest rates rise in the interim, as manifested in LIBOR, the FRN will decline in price, since it retains the recent "old" LIBOR. The converse applies for a decline in interest rates. The price will not change much, though, as the coupon is "fixed" for only three months (or shorter if the rate change occurred later than immediately after the reset date). In other words, price volatility of FRNs in response to market interest-rate movements (as opposed to credit changes) is similar to that of money market instruments.[6]

Floaters for Market Timers

We conclude earlier in this chapter that FRNs are not useful in expressing interest-rate views. Why? Because their prices are not sensitive to changes in market interest rates. We can now qualify that conclusion. True, FRNs are not responsive to shifts in LIBOR because their coupons adjust to market conditions, freeing their prices from bearing the brunt of the adjustment. But, as explained in the previous section, FRN prices certainly are sensitive to credit spread shifts. As such, they can be used to express a view as to changes in the creditworthiness of the issuer, or of the sector/industry the company is a member of. A speculator believing that an issuer's or sector's credit conditions are set to improve could buy the issuer's floating-rate note, if one exists. If the speculator's view proves to be right, the FRN's required spread narrows, causing the note's price to increase, as just explained. If credit deterioration is anticipated, the note should be shorted. When the price falls, as the expected spread widening materializes, the speculator buys the FRN, covering the short and pocketing the difference between the sale and subsequent repurchase price.

In this chapter we examine the basic, "plain vanilla" type of floating-rate note. There are many variations. Some are variations that keep the basic theme of FRNs— reset the floater's coupon in order to reflect current market conditions—intact. Some turn the basic theme upside-down. We explore a number of them in the next chapter.

16

THOSE NEWFANGLED FLOATERS

In years long past, government, agency, and corporate borrowers would issue securities consistent with their unique requirements (e.g., maturity, seniority, callability) and aligned with market conditions (e.g., coupon rate). Investors would express their satisfaction through their purchases or lack thereof. Today bankers have the ability to create securities at the direction of investors, a reversal of the traditional process. The process is known as "structuring," and the result is structured products. Structuring typically is targeted toward adding yield to an otherwise lower-yielding security or toward achieving a specific market exposure dictated by an investor or type of investor. We examine a few prominent structures in this chapter, all in the floating-rate note family, exploring their attractiveness to investors and their risks. Structured products are created every day. You should be able to apply the approach in this chapter to many new structures you're confronted with.

A note before we start. Our concern in this chapter is with interest-rate risk and structures that have been created around it. In practice, many of the issuers present credit risk to the investor as well. Hence, the securities should pay a credit spread. Since credit risk is not our concern here, we'll ignore the spread so as not to overcomplicate the issues. (Alternatively, you can think of the issuers behind these securities as having no default risk.)

Inverse Floaters

Remember the "plain vanilla" floater? Here it is again.

Floating-rate note: Coupon = LIBOR + fixed spread

The inverse floater's structure, on the other hand, is as follows.

Inverse floating-rate note: Coupon = fixed rate − LIBOR

For example, the note may have a maturity of three years and pay 8% less LIBOR, semiannually. Suppose the six-month LIBOR is set at 3% on the note's issuance date. The first interest payment will be half (because it covers six months) of 8% less 3%, or 2.5% of the principal amount. Six months later, a new LIBOR is set at, say, 4%. The next interest payment will be 2%.[1]

What's the point of an inverse floater? Let's address this from an investor's perspective by answering four questions. In fact, these are the questions that, at a minimum, you should ask when considering any structured product whatsoever:

1. What is the "carry?"
2. What do you earn if the market behaves as "expected?"
3. How does this investment compare to others in the same class?
4. What are the risks?

What Is the "Carry"?

We've come across the word "carry" before (for example, in Chapter 11). It refers to an investor's earnings from a security assuming nothing changes. Let's work with the three-year inverse floater above, paying 8% less LIBOR. Let's also simplify and work with annual frequencies. Assuming LIBOR begins at 3%, the inverse floater pays 5%. If LIBOR remains at 3%, you'll earn 5% until maturity; hence, 5% is the carry. Is this good or bad? Well, it would seem good if it's above the rate on other securities of similar credit quality. But the carry is just the starting point. Here's the catch: The 5% is not likely to persist, so you'll need to make the comparison in a smarter way, which is the next step.

What Do You Earn If the Market Behaves as "Expected?"

When we use the word "expected" in financial markets, we typically don't mean the expectations of the particular investor. Rather, we mean the "market's expectations." How do we know the market's expectations? From the yield curve, as explained in Chapter 8. Since forward rates, derived from long-term interest rates, reflect (to a first approximation) market participants' expected future short-term rates, we use forward rates as our expectations benchmark. The second column in Table 16.1 presents a hypothetical LIBOR yield curve, that is, the rates observed in the market for various maturities. The derived forward rates appear in the third column.[2] The final three columns present the coupon rates for the current and following two years for three investment alternatives, based on the market's expectations as given by the forward rates. Because the yield curve is upward sloping—the two-year rate is above the one-year, and the three-year is above the two-year (as you see in column 2)—we infer that the market expects interest rates to rise (column 3). Notice the inverse floater's coupon rates (column 5). Although showing a relatively high rate today, they are expected to provide declining rates over time, due to the subtraction of LIBOR from the fixed 8%

How Does This Investment Compare to Others in the Same Class?

Over the three years of its life, the inverse floater's rate of return is 4%. Compare this to the other two notes in the table. The coupon on the fixed-rate note is 4%, consistent with the notion that longer-term rates are averages of the short-term rates spanning its life (see

TABLE 16.1 Forward Rates and Implications for Alternative Investments

Year	Yield Curve	Forward Rates	Floating Rate Note	Inverse Floater	Fixed Rate Note
1	3	3	3	5	4
2	3.5	4	4	4	4
3	4	5	5	3	4

Chapter 8, "The Yield Curves"). The return over three years is, of course, 4% for this bond. It is 4% for the plain vanilla floater as well, since it pays whatever rate obtained in the market. In short, if market expectations are realized, all three instruments provide the same return.[3]

What Are the Risks?

There are two ways to look at interest-rate risk. One is to ask what would happen if rates turn out differently from what is expected. Suppose in year 2 the current LIBOR rate is 5% rather than 4%. The regular floater pays 5%. The fixed-coupon bond continues to pay its 4% coupon. But the inverse floater pays only 3%. Even if actual rates fall back in line with expectations for year 3, the inverse floater (IF) will turn put to be the worst performer of the three. Of course, if LIBOR in year 2 turns out to be 2%, the IF beats the other two.

Another way to compare risk is by looking at how the *prices* of the different bonds react to market shifts rather than their interest income. Suppose LIBOR in year 2 rises to 5%, defying expectations of 4%, and now the market expects it to remain at that level through year 3. The FRN is still at par, since its coupon rate rises with the market. We saw this in the previous chapter. The fixed bond declines in price because its coupon does not move with the market. How much does its price decline? Approximately 2%, since for the next two years its coupon is deficient by 1%. We saw this in Chapter 3. What about the inverse floater? Its price drops by nearly 4 percent. Why? Intuitively, it is "twice as bad" as the fixed coupon bond. Not only does the interest rate on the IF fail to keep up with the market—in this respect it is similar to the fixed-coupon bond—but its coupon actually *declines* one for one with the market. The same analysis applies in the other direction. Were LIBOR to equal 3 percent in year 2 and be expected to remain at this level the following year, the FRN would be priced at par, the fixed-coupon bond would rise by approximately 2% in price, and the inverse floater would *appreciate* by nearly 4%. In the language of Chapter 12, an inverse floating-rate note has a duration equal to roughly *twice* that of a fixed-coupon bond of equal maturity.

Capped Floating-Rate Notes

Compared to the inverse floating-rate note, a capped floating-rate note seems more intuitive, at least superficially. The structure is straightforward:

Capped floating-rate note: Coupon = LIBOR + spread, subject
to maximum coupon

For example, a three-year Capped FRN pays LIBOR each year plus 1.5%. However, it never pays more than 6%; 6% is known as the "cap." As long as LIBOR does not rise above 4.5% on any reset date, the note pays that LIBOR plus 1.5%. If, say, on a particular future coupon reset date one year LIBOR is 5%, the note pays only 6%. Were it not for the cap, the FRN's coupon could rise to any level. The spread on a capped floater, therefore, is the investor's compensation for accepting the cap (besides credit risk, if any). Let's go through the four steps, comparing our capped floater with an uncapped, or plain vanilla, FRN, of equal maturity.

Carry

To review, the capped FRN under discussion pays LIBOR + 1.5% to a maximum of 6%. As is the case with the inverse floater, the initial coupon on a capped FRN, or its carry, will exceed that of an otherwise equivalent uncapped FRN. In fact, that is typically the "draw" of the security. If LIBOR is 3%, then the capped FRN in our example pays 4.5%, while the regular floater pays that 3%.

Return If Expectations Are Realized

Table 16.2 extends the curve of Table 16.1 by one additional year. In order to illustrate the effect of the cap, the curve shows an accelerating slope from year 3 to year 4, resulting in a forward rate of 8% in year 4. The capped floater, if rates turn out as expected, is "stuck" at 6% for both final years. An uncapped floater, of course, rides the increase in market interest rates.

TABLE 16.2 Forward Rates and Implications for Capped (6%) and Uncapped Floaters

Year	Yield Curve	Forward Rates	Capped Floating Rate Note	Uncapped Floating Rate Note
1	3	3	4.5	3
2	3.5	4	5.5	4
3	4	5	6	5
4	5	8	6	8

Comparison to Other Bonds

Over the four years, the average expected rate of the capped floater (5.5%) exceeds that of the uncapped floater (5%). These are also the expected rates of return (RORs) for the two instruments.[4] Why, then, would an investor purchase the uncapped FRN? One reason is obvious: An investor whose expectations for future LIBOR rates exceed those implied by the forwards; that is, the investor believes that rates will rise by more than the market expects. For example, adding 1% to each of the rates in the third column of Table 16.2 beginning with year 2 produces an average of 5.625% for the capped FRN and 5.75% for the uncapped. But there is another possible reason. Let's consider what happens if future rates diverge symmetrically from expectations. In Table 16.3 we accept the forward rates as the *central* rates for each future year (denoted by •) but allow

TABLE 16.3 Scenario Analysis for Capped (6%) and Uncapped Floaters

Year	Future Rates	Capped Floating Rate Note	Uncapped Floating Rate Note
2 −	3	4.5	3
2 •	4	5.5	4
2 +	5	6	5
3 −	4	5.5	4
3 •	5	6	5
3 +	6	6	6
4 −	7	6	7
4 •	8	6	8
4 +	9	6	9

LIBOR to rise (denoted by +) *or* fall (denoted by −) by 1% beginning in year 2. That is, we're not changing our *average* expectations at all; the average rate expected for each of the future years is the forward rate as in Table 16.2. Table 16.3 omits the first row of Table 16.2, since that is known with certainty when the note is issued. It also omits the yield curve column. Each future year has three rows associated with it, for the three possible interest rate outcomes (the −, •, and + scenarios).

The average rate over the three future years is 5.67% for the regular floater. This is the same as its average rate in Table 16.2, excluding the first year—not surprising, since each row of Table 16.2 is the midpoint of the corresponding row trio in Table 16.3. Now look at the capped floater. Its average rate in Table 16.2, net of year 1, is 5.83%. But in Table 16.3 it is 5.72%—lower than in Table 16.2 and closer to the uncapped. Why? Because—and this is crucial—the cap imposes an asymmetry on variations around the central point, the expected future (or forward) rates. It limits the upside and allows full movement on the downside.

Table 16.4 performs the same calculations as Table 16.3, but allows 2% variation on either side of the midpoint for each future year. Again, the average rate for the uncapped floater is 5.67%. This is as it should be, since greater variations do not change the average outcome for a symmetric security (such as an uncapped FRN). But for the capped floater the average rate is only 5.5%; now it underperforms its counterpart, because the asymmetry produces more acute repercussions for greater variations. Here's our conclusion: The more volatile (the statistical term

TABLE 16.4 More Volatile Scenario Analysis for Capped (6%) and Uncapped Floaters

Year	Future Rates	Capped Floating Rate Note	Uncapped Floating Rate Note
2−	2	3.5	2
2•	4	5.5	4
2+	6	6	6
3−	3	4.5	3
3•	5	6	5
3+	7	6	7
4−	6	6	6
4•	8	6	8
4+	10	6	10

for variations) future interest rates are, the worse the performance of the capped versus the uncapped floating-rate note. Increased volatility is a negative for capped FRNs. Indeed, this is a conclusion we come across very often in the securities markets: *if an asset displays asymmetric return characteristics, the effect of the asymmetry becomes more pronounced at higher volatility levels.*[5]

Risk

We've examined what happens to the respective returns of the capped and uncapped FRNs when LIBOR turns out differently from what is expected. Let's look at risk from the perspective of an investor selling a note prior to its maturity, say, at the end of year 1. Suppose interest rates rise across all maturities (a "parallel shift" in the yield curve). Depending on the degree of the increase, some of the forward rates will hit the 6% cap. Others will not reach the cap rate but will be closer to it, which means that the chances of the next rate change piercing the cap are greater. As a result, investors will require a wider spread for the capped floater as compensation. Since the spread is fixed at issuance, the price of the note decreases. The uncapped floater's price, by contrast, remains at par. Conversely, a drop in interest rates lowers the necessary spread on the capped floater because the cap is less likely to kick in, hence is less onerous. With the spread fixed, the price of the FRN rises. Again, the uncapped floater is unaffected. Notice the similarity of the capped floater's price reaction to interest-rate movements to that of fixed-coupon bonds. Unlike an ordinary FRN, a capped FRN's price moves inversely with market interest rates. We might, therefore, even describe a capped floating-rate note as somewhat of a hybrid of a pure FRN and a pure fixed-rate bond.

Changes in the *slope* of the LIBOR yield curve affect the price of capped floaters independently of the effect of changes in the *level* of LIBOR. Suppose the slope steepens. From Chapter 8 (on yield curves) we know that this means that forward rates increase even though current short-term rates may be unchanged (or possibly lower). Forward rates, remember, reflect the market's expectations of future interest rates. Just as above, therefore, the steeper yield curve slope causes expectations of future rates to surpass or, at least, to push against the cap. This causes the price of the capped floater to decline. Conversely, a flattening of the curve results in a price gain for the capped FRN. In either case, the uncapped floater is unaffected.

Finally, we observed earlier that investors in a capped FRN suffer a lower expected rate of return in more volatile market environments (because more volatility increases the chances of the cap becoming effective and limiting return). In turn, this means that investors require a larger spread above LIBOR in the note's coupon when volatility is higher and a narrower spread when volatility is lower. Since the floater's spread is fixed at issuance, we arrive at the final implication for price risk: A capped FRN's price is sensitive to market volatility; an increase in expected volatility reduces its price; a decrease raises its price.

Variations

Capped floating-rate notes have a long history in the structured products area of the capital markets. A number of variations around the basic structure have been created:

- *Step-up cap.* The maximum rate on the FRN is not constant. Rather, it rises each year or on each coupon payment date. For example, instead of 6% throughout the floater's life, as in the above example, the coupon is capped at 6% for year 2, 6.5% for year 3, and 7% for year 4. This is particularly appropriate in a sharply sloped yield curve environment, because a fixed cap would quickly intercept the forward rates.
- *FRN with floor.* Rather than a maximum interest rate, this type of floater provides a minimum rate for the investor. The coupon, for example, can never fall *below* 2%. Whereas a cap benefits the issuer, who pays a higher rate in order to be capped, a floor, of course, benefits the investor. Hence the coupon is LIBOR *less* a spread.[6] An increase in rate volatility makes the floor more attractive to the investor, raising its price (or calling for a deeper spread).[7]
- *Collar.* This is an FRN with both a cap and a floor. The cap (paid for by the borrower) adds to the spread over LIBOR; the floor (paid for by the lender) subtracts from it. If the minimum and maximum rates are set so that the addition and subtraction cancel out, it is known as a "zero cost collar."[8]
- *Callable capped FRN.* (Now that's a mouthful, but it's quite a sensible innovation!)We learned above that a cap pushes the FRN

closer to behaving (on a price basis) like a fixed-rate bond. We also know that callable fixed-coupon bonds allow the issuer to refinance when interest rates drop below the bond's coupon. Now think about the capped floater. If LIBOR falls significantly (or if the LIBOR curve flattens) after the note is issued, the borrower will be paying a spread for a cap that is not necessary. Indeed, for this reason the note's price rises above par. A call feature embedded in the structure would allow the issuer to pay par for the note and refinance it by issuing an uncapped floater with no spread (except for credit risk). The issuer, of course, must pay for this privilege, similar to the call feature in a callable fixed-rate bond. Until the note is called, if at all, the callable capped FRN pays two spreads—one for the cap and one for the call feature!

Range Notes

Range notes are also found in fixed-coupon form. Their roots, though, are in the floating-rate note universe, so we'll analyze them in that framework. The structure is very interesting. Here are two examples.

1. Equity range floating-rate note:

   Coupon = LIBOR + 3%, only when $950 \leq$S&P500 index $\leq$990

2. Commodity range floating-rate note:

   Coupon = LIBOR + 4%, only when $50 $\leq$barrel oil $\leq$$60

The first note pays interest only for those days the Standard & Poor's 500 Stock Index closes no lower than 950 and no higher than 990. The second pays interest only for those days that a barrel of oil does not rise above $60 or fall below $50.[9] Interest is paid only for those days a referenced financial variable is within a *range*, hence the name.

Again we assume that the issuer presents little to no credit risk, so that we can concentrate on the unique aspects of these notes. A plain vanilla floating-rate note would pay LIBOR with zero or a token spread. Why do these notes pay so much more than LIBOR? Because the *most* the investor can receive is LIBOR plus 3% or 4%. Only if the reference price stays within the range the entire coupon period will the investor receive the stated interest rate. Movements in stock prices or the price of oil can only hurt, not help. Clearly, the investor is at risk of volatility:

Carry

Let's assume that the equity range-floating note pays its coupon quarterly. At the start of the quarter, three-month LIBOR is set at 2.5%. Although there are 91 days in a quarter (on average), there are fewer business days. Assume that there are 65 business days in the coming quarter. Say the S&P 500 index closed between 950 and 990 for 60 of those days. At the end of the quarter, the investor receives a coupon of $[(2.5\% + 3\%) / 4] \times 60 / 65 = 1.2692\%$ multiplied by the note's principal (the 4 divisor due to the quarterly frequency). A new LIBOR is now set for calculating the coupon for the second quarter, and this may be higher or lower than 2.5%. But even if it sets lower, the actual coupon paid to the investor may be greater than in the preceding quarter if the fraction of the new quarter that the index stays within its range substantially exceeds that of the previous quarter. Got it? The oil-based range floater works the same way.

Return If . . .

Just as the market as a whole expects future interest rates to follow a certain path (and we can glean this expected path from forward rates, as we've done many times), there is a level of future volatility expected by the market as well. Not only volatility of future interest rates, but future stock prices, commodity prices, etc. The buyer of the range note is at risk from this volatility. The *most* he or she can earn is LIBOR + 3% (or 4%). But the downside is steep; the coupon can fall to zero if the range is breached every day. The spread over LIBOR is the investor's compensation. Oil prices have recently displayed sharp volatility, sharper than equity prices. For this reason the spread over LIBOR for the oil range note is greater. Furthermore, because of its higher expected volatility, the range is relatively wider. Otherwise, the investor would be taking much more risk of oil breaking out of the range and thereby losing interest, and the spread would need to be markedly higher.

Comparison to Other Bonds

Range floating-rate notes were developed during periods of low interest rates. Investors looking for yield—and wary of accepting credit risk—embraced a product paying a wide spread over LIBOR issued by high-grade corporations or government agencies. Essentially, the factor providing the yield kicker is a set of options sold by the investor to the issuer. The payment for the options by the issuer is in the form of the wider spread on the note than for a plain vanilla floater. This is quite common in the capital markets. A callable bond pays a higher rate than an otherwise similar noncallable bond because the issuer has purchased an option to redeem the bond from the investor at par. In the same vein, the spread on a capped floating-rate note represents a series of "cap" options—one for each LIBOR reset date—paid for by the borrower. The range floating-rate note contains a veritable portfolio of options—two (the upper and lower bounds of the range) for each business day—sold by the investor to the issuer.[10]

Risk

An increase in the likelihood of the S&P 500 or the price of oil pushing outside the range reduces the expected coupon of the floater, hence lowering its price. In other words, similar to the capped floater, the investor is exposed to changes in the market's assessment of future volatility. But not interest-rate volatility—rather, volatility of the variable referenced in the range. Interestingly, another factor is at work here, one related to volatility. The investor is also exposed to movements in LIBOR, because the coupon changes each quarter as LIBOR does. If LIBOR and the S&P 500 index (or LIBOR and the price of a barrel of oil) are negatively *correlated*, the overall volatility, hence risk, is reduced. If they are positively correlated, overall risk is exacerbated.

A variation on the above structure places LIBOR as the variable in the range! For example, the coupon is set each quarter as three-month LIBOR plus 2.25%, payable for those days that *one-year* LIBOR stays between 4% and 6%. Furthermore, in some of these structures, the range itself "steps up" to reflect the yield curve; for example, in year 2 the range becomes 4.5% to 6.5%. Clearly, correlation is not an independent factor here as both the range and the rate relate to the same market.

17

INTEREST-RATE SWAPS

Do interest-rate swaps sound exotic to you? If they do, you're dating yourself. Swaps have been around for somewhat longer than a generation. But in that short time, they've transformed the fixed-income markets—all markets, for that matter.

Swap Structure

A swap is a derivative. Indeed, it is a *pure* derivative. What is a pure derivative? A derivative is simply a contract, an agreement between two parties to perform services for each other over a period of time. If it is a financial contract, the services involve monetary arrangements. A *pure* financial contract involves no payments between the counterparties at the contract's inception—only the signing of a contract. This makes sense when you look at a simple interest rate swap, as diagrammed in Figure 17.1.

Every swap has at least four parameters:

- *Term.* The length of time the contract is to be in effect.[1] The word "maturity" is inappropriate because there is no "loan" that is repaid at the end.
- *Notional.* The size, or face amount, of the contract. Included in this parameter is the particular currency chosen by the counterparties.
- *Counterparties.* The two parties to the contract. They can be investors, governments, banks and other financial institutions, individuals (though unusual), or swaps dealers.

FIGURE 17.1 Five-Year Interest Rate Swap

- *Cash flows.* The pair of payments that the two counterparties have agreed to make to each other during the term of the swap contract.

The swap shown in Figure 17.1 has a five-year term. Based on an agreed notional amount of, say, $100 million, X agrees to pay Y 5.75%, or $5.75 million, in return for Y paying X an interest rate that changes periodically. The most typical arrangement for this changing rate is that it be based on LIBOR. [LIBOR is explained in Chapter 14. It is the rate banks pay each other (the interbank market) for deposits, with a different rate each day for various maturities and currencies.] Since the 5.75% is fixed for the term of the swap (whereas LIBOR will change), this arrangement is known as a "fixed for floating interest-rate swap."

Table 17.1 displays the cash flows of the interest-rate swap in Figure 17.1. It assumes, for simplicity's sake, annual payment periodicities for both sides of the swap, even though the convention in the United States is, like the bond market, semiannual.[2] On the contract's inception date there is, fundamentally, no exchange of cash flows; the parties simply agree to and sign the contract. However, the two interest rates for the upcoming swap payments are set now. The example

TABLE 17.1 Five-Year Interest-Rate Swap Cash Flows, 5.75% versus LIBOR

Date	Fixed Rate	LIBOR	X's Payment to Y ($)	Y's Payment to X ($)
Inception	5.75%	4.00%	0	0
End of year 1	5.75%	4.50%	5.75MM	4.00MM
End of year 2	5.75%	5.25%	5.75MM	4.50MM
End of year 3	5.75%	?	5.75MM	5.25MM
End of year 4	5.75%	?	5.75MM	?
End of year 5	5.75%		5.75MM	?

assumes that one-year LIBOR on the swap's inception date was set in the market at 4%. Like most interest rates, rates are set at the beginning of the "borrowing" period (remember there is no actual borrowing of principal here), and payments are made on the anniversary dates. Hence, at the end of the first year, X, the fixed rate payer, sends $5.75 million (5.75% of the $100 million notional) to Y, and Y sends $4 million to X, since 4% was the floating rate set a year ago covering this period.

In addition to the exchange, or swap, of interest-rate payments taking place on the first anniversary date of the contract, the pair of rates is set for the *next* payment date. While the fixed rate is, of course, known in advance, LIBOR is not. The example assumes that one-year LIBOR rises one year after the swap's inception (perhaps due to increasing macroeconomic activity) to 4.5%. As a result, on the second anniversary date, the floating payment from Y to X will be $4.5 million. On this date a new LIBOR is determined, setting the floating payment for the next date. The example assumes 5.25% (perhaps reflecting accelerating macroeconomic activity). This process continues each year. The table contains question marks in the next two LIBOR rows simply to highlight the fact that the entries in this column are unknown at the swap's inception date, as are the corresponding dollar payments in the final column.

The first and final rows are different. There is no payment between the counterparties at the contract's inception, but the floating rate is set for the upcoming first payment. Symmetrically, while there is a final payment at the swap's termination, there is no rate that needs to be set on that date.

Another point before we analyze *why* X and Y have agreed to do such a weird thing. There is a possibility that one or both parties may not be able to fulfill their obligations at some future date. For example, one of them may become bankrupt. (Indeed, this swap may contribute, or even cause, the bankruptcy.) We will see that such an occurrence may be quite costly for the counterparty. To provide compensation in such an event, the parties are commonly required to put up collateral at the outset, and even update the collateral ("mark to market," as we will learn later) over time as market conditions change. This does not appear in Table 17.1 because it is not actually a *payment* from one party to the other.

One more point, a semantic one. Neither X nor Y is buying or selling anything (nor are they borrowing or lending). Hence, the terms "buyer" and "seller" are technically inappropriate for swap transactions.[3] X and Y are simply described as having *entered* a swap contract, as the fixed-rate receiver or payer (because the focus, typically, is on the fixed rather than floating, rate, as we will see later in this chapter and in Chapter 18).

The Swap Rate

Now let's get to the gist of the matter—why are X and Y doing this? A superficial look at Table 17.1 shouts a different question: Why has X willingly signed this contract? Remember, an interest-rate swap is a pure derivative; no cash is exchanged between the counterparties at the outset. So why is X agreeing to pay 5.75% to Y and receive LIBOR when LIBOR is 4%?

A closer look at Table 17.1 provides the answer. The LIBOR column changes, or floats—that's the point. X must believe that LIBOR will increase over the next five years. Indeed, X must expect LIBOR to rise, pass 5.75%, and average *at least* that rate over the next five years. X, you see, is not stupid. Neither are the thousands of swap market participants with trillions of dollars worth of contracts. If the fixed rate of the swap is 5.75%, then all the fixed-rate payers must believe that LIBOR will average at least 5.75% over the term of the swap. Conversely, Y in our example—and all the other LIBOR payers in the swap market—must be of the opinion that LIBOR will average *at most* 5.75% over the swap term.[4] Considering all the participants in the swap market as a group (and recognizing that there needs to be a fixed-rate payer for every fixed-rate receiver), we must conclude that "the market" expects one-year LIBOR to average 5.75% over the next five years. Or, more generally:

> *The fixed rate on an interest-rate swap represents the market's expectations as to what the floating rate will average over the term of the swap.*

Notice how perfectly consistent this conclusion is with the basic notion of the yield curve in Chapter 8: Long-term interest rates are fundamentally equal to the average of short-term rates spanning the longer term.

The Swap Spread

Consider the swap in the previous section. The fixed rate agreed upon by the counterparties is 5.75%. Some time later—days, or even minutes— the rate for five-year swaps changes, say, to 5.65%.[5] That is to say, new swaps are being contracted at a fixed rate of 5.65% against one-year LIBOR. The "old" swap between X and Y retains the 5.75% rate agreed upon. But note that in both the old swap and the new swaps being negotiated, the floating side is LIBOR. So what distinguishes existing swaps from ever-changing new ones is the fixed side. Hence the float- ing rate need not be mentioned when describing the dynamics of the market.

More to the point, swaps are quoted as a "spread" to U.S. Trea- suries (or the government bond benchmark of the currency the swap is denominated in) of similar maturity. Recall from Chapter 9 that this is the convention in the corporate bond market. Consider again the swap above. Suppose that at the same time that the fixed side of five- year swaps is paying 5.75%, the five-year Treasury bond is priced in the market to yield 4.65%. Market participants will describe the swap as trading at (or "yielding," despite the inappropriateness of the termi- nology as there is no money actually "invested" in the swap) 110 basis points over Treasuries, because that is the difference between the swap's fixed rate and the Treasury note's yield to maturity. What determines the swap spread? Recall that the swap's fixed rate should equal market participants' expectations regarding LIBOR over the term of the swap. Which LIBOR? The three-, six-, or twelve-month, depending on the periodicity of the contract. Hence, the spread between the swap inter- est rate and the associated Treasury rate is essentially the same as the spread between long-term LIBOR and Treasuries. As explained in Chapter 14, "Money Markets Instruments," LIBOR is the interbank borrowing/lending rate for major international banking institutions. Therefore, the swap spread represents the market's assessment of the risk of the (top tier) banking system.[6] The spread changes according to changes in this assessment. We conclude that the swap rate—being the sum of the risk-free Treasury rate and the swap spread—changes according to movements in the Treasury rate and/or in the spread. This is much like corporate bond yields changing because of changes in Treasury rates and the corporate's risk premium as reflected in the credit spread (as demonstrated in Chapter 9).

"Trading" Swaps

We've examined bond investing in a number of contexts; for example, in Chapter 4 regarding rate-of-return and Chapter 11 with respect to various investing strategies. As explained there, "investing" means buying bonds for a particular horizon, or holding period, and hoping to achieve a rate of return in which the return consists of the bond's coupon (as a percentage of its price), or its yield, plus the price change. The latter component, in turn, reflects the change in yield between the beginning of the investment and its termination. If the bond is a corporate, the credit spread becomes an additional element present in both the coupon and price change (as in Chapters 9 and 11). If the bond is denominated in foreign currency, exchange-rate movement becomes a third factor in rate of return (coming up in Chapter 19). What distinguishes trading or speculating, if you will, from investing is that the speculator's primary (and sometimes sole) focus is the price change. Furthermore, he or she has no "definable horizon." When the price target is reached (or the price declines enough to warrant exit), the position is liquidated. What we need to understand now is, what does speculating mean with respect to swaps?

Let's assume that a speculator anticipates a decline in interest rates (specifically LIBOR). She enters into an interest-rate swap as the fixed-rate receiver, floating-rate payer in order to profit when rates fall. Why? First off, notice the leverage. Were the speculator to do this trade with bonds, the bond would need to be purchased, requiring payment. Sure, the funds could be borrowed (we'll actually see how is done via a repurchase agreement in Chapter 22). But borrowing has to be available—and paid for! The swap, by contrast, simply requires signing a contract; no funds are necessary at the outset because there is nothing purchased. Yes, collateral likely must be posted, but as a relatively small fraction of the notional amount. Now let's make the application more concrete. We do this by examining the speculator's motivation a little more carefully, relate the dynamics to the swap spread, and see how profits or losses are realized with a swap in comparison to a bond.

The speculator—call her a hedge fund—anticipates that intermediate-term interest rates will decline soon. Which interest rates? Typically, this view relates to "pure" interest rates, that is, a Treasury rate. A corporate bond includes a risk premium, disqualifying it as a candidate. The fixed rate on a five-year interest-rate swap equals the five-year Treasury rate plus the swap spread. It is, therefore, an excellent candidate through which to express this view. Why not simply purchase a five-year Treasury note yielding 4.65% and sell it when the yield declines as expected? Because it requires funds, either the investor's own or borrowed, and a swap does not.

So, the hedge fund enters into a five-year swap, most likely with a swap dealer as counterparty, agreeing to receive 5.75% for the next five years in return for a series of LIBOR payments to the dealer, only the first of which is known now. No payment, no borrowing of funds, just collateral (and the dealer may well post collateral, too). Some time later, say a week, the five-year Treasury yield falls as expected, from 4.65% to, say, 4.5%, and the hedge fund believes this is as far as it will drop. Had the trader purchased the Treasury note, she would be selling now and realizing the profit. How much profit? The change in price of the bond due to the 15 basis point drop in yield—15 times the dv01, to use the bond trading apparatus of Chapter 12. Assuming the 1.1 percent swap spread has not changed over the week (more on this later), a new five-year interest-rate swap will have a fixed rate of 5.6%—4.5% new Treasury yield + 1.1% swap spread. What does the speculator do? Essentially the same thing he or she would have done with the bond. The bond would have been bought in anticipation of a yield decline and then sold to realize the profit after the actual decline. A sale reverses, or "offsets," a buy. The same is done with the swap. The hedge fund initiates the trade by agreeing to receive the fixed rate on the swap and then does the opposite swap upon realization of the decline in the fixed rate on new swaps. How? One week later, when Treasury rates decline, the fund trader enters into an "offsetting" interest-rate swap of the same term and size as the first, but agreeing to *pay* the new fixed rate and *receive* LIBOR, with another dealer. The trader now has two positions— the original and the offsetting swap—as shown in Figure 17.2.

FIGURE 17.2 Initial Swap With Offsetting Swap

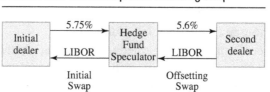

Initial Swap   Offsetting Swap

Although the speculator now has two *gross* positions, the net position is what matters. Every year for the next five years, she will be receiving 5.75%, representing the fixed rate of the initial swap, and paying 5.6%, representing the fixed rate of the offsetting swap.[7] The two LIBORs cancel each other out—whatever is paid to one dealer is received exactly from the other. Here we have it; we've accomplished our goal. The swap "trade" has allowed the speculator to profit from a correctly anticipated decline in the five-year U.S. Treasury yield. Every year she has net income of 15 basis points on the swap national amount. Furthermore, this was accomplished without her having to purchase the bond and then turning around to sell it. But is it really the same as transacting with the actual bond?

In terms of profit, essentially yes. Recall from Chapter 12 that the degree of price change in a bond brought about by a change in yield depends on its maturity, modified somewhat by the size of the coupon. This is quantified by the bond's dv01 (duration). Had the trader purchased the five-year Treasury when it yielded 4.65% and sold soon thereafter when it yielded 4.5%, her profit would have reflected the effect of the 15 basis point drop—15 times the bond's dv01. You know what? The trader with the pair of swaps in our example is now entitled to 15 basis points, net, each year multiplied by the face amount. And the present value of that is the same as the profit on the Treasury note! The five-year swap has the same dv01 (duration) as a par five-year bond.[8]

Of course, interest rates could have gone the other way, causing a loss for the hedge fund. But this would have happened had the trader purchased and then sold the Treasury note as well. Suppose that instead of declining, the five-year Treasury rate rises to 4.80%. Its price drops by 15 times the note's dv01, the speculator's loss. With an unchanged swap spread, new five-year swaps carry a fixed rate of 5.90%. The trader offsets the swap by agreeing to pay this rate in return for LIBOR. Net, the trader will be have a *negative* cash flow of 15 basis points per the size of the swap, the present value of which is the same as the loss on the Treasury note.

Swap Spread Risk

A caveat is in order at this point. Our hedge fund had a view about Treasury yields, the five-year maturity in particular. As we have seen, expressing a view of an imminent decline in yield can be done by way of receiving the fixed rate on a five-year interest-rate swap rather than purchasing an actual five-year Treasury bond. What if, in our example above, the five-year Treasury declines to 4.5%, but at the same time the swap spread widens by the same 15 basis points from 1.1% to 1.25%. Since the swap rate equals the Treasury rate plus the spread, the ending swap rate is unchanged. The trader will have zero profit when the position is offset with the second swap. Further, if the spread widens by 20 basis points, the ending swap rate actually is above the rate at the trade's initiation despite the Treasury rate having declined. The speculator's net position will produce a net loss for the next five years, whereas purchasing and liquidating the Treasury note would have produced a profit.

Conversely, when the Treasury yield rises (by the same 15 bps) to produce a loss on its purchase, the swap spread might narrow. Depending on the size of the narrowing, creating the same exposure via an interest-rate swap would produce a smaller loss (if the spread narrows by less than 15 bps), no loss (if the narrowing is exactly 15 bps), or even a profit (if more than 15 bps). Of course, the swap spread can move in the *same* direction as the Treasury interest rate. If the spread were to narrow at the same time that the five-year Treasury's yield declines, the fixed rate on the new, offsetting swap will fall more than the Treasury yield, thus producing greater profits in the swap trade than would have been produced for the actual bond. Conversely, if the swap spread were to widen just as the Treasury rate increases, the new swap rate would rise more than the Treasury, exacerbating the loss. In short, the swap position mimics an actual Treasury bond position—hence reflects a pure interest rate speculation—only if the swap spread is constant.[9]

We can express these ideas from a different perspective. The speculator may have a view concerning the direction of future swap rates rather than Treasury rates. Suppose she believes that five-year interest-rate swap rates are about to decline. She agrees to *receive* fixed on the swap just as above. A few days later, when rates move, she offsets the position with an opposite swap. The net position will be profitable if:

- The five-year Treasury rate falls, and the swap spread is unchanged.
- The Treasury rate is unchanged, but the swap spread narrows.
- The Treasury rate falls, and the swap spread narrows (*a fortiori.*).
- The Treasury rate falls, and the swap spread widens but by less than the Treasury rate declines.
- The Treasury rate rises, and the swap rate narrows by more than the Treasury rate increases (least likely).

The net position will show a loss if:

- The five-year Treasury rate rises, and the swap spread is unchanged.
- The Treasury rate is unchanged, but the swap spread widens.
- The Treasury rate rises, and the swap spread widens (*a fortiori*).
- The Treasury rate rises, and the swap spread narrows but by less than the Treasury rate increases.
- The Treasury rate falls, and the swap rate widens by more than the Treasury rate decreases (least likely).

Short Positions via Swaps

What does a speculator, expecting interest rates to rise or bond prices to fall, do? He *shorts* securities. The actual mechanism is described carefully in Chapter 22. Briefly, the trader acquires the bond that is expected to decline in price through a (reverse) repurchase agreement—essentially borrowing it—and then sells it at the current price. When the price actually falls (or rises, and the trader decides it's time to abandon the position), he buys the bond in the market at the now lower (higher) price, and returns it to the lender (the counterparty in the repurchase agreement). The profit (or loss) equals the difference between the original sale price and the lower (higher) purchase price.

There's a simpler way to accomplish the same goal, without the need to borrow securities (which necessitates a credit line plus other

FIGURE 17.3 Initial and Offsetting Swap Positions

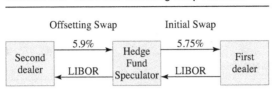

infra-structure for a repurchase agreement). That's right—an interest rate swap! Only this time the trade is reversed. The speculator enters a contract, agreeing to *pay* fixed on the five-year swap in return for receiving LIBOR. Then, when the swap rate rises, he enters an offsetting swap to receive the now higher fixed rate and pay the same LIBOR producing a net positive cash flow. Suppose, as above, the five-year swap rate begins at 5.75%, 110 basis points over the going five-year Treasury yield. The trader enters a contract to pay 5.75% against receiving LIBOR. A short while later, five-year swaps are at 5.9% (because the five-year Treasury yield has risen, the swap spread has widened, or some combination of the two). The trader then enters into a new swap, now to receive 5.9% and pay LIBOR. The two positions are displayed in Figure 17.3, where it is clear that the trader has a net profit of 15 basis points on the notional amount of the swap each year over the next five years.

The trade will produce a profit or loss depending on changes in the Treasury five-year yield and five-year swap spread, whether they moved together or apart, and to what degree. The ten possible outcomes given in the two lists above apply here as well, but with "rise" substituted for "fall" and vice versa, and with "widen" substituted for "narrow" and vice versa. Because there are so many possibilities, I've provided Table 17.2 as a summary. Each entry reports on the result of a swap position *relative* to what the trader would have experienced had he or she attempted to do the same with a Treasury bond.[10]

Counterparty Risk

We put a lot of effort in the last section into understanding that the pair of transactions—buy and then sell a five-year Treasury note—can be duplicated (except for possible movements in the swap spread) by entering into a five-year interest-rate swap contract as the fixed-rate

TABLE 17.2 Profit/Loss Outcome of Interest Rate Swap Compared to Straight Treasury Bond Position

Received Fix on Swap in Place of Treasury Purchase	Treasury Yield *Declines*	Treasury Yield *Unchanged*	Treasury Yield *Rises*
Swap spread narrows more than Treasury yield change	Profit increased	Flat becomes profit	Loss turns into profit
Swap spread narrows as much as Treasury yield change.	Profit increased	Flat becomes profit	Loss turns into flat
Swap spread narrows less than Treasury yield change	Profit increased	Flat becomes profit	Loss reduced
Swap spread unchanged	Profit unaffected	Flat remains	Loss unaffected
Swap spread widens less than Treasury yield change	Profit reduced	Flat becomes loss	Loss exacerbated
Swap spread widens as much as Treasury yield change	Profit becomes flat	Flat becomes loss	Loss exacerbated
Swap spread widens more than Treasury yield change	Profit turns into loss	Flat becomes loss	Loss exacerbated
Paid Fix on Swap in Place of Treasury Short Sale	**Treasury Yield *Declines***	**Treasury Yield *Unchanged***	**Treasury Yield *Rises***
Swap spread narrows more than Treasury yield change	Loss exacerbated	Flat becomes loss	Profit turns into loss
Swap spread narrows as much as Treasury yield change	Loss exacerbated	Flat becomes loss	Profit becomes flat
Swap spread narrows less than Treasury yield change	Loss exacerbated	Flat becomes loss	Profit reduced
Swap spread unchanged	Loss unaffected	Flat remains	Profit unaffected
Swap spread widens less than Treasury yield change	Loss reduced	Flat becomes profit	Profit increased
Swap spread widens as much as Treasury yield change	Loss becomes flat	Flat becomes profit	Profit increased
Swap spread widens more than Treasury yield change	Loss turns into profit	Flat becomes profit	Profit increased

receiver and then offsetting the contract. However, there is a subtle, yet crucial, distinction between the two positions. Take the example of the hedge fund speculating on a drop in interest rates. After the Treasury note is sold to complete what is known as a "round turn," the position is history. Profits (or losses) are booked, the dealers involved in the pair of trades are gone, and the hedge fund is on to the next trade. Not so with the swap. A look at Figure 17.2 shows clearly that, even after the round turn, the fund manager has two swaps on the books and, unless these are taken care of in one of the manners described below, a five-year relationship with these dealers. What's wrong with that, you ask? Counterparty risk.

The best way to appreciate what counterparty risk is—and what it is *not*—is by working through a couple of scenarios. Let's return to the speculator above. He signed a contract with a dealer to receive 5.75% for five years in exchange for paying LIBOR. Soon afterwards, five-year swap rates decline to 5.6%. He's really happy because now he can offset the swap and earn 0.15% on the notional amount for the next five years. But suddenly the swap counterparty is out of business! Default! We need to explore what default means in the context of a swap, what the cost of default is, and how it differs from a bond default.

With respect to the swap contract itself, it is dead. That is, the defaulting counterparty (in this case the dealer) stops making payments, and the speculator stops his payments as well. What has the speculator lost through this? Clearly, there is no point in offsetting the swap with a new, opposite swap. The speculator, therefore, loses the net cash flow that he would have received over the next five years had the dealer not defaulted. On a present value basis this amounts to $0.6388 per $100 of face value.[11] This is the loss caused by the counterparty's default. Note—and this is crucial—the trader has not lost the $100 face value of the swap. This money did not exist. There was no loan of $100 by either of the parties to the swap. Remember that a swap is a derivative. The only money put in place at the contract's inception is the collateral, which we discuss shortly. So, unlike a bond, there is no principal to lose. Indeed, if the five-year swap rate hadn't budged from its initial 5.65%, and the counterparty defaulted, *there would have been no loss at all* to the speculator because nothing occurred to create any value in offsetting the swap. The speculator, or any swap participant, *suffers a loss due to the counterparty defaulting only when there has been a change in rates* that would have produced a profit on the swap, but now cannot be realized because of the default. Contrast this with a bond. If a bond issuer defaults, the investor loses even if there has been no change in bond yields since the purchase. This is such a crucial concept—that without a change in the swap rate a counterparty default produces no loss—that we need to examine it from another angle. We need to consider the *value* of a swap.

Swap Value

At the swap's inception, there is no purchase of a security, hence there is no "sale." No payment by a buyer to a seller and no receipt of payment by the seller from the buyer. There is no loan, hence no borrowing. The two parties to the transaction—in our case the speculator and dealer—sign a contract, agree to the future cash flows called for by the swap, and that's it. (The collateral, if any, is not a *payment*. Both parties, if agreed, post funds, but these sit in escrow, to be drawn upon in case of default.) At inception, the cash flows expected to be paid by the two counterparties to each other are equal. That must be so, otherwise why would they agree to the contract? Indeed, that is how we proved earlier that the fixed rate of the swap must equal the average of the expected LIBOR rates over the term of the swap. In short, there is no *net* value in the swap.[12] An implication of this is that if the dealer were to default immediately after the swap contract's inception, the speculator would incur no loss (and if the speculator were to default, the dealer would suffer no loss), since there is no net value in the contract. Just write the same contract with another counterparty.

Things are very different after the swap is in place for a while. Let's return to the first example above. A short time, say a few days, after entering into a five-year swap to receive 5.75% fixed (and pay LIBOR), new five-year swaps in the market pay 5.6% fixed. Is the original swap "worth" anything now? It sure is. How do you know? Because the speculator can offset the swap by entering a new one to pay 5.6% (and receive LIBOR), which will produce 15 basis points of profit on the notional amount of the swap for the next five years.[13] How much is that worth in today's money (i.e., present value)? Bond math tells us $0.6388 for each $100. So this is the value of the swap. If the dealer were to default now, the speculator would lose this amount of money. From the dealer's perspective the swap is worth a *negative* $0.6388 per $100. It is a liability, or a loss, since offsetting the swap means having agreed to receive 5.6% for five years, and now paying 5.75% on a new swap. So, here's what we've learned:

1. Interest-rate swaps begin life with a zero net (present) value. If—and only if—there is a change in swap rates after the swap is in place will the swap have value. Whatever the *positive value* is to one counterparty, it is a negative value to the other counterparty.
2. Should the counterparty default on the swap, the contract terminates. A loss is suffered by the remaining counterparty only if the swap has *positive value*, which occurs only if there has been a change (in the beneficial direction) in swap rates since the contract's inception.
3. Since a loss is incurred only if default occurs once the swap has *positive value*, counterparty risk reflects the likelihood of default, and the amount lost in that event, when the swap has positive value.

Note the emphasis on *change* in these three points. Remember our characterization of a swap at the beginning of this chapter—a "pure" derivative. It has no monetary value at inception.[14] Only after a relevant change takes place is there value to the counterparties. Be careful: No monetary value does not mean no usefulness. We just saw that a swap is useful as a speculative tool. And we'll see in Chapter 18 how enormously useful swaps are to investors, even without a change in interest rates.

The two-sided nature of swap counterparty risk is worth emphasizing. The dealer also faces default risk—that the speculator will not perform. Of course, the scenario presenting risk to the dealer is the reverse of the above. Should the fixed rate on new swap *increase* after this swap was agreed to, the swap will have a positive value to the dealer (and a negative value to the speculator) as the fixed-rate payer. An offsetting swap, in which the dealer receives the now higher fixed rate, will produce a positive net cash flow for the succeeding five years. A default by the speculator negates this. Notice the profound difference between the swap and a loan. The lender faces default risk from the borrower, and on the entire amount of the loan. The borrower has no risk from the lender once the funds have been taken down. On the other hand, *both* parties to an interest-rate swap face risk from each other, and only on the value of the change (and the possibility of such), not the face amount.[15]

Swap Collateral

Let's now take a deeper look at the collateral for a swap. Just as with a loan or bond, collateral is posted to compensate for losses incurred in the event of default. With respect to a loan or bond, only the borrower can default, with negative consequences to the lender. With respect to an interest-rate swap, we've seen that each counterparty can potentially default. Not all loans or bonds are collateralized. Loans without collateral are "unsecured"; bonds lacking collateral are known as "debentures." The same applies to swaps. Both parties can agree at the outset to dispense with collateral. This is more likely when: (1) the term of the swap is very short; (2) the parties already have significant business relationships, hence exposure and credit lines with each other; or (3) both parties are well-capitalized.

If counterparties agree to collateral, how much should there be? Recall, with respect to a loan, that the entire principal is at risk of default. With respect to an interest-rate swap, we learned above that only after a change in swap rates is the counterparty with the positive value at risk of the counterparty with the negative value defaulting. Collateral should reflect the likelihood of default and loss in event of default. Therefore, based on our earlier analysis, the amount of collateral increases with:

- *Term of the swap.* Swaps have value only when there is a change. The longer the term of the swap, the greater the chance of a change occurring.
- *Volatility.* The more volatile the (fixed) swap rate, the greater the likelihood of a movement in the rate and the larger the likely change in the swap's value. Since the swap rate equals the sum of the Treasury yield and the swap spread, higher volatility in either component increases the chance of the swap having value, hence potential for loss in the event of default.
- *Creditworthiness of counterparty.* Whatever the term and volatility situation, the less creditworthy the counterparty is, the greater the risk of default.[16]

Mark to Market

Suppose two parties enter into an interest-rate swap, similar to the one above. Say the notional amount is $1million. Based on market conditions (which include expectations about future swap rate volatility), both parties post collateral, in the form of cash, equal to 3% of the swap's notional value, or $30,000. Some time later, swap rates rise, causing the value of the swap to decline by, say, 1%, for the fixed-rate receiver, hence rise by 1% for the payer. The original collateral would have compensated the fixed-rate payer had the receiver defaulted when the swap was worth up to $30,000. Now that the swap is already worth $10,000, there is only room for another 2% change in value to still cover default. In order to maintain this 3%, or $30,000, cushion, the fixed-rate payer demands another $10,000 in collateral from the receiver. This is known as "marking to market." Allow me to restate this crucial concept from a different angle:

At inception, interest-rate swaps have zero net value. Once swap rates change in the market, this swap will have a positive value to one counterparty and an equal negative value to the other. Even though the value is not *realized*—because the swap is not offset in the manner explained previously—it is still there. Mark to market forces the realization by adjusting the collateral. The party for whom the swap has achieved positive value receives additional collateral, while the other party pays it. Depending upon the agreement, the party credited with the marking to market may even withdraw and spend the funds! If swap rates then move in the other direction, collateral is adjusted the other way. The frequency of mark to market, along with the cash transfers, is negotiated in the swap contract.[17]

Hedging with Swaps

Abstract from the swap spread's movements, a change in the swap rate causes a mark to market in the swap's value. How much? Earlier in this chapter we show that a swap's dv01 (duration) is approximately the same as that of a par bond whose maturity matches the term of the swap and whose coupon equals the swap fixed rate.

The fixed rate on a swap equals the yield of a similar maturity Treasury bond plus the swap spread. Given a constant swap spread, the swap rate and the Treasury yield, therefore, move in parallel. Now we can draw on our knowledge of hedging from Chapter 12. Remember, hedging refers to reducing the risk exposure of a security without selling the security. A position in a bond can be hedged by selling short a different bond. The hedge works if the two bonds are correlated. If the price of the bond that is owned declines, so should the price of the bond shorted. Buying back the shorted bond at the lower price offsets the loss. Conversely, purchasing a bond hedges a short position in a different, but related, bond. Co-movements of swap rates and Treasury yields means that an investor, speculator, or dealer holding a bond position can hedge its interest-rate risk with a swap. Long a five-year fixed coupon bond? Pay fixed on a five-year swap. Short the bond? Receive fixed on the swap. How large should the swap position be? The ratio of the dv01s, as shown in Chapter 12. And what's better, unlike using a bond to hedge, swaps require no financing of a long position or borrowing of bonds to create a short position. It works in the other direction, too. An interest-rate swap position can be hedged with a bond.[18] However, because of possible movements in the swap spread, the hedge is imperfect. We call this "basis risk" (see Chapter 12).

Unwinding or Assigning a Swap

Let's return to the speculator who used the swap as a substitute for purchasing a five-year Treasury note. He agreed to receive a fixed rate on a five-year swap. When the rate on new swaps fell, he entered into an offsetting swap to lock in a net profit for the remainder of the swap's term. But he is exposed to counterparty risk if the dealer who is paying fixed to him defaults. And, until the five years are up, the speculator has two swap contracts to worry about. Here's an idea. Why not do the second offsetting swap with the same original dealer? Go back to Figure 17.2 and put the same dealer into both boxes. The hedge fund will now be receiving 5.75% and paying 5.6% on the same notional with one dealer. (The two LIBOR payments exactly cancel out.) A simple procedure suggests itself: Ask the dealer to pay a lump sum *and dissolve both contracts*. How much? The present value of 15 basis points times the notional amount over the next five years, which is exactly the "value" of the swap, as explained above. This is known as "unwinding" the swap.

While this method of offsetting and realizing the value of a swap is attractive because it avoids the counterparty risk for the remaining term of the swap contract, it creates another dilemma for the fund manager. She needs to deal with the original dealer to do the second swap. It would certainly be preferable to shop around in order to find the best swap rate. There is another alternative: Enter an offsetting swap with a second, different dealer and then exit the deal, leaving the dealers as counterparties to each other. This is known as an "assignment," and the steps are as follows, using our above example:

1. Hedge fund enters original swap with Dealer A, agreeing to receive 5.75% from dealer, paying dealer LIBOR.
2. After market swap rates decline, hedge fund enters an offsetting swap with Dealer B, agreeing to pay Dealer B 5.6% and receiving LIBOR from Dealer B.
3. Rather than signing the new contract as in step 2, the hedge fund notifies Dealer B that he will be taking over the hedge fund's swap with Dealer A; that is, Dealer B will receive 5.75% from Dealer A and pay LIBOR to Dealer A.
4. The hedge fund notifies Dealer A that from this point on Dealer B will be the counterparty to the swap, having taken over hedge fund's contract with Dealer A.
5. Dealer B pays the hedge fund the value of the contract (the present value of 15 basis points on the notional amount).

What the hedge fund has accomplished here is twofold: (1) the realization of the profit on the trade—she actually has a cash profit, as opposed to a security that has risen in value; and (2) the removal of counterparty risk—she is no longer party to any contract because it has been assigned away. A particular feature of the swap contract needs to be noted since it becomes prominent at this point. Technically, both dealers need to consent to the assignment. Since they will be assuming counterparty risk with respect to each other—parties with whom they did not initiate the trade—they may decline the assignment (perhaps because they already have enough credit exposure to that particular counterparty).

Bondlike Aspects of the Swaps Market

Back in Chapter 1 we discuss the "benchmark" status of government bonds. An important aspect of qualifying as the benchmark is the liquidity of Treasuries compared to other bonds, as reflected in their narrow bid-offer spreads.[19] There are degrees of liquidity among Treasury bonds. Bonds lying in the U.S. Treasury's auction cycle are more liquid than others. The U.S. government, for example, has not issued a seven-year note in quite some time. A five-year note, therefore, will be more liquid than a "seasoned" seven-year (a note issued three years prior as a ten-year). We find similar phenomena in the interest-rate swap market. While a swap dealer will accommodate a customer (i.e., quote a "two-way" market) in nearly any term requested, there is much more activity in two-, three-, five-, ten-, twenty-, and thirty-year terms, hence narrower bid-offer spreads than for other dates.

Interest rate swaps today come in many shapes and sizes. Over its relatively short lifetime, the swaps market has introduced nearly as many variations as its sister market, that for bonds. This should not be surprising. As explained above, swaps can be used as a substitute for actual bonds. And, as is explained in Chapter 18, swaps are employed by investors alongside bonds to achieve desired risk exposure. So it was quite natural for the market to develop new swaps to correspond with the various structures found in the bond market:

Amortizing Swaps

An amortizing bond repays part of its principal prior to the final maturity, according to a prearranged amortization schedule. Swaps, of course, entail no exchange of principal at inception, and hence no repayments at maturity. Swaps do involve a notional principal to which the fixed and floating rates refer in order to calculate the swap payments. An amortizing swap simply reduces the notional principal over time, according to an agreed-upon schedule, which serves to reduce the two sets of interest payments.

Zero Coupon Swap

Like its counterpart zero coupon bond, a zero coupon swap calls for no payments by the two counterparties during the term of the swap. There are, however, interest rates expressed in the swap contract (just as a zero coupon bond has a yield, yet no coupon). The stated fixed rate is compounded for each of the years. The floating rate is compounded as well but is not known in advance. At the swap's termination, the respective compounded rates multiply the notional amount, and only then are the cash flows exchanged.

Cancelable/Callable Swap

The technical name is *cancelable,* but it is essentially a callable swap, and you'll see why. Recall the elements of a callable bond. The call feature allows the issuer to repay principal prior to maturity on (or after, depending on the structure) the call date. This is a valuable right, since it provides the borrower with the option of refinancing at a lower rate, if available in the market, yet keep the existing bond should market interest rates rise. Upon exercise of the bond's call option, two things occur: the principal is repaid, and coupon payments terminate. A cancelable swap is a parallel instrument. Consider the following. A and B enter into a ten-year interest-rate swap; A is to pay 6% to B, B is to pay LIBOR to A, based on a notional $1 million. Three years later, new *seven*-year swaps are being created in the market at 5% against LIBOR. If A has the right of cancellation, he certainly would cancel; it's much better to pay 5% for the remaining seven years than 6%. What would cancellation entail? Both payments simply terminate. Unlike the bond, where exercising the call requires repayment of principal, there is no principal with a swap (hence the name "cancelable" as opposed to "callable"). A is now happy to enter into a new swap to pay 5%. B is, of course, sad. She must enter into a new swap to receive 5% instead of 6% for the remaining seven years and pay LIBOR.[20] Clearly A would much prefer this cancelable swap than an ordinary noncancelable swap of similar term. And B would not want it. So, just as a bond issuer pays the investor a higher rate for a callable bond than an otherwise equivalent noncallable (since the call feature is a potential benefit to the issuer at the expense of the investor—see Chapter 2), the fixed-rate payer in a cancelable interest-rate swap pays a higher swap rate than that of an ordinary noncancelable swap of equal term.

Can a similar swap be created to benefit the fixed-rate receiver? Sure. The ten-year swap entered into originally may instead give B the right to cancel. When would she do that? If, for example, after three years new seven-year swaps are trading, say, at 7%. B would love to cancel, replace the original swap, and receive 7% instead of 6%. This would hurt A. Hence, if the right of cancellation is conferred upon the fixed-rate receiver, the swap carries a lower fixed rate than it otherwise would.

Inflation Swap

What seems like an exotic product is actually one of the easiest to understand. X and Y sign a swap contract for, say, three years. As a pure derivative, the contract calls for no money to be exchanged at the outset. Based on an accepted notional value, X agrees to pay Y, for example, 2.5% each year. In return, Y agrees to pay X the previous year's inflation rate both multiplied by the notional amount.[21] If entered into on a stand-alone basis, X must be of the view that inflation will average *at least* 2.5% per year over the next three years. Y must be expecting inflation to average *at most* 2.5% over the same period. Extrapolating from this specific contract to all such contracts (and proceeding with the same logical argument as we did earlier in proving that the fixed rate on an interest-rate swap represents the market's expectations as to LIBOR over the term of the swap), we conclude that the fixed rate on inflation swaps reveals to us market participants' expectations as to inflation over the term of the swap, in this case 2.5% over the coming three years. Unlike the earlier three swap variations, an inflation swap has no direct counterpart in the cash bond market. However, as we will see in Chapter 18, combining an inflation swap with cash securities produces (synthetic) inflation-protected bonds.[22]

18

HOW INSTITUTIONAL
INVESTORS USE SWAPS

Swaps have completely transformed the investment landscape for the bond investor. They have enlarged the menu of available risk exposures and, at the same time, presented new ways to achieve traditional exposures. Looked at another way, the creation of swaps that target a variety of fixed-income products has removed almost all traditional constraints. Investment managers are no longer limited by the risk exposures placed before them by cash instruments; they can purchase an asset, retain the desired risk, and dispense with the undesired.

Traditional Investment Alternatives

Consider a portfolio manager with a five-year horizon, or holding period. As in Chapter 4, we take this to mean that, whatever the strategy employed, the assets and derivatives in the portfolio must be liquidated at the horizon date. Table 18.1 presents four traditional, "plain vanilla," investment alternatives.

An investor with no appetite for credit risk would choose between the first two. Would she buy a Treasury bill at 3.5% when 4.75% is available with the note? Only if it is her view that short-term Treasury interest rates will rise enough so that the average Treasury bill rate over the horizon will be at least 4.75%. The choice between the two, therefore, reflects interest-rate expectations. It can be alternatively described as a choice between floating (short-term) and fixed (long-term) rates.[1] The

TABLE 18.1 Traditional Investment Menu

Security	Yield
Treasury bill	3.50%
Five-year Treasury note	4.75%
Commercial paper	4.50%
Five-year corporate bond	6.00%

bill's rate changes over the horizon; the note's yield is fixed. A third alternative may be a ten-year Treasury note with possibly a higher interest rate, depending on the shape of the yield curve. In the context of the choices examined here, it is not a new alternative. It is a fixed-rate instrument lacking credit risk, just as the five-year note is, albeit for a longer term.[2] Hence, we will stick with the bill and five-year pair because they highlight the floating-rate–fixed-rate distinction which is one focus of this chapter.

Our investor may be prepared to accept some degree of credit risk. The second pair of assets in the table, involving corporate paper of similar credit quality issues, returns a higher yield as compensation for the risk of default. Notice the 1.25% spread between the Treasury note and the yield on the five-year corporate note. Compare this to the 1% difference between the Treasury bill and commercial paper. Credit risk, and the compensation for accepting it, generally increases with maturity, as the possibility of negative events multiplies with time. Choosing between the second pair of alternatives involves interest-rate expectations—floating versus fixed rate or short term versus long term—as did the first pair. In addition, the investor needs to choose between short-term and long-term credit risk. Purchasing the commercial paper locks the investor into the issuer's credit risk for only a few months. Should the firm survive but deteriorate, she can then roll over the paper at a higher rate or switch to another issuer. This is not the case with the corporate bond. (A default, of course, hurts both the paper and the bond.) Hence, the choice between the two is that of floating versus fixed credit spreads, as well as floating versus fixed interest rates.

With this distinction in mind between long-term (fixed) and short-term (floating) risk—be it interest rate or credit risk—the investor should be able to base her choice from among the four alternatives on pure economic expectations. An expected rise in interest rates should push her toward floating-rate exposure.[3] An expected deterioration in corporate earnings points to floating credit exposure. What if the investor's views produce a mutually exclusive pair of risk exposures? Suppose she believes that the economy will weaken, pushing down interest rates as the need for liquidity declines, yet widening credit spreads as corporate profits diminish. This scenario calls for fixed (long-term) interest-rate exposure and floating (short-term) credit exposure, a combination unavailable among the choices under discussion. Fixed credit exposure demands fixed interest-rate exposure—the corporate bond; a floating interest rate requires a floating credit spread—the commercial paper. There is no alternative in Table 18.1 that fits. The investment manager must compromise on one of the factors and accept a portfolio inconsistent with her views.

Table 18.2 summarizes the dilemma. With the traditional investment alternatives, there is no strategy that meets our investor's requirements. If fixed (i.e., long-term) interest-rate exposure is appropriate, fixed credit exposure must be accepted and vice versa. What is needed is an investment strategy that allows the interest-rate decision to be separated from the credit decision.

Enter Swaps

A simple interest-rate swap (IRS) is shown in Figure 18.1. The term is five years to match our investor's horizon, and the notional amount is equal to the amount invested in the assets listed in Table 18.1.

Now consider the following arrangement: The investor purchases the commercial paper and simultaneously enters the swap as

TABLE 18.2 Risk Exposure

Investment Strategy	Interest Rate Risk	Credit Risk
1. Treasury bill	Floating	None
2. Treasury note	Fixed	None
3. Commercial paper	Floating	Floating
4. Corporate bond	Fixed	Fixed

FIGURE 18.1 Five-Year Interest Rate Swap

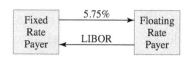

the floating-rate payer–fixed-rate receiver. The commercial paper pays 4.5% only until it matures. At that point, assuming that the firm survives, rolling over the paper will pay the investor a rate reflecting the issuer's creditworthiness as of that date. Any deterioration (or improvement) will be reflected in the new interest rate. We can think of commercial paper as paying LIBOR plus a spread, with the spread reflecting the issuer's current creditworthiness.[4] Contrast this with the corporate bond's coupon, which reflects the issuer's credit risk as of the issuance date and does not respond to changing market or company conditions. This paper/swap combination produces a combined interest rate of 5.75% plus the commercial paper's spread over LIBOR. LIBOR, as you can see in Figure 18.2, is netted out by the swap. The 5.75% is locked in through the swap; the spread is not because it will always reflect the current creditworthiness of the paper issuer. The investor's goal has been achieved: fixed interest rate and floating credit spread. It is worthwhile looking at this structure from another perspective: What the interest-rate swap has achieved is a *decoupling of the interest-rate decision from the credit decision.* The investor can make the credit risk decision as she pleases and not be beholden to the resultant interest-rate exposure—fixed or floating—that it entails.

What about the reverse situation? What if the investment manager believes that a strengthening economy lies ahead? In this case floating

FIGURE 18.2 Commercial Paper/Interest Rate Swap Combination

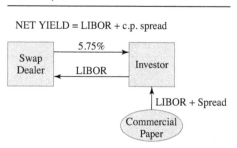

interest rate and fixed credit exposure are called for—the former in order to participate in the rise in interest rates typically accompanying an expansion (Chapter 5) and the latter to lock in a credit spread because spreads are likely to narrow with the increase in corporate earnings (Chapter 10). Once again, this pair of exposures is simply unavailable with the traditional alternatives contained in Table 18.1. The Treasuries provide no spread. Commercial paper and corporate bonds do pay a credit spread, but the pair of exposures does not fit the investor's views, as shown in Table 18.2. A simple floating-rate note solves this problem.[5] Assume it has a maturity of five years and pays LIBOR plus 0.50%. Purchasing this note locks the investor into the issuer's credit risk for five years; the 0.50% spread over LIBOR is fixed for the life of the note. Yet, the reference rate, LIBOR, adjusts to the market, just as the T-bill and commercial paper rates do. Perfect! Table 18.3 presents the expanded menu of investment alternatives now available and shows clearly that, with interest-rate swaps and floating-rate notes (FRNs), strategies 5 and 6, the choice set appears complete.[6]

Table 18.3 provides two additional strategies. Purchasing a floating-rate note and adding a swap as the floating payer converts the floating interest-rate risk exposure of the FRN into fixed, as did the commercial paper-IRS combination just discussed. Hence, strategies 5 and 7 both are "synthetic" fixed-rate investments. However, strategy 7 produces fixed credit risk exposure, since the FRN involves a long-term loan to the issuer. Said otherwise, a floating-rate note is only *partially* floating, as the 0.50% spread over LIBOR paid by the FRN is fixed

TABLE 18.3 Expanded Risk Exposure

Investment Strategy	Interest Rate Risk	Credit Risk
1. Treasury bill	Floating	None
2. Treasury note	Fixed	None
3. Commercial paper	Floating	Floating
4. Corporate bond	Fixed	Fixed
5. Commercial paper + IRS	Fixed	Floating
6. Floating-rate note	Floating	Fixed
7. Floating-rate note + IRS	Fixed	Fixed
8. Corporate bond + IRS	Floating	Fixed

FIGURE 18.3 Floating-Rate Note/Interest-Rate Swap Combination

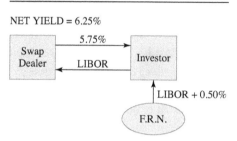

for the life of the note. Only the LIBOR portion floats (see Figure 18.3). Adding an interest-rate swap, therefore, produces a strictly fixed-rate investment. On the other hand, adding the IRS to commercial paper retains the floating credit risk exposure, since upon maturity of the paper, the new credit situation of the issuer will be reflected in a new spread over LIBOR.

Indeed, strategy 7 creates a synthetic corporate bond, as it perfectly duplicates the risk exposure in strategy 4. Strategy 5, on the other hand, does not because the credit risk exposure remains floating. Now move to strategy 8, purchasing a fixed-rate corporate bond and entering into an interest-rate swap as the fixed-rate *payer* (where the IRS position is shown as a negative in Table 18.3). It transforms the interest-rate exposure from fixed to floating, yet retains the fixed-credit exposure. The investor has committed funds to the borrower long term, and the spread over LIBOR is fixed. It qualifies, therefore, as a synthetic FRN.

An important question now presents itself. If combination 7 synthesizes strategy 4, and combination 8 synthesizes strategy 6, is there any reason to choose between the two alternatives of each pair? One simple reason is that the company the investor wishes to lend to has not issued the appropriate security. That is, while it is quite common for corporations to issue fixed-coupon securities, it is far less common for them to sell floaters. A synthetic FRN strategy may be necessary simply to get a floating-rate note of the desired corporation into the investment portfolio. That explains the need for combination 8. Similarly, though less likely, it is possible for an FRN of a particular issuer to exist but not a fixed-coupon bond, hence the need for strategy 7. There is, however, a more fundamental answer to the question.

Consider the following situation. An investor purchases a fixed-coupon corporate bond, strategy 4, and interest rates decline thereafter. In response, the bond's price increases, say, from par to $102. Then the corporation defaults. The investor's claim in bankruptcy court is for par, not for $102. Why? Hasn't the bankruptcy caused a loss of $102 in the portfolio? No. Bankruptcy triggers acceleration of debt; that is, the debt is due now, and the bond is therefore at par.[7] Now consider the alternative. The investor synthesized the same risk exposure as the bond by combining a floater with an IRS, combination 7. Interest rates subsequently decline, causing the swap—hence the FRN/IRS *combination*—to rise above par to, say, $102, for exactly the same reason as in option 4. But remember, there are two parts to strategy 7. The FRN, by its very nature of being an interest-rate–insensitive instrument, remains at par (see Chapter 12). What brought the combination to $102 is the swap's mark-to-market value going from 0 to +2, since it reacts to interest-rate changes just as a bond does (as we just learned in Chapter 17). With the issuer having defaulted, the investor claims $100 as the FRN creditor. *But the swap now decouples from the FRN.* It remains intact as the obligation of the counterparty—unrelated to the corporate bond issuer—and is worth $2 to the investor. This is where the FRN/IRS synthetic bond differs from a plain vanilla bond.

Conversely, suppose interest rates rise subsequent to the bond or the FRN/IRS purchase. In response, the corporate bond falls, say, to $98. Now the company defaults. The investor has a claim for $100 in bankruptcy, even though the bond was at $98 prior to the default. Again, this is due to debt acceleration. Not so with the FRN/IRS combo. Holding the FRN entitles the investor to claim $100. But the decoupling of the swap produces negative mark-to-market value of −$2. Parallel arguments explain the differences between a straight FRN, strategy 6), and the synthetic FRN, strategy 8), in the event of bankruptcy.

New Alternatives

Is there any exposure combination missing from Table 18.3? How about *zero* interest-rate exposure with short or long credit exposure? Until recently, this would have been impossible to create. Credit exposure requires lending money, which automatically creates nonzero

FIGURE 18.4 Credit Default Swap

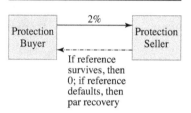

interest-rate exposure. The introduction of credit default swaps has solved this problem.[8]

We study credit default swaps (CDSs) in depth in Chapter 23. Figure 18.4, illustrating the basic CDS contract, will suffice for now. A "protection buyer" makes a periodic (typically quarterly) premium payment to the "protection seller," in this example an annualized 2%, on an agreed-to notional amount. In return, the buyer is compensated by the seller in the event the reference credit—the issuer whose credit risk is covered by the contract—defaults. The compensation equals the difference between the recovery value of the reference asset and the par notional. Until that time, and that time may never occur during the term of the contract, the protection seller receives the premium.

A protection buyer who also owns the protected reference bond has essentially removed credit exposure (subject to the risk of nonperformance by the protection seller). The net exposure, therefore, is equivalent to that of a Treasury instrument. It follows that this 2% premium must equal the credit spread of the issuer's bond over the Treasury, which is transferred by the protection buyer to the protection seller, who now bears the credit risk. Since the seller has not expended any cash, this "unfunded credit risk" includes no interest-rate risk. We have achieved our goal: zero interest-rate exposure along with positive credit exposure. Table 18.4 reproduces the main entries from Table 18.3 along with the two CDS positions which complete the menu. Both options 7 and 8 reflect protection-seller positions. The first uses a short-term CDS, where rolling over the contract results in credit spread payments which shift along with the risk of the reference corporation (similar to a commercial paper position, but without the cash investment). The second is a long-term CDS, where the credit spread is fixed for the horizon (similar to a corporate bond investment, but without the funds).

TABLE 18.4 Enlarged Menu of Risk Exposure

Investment Strategy	Interest Rate Risk	Credit Risk
1. Treasury bill	Floating	None
2. Treasury note	Fixed	None
3. Commercial paper	Floating	Floating
4. Corporate bond	Fixed	Fixed
5. Commercial paper + IRS	Fixed	Floating
6. Floating-rate note	Floating	Fixed
7. Short-term CDs	None	Floating
8. Long-term CDs	None	Fixed

Real Risk versus Inflation Risk

Interest rates must include a premium for expected inflation. As explained at length in Chapter 7, the stated, or "nominal," yield on a bond contains two components: the "real" interest rate and an additional payment covering the annualized inflation rate expected over the life of the bond. Purchasers of long-term debt, whether government, corporate, or the synthetic structure formed via a short-term instrument plus an interest-rate swap, necessarily take long-term, or fixed, inflation risk. This is because the expected inflation premium, once added to the coupon at the bond's issuance, or included in the swap rate, is fixed for the bond's life (just as the credit spread on a corporate bond is fixed). Should actual inflation turn out to be greater than the expected level built into the bond's interest rate, the investor's real return is lower. Conversely, if actual inflation is lower than expected, the real rate of return is higher.

A short-term investment, on the other hand, such as Treasury bills or commercial paper, presents floating inflation exposure to the investor. When the asset is rolled over, the investor will receive the new inflation premium,[9] along with the new real interest rate. Once again, traditional investment vehicles present us with a forced link between two risks, in this case real interest rates and inflation. By their very nature, long-term fixed-income investments fix both the real rate and inflation risk factors. Short-term assets allow both risk parameters to float. For any particular investor, these combinations may be undesirable given the investor's

TABLE 18.5 Disaggregated Risk Exposure

Investment Strategy	Real Interest Rate Risk	Inflation Risk	Credit Risk
1. Commercial paper	Floating	Floating	Floating
2. Corporate bond	Fixed	Fixed	Fixed
3. Floating-rate note	Floating	Floating	Fixed
4. Commercial paper + IRS	Fixed	Fixed	Floating

expectations. This is clear from Table 18.5, which repeats the four basic interest-rate risk/credit risk combinations (3 through 6) from Table 18.4, but further disaggregates risk by separating the real interest-rate component from the expected inflation component within the nominal interest-rate risk factor. Examining these four options, it is clear that we've solved the problem of separating the credit exposure decision from the (total) interest-rate exposure decision by introducing strategies 3 and 4. Yet real interest-rate risk seems to be linked with inflation—both need to be fixed or floating—whether desired or not.[10]

We are by now familiar with the economic scenarios which call for strategies 1 through 4. So consider the following. An investor anticipates a weakening of economic activity, yet it is accompanied by accelerating inflation (the result, perhaps, of rising oil prices). Long-term real rates should decline, if the investor's expectations are realized, since firms have less need for capital and the central bank may well ease liquidity to jump-start demand. The expected inflation premium, though, will likely rise, so the net effect on nominal rates, which equal the sum of the real and expected inflation rates, is not clear. In this scenario, the choice between standard fixed- and floating-rate assets is unhelpful. The appropriate response would be an asset with a fixed real interest rate to take advantage of the decline in real rates, yet one with a floating inflation premium. Inflation-protected notes address this need.

We've already examined inflation-protected securities and compared them to standard, or "nominal," bonds, in Chapter 7. Briefly, the coupon on a Treasury inflation-protected security (TIPS) bond equals a fixed "real" rate plus the *actual*—not expected—inflation rate recorded over the period ending on the coupon date.[11] The inflation component of the interest rate floats. A similar security issued by a corporate entity (corporate inflation-protected, CIP) would pay a higher fixed rate in order to include the credit spread plus the same actual inflation premium. Should real interest rates in the market decline, the fixed real coupon on the TIPS (or CIP) bond becomes relatively more attractive, raising the bond's price, just as it does to a nominal bond's price. Conversely, an increase in real interest rates reduces the price of an inflation-protected security. Movements in inflation rates, however, do not force shifts in TIPS (or CIP) bond prices. Indeed, the bond's cash flows change in consonance with inflation. Because the bond's nominal coupon will rise in response to an increase in inflation, higher nominal interest rates will not have a negative effect on the bond's price. Conversely, a decrease in inflation reduces the coupon as well as nominal rates, again with zero net effect. Strategy 5 in Table 18.6, therefore, is the investment strategy that conforms perfectly to the investor's parameters set out in the previous paragraph.

What about the reverse exposure? Suppose the investor expects an increase in real interest rates accompanied by lower inflation, say, due to an expanding economy supported by reduced commodity prices (a situation not unlike the world economy during the post–9/11 recovery). An

TABLE 18.6 Full Menu of Disaggregated Risk Exposure

Investment Strategy	Real Interest Rate Risk	Inflation Risk	Credit Risk
1. Commercial paper	Floating	Floating	Floating
2. Corporate bond	Fixed	Fixed	Fixed
3. Floating-rate note	Floating	Floating	Fixed
4. Commercial paper + IRS	Fixed	Fixed	Floating
5. Corporate inf.-prot. bond (CIP)	Fixed	Floating	Fixed
6. Commercial paper + INF	Floating	Fixed	Floating
7. Floating rate note + INF	Floating	Fixed	Fixed
8. Commercial paper + IRS – INF	Fixed	Floating	Floating
9. Treasury inf.-prot. security (TIPS)	Fixed	Floating	None
10. Treasury bill + INF	Floating	Fixed	None
11. Treasury bill	Floating	Floating	None
12. Treasury note	Fixed	Fixed	None

appropriate investment would be one with a floating real interest-rate exposure, to take advantage of the expected rise in real rates which accompanies strong business activity, but with a fixed inflation premium, since the investor expects inflation, hence the inflation premium, to decline and wants it locked in. Furthermore, the investor wishes to take credit risk in order to receive a higher yield than is provided by Treasuries. Purchasing and rolling over commercial paper provides the credit risk premium and the floating interest-rate exposure. The latter, though, floats both the real interest rate and the expected inflation rate. How is the investor to change the floating inflation premium in commercial paper to fixed? The solution lies in an inflation swap, introduced in Chapter 17.

Inflation Swaps

Figure 18.5 depicts a simple inflation swap (INF). In return for receiving a fixed rate on a notional amount (just like a simple interest-rate swap), the floating-rate payer sends the actual inflation rate multiplied by the notional to the counterparty.[12] If the swap has, say, a five-year term, then the fixed rate agreed upon represents market participants' expected average inflation rate over the next five years (similar to the fixed side of an interest-rate swap equaling the market's expectation for the average LIBOR over the term of the swap). This was proved in Chapter 17.

Suppose that our investor purchases commercial paper and simultaneously agrees to be the fixed-rate receiver on an inflation swap. Look at Figure 18.6. The inflation swap effectively transforms only the

FIGURE 18.5 Five-year Inflation Swap

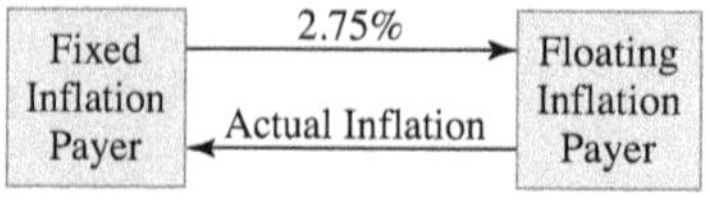

FIGURE 18.6 Commercial Paper/Inflation Swap Combination

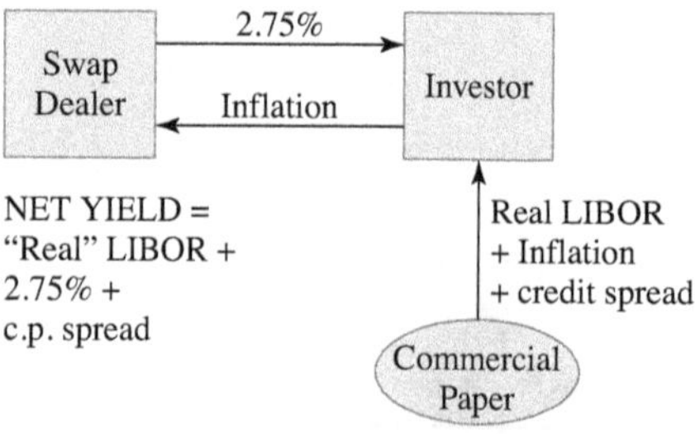

inflation component of the commercial paper rate from floating into fixed, which conforms to the investor's view. Compare this, shown as strategy 6, with the commercial paper/interest-rate swap combination, strategy 4, in Table 18.6. There, the interest-rate swap transformed the *entire* floating-rate exposure of the commercial paper investment into fixed. In our case, the inflation swap targets only the floating inflation rate that the paper buyer will receive, transforming it into fixed. The floating real-interest rate exposure is retained, and we have the desired result.

Strategy 6 turned the floating inflation exposure of commercial paper into fixed. Let's rethink the scenario. Expectations of expanding economic activity imply improving corporate creditworthiness. This implication points to a strategy that locks in credit spreads or takes fixed credit exposure, which commercial paper does not provide. Our investor would like the same real rate and inflation exposure as in strategy 6, but with fixed credit risk. Substituting a floating-rate note for the commercial paper meets this objective. As a long-term loan, the FRN presents fixed-credit exposure (the spread is constant for the life of the FRN). The inflation swap fixes the expected inflation premium, but the real component of the LIBOR exposure is maintained as floating. This is strategy 7 in Table 18.6.

There is one risk combination as yet uncreated: fixed real rate exposure and floating inflation, with floating credit risk. Recall that this strategy was called for by a scenario of weak economic activity (implying declining real interest rates and widening credit spreads) together with accelerating inflation (perhaps oil prices rising)—a "stagflation" environment. The corporate inflation-protected bond provides the proper fixed real interest-rate/floating inflation combination, but presents a fixed credit spread. What the investment manager is looking for can be accomplished with commercial paper plus an interest-rate swap, and paying fixed inflation on an inflation swap (strategy 8 in Table 18.6). The commercial paper produces floating credit risk, the swap transforms the paper's floating interest-rate risk into fixed (both real rate and inflation), and the inflation swap then turns the resulting fixed inflation exposure back into floating (but not the real interest-rate component). The choice set is now complete.

The final four strategies in Table 18.6 show how it is possible to avoid credit risk entirely and choose a desired real interest-rate/

expected-inflation premium combination. Purchasing a Treasury inflation-protected security provides a fixed real rate and a floating inflation rate exposure. Purchasing a Treasury bill and receiving the fixed rate on an inflation swap produces floating real rate and fixed inflation exposure. Both present no credit risk. Finally, simple investments in a Treasury bill or a longer-term Treasury note bring us full circle to the first two entries in Table 18.2.

PART VI

FOREIGN TRADE
AND INVESTMENTS

19

FOREIGN TRADE, FOREIGN EXCHANGE, AND FOREIGN BONDS

A foreign exchange transaction involves a sale/purchase of one currency for another at an agreed-upon rate of exchange. For example, if the dollar/pound sterling exchange rate is \$1.8/£, then it takes \$1,800,000 to purchase £1 million (1 million × 1.8) and £555,556 to buy \$1 million (\$1 million/1.8). At the risk of being trivial, we can equivalently say that you'd get \$1,800,000 for a million pounds, and £555,556 for a million dollars.[1]

Quotations

Foreign exchange (FX) becomes awkward (not complex) because the transaction involves exchanging two different kinds of money. In order to speak the same language, there must be agreement among market participants as to which of the currencies is considered the item being purchased and sold, and which serves as the means of payment. In the dollar/pound example above, the pound is taken to be the "item," or the commodity if you will, and the dollar is the "money," or means of payment. Thus the convention is to quote the number of dollars it takes to buy a pound (or the amount of dollars to be received for each pound). In fact, that is the market's rule for all currencies with respect to the pound—units of currency per pound sterling. This is true as well for the euro, the common currency of much of Europe: dollars per euro, Japanese yen per euro, etc.[2]

With respect to currencies other than the pound and euro, the convention is to use the U.S. dollar as the item or commodity. For example, at ¥105/$, it takes 100/105 = $0.9524 to purchase 100 yen or a yen denominated bond with a face value of ¥100.

Terminology

Suppose the dollar/euro exchange rate changes from $1.25/€ to $1.26/€. The euro is said to have *appreciated* compared to the U.S. dollar. If it changes to $1.24/€, the euro has *depreciated* against the U.S. dollar. It has neither appreciated nor depreciated *absolutely* since, at the same time its movement occurred versus the U.S. dollar, the euro could have depreciated or appreciated against, say, the British pound. Both terms are, therefore, only relative. Note also that in the first case, the U.S. dollar has depreciated versus the euro, and in the second case it has appreciated.

If the yen were to move from ¥105/$ to ¥106/$, then the yen has depreciated against the U.S. dollar, despite the number of yen being higher. This is because the yen is quoted in a way that is the reverse of the euro. Were it to change to ¥104/$, then the yen appreciated.

What about *devaluation* and *revaluation*? Devaluation is synonymous with depreciation, revaluation with appreciation. "Synonymous" is not "equivalent." The difference is subtle but important. Depreciation and appreciation are market events; that is, market participants expressing more or less desire to own particular currencies. These expressions are carried out through buying and selling, which results in currency price changes. What do these desires reflect, and why do they change? We address this later in the chapter. All we need to know now is that exchange rate movements reflect the changing preferences of market participants. Central banks also purchase and sell currencies. And they have desires as well, although theirs are profoundly different from those of the other market participants, as we will also see later, particularly with respect to their own currencies. Recall from the Chapter 6 that a country's currency is the IOU, or liability, of the central bank. So here's the rub: When a central bank buys foreign exchange, it is *creating* more of its own currency. When the U.S. Federal Reserve buys pounds, euros, or yen in the FX market, it pays for the foreign currencies with its own currency—dollars. New dollar bills are created. Because the Fed is the "issuer" of dollars, its balance sheet is changed—more liabilities (dollars) and more assets (foreign exchange) to match—when it transacts in the currency markets. If the result—and likely the intention—of this action is to raise the value of the purchased foreign currency versus the U.S. dollar, then the dollar has been *devalued* against that foreign currency. Conversely, were the Fed to buy dollars in the open market, using its reserves of foreign currency as payment, not only does this have a market impact, just like any participants transacting in the currencies, but it also effects a change to the central bank's balance sheet in the reverse direction; dollars outstanding are reduced so that its value has risen against foreign currencies and hence has been *revalued*. In short, market participants (other than central banks) *transact* in currencies with each other, and the *result* of their actions is an appreciation/depreciation; the net amount of currency is unchanged. Central banks *intervene* in currency markets, and the *purpose* of their actions is appreciation/depreciation; the net amount of currency is changed.[3]

The Currency Factor in Foreign Bonds

Our concern in this book is bond investing and trading. We care about foreign exchange because purchasing foreign bonds—bonds denominated in a foreign currency—necessitates accepting foreign exchange risk.[4] Let's see what's involved.

Consider a five-year bond issued by the Japanese government and denominated in yen. The coupon is 2%, and it's priced at par. We'll work with a face value of ¥100 to be consistent with our U.S. dollar bonds in the preceding chapters. Assume that the spot exchange rate is ¥112/$.[5] The yen bond, therefore, costs 100/112 = $0.8929. A coupon of 2% × ¥100 = ¥2 is received after one year. If the exchange rate is unchanged, this ¥2 translates into 2/112 = $0.0179, which equals 0.0179/0.8929 = 2% based on the dollar investment. So, with an unchanged exchange rate, the interest rate (or yield, were the bond not at par) expressed in yen terms is the same when translated into dollars.

Now allow a change in the exchange rate, assuming, for simplicity, that it occurs at year-end. Assume the rate goes to ¥113/$. Remember, with the yen expressed as foreign currency units per U.S. dollar, this constitutes a depreciation versus the dollar. If the bond's price is unchanged in yen terms—because interest rates in Japan have not moved in the interim—the bond's principal proceeds in dollars is now 100/113 = $0.8850, a drop of 0.89% compared to the initial investment of $0.8929. This decline in the bond's value in dollar terms matches the yen's depreciation: A change from ¥112/$ to ¥113/$ means that 1 yen buys 0.89% fewer dollars. This subtracts from the coupon earnings of the bond, so the net return is only 2% − 0.89% = 1.11%. Had the exchange rate gone the other way, say, to ¥110/$ − a 1.81% appreciation, the net return on the investment would be higher than the bond's yield, or 2% + 1.81% = 3.81%. Were the yen to drop to ¥115/$, a 2.61% depreciation, the rate of return would actually be a negative 0.61%, despite an unchanged bond price.[6]

What if the bond's yield does not remain constant? Then, separate from the exchange rate factor, the bond's price change affects the investor's rate of return (ROR). Suppose at the end of the year its yield rises by 5 basis points, to 2.05%. Remember that one year later our Japanese government note has a four-year remaining maturity, which requires the bond math to be so adjusted. The new price is 99.8098 *in yen terms*. Since the yield in the market has risen above the bond's coupon rate, the bond's price drops below par.[7] Assume at first an unchanged exchange rate. Then the proceeds in dollar terms are (99.8098 *principal* + 2 *coupon*) / 112 = $0.9090. Combined with the $0.8929 investment, the rate of return equals 1.81%. Because the yen is unchanged versus the dollar, this is the same ROR that would have been obtained with a U.S. dollar 2% five-year bond whose yield begins at 2% and one year later increases to 2.05%.

So what do we have so far? The return on a foreign currency-denominated bond contains three components:

1. Coupon (or yield, or "carry")
2. Price change (capital gain/loss) in foreign currency terms
3. Exchange rate appreciation or depreciation

What if the bond's yield changes simultaneously with an exchange rate movement? Table 19.1 examines the four possibilities, along with the base case of no change in either the bond's yield or currency exchange rate.

TABLE 19.1 Rate of Return (ROR) of Foreign Currency–Denominated Bond under Four Scenarios

Five-year, 2% coupon Japanese government bond, purchased at par, initial exchange rate ¥112/$, $ investment of ¥100/112 = 0.8929; one-year holding period

Scenario 0: bond yield and exchange rate unchanged

Bond price at ending yield = ¥100

Dollar proceeds = [¥100 + ¥2] / 112 = $0.9107

ROR = 2.0%

Scenario I: bond yield rises to 2.05%, yen depreciates to ¥113/$

Bond price at ending yield = ¥99.8098

Dollar proceeds = [¥99.8098 + ¥2] / 113 = $0.9010

ROR = 0.90%

Scenario II: bond yield rises to 2.05%, yen appreciates to ¥111/$

Bond price at ending yield = ¥99.8098

Dollar proceeds = [¥99.8098 + ¥2] / 111 = $0.9172

ROR = 2.72%

Scenario III: bond yield falls to 1.95%, yen appreciates to ¥111/$

Bond price at ending yield = ¥100.1906

Dollar proceeds = [¥100.1906 + ¥2] / 111 = $0.9206

ROR = 3.11%

Scenario IV: bond yield falls to 1.95%, yen depreciates to ¥113/$

Bond price at ending yield = ¥100.1906

Dollar proceeds = [¥100.1906 + ¥2] / 113 = $0.9043

ROR = 1.28%

Currency depreciation exacerbates the negative effect of an increase in bond yield (scenario 1); appreciation can mitigate the negative effect of the increase in yield (scenario 2). If the appreciation is large enough, it can potentially produce a positive ROR. Currency appreciation enhances the positive effect of a decrease in bond yield (scenario 3); depreciation can diminish the positive effect of the decrease in yield (scenario 4). If the depreciation is large enough, it can produce a negative ROR.[8]

It's time to summarize (and relate what we've done here to the other parts of this book). The rate of return on a foreign bond equals the sum of:

1. *The bond's yield.* As we've seen (Chapter 5) this reflects the country's position in its business cycle (i.e., its level of economic activity relative to potential), the central bank's reaction to it, and expected inflation. If this were a corporate bond (or other bond containing default risk), the yield would include a spread for credit risk, again reflecting the economy's position plus any factors specific to the risk of the issuer.

Plus or minus

2. *Bond price changes (in the home currency).* The change in the bond's price is a function of the movement in its yield between the start and end of the investment period. The degree of price response to the yield change follows the parameters set out in Chapter 12, namely, the bond's maturity, coupon, and any embedded derivatives. If it is a corporate bond, the price will also reflect any changes in perceived creditworthiness.

Plus or minus

3. *Currency appreciation/depreciation.* The final section of this chapter explains the primary drivers of exchange rate movements. As the example at the beginning of this section clearly shows, even a small movement in exchange rates has profound effects on rate of return.

A Common Mistake

We know now how currency movements affect rates of return. It's time to understand what makes currencies move. Before we make an attempt to do so, we need to clear up an, unfortunately, very common misconception. The misconception is this: After a foreign currency depreciates, even if the interest rate in that country remains the same, you'll earn more by investing in that country. Sorry, not true. The depreciation itself does not improve the yield on new investments.

Let's consider the Japanese bond again, with a 2% coupon and the yen at ¥112. Recall the base scenario above, in which both the bond's yield and currency's exchange rate against the dollar are unchanged at the holding period's end, which produces a return of 2%. Say instead that the yen significantly depreciates by approximately 3%, to ¥115/$. Are new investors better off? Can they not get more yen per dollar now, which will produce a greater return on their investments? No, not at all. Don't you see? In the base scenario, the exchange rate we started with does not matter. *Whatever the starting exchange rate*, if it remains the same at the horizon's end, the ROR will be 2%, assuming that the bond's yield is constant. And if the yield is not constant, producing a different ROR, that ROR will be the same regardless of the starting exchange rate. Convince yourself: At ¥115/$, it costs only $0.8696 to acquire ¥100 to pay for the Japanese bond, significantly less than the $0.8929 that it cost before the yen depreciation. Sure, but the ¥2 coupon and ¥100 in principal at the end of the year produce proportionately less proceeds — $0.8870, compared to $0.9107 in the original situation. Proceeds of $0.8870 on an investment of $0.8696 produces the same ROR of 2%. Finished. Myth dispelled.

Let's look at this another way, which will actually serve as a good entrée to the next section. You have $1 million to invest. At ¥112/$, you buy 1 million × 112 = ¥112 million, and invest in this 2% bond. At year's end, you receive 2% × ¥112 million = ¥2,240,000 in coupon, plus the ¥112 million principal. Assuming no currency or bond price changes, proceeds of [(112,000,000 + 2,240,000)/112] = 1,020,000 in dollars relative to the $1 million investment comes to a 2% dollar ROR. Now assume the yen depreciates to ¥115/$ and you invest $1 million again. Go through the same calculations: $1 million gets you ¥115 million; your end-of-year proceeds *in yen* are larger, but in dollars they are [(115,000,000 + 2,300,000)/115] = 1,020,000, for the *same* 2% rate of return.

So a cheaper currency, assuming everything else is the same, does not do anything for the foreign investor. Or does it? Let's think again, but from a different angle. After the decline in the yen from ¥112 to ¥115/$, $1 million buys you 3 million more yen. Sure, investing in the Japanese bond gives you the same 2% return on your dollars, as just proved, but you are able to purchase more bonds than before. If this were a company rather than a government, this would give you a larger claim on the company in case of default.[9] If it were a corporate convertible bond (see Chapter 10), you can get more stock. Indeed, if this were an investment in a Japanese company's stock, assuming unchanged stock price, dividend, and yen exchange rate, once again you'd earn the same return in dollars, but you'd own a bigger piece of the company. You can see this even more clearly with an investment in Japanese real estate. The cheaper yen gets you more property for the same dollar investment, even though your return in dollars is the same, assuming unchanged rent and price in yen terms. Extending this train of thought a bit further, *the depreciated yen buys you more Japanese goods and services*, thus affecting trade flows between the United States and Japan, the subject of a later section.

What Determines Foreign Exchange Rates?

I wish I knew what determines foreign exchange rates, believe me. I don't think anyone truly knows what makes currencies move on a day-to-day basis.[10] So what are we doing in this chapter? I'll make an attempt to explain the fundamental macroeconomic determinants of exchange rates, that is, the drivers of *longer-term movements* around which day-to-day rates oscillate.

Fundamentally, a currency is just a piece of paper. It has no inherent value. Goods (and services) have inherent value. How much value? At any moment in time and in any particular region, a ton of coal may be worth one hundred bushels of wheat—the market requires you to give up a hundred bushels of wheat to acquire a ton of coal, and vice versa. A computer may cost two coats. And a quarter of a coat gets you a visit to the doctor. Why? Where did these "rates of exchange" come from? They reflect the worker-hours and materials required to produce the item or perform one service compared to the other. They also include profits earned by the entrepreneur coordinating the production or provision and owning the capital used therein. Ultimately these relative values are driven by consumers' needs and tastes and a bunch of other "real" economic determinants. In a modern economy, instead of bushels of wheat actually exchanged for coal, computers for clothes, or worker-hours for any of them, we use "money." Based on these "real" relationships that the market determined, it must be that twice as many pieces of paper, called dollars, are needed to buy a computer than to buy a coat. So, it doesn't matter if a coat costs $250 and the computer $500, or the coat $300 and the computer $600. Only the relative value matters, not the absolute. Money is only a medium of exchange.

What, then, determines absolute prices—why is it $250 for the coat and not $300, as long as it trades for half the computer? The answer is: the amount of dollars in circulation. A dollar has no "value." It is just the agreed-upon unit of exchange. To use terminology from Chapters 5 and 6, it serves as the economy's liquidity. If nothing changes in terms of relative worker-hours and other inputs required to produce corn and coal, coats and computers, and if people's tastes and needs for these items do not shift, then an increase in dollars in circulation is required just to match the growth in production of these goods (and services). If more dollars are "produced," it just raises the absolute prices of all these items equally. (If they don't increase equally, then there must have been a real relative change.) This is inflation—an increase in the absolute price level. This explains why, *fundamentally, inflation is a monetary phenomenon.*[11]

A Digression on Gold and the Gold Standard

Let's think about gold for a minute, the original "money." A modern, growing economy, requiring a vast and ever-increasing amount of liquidity to operate, cannot be subject to the efforts of gold miners and the consumption of jewelers. To provide a base of expandable and, when necessary, contractible, liquidity, central banks were created to introduce and oversee paper money.[12] The risk, of course, is that the central bank expands liquidity faster than the level of economic activity, hence transactions necessitating liquidity are called for. And this, as just explained, means inflation. Gold, on the other hand, would provide an anchor. If the central peg fixes the rate of exchange between its currency and gold—it "pegs" its currency to gold—then even though the economy uses the paper currency for its liquidity, it is effectively bound by a "real" commodity. How does such a peg function?

Consider the Federal Reserve. The Fed would proclaim its readiness to pay, say, $35 per any ounce of gold (gold was the actual peg in the United States until it was abandoned decades ago) that someone brings to exchange. It would also stand ready to provide 1/35 of an ounce of gold to anyone bringing a dollar bill. Suppose the central bank added too much liquidity, the result being inflation. Gold would rise versus dollars just as the price of other commodities (and goods and services). People would present dollars to the Fed and demand gold at $35. This would reduce dollars in circulation, bringing inflation back down. Now think about the economy growing. It needs more liquidity as it does so. If the Fed does not supply it, the demand for liquidity will cause the price of dollars to rise versus gold (as well as other goods and services), i.e., deflation. That is, the price of gold falls below $35. The Fed will, therefore, purchase gold in the market, paying for it with $35, which is what the economy needs.[13] In short, anchoring the supply of dollars to gold insures, at least over time, that liquidity growth matches, but does not surpass, the pace of economic activity, thereby preventing inflation.

Back to the "Real" World

The Federal Reserve no longer pegs its currency to gold. Nor do almost all other central banks on our planet. The Fed buys and sells all kinds of assets as it carries out monetary policy. It does so in order to provide the economy with the liquidity it needs so that transactions to take place efficiently without the use of a physical commodity like gold. But it also engages in this activity in order to affect interest rates and possibly other variables that impact on the macroeconomy. That is not our concern here; it is covered in Chapter 6. What *is* our concern in this chapter is this: The liquidity created by the Fed, in the form of dollars, determines the absolute price level. The price of gold in dollars is no longer fixed. Hence, the overall absolute price level in the economy is free to vary, as is, by extension, the rate of inflation. The rate of inflation reflects the percentage change in the Fed's provision of liquidity.[14]

We could go through the same argument with the Bank of Japan, which provides liquidity in that country by introducing yen into the

Japanese economy. Yen is the liability of the Bank of Japan, just as dollars are the liability of the Federal Reserve. And we can conclude that the *relative* prices of Japanese-made computers versus coats reflect production and preferences in Japan, but that the *absolute* price level is a function of the amount of liquidity in the Japanese economy. The Bank of Japan does not peg the yen to gold, either. And, finally, Japanese inflation, fundamentally, is determined by the rate of growth in Bank of Japan liquidity creation.

What about the relative price of Japanese yen versus U.S. dollars—the ¥/$ exchange rate? Given what we've learned above (subject to some qualifications, which we get to later) the answer is pretty straightforward. Think about the U.S.-made computer. Say it costs $600. Assume that *exactly* the same computer, but made in Japan, costs ¥67,200 there. Ignoring transportation costs, a rational computer buyer would buy the cheaper one, since they are exactly the same. In this case, the exchange rate *must be* ¥112/$. If then yen were higher, no one—not Japanese, not Americans—would buy the Japanese computers. (For example, at ¥110/$ it would cost an American ¥67,200/110 = $611, so why buy it there? And a Japanese would pay only $600 × 110 = ¥66,000 to buy the American model, so why not?) If the yen were lower, no one would buy the U.S. model. (At, say, ¥114/$, it would cost an American only ¥67,200/114 = $589 to purchase the Japanese computer. And a Japanese would have to pay $600 × 114 = ¥68,400 for the American model, so why do it?) Since, by assumption, the computers are perfect substitutes, the yen/dollar exchange rate must be ¥112/$.[15] This is known as the "law of one price." And it must hold for every good (as long as it can be purchased in either country).[16]

We now derive a major implication from this law. Say inflation in the United States is 3% over the coming year. If there is no inflation in Japan, then for the law to hold, the yen must appreciate by 3% against the dollar. Otherwise the computer prices in the two countries will be "out of whack." And the same holds true for all (tradable) goods. Similarly, if inflation in Japan is 1%, the yen must appreciate by 2%. If, on the other hand, inflation in Japan turns out to be 5%, the yen must depreciate by 2% to abide by the law. In short, movements in the exchange rate between two countries' currencies must equal the difference in their inflation rates. This is known as "purchasing power parity" (PPP). It is a powerful concept.[17]

Implications of Purchasing Power Parity for Investing

Purchasing power parity (PPP) obviously has major implications for currency movements. To the extent that it holds true, a currency trader may base decisions on observed relative inflation rates. For example, say over the past year that inflation in the United States was recorded as 2.5%, and in Canada as 2%. Suppose that compared to one year ago the U.S. dollar/Canadian dollar exchange rate is unchanged. According to PPP, the U.S. dollar should have depreciated by 0.50%, suggesting that the trader buy the Canadian dollar. Or looking forward, perhaps the speculator forecasts inflation in the United States to be 1% over the next year, but 2% in Canada. This suggests a sale of the Canadian dollar. In the first scenario, the trader expects the market to "right itself" shortly. In the second, the speculator, even if correct, may have to wait up to a year for events to play out according to expectations.

PPP suggests a strategy for the global fixed-income portfolio manager. Earlier we learned that that the return to an investor from holding a foreign currency denominated bond is the sum of three factors:

foreign bond yield + bond price change +
currency appreciation / depreciation

Let's look forward and think about the bond's *expected* return, focusing on the *market's* expectations, not any one individual's. Since there is an equal likelihood of yields moving up or down, the bond price change factor, on a market expectations basis, equals zero. Recall now from Chapter 7 that every yield contains two components: a real interest rate and compensation for expected inflation. Thus the expected return from a foreign bond equals:

foreign real interest rate + expected foreign inflation rate +
currency appreciation / depreciation

Now we're ready for the punch line. Under PPP we saw that the currency's appreciation/depreciation equals the difference between inflation rates of the country in which the bond is issued and the investor's home country. Inserting this into the currency factor , we see that the expected ROR of a foreign bond, under a regime of PPP, is:

foreign real interest rate + expected foreign inflation rate +
(expected domestic inflation rate − expected foreign inflation rate)

Finally, since two of the factors cancel each other out, what remains of expected rate of return is:

foreign real interest rate + expected domestic country
inflation rate

This is a pretty amazing result. In a world governed by PPP, the inflation rate of the country issuing the bond is irrelevant! What is relevant to ROR. of a foreign currency denominated bond is, to be sure, that country's real interest rate. But added to that is the inflation rate of the investor's home country! Now consider what the investor would be receiving if he or she chooses to remain at home—the domestic interest rate. That, as we know, is equal to:

domestic real interest rate + expected domestic country
inflation rate

Do you notice the result? The investor choosing between purchasing a domestic and a foreign currency bond *needs only compare the real interest rates of the two countries*. Because PPP removes inflation expectations from the equations, it means that international portfolio choice becomes exclusively one of *real interest rate differentials*. This is known as the "real yield approach" to global fixed-income investing.[18]

Drivers of Exchange Rate Movements

There is nothing wrong with the above analysis, hence with the conclusion it inevitably leads to. It just doesn't work on a day-to-day, month-to-month, or even year-to-year basis. Purchasing power parity is a long-run concept, that is, one that predicts the direction of relative currency movements over long periods of time. It may also serve as a measuring rod of asset relative value, that is, relative to these long-run relationships.[19] But it does not explain short-run exchange rate shifts.

Why not? There are a number of reasons. Services constitute a far larger portion of a modern economy's output than do goods, and the inflation rates include goods and services. Most services, though, are not tradable across countries (unless the countries' geographic boundaries are easily—in the sense of cost—traversed). Furthermore, the goods that are traded, though nominally the same in both countries, are really not strictly the same. They can differ in substance (French wine is not California wine) or quality, actual or perceived (think about Japanese versus U.S. cars). This vitiates the "one-price" argument.[20] And there are barriers to trade—transportation, political, and regulatory. The assumptions underlying purchasing power parity, therefore, are not met.

Does this mean that we have nothing to say fundamentally about what drives exchange rates? No. It just means that we need to work harder in trying to explain FX movements and that at the end we won't have an elegant formula to rely upon. Instead:

> *Currency movements reflect the relative desires of citizens in one country for the goods, services, assets, and even central bank liquidity of another country.*

We spend most of the rest of this chapter trying to understand the source of these relative desires, how they are expressed, and how currencies may be affected by them.

Trade Deficits

I guess I should have titled this section "Trade Deficits and Surpluses." But the United States has been in a deficit for so long that the possibility of a surplus doesn't even enter our collective mind! A country's merchandise trade balance is simply the difference between its exports to and imports from the rest of the world. International transactions occur in many currencies, so each bilateral deficit or surplus is translated into the home currency, which allows summation and netting. For comparison purposes, the final result is then usually expressed in U.S. dollars.

We use the United States as our example. Why? Because it has a humongous trade deficit which makes it very interesting. And I live here.

The United States imports far more goods from the rest of the world than it exports, and this happens month in and month out. (Don't be misled. The United States is one of the largest exporters in the world. It just has a tremendous appetite for foreign goods and services. And, as we will shortly see, foreigners are more than willing to provide them.) The country does have a surplus in services. But remember, unlike domestic economic activity, which in industrialized countries is dominated by services, goods form the bulk of international trade. So the slight surplus in services hardly makes a dent in the trade deficit. Each month, therefore, U.S. importers are looking to purchase more foreign currency with their dollars to pay for imports than foreigners are looking to buy U.S. dollars with their currencies in order to pay for U.S. exports.[21] All else the same, this puts downward pressure on the dollar versus other currencies. Price matters as well. When the price of oil—which happens to be denominated in U.S. dollars on world markets—rises, the United States, being a net importer of petroleum, sends more dollars abroad. Downward pressure again.[22]

Currency transactions among countries are not limited to paying for imports and receiving payment for exports. Tourists take their home currency and exchange it into the currency of the visited country to pay for goods and services. The United States happens to have a surplus in tourism. But it is not nearly enough to offset the trade deficit. Governments send money abroad, not only for imports, but in the form of foreign aid. Private citizens working in a foreign country often remit some of their income back home, a very common occurrence when immigrants arrive from developing countries. This has the same effect as an import, since the currency will need to be sold in order to be used in the home country. Finally, interest, bond coupons, and stock dividends are paid to foreign holders of bank deposits, bonds, and equities. For example, Japanese are *net* investors abroad; they receive more of these payments than they send out. The reverse is now the case in the United States, which has become a net debtor.

If we add all these (and some other, smaller) items to the trade balance, we arrive at the "current account." The current account thus measures the net payments from one country to another. It stands to reason that a negative current account should put downward pressure on a currency relative to the currency of the country it has the deficit with. Of course, a country may be in a current account deficit position with respect to one country, and in a surplus position relative to another. The wider the deficit, the greater the pressure. This makes sense; it is simple economics. If a firm produces a product that, at its current price, elicits a shortage of buyers, the price falls until buyers are attracted (or the firm produces less). Similarly, if a country's products are not in demand internationally, its currency should decline until the products become more attractive on a net price basis, and/or other countries' products become more expensive, causing imports to decline and exports to rise.

Capital Transactions

Everything we say above sounds pretty logical. The problem is that current account surpluses and deficits don't explain currency movements well. For example, the United States has had a negative (and ever-widening) balance every year for well over a decade, yet the U.S. dollar hasn't depreciated year after year. The reverse is true in Japan; current account surpluses haven't consistently resulted in yen appreciation. So what's the story?

It's a bit of a complicated story, both satisfying and difficult. Satisfying because it should explain the perplexity pointed out in the previous paragraph. Plus it presents a foundation for understanding currency movements. Difficult because it's not obvious and perhaps, in part, is counterintuitive.

The discussion above dealing with cross-country purchases of goods and services, plus the other items such as tourism, etc., all involve transactions for the here and now; that is, "current." What is left out, as you probably noticed, are transactions for the "future," otherwise known as "investments." Cross-country purchases of stocks, bonds, deposits, real estate, etc. enter the "capital account" of the balance of payments.

Let's work with the United States again, recognizing that the analysis holds for any country. Suppose that over a full year the United States realizes a $500 billion deficit in its current account. Relative to all other countries taken together, U.S. individuals, companies, institutions, and even governments imported more merchandise, sent more tourists, extended more aid, and paid more interest to foreign countries than foreigners paid us, to the tune of $500 billion. This means that, when all is said and done, foreigners, at least temporarily, hold $500 billion worth of green pieces of paper with pictures of famous U.S. citizens on them. They can only do one of three things with these dollars (remember, they've already spent all they wish on U.S. goods, hotels, etc.). They can:

1. Purchase dollar-denominated stocks, bonds, bank deposits, etc.
2. Make direct investments in U.S. companies or real estate.
3. Hold the U.S. currency as is.

The first is known as "portfolio investment." The second is "direct investment." The last, termed "official investment," doesn't seem to make too much sense from the foreigner's perspective, since Federal Reserve notes do not pay interest. But note that foreign central banks hold U.S. dollars as reserves. And in many countries—especially those with emerging economies—individuals and firms prefer keeping their liquidity in dollars rather than in their home currency.

So there we have it! Because foreigners' excess receipt of dollars must be held in one of the above forms, the current account deficit must, by straightforward logic, be equal to the increase in foreigners' purchases of U.S. assets, otherwise known as "foreign investment." Here's the way economists say it: A country's current account deficit is "financed" by foreigners accumulating claims on the country via securities, direct purchases of assets, or simply holding the central bank's liquidity, or money. A country, therefore, becomes a debtor to other countries as a result of current account deficits. *Foreign debt equals the accumulation of current account deficits.* The converse is also true, of course. If the United States were running a surplus on its current account, it would be accumulating claims—via financial assets—on other countries. *The current account deficit or surplus equals the change in the capital account.*

Now we begin to have an understanding of why the dollar does not necessarily depreciate when the United States runs a trade deficit. Just as Americans are net purchasers of foreign currency when the current account has a negative balance, which should push the dollar down, foreigners' net purchases of U.S. financial assets require dollars, thereby pushing the currency up.

We could have started the analysis from the other direction. Foreigners are net purchasers of U.S. financial assets year after year. Why does this not cause the dollar to continuously appreciate? Because it must be balanced by a U.S. current account deficit. The capital account surplus means that U.S. individuals, firms, banks, and even governments have foreign currency in excess of their wishes to purchase assets denominated in those currencies. They must be using these currencies to purchase foreign produced goods and services, to send aid abroad, for tourism, and so on. The two flows must be in balance, hence the term, "balance of payments."

Great. But if the two sides must always balance—the dollars chasing foreign currencies because of the U.S. net deficit are matched by the foreign currencies chasing dollars because of foreigners' net purchases of U.S. assets—then what makes a currency go up or down? Ah, that's where economics comes in! Let me give you an analogy. At the end of every trading day, the number of stocks sold equals the number of stocks purchased. Right? Yet, stock prices go up, and they go down. Why? Because the *desired* amount demanded throughout the trading day is not equal to the *desired* amount supplied at any particular share price. If the former is in excess, the price of shares rises. If the latter is in excess, the price declines. The price moves until desired demand equals desired supply.

The same with respect to currencies. At any particular exchange rate, the amounts of imports and exports may produce a net deficit that is not matched by the excess of foreign demand for U.S. assets relative to U.S. demand for foreign assets. The exchange rate must adjust until there is a match. So when all is said and done, the accounts balance. But the balancing could only be arrived at by the exchange rate changing.

Determinants of International Trade and Capital Transactions

What determines relative demand for goods and services between countries, hence the trade deficit or surplus?

- *Economic activity.* The stronger an economy is, the greater its aggregate demand. Economic strength has fundamental meaning. An industrialized country has a larger appetite for goods and services – and the means to pay for them – than an emerging economy. It also has cyclical meaning. All else the same, a country in a business cycle expansion will import more than will a country operating below its potential. Recessions reduce trade deficits.

- *Relative prices.* The cheaper an item is abroad (including transportation costs), the greater the incentive to shun domestically produced items and import instead. In calculating relative prices, of course, the currency conversion needs to be taken into account, as we did above. For any price in local currency terms, the lower the exchange rate, the cheaper the product to foreign consumers.
- *Perceived quality.* This covers the expected life of the product; a longer life results in an effective lower price. Attractiveness as a tourist destination would be included here as well.

All else the same, movements in these factors affect foreign trade and put pressure on a currency. The parameters determining relative attractiveness of domestic versus foreign investments are:

- *Relative yield.* The greater the yield on foreign assets (adjusted for credit quality differences), the greater the desire to invest abroad. Yield includes interest rates on bonds, dividends from stocks, and net income from real estate.
- *Total return.* As shown earlier in this chapter, the total return from foreign investing adds capital gains/losses plus currency appreciation/depreciation to current yield. Hence, the greater the expected change in price of the foreign asset, and the more the currency of denomination is expected to appreciate, the more attractive investing abroad is compared to investing domestically.
- *Risk.* This includes price volatility, the likelihood of default, and the other risk elements mentioned in this book. With respect to investments abroad, new factors relating to the integrity of the financial system become important, such as property rights, bankruptcy laws, treatment of creditor claims, and the possibility of sovereign appropriation or other deleterious actions (crucial to emerging markets, as explored in Chapter 20).

Central Bank Actions

What have we got so far? Purchasing power parity, while an attractive theoretical construct, does not have operational value, certainly not in the short run. Relative prices of currencies—exchange rates—do not merely reflect inflation differences (in turn reflecting, in the long run, liquidity, or money, growth in the respective countries). Rather, they reflect real phenomena, summarized in the trade and current account balances on one side of the cross-country ledger and capital account transactions on the other.

We've ignored one big player in the market, the entity whose name is on the piece of paper we're talking about. Central banks have the potential to profoundly influence exchange rates. When they take action to do so, it is known as central bank "intervention." We examine direct and indirect intervention on the part of central banks. You will see that, ironically, direct intervention is more likely to have a fleeting impact on currency values, while indirect intervention can be long lasting.

Let's work with the U.S. Federal Reserve, but recognize that the process is the same for central banks generally.[23] Suppose that the Fed purchases foreign exchange, say euros and yen. How does it do so? The same way it purchases bonds and the other assets explained in Chapter 6 with respect to monetary policy. It buys the currency from an FX dealer, paying for it with IOUs drawn on itself, which we call dollars. What are the repercussions? We know that the very act of *any* market participant making a large purchase of an asset raises its price, at least temporarily. But there's more to it than that. Think of a company issuing more stock. It probably purchases assets with the proceeds of the stock sale. But the extra shares dilute the company's earnings and, all else the same, lowers the price per share. Now go back to dollars and the Fed. If market participants were to purchase euros and yen with their dollars, that would, of course, depreciate the dollar versus the two currencies. But it would not change the supply of the currencies in the marketplace. When the central bank does the same thing, it adds dollars, causing a more structural depreciation of the currency (hence the term "devaluation" is more appropriate than depreciation).[24]

Why would a central bank desire a lower value for its currency? Perhaps its economy is operating below potential and a cheaper currency would stimulate exports, in turn raising aggregate demand (see

Chapter 5), hence production to meet that demand. Or perhaps the central bank has chosen a target exchange rate (explained below). If market forces have caused the currency to appreciate, the central bank would be required to intervene to force a return to the target.

Let's go the other way. Suppose the Federal Reserve *sells* euros and yen in the open market. The bank is *purchasing* dollars, thereby causing dollars to rise relative to the foreign currencies. Furthermore, the Fed has removed dollars from the economy, so the scarcity of dollars increases their value. The analogy to a company's equity is a stock buyback which, given unchanged earnings, increases earnings per share outstanding, enhancing the stock's value. A central bank may desire an appreciation of its currency when the domestic economy is operating at capacity and needs to reduce aggregate demand (by making exports expensive). Alternatively, the exchange rate may have fallen below its target and the bank's policy is to keep it pegged. Buying dollars with the bank's foreign exchange reserves not only causes the dollar to rise in value due to the demand shift in the marketplace, but it also reduces the quantity in the marketplace (hence the term "revaluation").

Indirect Intervention

Direct intervention by a central bank in the currency markets in the manner described above is only a Band-Aid. It does not get at the root of the matter, that is, the fundamental factors forcing the currency's movements. Sometimes, though, a bandage is all that is required. If the central bank is convinced that the currency has only temporarily departed from its targeted exchange rate because the factors causing the move will dissipate soon, then the bank can buy or sell the currency to push the currency toward the bank's desired exchange rate for that limited amount of time. But if fundamental factors are driving the currency, these actions won't do the trick. Analogously, if investors are selling a company's shares and pushing the price downward because of deteriorating earnings, the company's buying back shares will not prevent the stock decline, except perhaps on the very day of the buyback.

What can a central bank do? It can change the fundamental factors. Suppose a country, having run a trade deficit for a number of months, is experiencing a decline in its currency relative to the currencies of its main trading partners. Foreigners are accumulating the country's assets, which they must be doing, in order for the accounts to be balanced, as we explain above. However, the *desired* purchase of assets has not been adequate to prevent deprecation of the currency. The central bank can increase that desire. How? By using its monetary policy tools to affect interest rates. The bank drains liquidity, in the manner described in Chapter 6, thus raising interest rates, which serves to increase the yield on the country's financial assets. Unless the other countries match the increase in rates, the relative interest-rate differential shifts in the country's favor, thereby attracting foreign purchasers. These investors must buy the currency in order to purchase the asset, which supports the exchange rate.

Conversely, a central bank may wish its currency to depreciate relative to currencies of its trading partners. In that case it can make the home currency less attractive to foreigners. It does this by lowering domestic interest rates, just as it would in a situation of weak economic activity. Lower interest rates make the home currency's assets less competitive in global capital markets, all else the same, thus reducing foreigners' demand for the currency and leading to a decline in the exchange rate.

A Caveat

Here's a caveat, and it's a major one. A central bank, through its monopoly on (pure) liquidity creation, has the ability to affect (if not determine) interest rates. In Chapters 5 and 6, we learned that the central bank establishes a target for interest rates in order to influence aggregate demand and thereby keep the country's GDP near its potential. We saw above that the bank can use interest-rate policy in order to achieve a particular exchange rate goal. It's tough to do both—one policy objective may compromise the other.

Suppose that the economy is operating significantly below its potential. Unemployment is high, and the central bank decides to add liquidity, thereby lowering interest rates in order to stimulate aggregate demand. At the same time, though, the bank wants to strengthen the currency. Why? Possibly because of inflation, since a stronger currency reduces import prices. Or the country may be committed to a peg (see below), and the weak economy has caused the currency to drop, reflecting foreigners' diminished appetite for the country's financial assets. This calls for raising interest rates to make domestic assets more attractive to foreigners. The bank can't have it both ways. It will have to make a painful choice. Conversely, an overly strong economy (growth above potential) may call for higher interest rates, while a trade deficit may necessitate a currency depreciation, which is prevented by the high interest rates. In short, central bank actions to affect exchange rates may compromise domestic economic policy.[25]

Currency Peg

Intervention is an activity; pegging is a policy. Central banks are not necessarily wedded to a particular exchange rate for their currency against those of their trading partners. At times the bank prefers the currency to weaken; at other times, to strengthen. The banks will intervene when necessary to achieve a goal, but the goal is dynamic. Some central banks concentrate on domestic economic policy, allowing the currency markets complete freedom to arrive at an exchange rate. This is known as a "freely floating" exchange rate. At the other extreme, a central bank may institute a policy that its currency should be exchanged with a particular foreign currency at a rate that remains fixed. This is known as a currency "peg."[26]

A central bank choosing a peg as its currency regime has committed itself to maintaining a particular exchange rate with respect to a foreign currency.[27] (You can readily see the analogy with the gold peg, or gold "standard," as explained earlier.) The chosen currency is typically that of a large economy, with substantial trade in goods and services and investment flows between the two countries. Suppose Mexico chooses to peg its peso against the U.S. dollar at 13 pesos per dollar. If the actual exchange rate in the FX market moves to 13.5 (say, because a larger than expected Mexican trade deficit was announced, or political turbulence in Mexico is causing U.S. investors to become less excited about investing there), the central bank of Mexico must step in. It might purchase pesos in the open market with its U.S. dollar reserves. But those reserves are finite, and that would not change the fundamental cause of the exchange rate shift. More likely, the central bank would act to raise interest rates in the country, hoping to attract U.S. (and other) investors who will need to purchase the peso in order to buy the now higher-yielding Mexican assets, thus raising the peso's value. Conversely, if the peso were to strengthen and trade below 13, the bank would lower interest rates in order to reduce demand for the currency.

I chose Mexico as the example because pegging regimes are found mainly in emerging economies. A peg, if adhered to, imposes discipline on a central bank; lack of discipline has characterized the central banks of many emerging economies in recent history. A disciplined currency policy, in turn, attracts foreign investors. Take the Mexican example again. As a developing country, Mexico needs foreign capital to expand (as we learn in Chapter 20). For that very reason, U.S. investors would purchase Mexican debt only if it pays a significant premium above interest rates in the United States (a credit spread, to use the language of Chapter 9). As we saw earlier in this chapter, currency fluctuations can quickly wipe out any yield advantage, erasing the attractiveness of Mexican debt instruments for U.S. investors. A peg is a promise by the central bank that this will not happen. It also means that if U.S. interest rates rise, interest rates in Mexico must also rise in order to maintain the required spread, and vice versa. In short, the peg means the Bank of Mexico has relinquished control over domestic monetary policy. Furthermore, to the extent that purchasing power parity holds, Mexico will be "importing" the U.S. inflation rate.[28] If the currency is stable (by virtue of the peg), then we saw earlier that PPP implies that the countries must experience equal rates of inflation.

20

EMERGING MARKETS

Years ago it was safe to refer to a less developed country as "less developed country," or LDC. But it became hard to identify any country as less developed without offending it, so the appellation turned into "developing country" or "emerging economy."[1] Hence, the name of this chapter.

Which are these countries? It's easier to say which they are *not*: They are not the industrialized economies of North America or Western Europe. They are not Japan, Australia, or New Zealand. Nor are they the group of "newly industrialized" countries of South Korea, Singapore, Hong Kong, and Taiwan. Which are they? Technically, all the rest. Our concern in this book, though, is only with those countries within that group whose governments, businesses, and/or financial institutions issue securities in the global capital markets. This would include a number of countries in Latin America (e.g., Brazil), in Eastern Europe (e.g., Hungary), in Southeast Asia (e.g., Thailand) and, of course, the giants of the class—China, India, and Russia.

What distinguishes these countries from the industrialized nations of the world? The risk that the governments may default on their debt (or force other entities in the country to renege on obligations). These fears are built on historical default experiences.[2] Market participants term this "sovereign risk." Emerging market debt instruments have become a significant asset class in many fixed-income portfolios, hence this chapter. The next section provides some general background on the economies of emerging market countries. This sets the stage for the analysis, in the final section, of sovereign risk.

Developing Countries: Economic Fundamentals

Macroeconomic dynamics of developing countries essentially flow from the poverty of its citizens. Since this is not a textbook on the economics of development, a synopsis will suffice. Remember, our concern is the implications for investing in the debt instruments of these countries.

- *International organizations (such as the World Bank) measure the economic well being of a country by its* per capita GDP, *or annual GDP divided by population.* The average figure for developing countries, while showing wide differences among individual nations, is far below that of the average industrialized country.[3]
- *Income (and wealth) show sharp dispersion within the country.* Of course, there are pockets of the rich, but the concentration of the population in the low end of the income scale results in a degree of *inequality* not present in industrialized economies. Furthermore, there tends to be little mobility from the lower stratus.[4] This situation has important implications for investors. The combination of poverty and inequality has historically led to social unrest, which often manifests itself in default on foreign obligations.
- *The composition of GDP is different from that of industrialized countries.* A significant percentage of the population in a developing country works in agriculture. Agriculture is subject to weather and supply disruptions. Further, goods typically account for a greater share of output than do services. Goods' prices are much more sensitive than services to global demand. As a result, macroeconomic activity displays greater volatility than it does in industrialized economies.
- *Infrastructure is lacking.* This refers to the physical means of getting goods, services, people, and information from their origins to where they can be used. It includes bridges and highways; canals, electric grids, and oil pipelines; and formal schools and other educational systems. (Deficient infrastructure interacts negatively with the previous point, in turn exacerbating the following point.)

- *Savings rates are low.* Although quite understandable, as the low income of citizens doesn't leave much over after spending on food and other essentials of day-to-day living, it means that capital must be imported in order for the economy to grow. Otherwise, the country remains stuck in poverty.
- *Procedures and institutions for investor protection are limited compared to what investors are accustomed to in developed economies.* (While technically not an economic fundamental, this point clearly relates to the risk of emerging market investments, the focus of this chapter.) These include property rights, laws requiring financial disclosure, and protection of creditor claims in bankruptcy.

The Central Bank and Exchange Rate Management

The low savings rates characteristic of developing economies forces them to import capital in order to grow out of their relative poverty. The other factors listed above translate into high risk for foreign investors supplying that capital. Developing countries, therefore, pay a high interest rate for the outside borrowing they desperately need.

All else the same, a developing country would prefer to borrow in its home currency rather than denominate its debt in a foreign currency. The latter imposes the burden of coming up with the foreign exchange to service the debt. Say the country borrows in U.S. dollars (the most common denomination). On top of the high interest rate it pays to compensate lenders for default risk, the country bears the risk of its currency depreciating against the dollar, which requires more of its own currency. If this were government borrowing, taxes would need to be increased. If it were corporate debt, profits would be reduced. Either way, the country is shifting more of its GDP to foreigners (in this case, the dollar lenders). Denominating the debt in its own currency shifts the burden of currency fluctuations to the U.S. lender. In this case, the lender demands an even higher interest rate: one premium for default risk plus another for foreign exchange risk.

In order to remove the FX risk faced by the U.S.-dollar–based (or other foreign) lender and thereby reduce the interest rate paid on foreign debt, central banks of emerging economies tend to "peg" their currencies to that of a large economy. That economy is typically a country with which the developing economy conducts substantial trade and/or is one that is relied on for investments. We cover the process of pegging in Chapter 19. Briefly, the central bank uses the tools at its disposal to keep its currency at a fixed exchange rate against the chosen currency. For example, suppose the Bank of Mexico chooses a peg of 13 pesos per U.S. dollar.[5] Say a widening of Mexico's trade deficit has temporarily pushed the exchange rate to 13.2 pesos/$. The bank may enter the FX market, purchasing Mexican pesos with its reserves of U.S. dollars, which serves to push the exchange rate back toward its target. If, after intervening, the rate reverts back above 13 for a number of days, the bank will likely conclude that the phenomenon is more than temporary, thus requiring a more fundamental policy adjustment than direct market intervention. It will raise short-term interest rates (by draining liquidity, as elaborated upon in Chapter 6). This makes Mexican peso debt securities more attractive than before, as the spread against U.S. bonds widens. The resultant shift to Mexican assets by U.S. investors requires purchasing pesos with dollars, again pushing the exchange rate back toward the bank's target.

So what's the problem? The problem is this: If the central bank is forced to conduct its monetary policy in order to keep its currency pegged, the bank loses its ability to influence domestic macroeconomic activity. Take the Mexico example again. Suppose the country is in recession. As we learned in Chapter 5, low interest rates are called for in order to stimulate aggregate demand. But the bank's hands are tied, since it must keep rates high to prevent the currency from depreciating below the peg. Something has to give—the domestic economy or the currency. It's a painful choice, particularly for a developing economy with a low savings rate and a poor population.[6]

Conversely, a country may be in the enviable position of its currency having appreciated *above* the peg and its economy expanding smartly (as the two often go together). To keep the peg, the central bank would lower interest rates. But that would add further fuel to the economy.[7] Alternatively, it could sell its currency and accumulate foreign reserves.[8] Either way, the stage is set for future inflation.

Emerging Market Debt Instruments

We now have some idea of the special features and difficulties of emerging market economies. Let's combine this with our knowledge of the economics of foreign exchange from Chapter 19 and examine the unique risks of emerging market debt instruments. We want to look at the risks of the developing *country*, not a specific borrower in the country, not a corporation, not even the central government of the country. Individuals, companies, and governments can default within the environs of a healthy economy. And economies can be in trouble even while particular borrowers are able to service their debt quite comfortably. Our concern is with the economy at large from the perspective of a foreign lender. Just for the sake of anchoring our discussion, let's consider a U.S.-dollar–based investor in a developing country. It is useful to think about three possibilities: (1) the debt is denominated in U.S. dollars; (2) the debt is denominated in the local currency, and the currency is pegged by the central bank to the U.S. dollar; (3) it is local currency-denominated debt, and the currency floats freely in the market.

Dollar Denominated Debt

Just as with any debt denominated in dollars, the yield equals the U.S. Treasury interest rate (for bonds of similar maturity) plus a spread for risk. Interest-rate fluctuations in the United States, therefore, will affect these developing country debt prices as they would any U.S. corporate, mortgage, or bank debt product. Ironically, interest rate dynamics in the local market will have no direct effect on the bond, except to the extent that they reflect factors playing into the spread. Similarly, the developing country's currency behavior will have no direct impact on the debt. It will, however, have an impact on the bond via the spread. Macroeconomic events that cause the currency to depreciate against the dollar will cause the spread to widen (and the price of the debt to fall), as the lower currency value means that the cost of acquiring dollars to service the debt has risen. In other words, muted day-to-day currency fluctuations will not have much effect on the bond's price. Substantial exchange rate shifts will cause market participants to question the country's ability to convert large amounts of the currency into dollars and hence be unable to honor the debt, which will have major repercussions on the bond's price.

Local Currency-Denominated Debt, Currency Pegged

Assume the country's central bank has not simply announced a peg to the dollar; it has actually maintained it for some years. Hence there is a level of comfort on the part of U.S. investors with the currency being stable against the dollar. Furthermore, the peg means that the country's interest-rate environment is linked to that of the United States. (Remember, the spread over U.S. interest rates needs to be maintained in order to keep U.S. dollars in the country.) So despite being denominated in the local currency, the interest rate on the debt equals the *U.S. rate* plus a spread for risk, similar to the above case. Yet, because the debt is denominated in local currency, the risk that the borrower will be unable to acquire dollars with the home currency is absent.[9] Where, then, lies the risk? In the possibility that domestic macroeconomic fluctuations, as explained in the previous section, may force the central bank to abandon the peg. In such a case, after a long period of stability, the currency depreciates markedly. In the extreme, the debt will be repaid in currency nearly worthless relative to dollars, or it simply will not be repaid at all. As investors begin to fear the peg abandonment, the bond default spread widens, and its price falls. Notice how in extreme situations, local currency-denominated and dollar-denominated emerging market debt behave similarly.

Local Currency-Denominated Debt with No Currency Peg

Fundamentally, local currency-denominated debt without a currency peg is no different from bonds issued, say, by the French government and denominated in euros or by a Japanese entity and denominated in yens. Interest-rate dynamics, hence movements in the bond's price, reflect domestic factors, such as inflation, stage of the business cycle, issuer characteristics, etc. On top of that lies the exchange rate risk. But wait. There is another very basic factor relevant to developing country debt that is essentially absent in debt from developed countries. The developing country is likely heavily indebted to the rest of the world. This introduces the possibility of default, which intensifies during periods of macroeconomic weakness. Thus own-currency-denominated emerging market bond prices are driven by standard macroeconomic-interest rate and exchange rate interactions plus default dynamics. A deeper understanding of the determinants of developing country default—known as "sovereign risk analysis"—is the subject of the next section.

Credit Default Swaps

Investors today can express a view on the risk of developing countries without buying and selling actual bonds. Credit default swaps allow market participants to take positions on a country's credit deterioration and default, speculate on credit improvement, and hedge existing developing country exposure without purchasing or shorting bonds. All the debt securities analyzed above subject the investor to both interest-rate and default risks. Credit default swaps react only to movements in market participants' views as to the likelihood of default.[10] This likelihood, reflected in the CDS "premium," encompasses macroeconomic, interest-rate, and currency factors, all elements of sovereign risk.

Sovereign Risk Analysis

Sovereign risk analysis—analyzing the possibility of default by a developing country—involves examining three categories of risk. Often labeled serviceability, solvency, and structural risk factors, they can synonymously be termed liquidity, cyclical risk, and fundamental risk. You'll see why.

Serviceability Risk

The definition of serviceability risk is self-evident: the possibility that the country cannot service its current debt obligations to the rest of the world. A widely used measure of this risk is the ratio of the country's export earnings to interest on its foreign debt. It is a sensible ratio because it measures "what comes in" relative to "what must go out." Serviceability risk is a short-term concept, since its focus is on the current situation. The analogy to corporate credit risk analysis is immediate. There we calculate the ratio of earnings to interest cost, known as the "coverage ratio" (Chapter 9), for exactly the same reason: Can the firm honor its obligations right now? The higher the ratio—for a corporation or sovereign nation—the more comfortable investors are.

A related measure—one without an obvious counterpart in corporate credit risk—is the ratio of the central bank's foreign reserves to the economy's monthly (or yearly) import costs. Reserves would include currencies of major industrialized countries, plus gold (the international currency) owned by the country's central bank. High-grade debt instruments of industrialized economies qualify as well. This is also a coverage ratio of sorts because it answers the following question: Assuming the worst case of zero export earnings, how many months (or years) of imports can the country pay for using its foreign reserves?[11]

Solvency Risk

A company, or an individual, is solvent when its assets are at least equal to its liabilities. How do we think about this concept with respect to countries? Market professionals examine the ratio of the country's foreign debt to its GDP. A country's assets are its resources—labor, physical capital, and endowed natural resources (the factors underlying an economy's potential GDP—see Chapter 5). There are no meaningful figures that put a monetary value on a country's resources. We use GDP as a proxy because it is a product of those resources. The greater the debt-to-GDP ratio, therefore, the closer the country is to "insolvency" and defaulting on its foreign obligations. Solvency risk is a medium-term measure. It is related to the business cycle of the country, as we will presently see, and is, understandably, sometimes described as cyclical risk.

Just as the leverage ratio is the one number market participants consider the most telling of a company's financial health, a developing country's debt-to-GDP ratio is probably the most scrutinized. It is worthwhile, therefore, to look inside this figure and examine what makes it move. The ratio obviously increases if foreign debt grows, and it decreases as GDP expands. The change in foreign debt each year, as we know from Chapter 19, equals the country's current account deficit for that year. Let's subtract interest on foreign debt from the current account since that represents payment for past deficits as opposed to newly incurred obligations. After a little math we arrive at a crucial conclusion: A nation's foreign debt-to-GDP ratio worsens according to

(1) an increase in its current account (net of interest) deficit *and* (2) the difference between the interest rate on its foreign debt and the country's GDP growth rate. This is a big deal. *Even if a country's foreign trade position is in balance, the ratio worsens if its interest rate exceeds its macroeconomic growth rate.* This is part of what has come to be known as the "foreign debt spiral." It is particularly difficult for developing economies to escape from this spiral. Why? The very fact that they are developing, as emphasized earlier in this chapter, forces a wide risk premium on their debt, and the premium widens as the ratio worsens! Thus their GDP needs to grow much faster than that of a country already developed in order to "grow out" of the same foreign debt problem. If not, the ratio gets larger, the default rate increases, the credit spread on debt jumps raising the ratio yet again—and so on.

Structural Risk

The factors entering into a country's structural risk equation are political and social as well as economic, each bearing on a country's fundamental health. It is, therefore, a long-term measure. There are many factors bearing on structural risk. Some of the more important follow.

Reliance on a single export is dangerous, even if it happens to be oil. Global economic fluctuations can reduce export earnings in a hurry, and oil is a perfect example of a macroeconomically sensitive commodity. A decline in exports leads to trade deficits, which result in foreign debt accumulation (solvency risk) which, unless grown out of as explained earlier, ends in serviceability risk. Other structural factors include the average level of educational attainment in the country and the degree of citizen enfranchisement in the political process. It seems, at least empirically, that the lower the level of each of these, the greater the likelihood of social unrest during periods of economic stress and the higher the probability of default on foreign debt. Finally, we return to unequal income distribution and low savings rates, two hallmarks of developing countries. The former contributes to political risk; the latter retards economic growth. Both, as do all the structural risk factors, widen a country's risk premium on its borrowings. This lowers the interest coverage ratio and ultimately increases solvency risk. It is a vicious circle.

PART VII

ADVANCED TOPICS

21

THE ROLE OF DEALERS

The economic and market upheavals of 2008–2009 have changed the basic nature of many financial institutions, their regulations and their interactions with the government and with each other. But the basic role of dealers is intact. Let me give you an analogy. People's diets change. Government regulations of the food industry evolve. Even the manner of eating is not fixed. But there will always be grocery stores. Securities dealers are the grocery stores. And you, the investor, are the customer.

Dealers versus Brokers

A dealer is not a broker. You need to understand that clearly. They are distinct entities with very different functions, particularly with respect to the customer. The job of a broker is to find: a buyer for a client who wishes to sell; a seller for a client who wishes to buy; a lender for a client who wishes to borrow; or a borrower for a client who desires to lend. During the search process, the price (or interest rate) can change. The broker tries to minimize this by conducting an efficient search, but *the risk is borne by the customer.*

A dealer, on the other hand, is a *principal* in the transaction (as opposed to a broker who acts as an *agent*, a representative, so to speak, for the buyer or seller). The dealer buys from a client who wishes to sell and sells to a client who wants to buy. He doesn't *match* a buyer with a seller; he *is* both the buyer and seller.[1] As such, the dealer's compensation is the difference between the purchase price and the sale price, much like any storekeeper who earns the difference between the price paid for goods and the price received from the customer for the goods. A broker's compensation, on the other hand, is commission—a fee for service. At any point in time, a dealer quotes a pair of prices: the price he is willing to pay for the security (bid) and the price he is willing to sell it for (offer). A grocery store also has two prices—the price for, say, milk that the storekeeper pays to the milk distributor or wholesaler, and the price for the milk asked of the customer. A car dealer likewise has two prices—the price of the car paid to the manufacturer and the price advertised to the potential customer. Enough. You get it. But here's the immediate implication that, despite the simple logic of it, many people just don't get: Bond dealers do not necessarily buy bonds because they think the market price will rise, no more than the grocer would order more milk in anticipation of a milk price increase, or the car dealer would put more cars in the lot because she expects car prices to rise. All three buy their goods—milk, automobiles and bonds—to sell at a higher price than purchased, *even when the market price is unchanged.* When purchased at the bid price and sold at the offer price, the three dealers earn their income, known as "margin," or "markup" or, in bond language, the "bid-offer spread."

This is not to say that bond dealers won't actively look to buy bonds when they think the price will soon rise. They surely will. But this would not be construed as a "pure" dealer activity. It is closer to speculating. On a practical level, though, it is difficult to discern a dealer purchase or sale due to pure dealing (known as customer-driven trading) or due to speculating for their own behalf. We'll return to this topic, albeit briefly.

To repeat—because it's so crucial—the most important difference between a dealer and a broker is this: The dealer owns the security in the time between the purchase and sale. The broker does not. Indeed, there is no time lag in a brokerage activity. While it takes time for the broker to find a counterparty, the buyer and seller transact simultaneously. The dealer, on the other hand, is exposed to possible price change during the time between her purchase and sale (or sale and subsequent purchase) of the security. Once the customer has done the trade with the dealer, the customer is finished—he has locked in a purchase or a sale price. The dealer now must find another party to sell to or buy from. During this "search" period the market is moving, and the bond's

FIGURE 21.1 Bid-offer Spread

price is subject to change. The longer the dealer searches, the greater the chance of a change in price. *This is the dealer's risk*, not the customer's. In short, the dealer is also a matchmaker, just as the broker is. But on top of that, the dealer is absorbing the price risk from the customer, and for this the dealer must be compensated. That compensation is in the bid-offer spread (see Figure 21.1).

Bid-Offer Spreads

Since the bid-offer spread is the dealer's compensation for assuming the price risk of the security as the dealer searches for a buyer or seller, it stands to reason that the spread will be a function of the degree of risk. Consider a dealer who has purchased a bond from a customer and is looking for a buyer. The dealer's risk depends upon:

- *Market "depth."* The longer the dealer expects to hold the bond, the greater the risk of a possible price change.[2] This length of time, in turn, will be shorter, the greater the number of potential market participants there are. "Potential," of course, is not measurable. A proxy is the security's average daily trading volume (ADTV). What determines the number of participants, hence the ADTV? Compare, for example, a corporate bond to a Treasury bond of similar maturity. Some investors are limited by regulation as to the amount of credit risk they may accept, if any. Some self-impose such a restriction. But all of them *could* buy Treasuries; that is, they are all potential buyers and, afterward, potential sellers. All else the same, the dealer will expect to hold the corporate bond longer than the Treasury, as the market is not as deep, and thereby be forced to accept more risk of price changes. The dealer, therefore, imposes a wider bid-offer

spread on the corporate.[3] Another factor is a security's uniqueness. The more standardized a bond is (for example, a bond
containing a straightforward coupon, has a fixed payment at
maturity and no embedded derivatives), the greater the universe
of potential participants. Conversely, the more unique it is (in
today's terminology, the more "structured"), the more time the
dealer will likely need to hold the paper until a buyer who is
comfortable with those particular parameters is found, hence
the wider the spread.

- *Volatility.* The more volatile the price of the security while it's
  in the dealer's possession, the more risk the dealer faces during
  the search process. More volatility means a wider bid-offer
  spread as compensation. Volatility, in turn, reflects: (1) "macro"
  factors, that is, general volatility in financial markets; (2) sector
  factors, that is, events concentrated in, (e.g., the market for
  corporate bonds as opposed to other bonds); and/or (3) issue
  factors, that is, occurrences unique to that particular issuer or
  that particular type of security.

- *Bond maturity.* One of the most fundamental principles of bond
  math (see Chapter 3) is the positive relationship between
  remaining maturity and price sensitivity to interest-rate
  changes. From the dealer's perspective, therefore, the longer the
  maturity of a bond, the more price risk is entailed in holding
  onto it while searching for a customer. Hence, the wider the bid-
  offer spread.

- *Dealer competition.* As with any business, healthy profits attract
  competition. Whatever the magnitude of the above three determinants, the more dealers there are, the narrower the bid-offer
  spread. Note that—and, again, this is true for any business—
  barriers to entry can reduce the number of dealers and hence
  keep bid-offer spreads higher than they otherwise would be,
  thus increasing transaction costs to investors.[4]

What I've more or less described above is "market-making." The
dealer provides an outlet—makes the market—for investors who are
looking to sell bonds and who are unwilling to bear the search risk associated with engaging a broker or acting on their own to locate a buyer.
Dealers provide a "two-way" market. They must also stand ready to sell

bonds to customers who do not wish to bear the risk of searching for a seller, either on their own or through a broker. In this case, the customer pays the dealer's offer price, and the dealer, who does not yet own the security, must then search for a seller of the security.[5] Again, the dealer's risk is a function of the very same parameters mentioned above, and in the same direction.

To sum up, investors buy bonds from dealers rather than search for sellers on their own (or they employ brokers to do so) and sell bonds to dealers rather than search for buyers on their own (or use brokers). They thereby transfer the search risk (the possibility that prices move during the search process) to the dealer. The dealer is compensated for accepting this risk, and relieving the customer of it, via the bid-offer spread. The greater the risk, the wider the spread.

Underwriters

When a dealer purchases *new* bonds from an issuer (notice the word "issuer" in this case replaces "seller"), the dealer is known as an "underwriter." Here, too, the issuer does not want to directly look for buyers. If the issuer/dealer agreement is one of "best efforts," then the dealer works to sell at the price prescribed by the agreement. The dealer in this situation is really acting as a broker, who is paid fees for the amount actually sold and is under no obligation to sell the amount underwritten. An alternative arrangement is one in which the dealer actually purchases the paper from the issuer and then distributes it to customers at the price that clears the market. In this case, the underwriter is acting as a true dealer—a principal in the transaction—earning a bid/offer spread and absorbing the search risk.

Dealer Options

Upon purchasing a bond from a customer (or underwriting an issuance), the dealer actually has a number of alternatives, only one of which (though probably the most profitable) is selling to an investor at the offer price. Suppose a dealer has purchased a bond and has had trouble finding a buyer who is willing to pay the offer price. The dealer is worried that the price will soon change. She has the following options:[6]

- *Reduce the offer price.* This, of course, eats into the bid-offer spread, the dealer's profit. But that's true of any business: If you need to get rid of the merchandise, you put it on sale. Furthermore, depending on the amount of time the dealer has already held onto the security, and her assessment of market conditions, the offer price may need to drop below the original bid price and thus entail a loss.
- *Sell to another dealer.* That dealer may have a customer the first dealer does not have, or she may be short the bond and need to cover (to be explained later), or she may simply want to hold the bond in inventory. The price will likely be below the original dealer's offer, since the second dealer needs to make a spread as well (which is one reason dealers prefer to trade with customers rather than with other dealers).[7]
- *Sell short a similar bond that the dealer does not own, since the dealer may be experiencing difficulty selling this particular bond at the offer price.*[8] In what way is the other bond similar? Same issuer, close maturity, corresponding characteristics (coupon, callability, etc.). What does this accomplish? Say the price of the original bond declines, forcing a loss upon the dealer when it is finally sold. Since the bond the dealer actually sold (short) is similar to the first, its price will likely decline as well. The dealer has sold it without owning it, so it needs to be repurchased, but now at a price below the sale price. This lower price compensates the dealer for the loss on the original bond. This procedure is known as a "hedge," and is explained in Chapter 12.[9]
- *Enter into any of a variety of derivative contracts as an alternative to hedging by selling short a related bond.* Remember, derivative contracts are structured so that they produce profit or loss to the contract counterparties in the event of a *change* in the price of the underlying instrument (see the explanation of interest-rate swaps in Chapter 17). The dealer is worried about a change in the price of the bond between the time she purchased it from one customer and finally finds a second customer to sell

to. An appropriate derivative will offset the loss. Once the bond is finally sold, the derivative contract is unwound or offset. (Chapter 17 shows how this is accomplished with interest-rate swaps.)

Why might a dealer have trouble locating a buyer at the offer price? The market may have shifted abruptly after the original purchase from the customer. Perhaps the dealer misassessed the market and put too strong a bid on the bond to begin with. Or, quite simply, liquidity has diminished—the presence of customers, hence the volume of activity, turned lower than what the dealer has come to expect (without the price changing).

What about the other direction? Dealers, as stated above, quote a two-way market. What if a dealer sells a bond to a customer, and the dealer does not own it yet?[10] The dealer would look to buy the bond at the bid price from another customer looking to sell and thereby earn the bid-offer spread. What if a customer is not around or is unwilling to sell at the dealer's bid? The dealer has options similar to those above: wait and search, accepting the risk of a price increase; raise the bid price; buy from another dealer; buy a different, but related bond; or enter into a derivative contract that would produce profit in case the market price of the bond rises in the interim.

Dealer Financing

What happens if, after the dealer has purchased the bond, none of the above options is attractive? Perhaps they are too expensive or simply unavailable. Or what if the dealer actively wants to keep the bonds, anticipating a positive market movement?

Let's assume that any of these conditions apply and that the trading day is over. The bond needs to be paid for, yet the dealer hasn't sold it. What to do? What do any people do when they've bought something without the funds to pay for it? Borrow the money. Dealers borrow lots of money because they hold lots of inventory. Recall the grocery store and car dealer analogies earlier. Both buy goods in advance of their sale. The supplier or manufacturer wants to get paid soon after delivery. Grocers and auto dealers don't sell all the cereal or cars the day they arrive.

How do they bridge the gap? They borrow money until the items are sold, at which time they repay the loan.[11] The same is true with bond dealers. This activity is known as "financing" and is the responsibility of the financing, or funding, desk at the dealer firm.

The actual instrument used by dealers is known as a repurchase agreement, or "repo." Repos are discussed extensively in the next chapter, but for present purposes you can think of a repo as a loan collateralized by a bond, the very bond the dealer has acquired and must pay for. The dynamics surrounding the transaction are straightforward (see Figure 21.2).

> *Step 1.* A dealer buys a bond, has not sold it by the end of the trading day, and needs to pay for it.
>
> *Step 2.* Using the bond as collateral, the dealer borrows the funds from a short-term lender and pays for the bond.
>
> *Step 3.* When the bond is finally sold, the dealer repays the principal plus interest to the repo trader.
>
> *Step 4.* The dealer retrieves the bond collateral and sends it to the bond buyer.

Figure 21.3 illustrates the completed process.

You need to know a few more things about repos as they pertain to dealers (for elaboration see Chapter 22).

- *"Haircut."* The lender of funds to the dealer via the repo transaction is at risk that the dealer will not be able to repay the loan. The lender will, therefore, lend less than the market value of the bond. This way, should the dealer default on the loan and the collateral be sold to meet the dealer's obligation, there is some room for the collateral to fall in price and for the lender to still

FIGURE 21.2 The Dynamics of a Repurchase Agreement

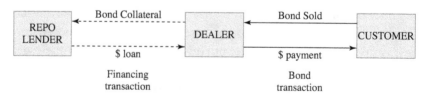

FIGURE 21.3 Completion of a Repurchase Agreement

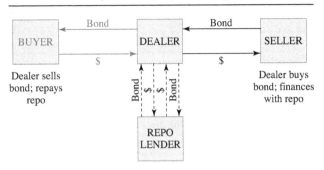

be made whole. This discount to the bond's value is known as the repo "haircut."

- *Net carry.* During the period that the dealer owns the bond (until it is finally sold to an investor or to another dealer), the dealer is entitled to the interest the bond pays, known as the "carry."[12] Over the same period of time, the dealer owes interest, according to the repo rate—the financing rate—to the lender of the funds. The difference between the two rates is the "net carry." Note that repo is a very short-term instrument, and hence it carries the short-term interest rate in the marketplace. The bond's interest rate is essentially its yield.[13] The yield depends on the bond's position on the yield curve (as in Chapter 8). Hence, the more positively sloped the yield curve is, the greater the dealer's (net) carry profits. Conversely, a negatively sloped yield curve would entail negative net carry, or a loss to the dealer while he or she is holding the bond.[14]

- *Term repo.* While most repurchase agreements are for overnight, there is a longer-term market, known as "term repo." Typically, the funding desk will look to lock in a longer-term borrowing rate when it expects that the security (or group of securities) will be held in the dealer inventory for longer than one day. This may happen if, for example, the bond is one for which there is not a large customer base. Or the funding desk has been made aware that the dealer intends to keep the security (or group), anticipating a market shift.[15] The interest rate on term repo will differ from that on overnight, reflecting the yield curve in the money market (see Chapter 14).

Repurchase agreements are not the only financing vehicle available to bond dealers. But they typically are the cheapest, since a specific, liquid security (or part of a portfolio of securities) collateralizes the borrowing. If repo financing is unavailable, the dealer can use its credit line at a bank. The interest rate would typically be higher because the bank needs to pay interest to depositors and earn a profit. The dealer may also issue commercial paper, if it has access to that market. Since it is uncollateralized (see Chapter 14), its rate is above that on repos.[16]

Reverse Repos and Short Positions

The previous section examines a common bond dealer problem—how to pay for bonds purchased but not yet sold—and its solution via repo financing. What about the opposite situation? What if the dealer sold bonds to satisfy a customer request, but has not purchased them by day's end? The bond still must be delivered.

The answer is almost obvious. The dealer's dilemma here is the opposite of that in the previous section. There the dealer had the bond, but needed money to pay for it. Here the dealer has the money—the bond is sold and will be paid for upon delivery—but needs the bond. So the dealer does the opposite from what the previous dealer must do. Instead of borrowing money using the bond as collateral, the dealer borrows the bond using money as collateral. The only reason this is "almost" obvious is that borrowing bonds is not as intuitive as borrowing money.

Now it's time to recognize that a repurchase agreement is not simply a collateralized borrowing. It is much more than that. In a normal borrowing situation, the holder of the collateral—the lender—has no rights to the collateral other than the right to take possession in the event of default by the borrower. He certainly can't sell it in the absence of default. Not so with a repo. As explained more fully in Chapter 22, the structure of the repo actually allows the lender to sell the bond collateral (because he actually "owns" the security while the loan is outstanding). The bond must be returned (resold to the borrower) when the loan is repaid.

The problem is solved. Recall that our dealer has sold a bond but has not purchased it. This is what he (that is, the funding desk) does.

He searches for a party in need of financing (remember, our dealer has money, having sold the bond) and who has that particular bond to supply as collateral.[17] Our dealer makes the loan, takes the bond as collateral, and delivers the bond to the customer who purchased it, which started this whole process. Here are the dynamics, the mirror image of the earlier situation, in which the dealer needed to borrow money:

Step 1. A dealer sells a bond, has not purchased it by the end of the trading day, and needs to deliver it.

Step 2. Using the cash from the sale, the dealer lends to a party looking for financing, and willing to supply the bond as collateral. The dealer delivers the bond to the purchaser.

Step 3. When the bond is finally purchased in the market, the dealer returns it to the bond lender/money borrower and retrieves the cash.

Step 4. The cash is used to pay for the bond purchase, plus interest accrued on the bond in the interim.

Note that during this process—that is, after Steps 1 and 2—the dealer is "short" the bond. True, the dealer has delivered the bond to the seller, satisfying his obligation. But it was a bond the dealer did not own; it was just borrowed. Ultimately, the dealer needs to buy the bond and pay off the borrowing—Steps 3 and 4.

Some terminology is necessary here. There are, obviously, two parties to a repo transaction, as there are to all trades. In this second case, the dealer is acting in the opposite capacity compared to the first case. The dealer is, therefore, said to be doing a *reverse* repurchase agreement. The repo counterparty in this case—the borrower of the funds, supplier of the collateral—is doing the repurchase agreement.

In the previous case the dealer was "long," that is, the dealer owned the bond during the repo period. As such, the dealer earned the bond's interest rate, or yield, and paid the repo rate, during the time period of the transactions. What are the corresponding dynamics here where the dealer is short of the bond? Again, the answer is very sensible. Between Steps 1 and 3, the bond has earned interest. The dealer sold it first and then bought the bond some days later. The dealer, therefore, will *pay* the bond's interest for those interim days. When the dealer is long, he receives the bond's yield; when the dealer is short, he pays the bond's yield. At the same time, the dealer in our case has lent funds to a borrower—the supplier of the bond (Step 3). The dealer *receives* the repo interest rate. Therefore, the net carry is the reverse of the previous case—it is the repo rate less the bond's yield. And the more positively sloped the yield curve, the more *negative* the net carry for a dealer who is short. A negatively sloped curve produces positive carry!

Proprietary Trading

We might term the above situations requiring dealer financing— whether of money or of bonds—as *passive* positions. In response to a customer purchase or sale, the dealer, unable to effect the opposite trade, had to go out and either borrow money to pay for bonds not sold, or borrow bonds to deliver on an uncovered sale. The dealer didn't intend to be long or short. His market-making activity simply required it.

Most bond dealers are empowered to take *active* long or short positions. Although not a pure market-making task, acting on an expected future bond price movement is quite natural for an entity involved in the markets. For example, a dealer expecting an imminent price increase would raise the bid (and the offer) to induce selling interest on the part of customers (or other dealers). If the dealer is successful in attracting sellers, and is correct in her expectations, she would look to sell the bonds once the market price increases. Should the anticipated price movement not occur before day's end—and the dealer has not altered her view—the bond will be carried to the next day. The funding desk, therefore, will need to finance the bond overnight, employing a repurchase agreement. The dynamics (including the net carry) are the same as above; the driving force is different.

Conversely, a dealer expecting a bond's price to decline would lower his offer (and the bid) to attract buyers. If successful, the dealer would wait to cover the sale of the bond with a purchase only after the expected price drop occurs. Should the trading day end without the realization, the bond still must be delivered. The funding desk will enter into a reverse repo in order to acquire the bond, using the cash from the bond sale. Again, this is an active short compared to the passive one examined above, but otherwise works the same way.

Risk and Hedging

Let's return to the dealer who bought a bond to satisfy a customer's need to sell. Let's assume that the dealer is unable to sell that day and is unwilling to take a proprietary position in the bond. The bond is financed with a repo. The dealer is subject to the risk that the bond price may decline between its purchase and sale dates, possibly by more than the bid-offer spread. What can the dealer do in the interim?

The dealer can hedge. Hedging is elaborated upon in Chapter 12. Briefly, hedging refers to entering into a supplemental trade in which the resultant risk position is in the opposite direction of a trade already in place. Suppose our dealer purchased a five-year Treasury note and hasn't sold it. To hedge its exposure to interest-rate movements, the dealer may borrow and sell short a different Treasury note with similar remaining maturity. As we learned previously, this is accomplised through a reverse repurchase agreement. Why? Suppose interest rates, as feared, do rise, causing the yield of the newly purchased five-year note to increase and its price to decrease. Since they are both Treasuries and are situated on the same point of the yield curve, the yield on the hedging note should rise as well, causing its price to decline in consonance with the price of the original note. So:

- When the dealer finally sells the first note, it will absorb a loss because of the lower price;
- At the same time the dealer will close out the short—by buying the second note in the market at its now lower price and returning it to the lender to retrieve the original, higher price—and earn a profit.

That's the goal of the hedge—the loss on the bond purchased is offset by the gain on the bond acting as the hedge. Of course, the opposite may occur. Interest rates may fall in the interim so that dealer profits by selling the original bond at a price above that paid for. In that case, though, the dealer will pay a *higher* price for the hedging bond to close out the short position. Now the loss on the hedge offsets the gain on the original bond at risk. But that's what hedging is all about—it works in both directions as a position that offsets risk.

Conversely, the dealer may have sold a bond and is short, not having succeeded in buying it before the close of trading. As we've seen, this necessitates borrowing the bond (via a reverse repo). In this situation the dealer is at risk of the bond's price *rising* before the short is covered by buying the bond. To hedge, the dealer *purchases* a similar bond (that is, the same maturity range, coupon, issuer sector, etc.). If the first bond should rise in value:

- The dealer will incur a loss when the bond is purchased in order to return it to the bond lender, covering the short.
- The second, hedging, bond will likely rise in value as well, producing a profit when sold and offsetting the loss.

Note that a dealer's hedging activity is not confined to a position that must be open overnight or longer, hence requiring repurchase agreements. Suppose the dealer purchased a bond in the morning and sold it in the afternoon. No financing is required. But the dealer faced price risk during the intervening hours. To hedge that risk, the dealer would sell short the companion bond soon after the original bond was purchased. Once the original bond is sold, the dealer buys back the hedging bond. No borrowing of money or bonds was necessary because all the activity took place on the same day.

Residual Risk

No hedge is perfect. Not even a dealer's hedge. The reason is that no two securities, or no two financial instruments in general, correlate perfectly with each other. (If they did, they'd be the same security!) Go back to the dealer who purchased a bond from a customer, say, a five-year note. Let's recall something about Treasury bonds from Chapter 3. The U.S. government issues five-year notes regularly. Suppose the most recently issued note carries a 4.25% coupon. It is the most actively traded Treasury bond in that maturity range; indeed it is the benchmark.[18] However, the dealer did not purchase the benchmark five-year Treasury. Instead, the "five-year" note the customer sold to the dealer was issued by the Treasury three months ago. It still carries the label "five-year" since the issue date is only three months removed. Its coupon could very well be different, for example, 4%.[19] Upon purchasing this "old" five-year, a reasonable hedge would be to sell short the benchmark five-year, as (1) their maturities are close to each other; (2) their coupons are not very different; and (3) they share the same issuer (the U.S. Treasury). Their price movements should display a high degree of correlation, but not a perfect correlation because they're not the same bond. Okay. Let's examine the dynamics of a common scenario from the dealer's perspective. Assume the pair of trades (the note plus the hedge) are initiated on day 1, and unwound some days later, day 2. The following scenario would have taken place:

Day 1

1. The dealer purchases the old five-year note from the customer at a yield of 4.22%. The dealer then finances the purchase with a repurchase agreement.
2. The dealer sells short the benchmark five-year note at a yield of 4.25%. The dealer then borrows on the note through a reverse repurchase agreement.

Day 2

1. The old five-year note is sold, but its yield has risen to 4.29%. The borrowing on the repo is repaid.
2. The short position in the benchmark five-year note is covered by the dealer purchasing the bond at a higher yield of 4.30%. The bond is returned to close out the reverse repo.

Between the purchase date and sale date, the old five-year note rose in yield, just as the dealer worried would happen. Its price fell, reflecting the yield increase. The dealer lost some money on the bond. On the other hand, the yield on the hedge rose as well. Therefore, when the dealer buys it back, it will be at a *lower* price than the one at which the dealer sold it. The dealer will make money on the hedge, offsetting the loss on the bond purchase. However, one does not completely offset the other. The yield increase on the hedge—the benchmark five-year note—was only 5 basis points, whereas the yield increase on the bond purchased from the customer was 7 basis points. Hence, the price decline on the old five-year exceeded that on the benchmark. The profit on the hedge, therefore, only partially offset the loss on the original bond. Still, had the dealer not hedged at all, the loss would have been greater, as nothing would have been offset. The possibility that a hedge is less than perfect—reflecting the fact that the two instruments involved are not perfect substitutes—is known as "basis risk."[20]

Similar risk, but in the opposite direction, exists when the dealer is short a bond and hedges with a different issue. Suppose a dealer sells a bond to a customer, but has not purchased it. The dealer is at risk that the price of the bond will rise by the time it is purchased. To hedge, the dealer *buys* a bond correlated with the bond posing the risk. If a shift in interest rates occurs in the market, the two bonds should move in the same direction so that a loss on one is balanced by a gain on the other. But they will not necessarily change equally, which results in basis risk.[21]

Underwriting Corporate Bonds

We learned earlier that dealers purchase bonds from a corporation that is looking to issue new securities in order to raise cash. This process, known as "underwriting," presents a risk to the dealer similar to the one we've just discussed. The corporate bonds are not sold out immediately. The dealer will end up holding a sizable amount of securities in inventory for a time, during which the dealer is exposed to the risk that the price will fall below what the dealer paid the issuer.

The standard procedure—and now you can see how sensible it is—involves the underwriter selling short Treasury bonds of similar maturity to hedge the corporates purchased. Why? For the same reason that the dealer above shorted a bond in response to a bond purchased from a customer. Should yields rise in the marketplace, causing the corporate bond inventory to decline in value, the Treasury bonds shorted should decline in price as well. When the corporates are finally sold at the now lower price, the underwriter recoups the loss by purchasing and covering the short with now cheaper Treasuries.[22] This way the underwriter preserves his or her bid-offer spread.

Wait. Things are not so easy. The yield on a corporate bond equals that of a similar maturity Treasury plus a spread for credit risk (Chapter 9). Sure, when yields rise on Treasuries, they do so on corporates. But if the credit spread widens at the same time, the price of the Treasury bond sold short as the hedge will not decline to the extent that the corporate bond will, thus mitigating (though not erasing) the effectiveness of the hedge. This is exactly the same scenario as experienced by our dealer in the previous section, who hedged an "old" five-year Treasury note with the benchmark Treasury. In this case, too, the corporate bond's yield might increase by more than the Treasury's. In fact, it is possible for the spread to widen even as Treasury yields are stagnant. In that case the corporate bonds will decline in value, and the Treasury hedge will do nothing. So here is our second source of basis risk—credit spread.[23]

A third common basis risk for the dealer involves the yield curve. Suppose that the dealer purchases a seven-year bond from a customer and hedges by selling short the benchmark five-year Treasury note. The hedge will work only if the yields on both bonds move in the same direction and to the same degree.[24] Movement in the same direction is likely, but degree of movement is another story. We've investigated this in Chapter 8 on yield curves and learned that yields across maturities do not correlate perfectly, hence, yield curve basis risk.

Swap Market-Making

Were we to finish this chapter with the previous section, it would belong in last generation's book. A financial institution with a significant presence in the market as a bond dealer is likely to be a swap dealer as well. Although a bit less natural, since swaps are not really a security that is bought and sold, the basic principles about dealers do apply quite directly to swaps. We'll look at an interest-rate swap dealer, but the mechanics are similar for the other swaps discussed in this book. Because of the similarities to bonds, we can go through this relatively briefly (but we elaborate when the swap dealer structure differs from that of a bond dealer).

A bond dealer stands ready to purchase bonds from a customer when the customer wants to sell (even though the dealer does not necessarily want to buy) and to sell bonds to a customer when the customer wishes to buy (even though the dealer does not necessarily wish to sell). A swap dealer stands ready to write a contract to pay the fixed rate and receive the floating rate *when* a customer wants to receive the fixed rate and pay the floating, and write a contract to receive the fixed rate and pay the floating *when* the customer desires to pay the fixed rate and

FIGURE 21.4 Swap Dealer's Relationship with Each of Two Counterparties

receive the floating. Figure 21.4 shows the dealer's relationship with each of the two customers. Notice the similarities with the basic bond dealer structure of Figure 21.1.

The swap dealer provides a "risk removal" service to customers, or counterparties. Without the dealer, swap participants would need to search for counterparties on their own. During the search period, swap rates can change. The dealer offers a rate to the customer, and, if accepted, the customer is done. Now it's the dealer's burden to find a counterparty, thus taking on the risk of rate change during the process. For this the dealer is paid the bid-offer spread on the swap. The similarity—perhaps the word is parallel?—to bonds should be clear. Therefore, just as with bonds, the swap bid-offer spread is a function of market depth, swap rate volatility, term (maturity) of the swap, and dealer competition.

Counterparty Risk

The bid-offer spread on an interest-rate swap (as well as other types of swaps) compensates the swaps dealer for all the risks found in bond market-making, plus one not found there: counterparty default risk. Compare Figures 21.1 and 21.4. Both show the dealer between two customers, acting as intermediary in the pair of transactions. But there's a subtle, yet crucial, difference. In Figure 21.1, once the bond dealer has sold the bond to the second customer after purchasing it from the first (or purchased it from the second customer after selling it to the first), the dealer is out of the picture. The seller has his money, the buyer has her bond. Any risk the bond might present thereafter— interest rate, credit, volatility, etc.—is the customer's to bear; the dealer is done. Now examine the situation in Figure 21.4, which continues even after the swap dealer has found the second counterparty. *The relationship of the swap dealer to each counterparty remains.* The dealer is definitely *not* out of the picture. Sure, the dealer has no interest rate risk; an increase in LIBOR requires more payment by the dealer on one side, but exactly the same increase in receipts on the other side. Furthermore, the dealer has no loans extended to either of the counterparties, as swaps involve no principal. So there is no interest-rate, credit, or other risk in the traditional sense. However, one of the counterparties can go out of business. He or she no longer performs on the swap. What happens? As we concluded in Chapter 17, the swap terminates. But wait! The swap on the other side is left standing! So, what's wrong with that?

Here is the problem. Suppose the swap is for five years, 6% against LIBOR (ignoring the dealer's bid-offer spread). So A pays 6% to, and receives LIBOR from, the dealer. B does the reverse with the dealer. Two years after the swap's inception, B is gone. If new three-year swap rates at that time happens to be 6% against LIBOR (a pretty strong coincidence), the dealer just enters a new swap for the same notional amount, with C, who pays the dealer LIBOR and receives 6%. But what if the three-year swap rate is 7%? The dealer will now lose 1% per year for the next three years.[25] Conversely, the dealer loses should A go out of business when swap rates decline.

How do dealers address this counterparty risk? The same way all swap market participants attempt to—they ask for collateral. Note that the customer, facing the risk of the dealer not performing on the swap at some later date, theoretically has the right to request collateral from the dealer as well. Issues such as who posts collateral, the amount of collateral as a percentage of the notional size of the swap and mark to market of the collateral are discussed at length in Chapter 17.

The Swap Dealer's Options

Suppose a swap dealer, in response to a customer request, has entered into a five-year interest-rate swap to pay the customer fixed and receive floating, say 6% against three-month LIBOR, properly collateralized. The dealer then searches for another customer who would be willing to pay fixed to the dealer, preferably 6.05% so that the dealer can earn his or her bid-offer spread and receive LIBOR. No one is coming forward. The dealer has a number of options. The discussion is brief (except for the last point) as you will readily see the similarities with the dealer's options in the bond scenarios above (again except for the last option).

- *Lower the offer, that is, agree to accept a lower fixed rate from customers in order to attract a counterparty.* The rate may even need to be lowered to the point of the dealer taking a loss on the swap.
- *Enter the second, offsetting swap with another dealer.* This will likely compromise the original dealer's bid-offer spread.
- *Find a customer willing to be the counterparty to, say, a seven-year interest-rate swap.* Rather than accepting the market risk of continuing to search for a five-year swap counterparty, the dealer agrees to the seven-year swap, receiving fixed and paying floating. Later—hours or days—when a five-year counterparty is finally located, the dealer will also offset the seven-year swap. In this way, the dealer is hedged against swap market movements during the interim. However, the dealer is exposed to the basis risk that the five- and seven-year swap rates do not move perfectly in tandem.
- *Purchase the benchmark five-year Treasury bond, and finance it with a repurchase agreement.* What will this accomplish? It's not a swap! Remember, our dealer is paying fixed and receiving LIBOR in response to the customer's request. Doesn't a bond purchase/repo financing arrangement produce a fixed rate (the bond's yield) receipt and a floating rate (the repo rate) payment? Is this not the opposite of the swap the dealer just entered into? Yes, it is. Doesn't this, therefore, constitute a hedge? You bet it does. Once the dealer locates a swap counter party, the dealer sells the bond and repays the repo loan. Should the five-year swap rate fall in the interim, causing the dealer a loss, chances are the bond yield will fall as well, thus providing the dealer with an offsetting gain.[26]

Now you can go through the same four alternatives—but in reverse—facing a dealer who has entered into a five-year swap to receive fixed and pay floating but who has not found another customer with whom to do the opposite. The fourth option would then be to sell the five-year Treasury short with a reverse repo. Keep in mind that an "inventory" of swap positions, unlike bonds, entails no financing or securities borrowing by the dealer. The bond hedge does.

22

REPURCHASE
AGREEMENTS

Look at the building you're in. You see the walls, the ceiling, the floor. You might see elevators, electric fixtures, windows, and so on. You probably *don't* see the building's foundation or the beams that hold up each floor and which rest on the foundation. But you're surely aware that without the foundation, there is no building! Well, the same thing applies to the fixed-income market. Participants see bonds of all types and sizes. They see money market instruments, a host of derivatives, foreign currencies, and on and on. But supporting all this is the repurchase agreement market. The bond market, so to speak, rests on the repo market.

This chapter provides an excursion into the world of repos. Repos are crucial for dealers, as we've seen in Chapter 21. They are crucial for hedge funds, as we will see in Chapter 24. But they are equally important for all fixed-income investors who:

- Transact with dealers, who in turn rely on repos to "make markets."
- Invest excess cash in repurchase agreements.
- Use repos for leverage, if necessary.
- Can be party to reverse repurchase agreements.
- Own bonds whose yields are influenced by their specific repo financing rates.

I use a bond dealer as the platform to explain all about repos because it makes the structure of the instrument and the dynamics of its applications more intuitive. Along the way I make clear the relevance to investors.

Financing Long Positions

Suppose a dealer is asked to purchase a bond from a customer. Let's work with a specific bond, say, the U.S. Treasury benchmark ten-year note. The customer is happy with the dealer's bid of par, and the trade takes place. Working with a calendar will make everything clear. Suppose this trade occurs on Monday. U.S. Treasuries settle "next day." This means that the dealer sends payment to the customer, and the customer delivers the bond to the dealer, on Tuesday. What does the dealer now (Monday) do with the bond? Since the dealer did not purchase it in anticipation of a price increase (which would constitute "proprietary trading" as described Chapter 21), the salesforce will attempt to sell the bond at the dealer's offer price, say, 100.1.[1] Suppose they are successful. Both trades settle on Tuesday—the dealer takes delivery of the bond from the first and delivers it to the second customer; the dealer is paid by the second customer and pays the first—and the dealer earns the bid-offer spread. This is shown in Figure 22.1. Note that no repo is necessary in this situation.

Not all bonds purchased are sold "same day." Suppose that the bond in question is purchased on Monday, but it is not until Tuesday that the salesforce has found a buyer at the dealer's offer price. The bond still needs to be paid for by the dealer—on Tuesday—but revenue from the sale won't arrive until Wednesday, as shown in Figure 22.2. The firm needs

FIGURE 22.1 Offsetting Trades: No Financing

MONDAY	TUESDAY
• Customer I sells 10-year note to dealer at 100	Customer I
• Customer II buys 10-year note from dealer at 100.1	Bond ↓ ↑ 100
	Dealer
	Bond ↓ ↑ 100.1
	Customer II

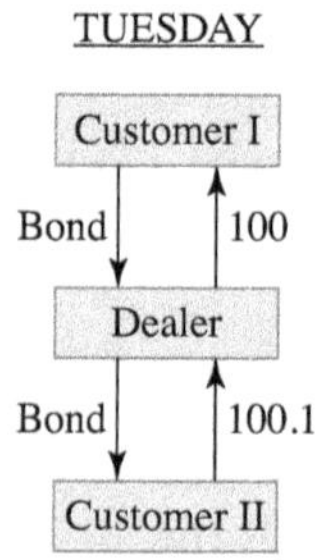

money for one day. Many lenders, known as "money market investors" (as discussed in Chapter 14), are in the business of lending overnight. A clever way for the dealer to get financing is by offering this very bond as collateral. Isn't it a perfect arrangement? The dealer owns the bond between Tuesday and Wednesday—look at the solid arrows in Figure 22.2. So the dealer borrows the funds on Tuesday for one day and provides the bond as collateral. Crucially, repurchase agreements "settle same day," so the dealer gets the funds that day. When the second customer pays for the bond on Wednesday, the dealer takes the money, repays the repo lender, retrieves the collateral, and delivers the bond to the customer. The pair of repo transactions are denoted with dashed arrows in the figure.

Question: When would the dealer not be able to repay the borrowing? Only if the second customer cannot honor his or her commitment to purchase the bond on Wednesday. In that case the dealer, of course, does not deliver the bond. Rather, it is turned over to the money market lender, who becomes an owner in place of a collateral holder.

Pretty straightforward? It is. Except the actual market and legal mechanics are not exactly as described above. And that is where repos differ from all other money market instruments and, as you will see, where the name repurchase agreements comes from.

FIGURE 22.2 Long Position: Dealer Financing with Repo

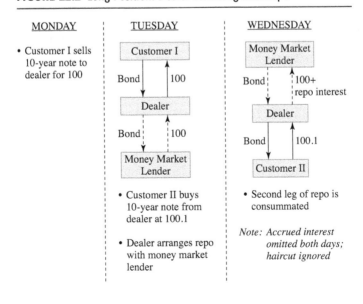

The True Nature of Repos

A repurchase agreement is, technically, not a loan. Read the words carefully. "Agreement" signifies a contract, a contract to do something *later*. A repo actually consists of two transactions—a *cash transaction* and a *forward contract*. This is what happens. On Tuesday, the dealer *sells* the bond to the money market lender (MM). This is the first leg of the repo. *At the same time*, the dealer and MM enter into a contract calling for the dealer to *repurchase* the bond from MM on Wednesday. The dealer uses the money received from MM on Tuesday (the repo settles same day) to pay for the bond purchased from the first customer (C1). On Wednesday, the second leg of the repo—that is, the forward contract— is fulfilled. The dealer repurchases the bond from MM, sends it to the second customer (C2), whose payment for purchasing the bond is used by the dealer to pay MM. Figure 22.2 shows this clearly.

What is MM's compensation? Since it is providing funds to the dealer for one day, MM is effectively an overnight lender and deserves an overnight interest rate. The interest rate—known as the "repo rate"—is implicit in the prices of the pair of transactions between MM and the dealer. That is, the repurchase price that the dealer pays MM on Wednesday equals Tuesday's purchase price plus an additional amount equal to one day's interest.[2]

Compared to Tuesday, on Wednesday the bond is one day closer to its coupon payment date. Therefore, even if the bond's *quoted* price is unchanged between the two days, it is worth more. This phenomenon, known in the bond market as "accrued interest," has major implications for repo dynamics. On Tuesday, when the dealer pays C1 the bid price of the bond, all the bond's accrued interest since the last coupon date is added to the quoted price to produce the invoice price. On Wednesday, when the dealer sells the bond to C2 at the offer price, all the bond's accrued interest is again added. Now, though, there is an extra day of accrued interest. The dealer, therefore, earns this one day of accrued interest, separate from the bid-offer spread. This is sensible. Look at Figure 22.2. The dealer has bridged the one-day time gap between the sale by C1 and the purchase by C2. Hence, the dealer is entitled to interest for that day.[3] Annualized, this equals the bond's yield.[4]

Net Carry

We conclude above that during the time period under discussion, when the dealer owns the bond and finances it via a repo, the dealer earns the bond's yield (via its accrued interest) and pays the repo "lender" the repo interest rate. Suppose the yield on the bond is 4% and the repo rate 2%. The dealer's net carry on the position is the difference, or 2%. It seems like a wide spread, and for little risk. After all, this is on top of the dealer's bid-offer spread, which is the dealer's compensation for acting as a dealer. Not exactly. You need to be reminded of two points. First, interest rates are annualized, and our time period is only one day. So the size of the position has to be pretty large for 2% to produce anything of significance. Furthermore, the bid-offer spread is not a certainty. The dealer can't be sure, when asked by the customer to bid on the bond, that the bond can be sold at the offer. And the larger the position, the greater the risk. This is one of the main themes of the previous chapter.

One thing is clear. The size of the net carry depends on the *shape* of the yield curve, not the *level* of interest rates. Repos lie on the shortest end of the yield curve. The bond's yield depends on its maturity. If the yield curve is positively sloped, as it is in our example, net carry is positive. Consider a different situation in which rates are much lower, say, because the economy is in recession. The repo rate may be at 1%, and the dealer may be financing a five-year note, shorter than the example above, yielding 3.5%. Net carry is 2.5%, better than in our example, despite lower rates in the market. Why? Because the section of the yield curve relevant to the position is steeper. Conversely, a negatively sloped yield curve produces negative net carry—the bond yields less than the cost of repo financing.

Leverage

Dealers do not purchase bonds solely for customer purposes. If the trader anticipates a price increase she may take the bond into "position," that is, purchase the bond for her own account in order to hold until the price increase materializes. In that case the dealer will likely raise the bid in order to attract sellers. Referring to the timeline in

Figure 22.2, the dynamics are the same. Say the bond is purchased on Monday and delivered to the dealer and paid for on Tuesday. In this case, the dealer will not look to sell the bond Monday. She would prefer to wait for the anticipated price increase. Assume for the sake of simplicity that the price does rise on Tuesday. The dealer sells, for settlement Wednesday. Again, the bond needs to be financed via repo overnight Tuesday, and the dynamics play out as above. In short, the dealer employed a repo in order to actively establish a position with another party's money, as opposed to passively respond to a customer order. This is leverage.

Investors employ repurchase agreements for leverage the same way dealers do. An investor with, say, $1 million, can purchase a bond with the cash, and then double the purchase by financing the second bond with a repo exactly as above. More than likely, the dealer who sold the bond to the investor will also be the repo lender to the customer. (Where did the dealer get the funds to lend? We get to that later in this chapter.)

Risk and Haircuts

Before going on to short positions, we need to examine the unique risks of repurchase agreements and how the market handles them. Recall that the money market lender has provided funds to the dealer overnight. The dealer's obligation is to repurchase the bond on Wednesday, paying the original purchase price plus the repo interest, economically equivalent to "repaying" a loan with interest. MM faces the risk that the dealer will be unable to honor its obligation. Suppose the dealer defaults. Clearly, if the dealer cannot repurchase the bond, MM is not obligated to deliver it to the dealer. Looking to recover its money, MM sells the bond in the market (economically equivalent to selling the collateral on a defaulted loan). The risk to MM, therefore, is that the proceeds from selling the bond fail to meet the loan obligation. This is a relatively low order of risk. *The lender of funds in a repo transaction stands to lose money only if the borrower defaults* and *the bond declines in value at the same time.*[5] In the event of default, the amount lost equals the difference between the loan amount and the market value of the bond. To ensure that the market value of the bond will be able to match the amount of the loan, MM will not extend funds to the full value of the bond; MM will take a "haircut."

The purpose of the repo haircut is to allow room for price declines in the collateral and nonetheless make the money market lender "whole" should the repo counterparty—in this case the dealer—default. As such, it is understandable that the size of the haircut will be a function of the riskiness and price volatility of the bond/collateral. Long-term bonds require greater haircuts because their prices fall faster when interest rates rise (Chapter 3). Similarly, if, instead of government bonds, the repurchase agreements involves corporate (or other credit risky) bonds, the haircut will be deeper, since, besides pure interest-rate risk, the price of the bond can fall in response to credit shifts.[6]

Creating Short Positions

Let's reverse the situation. A dealer on Monday is asked by a customer to *sell* a ten-year note, and the note is not in the dealer's inventory.[7] If the dealer wants to stay in business, he will offer the bond to the customer and worry about acquiring it later. Say the dealer offers the bond at 100.1, and the customer agrees to purchase. The bond is to be delivered for payment on Tuesday. The salesforce will attempt on Monday to buy the bond from another customer, preferably at the dealer's bid price of par. If successful, both trades settle Tuesday, and no repurchase agreement is necessary. The pair of trades will match exactly as the first case above (shown in Figure 22.1), despite the fact that in this case the dealer sold prior to purchasing.

What if the salesforce is unsuccessful in acquiring the bond Monday? The bond must be delivered on Tuesday regardless. That's the dealer's problem, not the customer's. Suppose a seller is found on Tuesday. That's no help for that day's delivery, as the dealer will receive the bond on Wednesday. Instead of borrowing money to bridge the gap between Tuesday and Wednesday, as in the long position above, the dealer now needs to borrow the *bond* for a day. In the previous situation, the dealer had the bond, but needed money. Now the dealer has the money (the bond is sold and will be paid for on Tuesday) but needs the bond. Above, the dealer entered into a repurchase agreement to solve the problem. Here the dealer does the opposite—a *reverse* repurchase agreement. This is shown in Figure 22.3.

What exactly is a "reverse repurchase agreement"? Every bond transaction, as you know, involves a buyer and a seller. Every loan brings

FIGURE 22.3 Dealer Short Position

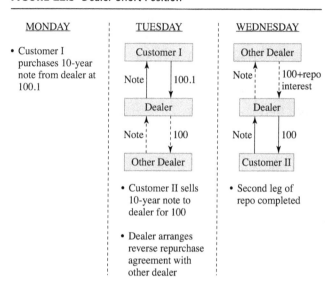

together a borrower and a lender. Every repo, by definition, requires a reverse repo. Here's how it works. On Tuesday, the repo desk searches for a counterparty who is looking for funds to finance that particular ten-year note that our dealer sold yesterday for delivery today. That counterparty may be another dealer who purchased the bond on Monday and had not sold it; that is, *that* dealer is in the same position now that our dealer was in in the previous example—in need of money. Or it may be a hedge fund borrowing money to leverage a long position in the ten-year note. Let's assume our dealer (D1) enters into the repo transaction with the other dealer (D2) as the counterparty.[8] As part of the first leg of the repo, D1 purchases the bond from D2. The funds come from D1's customer who initiated this entire process. Upon taking delivery of the bond on Tuesday, D1 delivers it to the customer in fulfillment of the original trade. (D2 uses the money received from D1 to pay *its* customer, but that is not our concern here.) D1 is now "short" the bond. The second leg of the repo takes place Wednesday. D2 *repurchases* the bond from D1. Where does D1 get the bond from, having delivered it yesterday to the initiating customer? From the second customer, who sold it to the dealer on Tuesday for delivery on Wednesday. D1 pays for the bond with the maturing repo money from D2. Got it? It's all in Figure 22.3.

Let's review the terminology. Both dealers have entered into a repo contract with each other. D2 did a "regular" repo—borrowed money to pay for a bond, using the very bond as collateral. D1 did the opposite—supplied the money and took the bond as collateral. (Technically, of course, and legally, D2 sold the bond and entered into a contract to repurchase; D1 bought the bond and agreed to resell.) Another word for opposite is "reverse." In sum, a reverse repurchase agreement is the vehicle for creating short positions.

Short Traders

No, short traders are not munchkins with a trading account. Dealers do not create short positions solely to accommodate customer purchases of bonds that aren't in the dealer's inventory, as in the scenario that concluded the last section. Dealers may actively initiate a short position. Suppose a trader anticipates a decline in a particular bond's price. She will instruct the salesforce to look for buyers of the bond, perhaps reducing the offer price to stimulate interest. When the bond is sold, the dealer will not initiate a search for a buyer immediately. Rather, she will wait until the expected market movement transpires. If it does not occur before the end of the day, the dealer will enter the next day short, and the bond will need to be borrowed, just as above. Alternatively, after responding to a customer's initiation of a buy order, just as the previous section, the dealer may decide to wait for a price decline, possibly into the next day. Once the price does decline (or the dealer no longer wishes to wait), a seller is sought, covering, or "unwinding," the short, just as was done above.

Hedge funds and other nondealer traders engage in short trades as well. Expecting a price decline, they will acquire the targeted bond through a reverse repo and sell it. The supplier of the bond—the repo counterparty—is typically a dealer, and is quite likely the same dealer to whom the bond is sold. The short position is later covered in a way similar to our dealer example above.

Net Carry Again

Let's examine the net carry of a short position, be it a dealer, hedge fund, or any other entity. Return to Figure 22.3. Our dealer's position in this situation is the same as the money market lender's position in

Figure 22.2. Both MM there and our dealer here are the suppliers of money and receivers of the bond on Tuesday. Their motivations, of course, are different. MM simply had cash to lend, and took the bond as collateral, structured as a repurchase agreement. Our dealer *needs the bond,* and uses the money as the vehicle to acquire it via the repurchase agreement. Indeed it must be via a repo, because if it would simply be a loan with the bond as collateral, how could our dealer then go ahead and deliver the bond to the customer? Structured as a repo, this becomes doable, since the dealer is now the owner—she actually *purchases* the bond on Tuesday. Observe that our dealer is the lender of the money in the (reverse) repo from Tuesday until Wednesday, just as MM was earlier. *The party doing the reverse repo earns the repo interest rate from the party doing the repo.*

The repo rate is the income for the short position. What's the cost? Recall our discussion of accrued interest for the dealer's long position earlier. The same thing applies here, but now the dealer is on the opposite side. On Tuesday our dealer, having sold the bond to the customer, receives the bond's quoted (offer) price plus the bond's accrued interest through Tuesday. On Wednesday our dealer purchases the bond from the second customer, paying the quoted (bid) price plus accrued interest through Wednesday. The dealer is effectively being charged one day of accrued interest. On an annualized basis, this is the bond's yield. Thus, we have shown that the net carry of a short position equals the repo rate less the bond's yield, just the reverse of a long position. But this is as it should be—it involves a *reverse* repo. Everything said earlier for the long financing position is now turned on its head. In particular, since bond yields are typically above repo rates, net carry on short positions tends to be negative, a loss. On the other hand, during negative yield curve periods, net carry for shorts will be positive, as repo rates then exceed bond yields. And the more negative the better!

Summary Thus Far

You probably are beginning to appreciate my characterization of repurchase agreements as the "foundation" of the bond market. Imagine our customer looking to sell a bond to a dealer and hearing the dealer say, "Hold on. I can't give you a 'bid' on your bond until I find out if we have enough money to pay for it." That is not the response of a market *maker*. There would be no market. The dealer does not respond that way because she knows that if, after buying the bond from the customer the bond cannot be sold that day (or even for a number of days), the dealer's financing desk can acquire the cash to pay for it through a repurchase agreement using that very bond. Similarly, imagine a customer's chagrin upon hearing the dealer, responding to the customer's need to purchase a bond, say, "Please hold while I look for the bond." In normal circumstances (we'll see some exceptions below), the dealer can offer the bond without checking whether it is in his or her inventory or not. Because even if it is not, the repo desk can acquire the bond via a reverse repurchase agreement, using the very cash generated from the sale as the means to borrow the bond. Repos, in short, give dealers the wherewithal to be dealers.

Repos for Institutional Investors

We know now how important repurchase agreements are for dealers. We've also mentioned that hedge funds can use repos to leverage long positions and to establish short positions, and we'll see more of this in Chapter 24. What about portfolio managers who don't short or use leverage? What's the benefit of the repo market to them? First, portfolio managers indirectly need repos because they require dealers to be able to bid for securities at any time and offer securities without owning them, which dealers can do only because there is a repo market behind them. Separately, investment managers typically have cash that needs to be invested short term (for example, funds that they've received but have not yet committed to securities purchases). Lending the funds via a repo produces income and provides collateral. Repos also allow investors to make efficient use of their securities. Here's what I mean. Suppose a pension fund (an example of an institutional investor) owns the ten-year Treasury bond. A dealer or a hedge fund might be looking for that bond, having sold it short. Buying it is not an option for either of them because: (1) the dealer sold it yesterday, was not able to purchase it, and it needs to be delivered today; or (2) the hedge fund is speculating that the bond will fall in price, so wants to be short, but must deliver the bond having sold it. The dealer or hedge fund requests to enter into a reverse repo,

332 • Advanced Topics

buying the bond from the pension fund (and delivering it to satisfy its short obligation) and agreeing to sell it back to the pension fund the next day. The pension fund manager, having entered into a repo (the opposite of the dealer or hedge fund's reverse repo), has cash for a day, which can be invested, say, in overnight commercial paper. If the commercial paper rate exceeds the repo rate (which the pension fund pays to the dealer or hedge fund)—which should be the case since commercial paper is an uncollateralized loan—the pension fund manager will add income to the bond position.[9]

Other Repo Applications

Let's return to the very first example, where the dealer, having purchased the bond to accommodate the customer, cannot sell it on Monday. Rather than going into Tuesday exposed to the risk of the bond falling in price, the dealer sells a different bond before the close of business Monday. For example, the bond purchased may be the Treasury's "old" ten-year note (issued prior to the current ten-year note), and the dealer sells short the benchmark ten-year. Why? Should interest rates rise between Monday and Tuesday, hurting the price of the old ten-year just purchased by the dealer, the price decline on the benchmark ten-year short position will produce profits, offsetting the loss.[10] The acquired old ten-year note is financed through a repo; the benchmark is shorted via a reverse repo. Conversely, recall the second example earlier in which the dealer sold the old ten-year note at a customer's request and was not be able to purchase it the same day. The dealer may buy the benchmark ten-year as a hedge while she is short the old ten-year. The next day, when the short on the old ten-year is covered through a purchase, the benchmark is sold. This way, if yields decline in the interim and the dealer loses money having to purchase the old ten-year at a higher price than it was sold to the original customer, the benchmark ten-year will be sold at a profit. The old ten-year is acquired through a reverse repo, and the benchmark is financed with repo.

We discuss underwriting briefly in Chapter 21. Dealers purchase new bonds from corporations, holding them in position while they are being distributed. Dealers also make mortgage loans (or buy mortgages from others who have made the loans) and then package them into securities for sale to investors as mortgage-backed bonds. In either case, dealers need to finance the inventory until the bonds are fully distributed. Again, repurchase agreements are an ideal vehicle, with the corporate or mortgage bonds used as the collateral. Dealers also purchase these securities in the secondary market, and, if they are to unable to sell them on the same day, they finance them with repo, just as above. While the bonds are held, the dealer faces interest-rate risk. To hedge, dealers short Treasury bonds of similar maturity by acquiring them through a reverse repo.[11] Conversely, were the dealer to sell more of these corporate or mortgage-backed bonds to meet customer orders than the dealer owns, the securities can be acquired via a reverse repo. The dealer would then hedge the interest-rate exposure by *purchasing* Treasury bonds, financed through a repo.[12]

Hedge funds construct relative value trades.[13] As explained in Chapter 24, these trades can involve the purchase of one security and the short sale of another, related security. The hedge fund trader is expressing a view as to the *relative* yields of the two securities. One example is buying a ten-year Treasury note and shorting a five-year. Another is purchasing the secured bond of a corporation and selling short an unsecured issue. The long position is financed with a repurchase agreement; the short is created through a reverse repo.[14]

"Specials"

Wall Street uses funny words. In repo land, some bonds are deemed "special," but not because they look good, are printed on special paper, or have nice coupons. Here's how they get that title.

A customer calls a dealer and asks for an offer on a Treasury bond that hasn't traded in a while. Perhaps it is a 20-year bond. The U.S. Treasury hasn't issued these maturity bonds in many years. They exist, of course, but only in the secondary market as very old 30-year bonds. The customer asks for $50 million of the bonds. Our dealer must offer them or risk losing this customer's business in the future—or, worse, gaining a reputation that the dealer doesn't deal in "difficult" bonds, which may impugn its very status as a dealer. Not owning the bonds, the dealer presents a high offer price compared to what the yield curve would imply. (Too high is no good; that would be tantamount to not offering.)

Suppose that the customer accepts the offer. It is Monday, and the bonds must be delivered Tuesday. The salesforce will get to work trying to buy the bonds from other investors, but it will have a difficult time because these bonds don't trade actively due to their age. Suppose $40 million remain unpurchased by the end of day Monday. The repo desk's job on Tuesday is to find these bonds and acquire $10 million through a reverse repo in order to deliver that day. Now it gets interesting.

The bonds exist, of course. But the same factors preventing the dealer from buying the necessary amount on Monday will frustrate the repo desk's search to borrow the bonds on Tuesday.[15] Whoever does have them and is willing to lend them will be in the driver's seat, so to speak. Say dealer D owns the bonds, or is representing investor I who owns them. Remember, our dealer is looking to do a reverse repo—lend money, take the bonds as collateral (or, technically, buy the bonds for Tuesday delivery with an agreement to resell them Wednesday). Since our dealer A is eager to lend money and dealer D is sitting pretty, dealer D can extract a concession from dealer A. If the general repo lending/borrowing rate is, say, 2.5%, a dealer may be forced to accept a significantly lower rate, perhaps 1.5%. That's what traders mean by "special." A bond trading special is one whose repo rate is below the general repo rate in the market. The reason for the specialness is the bond's scarcity, but not so much in the bond market, rather in the market for collateralized financing.[16]

While this dramatization is a good way to explain how a bond becomes "special," it is not the most common scenario. A more likely occurrence is a large short position in a bond by many market participants. For example, dealers create and underwrite mortgages and mortgage-backed securities. They hedge the interest-rate risk inherent in these bonds by shorting Treasury securities. Hedge funds as well buy these mortgage products and sell short Treasuries in order to create relative value trades (Chapter 24). The Treasury instrument typically used as the short is the benchmark ten-year note, because its maturity is similar to a new mortgage's "weighted-average life."[17] With many dealers and others looking to borrow these Treasuries via reverse repo, a scarcity is created, which becomes manifested as a relatively low (reverse) repo rate, following the same logic as above and hence its "specialness."

The U.S. Treasury sells its bonds at auctions. Each issue—T-bills, two-year notes, five-year notes, etc.—follows a regular calendar, some weekly, some monthly, some quarterly. Bond dealers participate in the auctions by buying for their own inventory as well as placing orders on behalf of customers. Investors can contract to purchase bonds from dealers prior to the auction. These are known as "forward trades" or "forward contracts," in which the dealer quotes a price (or yield) for the customer but will deliver the bonds only after the auction.[18] If there is substantial demand for the issue leading up to the auction, plus a strong actual auction, it is quite likely for the sum of cash (i.e., regular) and forward trades to have exceeded the number of bonds than the Treasury actually issues. In this case, dealers will be forced to short a large number of these bonds because there are more bonds sold than actually exist! They will need to acquire the bonds via reverse repurchase agreements. This pressure in the repo market by the bond borrowers/ money lenders seeking to acquire a large number of a specific bond gives holders of that bond—in this case the recently auctioned Treasury benchmark—the upper hand. They will be able to negotiate a lower interest rate for their borrowing. Since the repo rate using this bond as collateral is lower than the general repo rate, the bond is on special. Over time, as the auction date fades, some holders of the bond agree to sell (they will be enticed by the bond's higher price – see the next section) and the "specialness" dissipates; that is, the bond's repo rate approaches that for general collateral.

Repo Specialness and Bond Price

A bond trading on special is a repurchase agreement market phenomenon. Yet it will force repercussions on the bond itself. Suppose that the general repo rate is 3%. The Treasury ten-year, 5% note is on special, with a repo rate of 0.5%, and it is expected to continue this way, say, for three months (until the next ten-year auction). Dealers, as well as leveraged investors, find this note to be more attractive, all else the same, than other Treasury bonds, which need to be financed at the much higher general repo rate. How much more attractive? Per $100 of face value (ignoring the haircut), the cost savings equals $(3\% - 0.5\%) \times 100 \times 91/360 = 0.6319$.[19] Using the bond price sensitivity tools covered in Chapter 12, this translates into a yield difference of 0.08%, or 8 basis points.[20] The bond's "specialness" is worth 8 bps. What does this mean? Because of its cheaper financing rate, market participants bid up the price of the bond until this advantage is factored into the bond, forcing its yield to be 8 bps lower than it otherwise would.

This has an important implication. When choosing bonds to purchase (or sell short), investors and traders compare relative yields. They will observe this bond's yield as possibly being lower than that of its peers. With the above analysis, they can attribute 0.08% of this lower yield to the fact that the bond is trading special in the repo market. When the specialness subsides—very likely as a new auction of ten-year notes approaches—its yield will rise back up by 0.08% to "normal."

Term Repo Financing Decision

Return to the event that began this chapter: our dealer's customer wishing to sell the Treasury ten-year note on Monday. The dealer purchases it at the bid price and, not having sold it, turns to the repo desk for financing on Tuesday. Let's take another step. Since there is no guarantee that the dealer will sell the bond that day, the repo desk recognizes that it may be in the same position tomorrow. Suppose the desk concludes that it will likely need to borrow money for a week. Rather than enter into a repo contract for one day, which will require repaying the funds on Wednesday, then entering into a new repo, then doing the same on Thursday, and so on, the financing desk enters into a *term* repo contract—a repurchase agreement for longer than overnight, in this case one week. The repo counterparty purchases and pays for the bond on Tuesday, with an agreement to resell the bond—the repo desk agrees to repurchases it—the following Tuesday. Again, the repurchase price includes the repo interest rate. In this case, whereas the overnight repo rate is 3%, the one-week rate may be 3.1%, reflecting an upward sloping money market yield curve. If the bond is at par (again ignoring the haircut), the dealer will repurchase it for par plus $100 \times .031 \times 7/360$. By the end of the contract's term, the financing desk expects the bond to be sold by the dealer, thus providing the desk with the funds to repay the repo (and retrieve the bond).

The repo desk does not *have* to enter into a term repo if it anticipates needing funds for a week. It may choose to borrow overnight and roll over the repo. Of course, this places the dealer at risk of increasing repo rates while the position is being financed. But it also provides the opportunity of borrowing at lower rates should repo rates decline during the week. Determining the best course of action is part of the repo desk's job. It bears the burden of choosing whether to "lock in" financing via term repo or fund overnight and be subject to interest-rate movements.[21]

The funding desk must make a parallel choice with respect to reverse repurchase agreements. Suppose the dealer sold the 10-year Treasury on Monday to a customer and was not successful in purchasing it in the market (or intentionally wanted to be short the bond). On Tuesday, using the funds generated from the sale, the firm will need to do a reverse repo to acquire the bond. Expecting the dealer to be short, say, for two days, the repo desk can enter into a two-day reverse repo, lending the funds and thus acquiring the bond, for a fixed interest rate. Or, if the desk expects the repo rate to increase, it can lend overnight to acquire the bond and do another reverse repo Wednesday.

Matched Book

Go back to the first case once more, where the dealer needs to finance the bond it purchased but has not yet sold. Suppose the repo desk, expecting the bond to be held by the dealer for more than one day, borrows money for a one-week term, that is, until the following Tuesday. On Wednesday, however, the dealer sells the bond. The bond will need to be delivered Thursday. But it is in the hands of the repo money lender as collateral for another five days. The repo desk will need to arrange a five-day reverse repo for the same bond. On Thursday it acquires the bond from the reverse repo counterparty and delivers it to the customer who has purchased the bond. The customer's payment serves as the collateral for the reverse repo. This is shown in Figure 22.4. Between Thursday and the following Tuesday, the funding desk has both a repo and a reverse repo for the same bond, known as a "matched book" transaction. After the five days, both positions unwind symmetrically.

Here's another way to look at the funding desk's position. On Thursday, having received cash from the customer who purchased the bond, the desk has money to lend. At the same time, the desk still owes the money it borrowed from the first repo counterparty, RP1. That

FIGURE 22.4 Customer's Payment Serves as Collateral for Reverse Repo

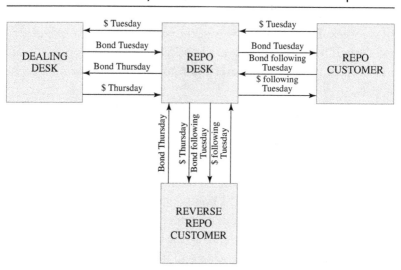

money is not due until the coming Tuesday because the original one-week term repo has not matured. Furthermore, that repo borrowing requires collateral, which the dealer has just delivered to the customer who purchased the bond. By acquiring the bond through a reverse repo for five days with a new counterparty, RP2, the desk has accomplished both tasks: It will be lending the available cash to RP2 and using the bond acquired to deliver to RP1 as collateral. For the next five days—Thursday through Tuesday—the funding desk is both a borrower (from RP1) and a lender (to RP2). It earns the repo rate from RP2 and pays the repo rate to RP1. The two transactions are "matched," as illustrated in Figure 22.5. In effect, the repo desk is acting as a financial intermediary. Like a bank, it is earning interest on loans and paying interest on borrowings. Whether the pair of repos is profitable or not—if

FIGURE 22.5 Matched Book

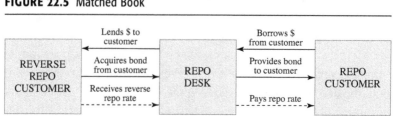

the spread between the rate on RP2 and that on RP1 is positive or negative—depends on the dynamics of the repo market between the initial funding date, Tuesday, and the current day, Thursday.

It is not uncommon for financing desks to intentionally create a situation of matched repurchase agreements. Let's revisit the above case from the start. On Tuesday the desk needs to borrow funds to pay for the dealer's purchase of the bond. Assume the desk fully expects the bond to be sold within a day or two, so that it needs to borrow for only two days. Yet it arranges a one-week term repo. Why? There are three possible reasons:

- *The desk wishes to act as an intermediary in the repo market.* Just as the market maker earns the bid-offer spread on the bond, the repo desk looks to earn the bid-offer (i.e., borrowing-lending) spread on repo financing. The desk expects funds to come in from the bond sale on Thursday. Since it has arranged financing until the following Tuesday, it plans to lend the money to a new repo borrower for five days.
- *The desk expects money market rates, particularly repo rates, to rise between Tuesday and Wednesday.* By doing a one-week repo on Tuesday, knowing full well that the funds will not be needed past Thursday, the desk has locked in a borrowing rate. Should rates rise as expected, the funding desk will then lend at the higher rate and earn a profit on the spread.
- *The repo desk does not have a view on repo rates generally.* It does, however, believe that this bond will soon go on "special." To appreciate this, we need to consider the reverse case. Suppose the dealer sold this ten-year Treasury note without owning it and fails to purchase it by the end of the day. On Tuesday, the repo desk needs to engineer a reverse repo in order to acquire the bond. Remember, it will be *receiving* the (reverse) repo rate. Although it expects the dealer to acquire the bond in a day or two, requiring only a two-day reverse repo, it enters into a one-week contract. The dealer succeeds in buying the bond and it arrives on Thursday. But the repo desk does not need to return it to the bond lender for another five days. By this time, if the repo desk is right, the bond is on special. That is, as we learned earlier, it can be used in a reverse repo to borrow money at a

rate well below the general repo rate. The repo desk, therefore, enters into a five-day special repo with a counterparty in need of this particular bond (reverse repo from the perspective of this counterparty). For the remaining five days the repo desk will be receiving the (higher) general repo rate, having arranged that when the bond was not on special, and paying the (lower) special repo rate, having correctly anticipated the bond's impending specialness.

In short, repo desks need not be passive accommodators to the market-making function of a bond dealer, providing funds or bonds as the case may be. Rather, by acting on both sides of a repo, they may be profit centers in their own right. In fact, *they don't even need the dealer at all.* Here's what they do.

On Monday morning our repo desk (Desk 0) lends money to the repo desk of another dealer (Desk 1) for, say, two weeks, at a repo rate of 2.5%. It takes the ten-year note as collateral. Where does it get the money? It finds another dealer (Desk 2) which needs this note for its short position. Desk 2 does a reverse repo with Desk 0; that is, in return for borrowing the bond, Desk 2 lends Desk 0 money for two weeks at, say, 2.45%. Desk 0's balance sheet, or "book," is matched, and it earns a 5 basis-point bid-offer spread. Alternatively, Desk 0 borrows for one week from Desk 2, using the note as collateral, perhaps at the same 2.5% rate at which it lent to Desk 1. Why is Desk 0 doing this? It believes repo rates will decline before the week is over. Next Monday it will roll over this repo with Desk 2 (or approach another repo desk) at a lower rate, say, 2.25%, but continue to earn 2.5% from Desk 1. Or Desk 0 has no view about repo rates changing. It thinks, instead, that this particular bond will go on special next week. When Desk 2 returns the bond, Desk 0 will, if correct, have one more week to use the bond in a reverse repo and pay a sharply lower rate of interest. We could have worked through this exercise with Desk 0 initiating the process from the other direction, as a money borrower/bond lender, anticipating a rise in repo interest rates. The analysis and reasoning for the cases are the same. They all constitute the funding desk's matched book.

23

CREDIT DERIVATIVES: THE FINAL FRONTIER

Why are credit derivatives considered the "final frontier"? All financial sectors—foreign exchange, interest rates, mortgages, equities, and commodities—have seen tremendous growth in derivatives over the decades. All except one: the credit sector.[1] But they've finally arrived, and with a vengeance. There are plenty of them. We cover four: total return swaps, credit default swaps, credit-linked notes, and collateralized debt obligations. An understanding of how these work will provide you with the foundation for understanding all the others.

Total Return Swaps

You already know the basic form of a swap from Chapter 17. It is a contract between counterparties that extends over an agreed-upon number of years, covers a specific notional amount of money, and in which the two parties promise to exchange—swap—payments to each other according to a predetermined formula. What distinguishes one swap from another is the precise formula. A total return swap (TRS) is shown in Figure 23.1.

The payments on total return swaps (and this is true generally of credit derivatives) refer to a particular security or portfolio (or index) of securities, known as the "reference security" (index). The security or portfolio referenced by the swap—and this is what makes it a *credit derivative*—contains credit risk. In Figure 23.1, the reference entity is

FIGURE 23.1 Total Return Swap

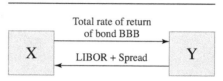

corporate bond BBB, with a four-year maturity and a 6% coupon. At the end of an agreed-upon term, say, six months, the total rate of return (coupon plus capital gain/loss) of BBB is calculated for the six months prior. Counterparty X pays counterparty Y that rate multiplied by the notional amount of the swap. In return, Y pays X six-month LIBOR, possibly plus a spread. Note that Y's payment to X, LIBOR, is set at the beginning of each period. X's payment to Y is not known until the period is over.

A couple of examples will be helpful. Say the contract begins on March 1. The bond is at par and six-month LIBOR 2.5%. Assume the spread over LIBOR in the TRS is 1%.

- On September 1, the bond has risen to $101, and LIBOR is at 2.25%. The bond's total return equals 3% (half the coupon) plus the 1% capital gain. X pays Y 4% times the notional amount. Y pays X 1.75% (half of 2.5% and 1%) times the notional.
- If instead the bond falls to $99, its total return is 3% less the 1% capital *loss*. X pays Y 2%.[2] Y pays 1.75%.
- What if the price declines to $95? The bond's capital loss is 5%, which exceeds the coupon. The total return is a *negative* 2%. Y pays X the 2% in addition to the 1.75%.
- Suppose company BBB defaults during the period the swap is in place. What happens to the swap agreement? Simple. It is treated just like a price decline. At default, bonds trade at a "recovery value" (see Chapter 9). If the recovery rate is 60%, the loss is 40%, which Y owes to X (plus the 1.75%).

Okay, we know what the contract does, but what's the point? By agreeing to receive the total return of bond BBB, the counterparty has achieved the same exposure to company BBB as purchasing the bond would have produced. Total return swaps, in other words, are "synthetic securities."[3] As such, they have quite a few applications in the market-place.

For Investors

At its most basic level, a TRS is transactionally efficient. There is no purchase of a bond, hence no delivery of the security or payment for it. No broker need be employed to search for the bond (see Chapter 21 on "search risk") and there is no dealer bid-asked spread to pay.[4] For the investor seeking to enhance return, there is another, more profound, benefit. Rather than purchase bond BBB outright, the investor can:

1. Enter the swap, receive the bond's total return, and pay LIBOR as well as the 1% spread.
2. Use the funds (since they have not been spent on the bond) and invest in a six-month money market instrument paying LIBOR plus a higher spread, say, 1.5%.

The TRS adds the credit risk of the counterparty to the investor. But the key idea is that the combination of points 1 and 2 increases the investor's return by 0.50% over what the bond would provide.

For Speculators

Speculators, as we've seen a number of times, purchase bonds in antic-ipation of price increases. They're less or not at all concerned with the coupon income. When the price reaches a target, they sell, hopefully for a gain. They typically borrow to fund the purchase, paying a short-term borrowing (usually repo) rate. In other words, they use other peo-ple's money to construct their portfolios. The TRS accomplishes the same thing. Receiving the bond's total return and paying LIBOR plus a spread mirrors the purchase bond/borrow short-term position. And it will be superior if the hedge fund's borrowing rate exceeds the LIBOR + spread that is required on the swap.

Suppose the speculator expects the bond to decline in price. Rather than borrow the bond (via a reverse repo) and sell it, he enters into a TRS to pay the bond's total return and receive LIBOR. As just explained above, if indeed the price of the bond falls by more than the coupon amount, the speculator will earn a profit on the TRS, just as he would by selling the actual bond short. In addition, if LIBOR is above the rate the speculator receives on the cash supplied as collateral for the bond (reverse repo) borrowing, the TRS alternative is superior.

For Dealers

Suppose a dealer has underwritten a bond issue of company BBB. The dealer has sold most of the bonds, but some remain on her books. Until they are sold, they present default risk. The dealer enters into a TRS referencing this bond to pay the total return. Should the price decline while the dealer is holding the bond (due to deterioration in BBB's creditworthiness), the dealer receives payment on the swap, covering the loss. Conversely, dealers sometimes sell more bonds than they hold in inventory. Until they cover their short, the price of the bond may *rise*, causing a loss when the short is covered. By agreeing to *receive* the total return on a TRS on bond BBB, the dealer is hedged.[5]

Credit Default Swaps

Credit default swaps (CDS) have taken the financial markets by storm. Although not as widespread as interest-rate swaps (IRS), their growth rate far exceeds that of interest-rate swaps at the same stage of development. CDS have wide applications as investing, trading, and hedging vehicles. They also serve as the basis for a number of other credit derivatives (e.g., credit-linked notes in the next section).

Figure 23.2 portrays a basic credit default swap. The similarities to interest-rate swaps covered at length in Chapter 17 should make the structure quite easy to grasp, but the differences will be obvious as well

FIGURE 23.2 Basic Credit Default Swap

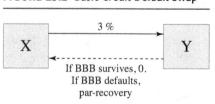

as profound. Whereas an IRS revolves around the fixed rate stated in the contract, a CDS revolves around a "reference entity." For the next five years (the "term" of the swap), counterparty X agrees to pay counterparty Y 3% of, say, $25 million (the notional amount). Most commonly, the $750,000 is apportioned quarterly. What does X receive in return? Unlike an IRS, X *does not* receive a regular stream of payments from Y. Instead, Y agrees to pay X in the event company BBB—the reference entity for this swap—defaults on its debt. How much? For simplicity, assume the CDS contract refers to a specific bond issued by BBB, a five-year 6.5% coupon. We know from Chapter 9 that postdefault, bond holders recover some money in bankruptcy court, depending on, among many variables, the firm's assets and where this particular bond stands in the company's capital structure (e.g., is it senior or subordinated). This is known as the "recovery value." Prior to the completion of the bankruptcy process, the firm's debt instruments trade in the "distressed debt" market, with the price reflecting traders' expectations as to the eventual recovery value. Suppose the recovery rate on bond BBB is 60%. Under the terms of the CDS contract, Y will pay X the difference—40%—or, for this particular contract, .40 × $25 million = $10 million.

Why have X and Y entered into this contract? In return for a steady income, Y is willing to accept the risk of a BBB default and the duty to pay up in that event. X's position is easy to understand as well. He owns $25 million of BBB's 6.5% bonds and seeks protection. Indeed, in the language of the marketplace X is identified as the "protection buyer," and Y is the "protection seller." X pays Y a protection "premium," 3% in this case. As long as BBB survives, X receives the 6.5% coupon and 100% at maturity from the company. Should company BBB default during the five years the contract is in place, X receives the recovery value of the bond (from BBB, via bankruptcy court, or by selling it in the distressed debt market) plus the difference between par and the recovery rate from counterparty Y. So X is covered whether BBB is dead or alive. But wait! This cannot be the sole motivation behind all Xs in the market. In many cases, perhaps even the majority of them, there are more CDS contracts outstanding on particular reference entities than there are bonds issued by those entities! Why are these Xs buying protection on bonds they don't own? We answer that fascinating question after we get a feel for what determines the cost of protection.

Determinants of the Cost of Protection

Let's examine X's position a little more carefully. X owns bond BBB and buys protection on it through a CDS from Y. Let's assume that the five-year term of the swap matches the maturity of BBB. If BBB survives the five years, X receives the bond's coupon plus $100 at maturity from BBB. If BBB defaults, X receives the coupon until that point, and now Y pays X the difference between BBB's recovery value and par. Again X receives $100 in total. Isn't this equivalent to a government five-year bond—coupons plus $100 guaranteed? (The "guarantee," though, comes from Y, not Uncle Sam. We return to this point later.) It certainly seems so. Therefore, we can appeal to the famous YCGSFN rule in finance: "You can't get somethin' for nothin'." In our context, this translates into the following: since X effectively takes no credit risk, she deserves no compensation for it. Why is the cost of protection—the CDS spread—3%? Because BBB's coupon is 6.5%, and the yield on a five-year Treasury note happens to be 3.5%. The cost of protection must be such that the buyer of protection's net yield is no better than that of a Treasury instrument of equal maturity—the 6.5% coupon less 3% protection leaves 3.5%. With the corresponding maturity Treasury yielding 3.5%, and the reference bond paying 6.5%, the bond's credit spread equals 3%. In short, the CDS spread on a reference bond must be the same as the bond's credit spread over a Treasury bond.

This is a crucial result. But it needs to be qualified. A number of factors prevent the perfect equality of a company's CDS spread and the credit spread of its bonds. The most obvious is CDS counterparty risk. YCGSFN is not totally applicable because the combined position of bond BBB and a CDS is not strictly a Treasury bond—Y might fail to pay in the event of BBB's default. And the lower the recovery value on the bond in event of default, the greater the likelihood of Y's inability to honor the CDS contract, since the payout is larger. Indeed, this risk of nonperformance by the protection seller of a CDS is of an order of magnitude greater than the performance risk faced by interest-rate swap counterparties. In an IRS, the risk is a function of interest-rate differentials, a relatively small amount. In a CDS, the risk reflects the debt principal (less recovery). X, therefore, will demand collateral from Y at the contract's inception. However, as we learned with respect to interest-rate swaps, collateral cannot completely remove performance risk, just as collateral on a bond is far from a perfect substitute for actual repayment.

Other factors may force a departure of the CDS premium from the bond's credit spread. One relates to the mechanics of the contract when the firm defaults. Firms, especially larger ones, have a number of debt securities outstanding. The protection buyer, in some cases, may have a choice as to which liability of the reference entity to claim compensation for. This can confer a valuable right on the CDS buyer. How so? The contract calls for the protection seller to pay par less the security's recovery value. Different debt instruments can have different recovery values. Another factor involves financing rates for purchasing the reference corporate bond.[6] These factors combine to create a differential between the CDS premium and the bond's spread, known as the "CDS basis." Because of the basis, investing in a corporate bond and buying CDS protection on it is not a perfect substitute for a Treasury bond. Still, in the big picture, since the basis is relatively small, movements in the CDS premium do mimic the reference credit's bond spread. Because of this result, the trading strategies described in the next section exist.

Speculating on Default

For many corporations, there are more CDS contracts outstanding than there are bonds—by a wide margin! This implies that there are many "investors" in the marketplace who have purchased protection on bonds that they do not own and, therefore, do not need to protect. What the heck are they doing?

They're speculating on default by company BBB. By purchasing five-year protection via a CDS contract, these investors will receive par less BBB's bond's recovery value should BBB default any time within the five years. Of course, the investors/speculators will be paying the protection premium to the counterparty until the time of default. But this is a small amount (3% per $100 of notional value in our example) compared to the receipt of $100 less a recovery value, which is typically no higher than $60. With the introduction of the CDS contract, *market participants for the first time have a vehicle through which they can speculate on a company defaulting.*[7] In short, a view that a company's prospects for survival are dim can be expressed via credit default swaps.

Must the speculator await actual default by the reference entity in order for his correct negative assessment of the company to bear fruit? Not at all. Suppose speculator S enters into a five-year CDS with a dealer, referencing Xerox Corporation, for a notional $10 million. Based on Xerox's creditworthiness, as perceived by market participants, the cost of protection is 4% annually (which is also the credit spread on Xerox's five-year bonds in the market). S does not own Xerox bonds. One year goes by (S has paid the dealer $400,000). Xerox is alive, but its earnings have deteriorated. So much so, that the spread on Xerox's bonds has widened by 1% and, concomitantly, new Xerox CDS contracts are written with a protection premium of 5%. Investor S had purchased protection on Xerox when protection was relatively cheap, 4%. Now that it has risen, S can profit in a manner similar to purchasing any asset at a lower price and holding it until the price rises—by selling the asset, in this case protection, at the higher price. S has four years remaining on his Xerox CDS contract with the dealer, correct? Assuming the 5% cost of protecting Xerox applies to new four-year CDS contracts, S simply enters into an offsetting CDS contract, this time *selling* protection on $10 million notional of Xerox debt for four years to another dealer. Figure 23.3 shows S's two CDS contracts. For the next four years, if Xerox survives, S will be paying $400,000 to the initial dealer and receiving $500,000 from the second dealer. If Xerox defaults, S is obligated to pay the second dealer the difference between par and the recovery value of $10 million face value of Xerox debt. But S will also receive exactly that same amount from the first dealer in the event of Xerox's default. Hence, having purchased protection on Xerox at 4% and now selling protection at 5%, investor S will be receiving a net cash flow of 1% on $10 million for the next four years (assuming, of course, the two dealers can honor their respective obligations).

FIGURE 23.3 Offsetting CDS Positions

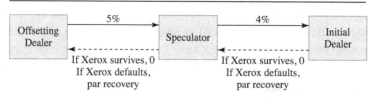

Offset, Unwind, or Assign

In the example above, our speculator has profited from making a correct call—credit deterioration at Xerox Corporation. He bought credit protection when it was cheap (4%) and sold it when it became expensive (5%). The second CDS offset the first. Indeed, this is known as an "offsetting transaction," as the net position of S with respect to Xerox is now "flat," and the money rolls in. This is just like buying a stock at a low price and selling it at a higher price, isn't it?

No. A speculator buying General Electric stock for $20 a share and then turning around and selling it for $24 a share has pocketed the $4 per share. Whatever happens to GE subsequently is of no concern to the speculator. Furthermore, the two entities taking the other sides of the two trades are then irrelevant. Not so with the CDS trades. It is clear from Figure 23.3 that our speculator now has a pair of CDS contracts to worry about. Only if both dealers make it through the next four years is our speculator home free.

Is there a way around this? Sure. Do the second, offsetting swap with the original dealer. Now the speculator has two four-year contracts with one dealer. The first requires payment of 4% to the dealer annually in return for Xerox default protection from the dealer. The second calls for *receipt* of 5% annually from the dealer in return for Xerox protection to the dealer. They're a "wash." Rather than keeping both contracts in place, the dealer simply pays the speculator a lump sum equal to the present discounted value of 1% (the difference between the two contracts) on $10 million over four years.[8] This is known as "unwinding" the CDS contract.

There is yet another alternative that is perhaps more attractive to the investor than unwinding. The investor may prefer searching among a number of dealers for the offsetting CDS rather than be beholden to just one, the dealer (D1) with whom the original contract was initiated. Say our investor enters into the offsetting CDS contract with a second dealer (D2). He now has two CDS positions: paying 4% to and receiving protection from D1; earning 5% from and offering protection to D2. The positions are as shown in Figure 23.3, where it is clear that our investor is effectively an intermediary between the two CDS dealers. Rather than face performance risk on the pair of contracts, the investor notifies D2 that D2 will simply take over the speculator's position in the original contract with D1. This is known as an "assignment," and the investor is now completely out of the picture.

D2, of course, is pretty happy with this arrangement. Rather than paying 5% for Xerox protection as agreed to with the investor, D2 is paying 4% to D1. Our investor is not stupid, however. He is transferring a valuable position to D2. How valuable? 1% of $10 million for the next four years. D2 will, therefore, pay as a lump sum the present discounted value of this future cash flow, which represents the value of the *original* CDS based on the *current* cost of Xerox protection, to the speculator.[9]

Marking to Market

The concept behind unwinding (or, for that matter, assigning) a CDS position is exactly the same as marking a position to market. Suppose our speculator decides to retain the Xerox CDS contract following the company's credit deterioration as documented above. Had the contract been unwound (or assigned), he would have received a lump sum payment equal to the present discounted value of 1% on $10 million over four years. Say this is worth $327,560.[10] This is the mark-to-market value of the CDS position to the speculator. Why? Based on current market conditions, the contract can be sold—that is, unwound or assigned—resulting in a payment of $327,560.

The idea, and calculation, of the mark-to-market (MTM) value of a CDS contract is useful in determining the degree of counterparty performance risk. If the contract is worth $327,560 to the speculator, it must be worth *negative* $327,560 to the counterparty. In order for the counterparty to get out of the contract with the speculator, he or she would have to pay the speculator this amount (since the speculator could receive this amount by assigning it). In a sense, $327,560 is what the counterparty *owes* the speculator now based on Xerox's condition. At the contract's inception, the counterparty owed the speculator nothing—both parties signed the contract without exchanging anything of value (other than their promises of future performance). But now that events have moved in his favor, the speculator wants to make sure that the counterparty has the means to fulfill this $327,560 obligation. He can ask the counterparty to increase the amount of collateral he or she initially posted by $327,560 (which might be termed a "margin call").[11]

Unfunded Credit Risk

Let's look a little more closely at the position of the credit protection seller—not the intermediary dealer, but the ultimate seller (party Y from way back at the beginning). In return for compensation to the buyer in the event of the reference credit's default, the seller receives the protection premium, 4% annually in our example. From the above analysis, we know that 4% equals (approximately) the credit spread of Xerox debt over the yield on a Treasury bond of equal maturity. Had this seller purchased the Xerox bond, she would be earning 7.5%—a 3.5% "pure" interest-rate payment (the yield on the Treasury) plus 4% for accepting the credit risk of Xerox. Instead, she is earning 4% from the CDS. Why not the other 3.5%? Because she is not lending any funds. Since no money is being extended to Xerox by the CDS seller, she is not entitled to any "time value of money" compensation. She *is* entitled to the 4%, because she is taking the same credit risk as the Xerox bond buyer. In short, credit default swaps allow for the separation of the two elements of a corporate bond—pure interest-rate risk and credit risk. The seller of protection via a CDS has taken "unfunded credit risk." So, here's another important conclusion: *Fixed income investors can now expand their portfolios—that is, diversify their exposure among more companies and/or industries—without tying up additional funds.*[12]

Credit-Linked Notes

The past decade witnessed a boom in "structured products."[13] These securities are so termed because, like a building, they comprise many interrelated parts. Structured products come in two types: a combination of instruments, typically a cash product plus one or more derivatives; and a decomposition of a security, or a portfolio of securities, into various offspring securities. Credit-linked notes are a prominent example of the first type. Collateralized debt obligations (CDOs) are the most famous example of the second.

The basic structure of a credit-linked note (CLN) is shown in Figure 23.4. A "special purpose entity" (SPE) is formed by the "structurer," typically an investment bank. The SPE is, for argument's sake, a company whose sole purpose is to issue bonds to investors and use the proceeds of

FIGURE 23.4 Credit-linked Note

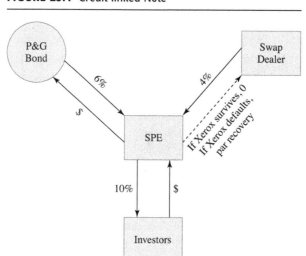

the issuance to purchase securities and, possibly, enter into derivative contracts. This particular SPE has issued $100 million of a five-year note to various investors, each purchasing the same note. We'll get to the coupon soon. The key is what the SPE does with the $100 million it raised.

The SPE purchases $100 million in five-year bonds of Procter & Gamble (P&G), an investment grade (AA) rated issuer. The bond pays 6% (2.5% more than the Treasury's 3.5% yield). This means that the SPE has $6 million each year to pass on to the noteholders. Well, they could have done that themselves. So, in addition, the SPE enters into a five-year credit default swap, as a protection seller, on $100 million notional of Xerox Corporation. For this it receives 4% per annum, just as above. It passes this on to the bond investors as well. The bond's coupon, therefore, is 10%. Not bad.

Let's take stock. If everything goes well, P&G pays its coupon, and Xerox survives the five years. The investor earns 10%. This is the investor's motivation for purchasing the CLN. What if Xerox defaults at some point within the term of the CDS contract or, equivalently, the life of the CLN? As the protection seller, the SPE pays the CDS dealer the difference between par and Xerox's recovery value. Where does the SPE get the funds to pay off the dealer? The CLN agreement specifies that the P&G bond is sold, the proceeds are used to pay the CDS counterparty—the protection buyer—and the investors keep what remains. This is why the CDS dealer does not worry much about counterparty risk—he holds the P&G bond as collateral. In short, if Xerox survives the five-year term of the CLN, the note investor receives 10% plus principal at maturity. Should Xerox default, the investor earns the 10% until that time, and then gets the recovery value of the Xerox debt referenced by the CDS embedded in the CLN.

Let's hold off for a moment considering what happens should P&G default. More importantly, let's ask why the investor is receiving this high yield. The answer seems obvious: He's accepting both credit risks, that of Xerox and P&G, hence is entitled to both credit spreads:

3.5% Treasury yield (pure time value of money)
2.5% P&G credit spread
4 % Xerox credit spread
_____
10 % total yield

It is very instructive to compare this investment with a portfolio consisting of one P&G bond and one Xerox bond. Isn't the investor accepting credit risk from both P&G and Xerox in that portfolio as well? If she were to take $100 million and put half into the P&G bond and half into Xerox, the yield would be 6.75%—half of P&G's yield (6%) and half of Xerox's (7.5%). With the CLN, on the other hand, the investor is spending the same $100 million and earning 10%! Why?

Here's the reason: In the portfolio, half of the $100 million is exposed to P&G and half to Xerox. If *either* defaults, the investor is exposed only up to $50 million. So the yield is the average of the two, just like any portfolio equally allocated to two investments. In the CLN, however, the *full* $100 million is exposed to Xerox, and the *full* $100 million is exposed to P&G. Should *either* default, the investor loses $100 million (less the recovery value). *That* is what distinguishes a CLN, my friend.[14]

One last thing. What if P&G defaults? The investment grade bond serving as the collateral for the CDS in a CLN, and providing some income as well, is typically of better quality than the CDS reference credit (as it is in our example, P&G compared to Xerox). But, of course, default is possible. In that case, the CLN matures, the investment grade bond fetches its recovery value, the CDS is unwound at its market value, and the net proceeds are distributed to the investors (unless the agreement stipulates that the dealer/structurer can replace it with another approved bond). What if both bonds default? The CLN investors cannot lose more than the initial value of their investment. Therefore, if the recovery value of P&G is less than the amount owed by the SPE to the CDS dealer for Xerox, the dealer suffers that loss. It is for this reason that the CLN's coupon is actually slightly less than 10%. The CLN investor does not quite take *both* P&G and Xerox default risks. The greater the correlation between Xerox and P&G default probabilities, the more likely a common default will occur, and the lower the CLN yield. This idea of correlation reappears in the next section, in a more profound way.

Collateralized Debt Obligations

Collateralized debt obligations (CDOs) evolved from collateralized mortgage obligations (CMOs), probably the first of its genre. CMOs took mortgage securities and sliced them up into pieces (tranches) with various types and degrees of risk, each of which attracted a different type of investor. CDOs do the same sort of thing with corporate debt obligations, loans, or bonds (or asset-backed securities). Enough with the background. Let's get to work.

The basic CDO structure is pictured in Figure 23.5. An SPE is formed to purchase corporate obligations. It is a "company" that owns nothing but financial assets. It acquires the funds with which to purchase these assets by issuing bonds. These bonds are the CDOs—debt obligations of the SPE, collateralized by the SPE's financial assets. So far, it is similar to the SPE above which issued the CLN. But here's the crucial difference. All the purchasers of the CLN own the same security, perhaps of different amounts. The whole point of the CDO structure, by contrast, is the issuance of *different* types of bonds—known as "tranches"—in order to appeal to investors with different risk appetites.

There are three fundamental elements to every CDO structure:[15]

1. The assets—the collateral—purchased and owned by the SPE, consisting of loans, bonds, and derivatives, if any.
2. The liabilities, or debt instruments (tranches), issued by the SPE—the CDOs.
3. Rules—similar to corporate bond covenants—governing the behavior of the SPE and its obligations to the bondholders.

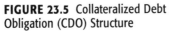

FIGURE 23.5 Collateralized Debt Obligation (CDO) Structure

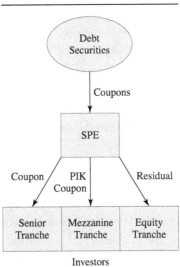

We'll work with a simple, unadorned CDO which will serve to highlight the basic structural concepts, attractiveness to investors, and risk. This CDO owns four assets, shown in Table 23.1. X and Y are portfolios of investment grade bonds, with Y of a lower order. For example, X might contain noncyclical firms, while Y includes cyclicals. Z is a speculative grade portfolio, which explains its high yield.[16] CP denotes commercial paper. It is of prime grade, providing liquidity to the SPE, as well as serving another function to be explained below. Coupon in the table means the average rate in each group.

TABLE 23.1 Assets of CDO

Bond Portfolio	Amount	Coupon
X	$120 MM	6 %
Y	$180 MM	7 %
Z	$ 90 MM	9.5%
CP	$ 10 MM	4 %

CDO Tranches

The SPE in our example sells three tranches of debt securities:[17]

- $300 million senior, 5%
- $80 million mezzanine, 7.25%, PIK (payment in kind)
- $20 million "equity"

The first tranche is *senior* in the following sense: Moneys received by the SPE from its assets are distributed first to this tranche to make interest and, later, principal payments. Hence, it is similar to a senior bond in a corporate organization. Under this structure, in order for the senior tranche holders to lose any money at all, $100 million of the assets need to default, *plus* they provide *zero* recovery value in event of default.[18] X, Y, and Z are all diversified portfolios. The chances of a one out of four default rate of that intense type are extremely slim. Investors recognize this. So do the rating agencies. The senior tranche, therefore, will probably receive a AAA rating, *even though the assets in the SPE themselves are rated below AAA*, and some substantially so. Because of the low risk, the interest rate on the senior tranche is relatively low, 5%. It is important to note that this low rate is the major "driver" of the deal. With the SPE'S assets earning much higher rates and three-quarters of the debt receiving just 5%, there is quite a bit left over. We'll, of course, come back to this later.

The *mezzanine* tranche is subordinate to the senior. However, it is senior to the equity tranche, hence it has some cushion. In our example, mezzanine holders are paid 7.25% by the SPE, to reflect their greater risk compared to the seniors—quite similar to a corporate bond subordinated to the senior secured. But here's a crucial difference between this bond and a normal corporate subordinate bond. If a corporation has earnings to pay interest on its senior obligations, but not to the subordinate bondholders, it defaults, triggering bankruptcy with all its ramifications regarding restructuring, asset liquidation, and the like. Not in this case. As long as the SPE services the senior tranche (and other stipulations are met, discussed below), even if it misses a payment to the mezzanine bondholders, this does not constitute default. Rather, the missed interest payments are added to the bond's principal. In short, the mezzanine tranche functions as a payment-in-kind (PIK) bond, allowing an issuer to pay interest in the form of more bonds.[19]

The *equity* tranche is technically not "equity"; it is a debt instrument as are the others. It is referred to this way because it behaves like equity. The equity tranche holders receive the net income of the SPE after all expenses, including interest and principal to the senior and mezzanine tranches, are paid. In market terms, equity tranche holders are entitled to the "residuals," just like the stockholders of a corporation. Indeed, now you can see that the structure of the SPE is similar to a corporation. Compare the SPE's balance sheet, shown in Table 23.2, with that of the shoe producer in Chapter 9. The similarity of the hierarchies of the liabilities is obvious.

One expense the SPE must pay is fees to a bond manager. Why a manager? The assets in the SPE are dynamic, not static. A manager is hired to:

- Trade the bond portfolio, that is, attempt to anticipate downgrades, price declines, etc., as well as ensure that the "tests" (see below) are withstood.
- Maintain a minimum degree of asset diversification.[20]
- Sell bonds to pay off portions of the senior tranche in response to certain events ("triggers"—explained below).
- Reinvest maturing bonds, recovery values following any default, and cash received from calls (unless the CDO is near maturity).

As compensation for performing these services, the manager is paid an annual percentage fee (plus a potential bonus at the end of the CDO's life). We ignore this in our calculations.

TABLE 23.2 Balance Sheet of Special Purpose Entity (CDO)

Assets		Liabilities	
X bonds:	$120 MM	Senior Debt:	$300 MM
Y bonds:	$180 MM	Subordinated Debt:	$80 MM
Z bonds:	$90 MM	Residual Owners:	$20 MM
Commercial Paper:	$10 MM		

Rules and Tests

The third element in a CDO is the set of rules governing the allocation of cash received from the assets by the SPE to the various claimants and, in some cases, their retention by the SPE. Most of these rules involve "credit enhancements." They are so termed because their purpose is to reduce the credit risk faced by senior debt investors. Less risk means lower required yield, thereby increasing the residual. Common rules include:

- *Overcollateralization (O/C) test.* From the perspective of the senior debt holders, O/C equals the ratio of the assets held by the SPE to the face amount of the senior debt.[21] It measures the degree of protection—the buffer, if you will—enjoyed by the senior tranche from potential defaults of the SPE's assets. Should the ratio fall below a predetermined minimum level, a portion of the senior tranche is paid off—known as "early amortization"—until the ratio is reestablished.
- *Interest coverage ratio test.* Similar to the coverage ratio for corporate bonds, this measures the income generated by assets relative to the senior tranche's interest expense. If it drops below a specific level, payments to the equity holders are diverted to the senior tranche.
- *Reserve account.* Funds invested in commercial paper (or other money market instruments) are considered "reserves." Some CDO structures specify that in certain situations relating to the quality of the portfolio, the SPV must add to the reserve account rather than pay the equity holders. Notice the similarity between this and retained earnings in a corporate structure. However, whereas retained earnings of a corporation are usually invested in assets targeted to achieve a high return for shareholders (unless they're used to build up the firm's liquidity), in the CDO structure the funds diverted to commercial paper earn a low rate. Hence, it builds a greater cushion for the senior debt holders at the expense of the equity tranche's desire for income.
- *Callability.* The equity tranche investors have the right to call the deal, that is, sell the SPV's assets and pay off the senior and mezzanine debt, pocketing the difference. They will do so only

if it is in their interest, for example, if the assets have risen in value significantly.

- *Management fees.* The portfolio manager employed by the SPE is typically paid in parts. For example, $\frac{1}{8}$ of 1% of the assets as a senior obligation, plus $\frac{3}{8}$ of 1% only after all tranches (except equity) have been paid their coupons. There may be a performance bonus at maturity if a hurdle rate of return for the equity holders is achieved.

Our CDO example ignores the interest coverage test; the O/C test will be enough to illustrate the implications of this sort of rule. At the deal's inception, as can be seen from the balance sheet, the senior tranche is 33% overcollateralized ($400/$300). We will assume that the O/C test requires a minimum of 30%. As stated earlier, we'll omit the manager's fee in the calculations, and we'll also assume that the deal is not called. Let's work through a number of scenarios, which is the best way to illustrate how the cash from the collateral is distributed to the tranches, what happens when the O/C test fails, and the effects of default.[22]

Scenario Analysis

Scenario 1: Everything's Cool

The assets owned by the SPE pay what was promised each year.
From Table 23.1, the SPE's income is:

$$6\% \times \$120 \text{ million} + 7\% \times \$180 \text{ million} + 9.5\% \times \$90 \text{ million}$$
$$+ 4\% \times \$10 \text{ million} = \$28.75 \text{ million}.$$

Interest distributions, for each of the two years, to the tranches shown in Table 23.2, are:

- Senior tranche holders receive 5% × $300 million = $15 million.
- Mezzanine tranche holders receive 7.25% × $80 million = $5.8 million.
- Which leaves $28.75 million − $15 million − $5.8 million = $7.95 million for the equity tranche investors.

Even if we subtract portfolio management fees plus other expenses incurred in maintaining the SPE, the return to the equity tranche is stellar. Just to keep things simple (since they are complicated enough), we'll keep the CDO's life to two years. Assuming that the assets are sold at par at that time, consistent with this perfect scenario, the senior and mezzanine tranches receive their principal, and the equity tranche gets what's left over. In this case, this equals the equity tranche holders' original $20 million investment, since the assets are intact.

Scenario 2: Improvement

The assets appreciate in value, due, possibly, to an improvement in credit quality.

Income to the senior and mezzanine tranches is unchanged compared to the previous scenario, since the appreciation does not affect the bonds' coupons. Furthermore, at the end of two years, these tranches are entitled only to their principal. Since the assets are sold above par, only the equity investors benefit. Just like the bondholder-stockholder arrangement in a corporation, the bondholders' income is capped by the promised payments, while the stockholders are entitled to all the upside.

Scenario 3: Deterioration—Downgrade

Some of the firms in the Y group deteriorate after the first year. Recall that Y contains cyclical companies, so this might be the result of a macroeconomic downturn. In response, their credit ratings are lowered. Let's examine the implications for the CDO.

- *Deterioration is not default.* The bonds are still paying their coupons to the SPE. However, their reduced credit quality means that investors demand a wider spread over Treasuries than the bonds are currently yielding. Since the bonds' coupons are fixed, their prices fall. But lower prices do not affect the cash flows to the SPE; hence the SPE maintains its interest payments to the tranches.[23] At the end of the second year, if prices do not recover and the bonds have not matured, they will be sold to meet the SPE's termination. In that case, any losses on principal are first absorbed by the equity tranche, then the mezzanine, before the senior holders lose a penny.

- *The deterioration of the collateral causes the prices of the CDOs—that is, the bonds issued by the SPE—to decline.* This is even though the tranches are still receiving their promised payments. The equity tranche suffers most, the mezzanine less so. Note that even though the mezzanine tranche has declined in value, at this point it is "still good for the money." That is, since none of the bonds have defaulted, the mezzanine tranche will be paid in full at the end of the second year.[24] Were a holder of the mezzanine tranche to sell *now*, the price would be below par. The senior tranche may not decline in price at all, depending on the depth of the decline in collateral value. For example, if the bonds in group Y fall by 10%, or $18 million, there is still quite a bit of room before the senior tranche suffers any loss.

- *Since none of the SPE's assets have actually defaulted, their "book value" is unaffected.* Hence, the O/C ratio is unchanged, and the payments to the tranches proceed as stated. (An O/C test based on market value would show a decline.) The next scenario examines the result of an O/C test failure.

- *A cash reserve adjustment may be triggered.* Some CDO covenants call for additions into reserves in response to asset deterioration without waiting for default. Indeed, this is meant to protect senior tranche holders against *future* default. For example, the rule may state that for every bond owned by the SPE that is downgraded, the cash reserves—commercial paper in our case—must be increased by 5% of the face value downgraded. Suppose that $20 million of bonds were downgraded in year 1. Then $1 million (5% × $20 million) of the equity tranche's payment is diverted to purchase commercial paper, leaving them only $6.95 million. If the deterioration remains just that—deterioration, not default—then the equity holders will recover their diverted payment next year.

Since there are no defaults, the senior and mezzanine tranches receive the same interest payments in year 2, and their full principals. The SPE's earnings in year 2 are somewhat higher, $28.79 million, as it owns $1 million in additional commercial paper. The equity tranche's residual cash flows at the end of year 2 are, therefore, $28.79 million − $15 million − $5.8 million, or $7.99 million in interest and now $21 million in principal. The tranche's rate of return is somewhat lower because commercial paper earns less than the primary assets in the SPE's portfolio.

Scenario 4: Deterioration—Default

This is where the risk to the tranches ultimately lies (if the investors hold on until the CDO's maturity). We need to analyze this carefully, so we'll proceed by degree of default. Assume that the defaults occur just before coupon payments are made to the tranches at the end of year 1. We'll also assume that the default figures in each case below are net of the recovery value. Finally, we'll ignore additions to the cash reserve, as the bond liquidations will be more than adequate.

Scenario 4a: $5 Million of Bonds in Group Z Default

The book value of the SPE's assets is lower by $5 million (hence, so is the equity). The O/C ratio is 395/300 = 1.317, which is above 1.3, so the portfolio manager keeps the remaining bonds intact. Interest received by the SPE is:

$$6\% \times \$120 \text{ million} + 7\% \times \$180 \text{ million} + 9.5\% \times \$85 \text{ million}$$
$$+ 4\% \times \$10 \text{ million} = \$28.275 \text{ million}.$$

- Senior tranche holders receive 5% × $300 million = $15 million.
- Mezzanine tranche holders receive 7.25% × $80 million = $5.8 million.
- Which leaves $28.275 million − $15 million − $5.8 million = $7.475 million for the equity tranche investors.

At the end of year 2, the CDO terminates. Assuming no further defaults, the interest received by the SPE and coupon and residual payments made to the tranches are the same as above. With respect to the principal, both the senior and mezzanine tranches are paid in full ($300 million + $80 million) while the equity tranche receives $15 million, due to the defaults. Note, however, that with the two residual payments of $7.475 million each year, the equity holders still enjoy a sizable return (see Table 23.3 on page 368).

Scenario 4b: $15 Million of Bonds in Group Z Default

The book value of the SPE's assets is lower by $15 million. This makes the O/C ratio 385/300 = 1.283, below 1.3. With $385 million in assets, the senior tranche can be no larger than $296.154 million (385/296.154=1.3). This triggers an "early amortization." Rounding to $296 million, this means that $4 million of the SPE's cash flows are diverted (from the equity tranche) to pay off senior tranche principal. Let's do the arithmetic.

The interest received by the SPE at year 1 is:

$$6\% \times \$120 \text{ million} + 7\% \times \$180 \text{ million} + 9.5\% \times \$75 \text{ million} + 4\% \times \$10 \text{ million} = \$27.325 \text{ million.}$$

- Senior tranche holders receive 5% × $300 million = $15 million in coupon; in addition, they receive $4 million in principal repayment.
- Mezzanine tranche holders receive 7.25% × $80 million = $5.8 million.
- Which leaves $27.325 million − $15 million − $4 million − $5.8 million = $2.525 million for the equity tranche holders.

Assuming no further defaults, interest received by the SPE in year 2 is the same $27.325 million. But there are fewer liabilities because of the early amortization:

- Senior tranche holders receive only 5% × $296 million = $14.8 million because the size of the tranche has been reduced (amortized) from $300 million to $296 million.
- Mezzanine tranche holders receive 7.25% × $80 million = $5.8 million.
- Which leaves $27.325 million − $14.8 million − $5.8 million = $6.725 million for the equity tranche holders.

With respect to principal repayments, both the senior and mezzanine tranches are paid in full ($296 million + $80 million = $376 million) while the equity tranche receives only $385 million − $376 million = $9 million, for a negative rate of return on the $20 million investment. *All the losses were borne by the equity holders in this scenario.*

Scenario 4c: $25 Million of Bonds in Group Z Default

The book value of the SPE's assets is lower by $25 million (which, on paper, wipes out the equity). The O/C ratio is 375/300 = 1.25, below 1.3. The senior tranche now can be no larger than $288.462 million (375/288.462 = 1.3). This triggers a larger early amortization than in the previous case. Rounding, $12 million of the SPE's cash flows are diverted in order to get the senior tranche's principal to $288 million. However, in this scenario approximating the equity tranche's interest payment *will not be enough.* Let's do the arithmetic.

The interest received by the SPE at year 1 is:

$$6\% \times \$120 \text{ million} + 7\% \times \$180 \text{ million} + 9.5\% \times \$65 \text{ million} + 4\% \times \$10 \text{ million} = \$26.375 \text{ million.}$$

- Senior tranche holders receive 5% × $300 million = $15 million in coupon; in addition, they receive $12 million in principal repayment.
- Mezzanine tranche holders *should* receive 7.25% × $80 million = $5.8 million.

But $27 million needs to be paid to the senior tranche. There is not enough cash flow to pay the mezzanine tranche holders their interest. Here's what is done:

- The entire $26.375 million of SPE cash flow is paid to the senior tranche. The remaining $0.625 million is taken from the reserves—the commercial paper.
- This is where the payment-in-kind (PIK) feature kicks in. The $5.8 million due to the mezzanine tranche holders, as the subordinated class, *is added to their principal.*
- Equity tranche holders get nothing.

Now let's look at the payments for year 2, again assuming no further defaults. The interest received by the SPE in year 2 is only a little less than that in year 1, $26.35 million, because of the commercial paper drawdown. But the SPE's liability structure has changed significantly— fewer senior bonds (via the early amortization), more subordinated (via the PIK):

- Senior tranche holders receive only 5% × $288 million = $14.4 million.
- Mezzanine tranche holders now receive 7.25% × $85.8 million (recognizing the additional $5.8 million to their principal) = $6.2205 million.
- Which leaves $26.35 million − $14.4 million − $6.2205 million = $5.7295 million for the equity tranche holders.

With respect to principal repayments, both the senior and mezzanine tranche holders are paid in full ($288 million + $85.8 million = $373.8 million), leaving a token $1.2 million for the equity tranche.

Scenario 4d: $50 Million of Bonds in Group Z Default

The O/C test certainly fails. It will need to be cured through early amortization of the senior tranche as in the previous scenario. Let's start as we've done throughout, by examining how much money is available from the SPE's interest cash flow:

$$6\% \times \$120 \text{ million} + 7\% \times \$180 \text{ million} + 9.5\% \times \$40 \text{ million} + 4\% \times \$10 \text{ million} = \$24.0 \text{ million.}$$

- Of this, 5% × $300 million = $15 million coupon, which needs to be paid to the senior tranche holders. This leaves $9 million for amortization. Not enough.
- The mezzanine tranche holders obviously will receive no coupon and will have its $5.8 million PIKed.
- Equity tranche holders, of course, receive zero.

Let's assume for simplicity that the commercial paper is left intact by the manager (indeed, if anything, the reserve account will need to be enlarged). Diverting interest from the other tranches in order to amortize the senior tranche is not enough to comply with the O/C test. The portfolio manager will need to sell $94.3333 million of the SPE's bonds in order to comply.[25] Say he liquidates $95 million of the Y group's bonds at par, using the proceeds to further amortize the senior tranche, the SPE's assets now are:

$$\$120 \text{ million } X + \$85 \text{ million } Y + \$40 \text{ million } Z$$
$$+ \$10 \text{ million CP} = \$255 \text{ million.}$$

With the senior tranche now down to $300 million − $9 million − $95 million = $196 million, the new O/C ratio is 255/196 = 1.301. Passed.

Interest received by the SPE in year 2 is significantly lower, due both to the asset defaults and liquidation:

$$6\% \times \$120 \text{ million} + 7\% \times \$85 \text{ million} + 9.5\% \times \$40 \text{ million}$$
$$+ 4\% \times \$10 \text{ million} = \$17.35 \text{ million.}$$

This is distributed to an entirely new liability structure. Recognizing the senior amortization and the mezzanine PIK event:

- Senior tranche holders receive 5% × $196 million = $9.8 million.
- Mezzanine tranche holders receive 7.25% × $85.8 million = $6.2205 million,
- Which leaves, tentatively, $17.35 million − $9.8 million − $6.2205 million = $1.3295 million for the equity tranche holders.

With respect to principal repayments, the senior tranche is paid its remaining $196 million in full. This leaves $255 million (out of the original $400 million, $50 million defaulted and $95 million was liquidated to early-amortize the seniors) − $196 million = $59 million for the mezzanine tranche holders. Since their principal is $80 million, the $1.3295 million in residual SPE income is paid to them, not to the equity holders). They suffer a loss of $80 million − $59 million − $1.3295 million = $19.6705 million in principal. The equity tranche holders recover nothing.

Scenario 4e: $80 Million of Bonds in Group
Z Plus $30 Million in Group Y Default

Before we get to the O/C ratio, let's go right to the cash flows. The SPE receives:

$$6\% \times \$120 \text{ million} + 7\% \times \$150 \text{ million} + 9.5\% \times \$10 \text{ million}$$
$$+ 4\% \times \$10 \text{ million} = \$19.05 \text{ million}.$$

As always, the $15 million coupon needs to be paid to the senior tranche, which leaves $19.05 million − $15 million = $4.05 million for amortization of principal. The SPE is left with $290 million in assets because of the defaults. It owes $300 million − $4.05 million = $295.95 million to the senior tranche holders. The O/C ratio is irrelevant; the SPE is in default. The portfolio manager liquidates the assets, giving the recovery value to the senior tranche holders, who suffer a relatively small loss, and nothing to the mezzanine (and equity, of course) tranche holders.

Table 23.3 summarizes all the cash flows of the different tranches for the various scenarios. It includes rates of return (RORs) in order to highlight how the pain of default is distributed among the tranches.

The Crucial Role of Correlation

Let's devote the remainder of this chapter to a deeper understanding of the default risks faced by the mezzanine and senior tranche holders. The mezzanine tranche holders suffer a loss in scenario 4d and are wiped out in scenario 4e. The senior tranche investors lose only in scenario 4e, but they recover most of their principal.

The default of $50 million group Z bonds in scenario 4d produced a loss of $19.67 million to the mezzanine tranche holders. Had $50 million in group Y defaulted instead of in X, the loss would have been the same.[26] Let's assume for a second that the firms in groups Y and Z are perfectly negatively correlated. That is, if one survives, the other defaults, and vice versa. In such a world, *one of the groups will definitely default!* We immediately conclude the following: The more negatively correlated the companies in the SPE's portfolio, the more default risk faced by the mezzanine tranche holders. And, therefore, the higher the yield demanded by the mezzanine tranche investors.

TABLE 23.3 Cash Flows ($ MM) and Returns for CDO Tranches (Held to Maturity) Under Multiple Scenarios

	Senior Tranche				
Scenario	Year 1 Interest	Year 1 Amortization	Year 2 Interest	Year 2 Principal	ROR (%)
1, 2	15	0	15	300	5
3*	15	0	15	300	5
4a	15	0	15	300	5
4b	15	4	14.8	296	5
4c	15	12	14.4	288	5
4d	15	104	9.8	196	5
4e	15	294.05	0	0	−1.98

	Mezzanine Tranche			
Scenario	Year 1 Interest	Year 2 Interest	Year 2 Principal	ROR (%)
1, 2	5.8	5.8	80	7.25
3*	5.8	5.8	80	7.25
4a	5.8	5.8	80	7.25
4b	5.8	5.8	80	7.25
4c	0	6.2205	85.8	7.25
4d	0	6.2205	60.3295	−8.79
4e	0	0	0	−100

	Equity Tranche			
Scenario	Year 1 Interest	Year 2 Interest	Year 2 Principal	ROR (%)
1, 2	7.95	7.95	20	39.75
3*	6.95	7.99	21	39.02
4a	7.475	7.475	15	26.5
4b	2.525	6.725	9	−4.8
4c	0	5.7295	1.2	−41.1
4d	0	0	0	−100
4e	0	0	0	−100

*With cash reserve trigger

We are now ready to think about "first-to-default" swaps. This is a type of credit default swap in which the protection seller pays the buyer in the event of default of any one member of a *portfolio* of reference credits. You can easily see that the more negatively correlated the credits, the greater the chance of any one defaulting. Hence the greater the risk to the swap seller, and the higher the protection premium demanded. Indeed, now you can understand that the investor in the credit-linked note above faces a similar risk. He or she essentially is subject to the first-to-default of *either* the bond owned by the SPE *or* the issue referenced by the CDS on which the SPE has sold protection.

Turn now to the senior tranche holders. Their loss occurred in scenario 4e, when bonds in *both* groups Y and Z defaulted. A default by only one (unless it is the *entire* group Y, or X for that matter) will not hurt them, as is the case in scenario 4d. The senior tranche holders face the risk of *positive* correlation. They worry that there will be a convergence of defaults, enough to produce a loss. Negative correlation is beneficial, since that precludes convergence of defaults. We've come across this idea before. In Chapter 10 we examine the true nature of a secured bond—that is, a corporate bond collateralized by a firm's real asset, such as a building. We concluded that if the firm's business line and the real estate are perfectly negatively correlated—that is, if one defaults the other survives—the secured bondholders face no risk. Their risk, as is the case with senior tranche CDO investors, increases with positive correlation.

24

HEDGE FUNDS IN THE FIXED-INCOME SPACE

Introduction

A good hedge funds book has yet to be written, and I'm not about to do it. Understanding the role of hedge funds in the fixed income market requires an understanding essentially of everything in this book, plus more—the funds' structure, their goals, their constraints, their operations. Indeed, a discussion of hedge funds is a fitting end to this book because it incorporates many of the concepts, instruments and techniques discussed in these pages. It is but one chapter, so its goal will be modest, but pretty exciting, I think. After a brief "big picture" description, I take what we've learned in this book and illustrate what a hedge fund might do with all that knowledge.

A hedge fund might be described simply as an unregulated pool of capital. This stands in sharp contrast to a mutual fund. Both draw funds from the investing public, and both hire a manager to handle the investing. Mutual funds, with no requirements as to investors' minimum income or net worth, draw from the average Joe and hence are strictly regulated. Hedge funds, besides being open only to qualified investors, typically impose a minimum investment hurdle through which only a small minority can pass. Their clients, as a result, are presumed to be financially "sophisticated" (as well as capable of absorbing losses). Compared to mutual funds, hedge funds have essentially no regulatory constraints with respect to:

- Asset concentration
- Leverage
- Short sales
- Derivatives use
- Liquidity

Of course, the hedge fund manager is constrained by the market, if not by regulation. For example, leverage requires a lender's willingness to lend. Derivative contracts require counterparties. Importantly, the compensation schemes for the two fund manager types differ sharply. Mutual fund managers are paid largely for assets under management. The bulk of the hedge fund manager's compensation comes from performance-based arrangements. In short, risk taking by hedge funds is available, and is rewarded.[1]

In their quest to achieve high returns on capital invested, hedge funds engage in the following broad categories of activities:

1. *Yield enhancement.* The goal here is to earn substantial regular income. Hedge funds use leverage and derivatives to maximize current yield.
2. *Market timing.* Another term for this type of activity is "positioning" or, simply, speculating. Hedge funds take positions in anticipation of a price increase or decrease.
3. *Relative value.* Trades belonging to this category target the *relative* price positions of two (or more) securities or derivatives, as opposed to their absolute price level. These trades are also described as being "market neutral" (in some cases known as "risk arbitrage").

The rest of this chapter illustrates a number of examples for each of these categories, using instruments we've already seen and introducing some new concepts along the way.

Yield Enhancement

There are simply too many yield enhancement strategies to include in one chapter. So I provide just an example or two for each major class.

Spread Instruments

Hedge funds as a group, with their substantial appetite for risk, are one of the largest (and sometimes *the* largest) purchasers of credit risky securities . These are known as spread products because, as we've come across many times, their yield equals the equivalent maturity government bond interest rate plus a spread for credit risk. Most common are speculative grade corporate bonds, which pay a wide spread because of their high risk of default and low recovery value in the event of default. A more recent addition to hedge fund high yield portfolios is the more risky tranches (see Chapter 23) of asset-backed securities/collateralized debt obligations. The more credit risk that is accepted, the more that yield is enhanced.

Repurchase Agreements

Repurchase agreements are somewhat more complicated than spread instruments, so I'll go through the dynamics step-by-step:[2]

1. A hedge fund uses its own capital to purchase, say, a 10-year government bond with a yield of 5%.
2. The fund borrows the same amount of money via repo, using the bond just purchased as collateral; it pays a 3% repo rate for the borrowed funds.
3. The hedge fund uses the borrowed money to purchase commercial paper and earns a 3.5% rate.
4. Net yield = 5% − 3% + 3.5% = 5.5%, a half-percent enhancement over the pure government rate of 5%.

Not much enhancement, but not much risk. The "core" yield (5%) comes from the government bond. The enhancement reflects the spread between the commercial paper rate and the repo rate. The hedge fund is, effectively, borrowing from short-term lenders (using the bond as collateral) and lending (uncollateralized) to short-term borrowers. The enhancement (0.5%) reflects the credit risk of the commercial paper issuers the hedge fund is accepting. Subprime commercial paper would provide a wider spread and hence a greater yield.

Leverage

A step-by-step presentation is worthwhile here as well:

1. A hedge fund purchases, with its own capital, a government bond yielding 5%.
2. The fund borrows the same amount of money via repo, using the bond just purchased as collateral and pays a 3% repo rate.
3. The fund buys another of the same government bond, yielding 5%, with money from step 2.

   So far, the hedge fund earns 5% − 3% + 5% = 7%. But why stop there?

4. Repeat step 2 with the second bond purchased as collateral.
5. Repeat step 3 with money from step 4.

Where are we now? 5% − 3% + 5% − 3% + 5% = 9%. Let's do it again, and earn 11%. Then again for 13%, and again . . . and so on. What's wrong with this picture? What's wrong is that we've omitted an important factor in collateralized lending to hedge funds. Indeed, this applies generally to all types of private sector borrowers. The lender demands collateral in excess of the loan amount. For example, the repo lender in the scenario might lend only $90 against the $100 bond purchased by the hedge fund and offered as collateral. The hedge fund, in other words, can finance only 90% of the bond's cost; 10% must come from the fund's own capital (that is, the investors in the fund). This 10% is known as the "haircut" in bond market language.[3] In the stock market it is known as "margin." In real estate the corresponding term is "down payment." The general term is "equity." The hedge fund, in our example, employs $10 of equity and $90 of debt to purchase the bond. If the hedge fund has $100 million of its own capital, then the 10% haircut allows it to purchase $1 billion worth of bonds and borrow the remaining $900 million. The leverage ratio—defined as assets to equity—you see is the inverse of the haircut: 1/10% = 10. The fund's $100 million is "leveraged up" to a portfolio of $1 billion, ten times its size.

What is the net yield, recognizing the maximum leverage? The $1 billion of bonds pay 5%, or $50 million. Interest on the repo borrowing equals 3% × $900 million =$27 million. As a percentage of the amount invested, the hedge fund therefore earns $23 million/$100 million = 23%. The greater the difference between the yield on the bond and the repo rate—the "net carry"—the greater the return to the fund.[4] And the smaller the haircut, the higher the return. A 5% haircut would require only $50 million of the fund's capital. $950 million of debt would cost $28.5 million in repo interest for a return on capital of (50 − 28.5)/50 = 43%. Hey, even 23% is not bad for a day's work.

If recognizing the limit on leverage imposed by the haircut still produces outsized yield, what's the catch? The catch is the risk, of course. Repo rates are not necessarily locked in for the life of the investment. If short-term financing rates rise, the net carry narrows and may even turn negative. Furthermore, bond yields change. An increase in yield lowers the value of the bonds. If severe enough, the value of the bonds can fall below the debt owed by the hedge fund. The position is insolvent, and the fund's equity is wiped out.

Derivatives

Hedge funds employ a variety of derivatives in their quest for yield enhancement. I'll illustrate two strategies using derivatives that we've covered in this book. Each one is described as a two-step procedure. The first step involves the cash asset that forms the basis of the yield. The second is the derivative that provides the enhancement:

1. Purchase agency bond (e.g., the debenture of Fannie Mae or Farm Credit Bureau—see Chapter 1), yielding Treasury rate plus slight spread for agency risk.
2. Enter interest-rate swap as fixed-rate receiver/floating-rate payer (see Chapter 17 for the payments made and received). Net yield = agency debenture interest rate + swap rate − LIBOR. But since the debenture rate = Treasury rate + agency spread, and because the swap rate = Treasury rate + swap spread, we therefore have:

Total net yield = twice Treasury rate + agency spread + swap spread − LIBOR

Alternatively:

1. Purchase a high grade corporate bond, yielding Treasury rate plus credit spread.
2. Enter credit default swap as protection seller on a reference credit (other than corporate issuer in step 1). The protection seller receives the regular protection payment, or the spread:

$$\text{Net yield} = \text{Treasury rate} + \text{corporate credit spread} + \text{reference credit spread}$$

Note that in either example, the derivative, requiring no investment of funds, has effectively permitted the hedge fund to create two exposures, with the attendant yield/spread compensations, using just one investment. Compare this with the earlier repurchase agreement example. It should be clear that derivatives are simply a disguised form of leverage.

Bonds with Embedded Options

Callable bonds give the borrower the right to pay the bond's principal prior to its stated maturity. Payment-in-kind (PIK) bonds provide the issuer with the choice of paying the bond's coupon in cash or with additional bonds. The callable bond grants the company the ability to refinance at a lower rate of interest, if available (analyzed in Chapter 21). The PIK bond allows the issuer to choose the cheaper alternative with which to pay interest (Chapter 9). In each case, the borrower pays the investor a higher interest rate than otherwise. The extra yield represents payment for the call or PIK option *embedded* in the bond. Hedge funds purchase these bonds, earning the higher yield for assuming the risk of the option they've effectively sold to the borrower.[5]

Market Timing

Hedge funds concentrating on market timing strategies are also known as "macro" funds, as they typically target macroeconomic variables, such as interest rates and exchange rates.

Leverage Again

Consider a fund manager who has purchased $100 million of U.S. Treasury notes with $10 million of the fund's own capital, having borrowed the rest. Think for a moment about the hedge fund manager in the previous section who appeared to be doing the same thing. She had an entirely different motivation. She created the position in order to capitalize on the spread between the repo rate and the bond's yield in order to produce net carry. The manager in the current example believes that the bond's yield will decline. Whereas the previous fund manager would be perfectly happy if interest rates stay constant and the fund would thereby earn the enhanced net carry while holding on to the position, this fund manager is banking on *changes* in rates. If his beliefs hold true, the bond's price will rise. The bond will then be sold and the profits realized. Many hedge funds look for small yield changes, as their holding periods for trades can be quite short. Profiting from small price movement requires large positions relative to the amount invested; that is, leverage.

Let's analyze the hedge fund's risk. In Chapter 9 on corporate bonds, we introduced the leverage ratio—the company's assets divided by its equity—as a measure of risk of the corporation. The greater the ratio, the greater the chance that a decline in the company's assets will prevent it from repaying its debts. The same applies here. A higher leverage ratio raises the likelihood of the hedge fund defaulting on its obligations because it takes less of a downward movement in the bond's price to wipe out the equity. But unlike a nonfinancial corporation, the standard leverage calculation is not quite the right measure for a hedge fund. Consider two hedge funds, both with the same leverage ratios. One owns five-year notes; the other owns thirty-year bonds. Clearly, the second fund presents greater risk because thirty-year bond prices are more volatile than five-year prices. How can we account for this? Simply by multiplying the hedge ratio with the duration of the bond (or the duration of the bond portfolio, as the hedge fund likely has more than one bond in its position). The numerator of this "risk-adjusted" leverage ratio, therefore, is the bond's (or bond portfolio's) dollar-duration, which is the proper risk exposure for bonds, as we show in Chapter 12.

We need to take this a step further. Recall that a bond's duration measures only its price reaction to a supposed shift in interest rates. It says nothing about the *likelihood* of such shifts. Clearly, risk needs to reflect the degree and associated probability of change. A high-duration bond portfolio does not pose risk if interest rates show little chance of movement or if potential movements are contained in a narrow range. Conversely, the portfolio may contain low-duration bonds, but the environment may be one of high volatility. Hence, a more complete measure of (interest-rate) risk for a hedge fund bond position would factor in all the above variables:

$$\text{Risk} = \text{leverage} \times \text{portfolio duration} \times \text{interest rate volatility}[6]$$

Interest-Rate Swaps

In Chapter 17 we learned how an interest-rate swap can be used to create the same market exposure as a fixed-coupon bond. A hedge fund, for example, anticipating a decline in interest rates would enter a swap as the fixed-rate receiver (floating-rate payer). A correct bet would produce profits the same way as a long government bond position would. After the swap rate declines, the fund manager enters into an offsetting swap as a fixed-rate payer. In fact, as shown in Chapter 17, a swap's duration (and dv01) matches that of a bond whose maturity equals the swap's term. Interest-rate swaps require no "investment" (except for margin), hence no financing. Put these two points together and it is clear that interest-rate swaps serve as an alternative to leverage.

This presents a major implication: In a world of derivatives we need a more up-to-date measure of leverage than the traditional ratio of assets to equity. An interest-rate swap is not an asset in an accounting sense, since no funds have been invested. Yet, as the purpose of the leverage ratio is to summarize an entity's risk, swaps need to be recognized just as bonds are. A solution is to redefine leverage. Leverage is traditionally defined as:

$$\text{Leverage} = \frac{\text{Market value of bonds}}{\text{Funds required as margin for bonds}}$$

A more complete measure, however, would be:

$$\text{Adjusted Leverage} = \frac{\text{Market value of bonds} + \text{Notional value of swaps}}{\text{Funds required as margin for bonds} + \text{Collateral required for swaps}}$$

Inverse Floating Rate Notes

The wide variety of structured products developed in recent years allows hedge funds to create leveraged positions without borrowing and without derivatives. One example will suffice, so let's use a security we've already worked with, the inverse floating-rate note of Chapter 16. There we learned that a three-year inverse floater, for example, exhibits a degree of price responsiveness to interest-rate movements (i.e., has duration equal to) approximately *twice* that of a three-year ordinary bond. Voilà! Exposure, or leverage, has been magnified. We can summarize these three strategies in the following way:

> *A hedge fund targeting a high-duration portfolio in order to achieve maximum interest-rate exposure can today achieve similar outcomes through leverage, swaps, or structured notes.*

Short Positions

A hedge fund anticipating a rise in interest rates will sell bonds short. The dynamics of creating a short position are explained at length in Chapter 22 on repurchase agreements. The strategy is employed in Chapter 21 by dealers who sell short as a part of their market-making function as well as in various other places in this book (see, for example, Chapter 12) that discuss hedging. Shorting is effected via a reverse repurchase agreement. In a sense it is the opposite of the leverage trade discussed earlier. Rather than borrowing money to purchase bonds (and the bonds serving as collateral), the hedge fund borrows bonds in order to sell (with the money generated from the sale serving as collateral). The hedge fund's risk is that the bond's price will rise. The lender of the bond to the fund is at risk, in a manner similar, yet opposite, to the lender of money to the hedge fund. Should the price of the bond borrowed and shorted rise significantly, the hedge fund may be unable to buy it back and hence default on the reverse repo. The bond lender then must add her own cash to the cash collateral in order to purchase the now higher-priced bond in the market. And, in a mirror image to the measure of the risk of a long bond position presented earlier, the risk of a short bond (or portfolio of bonds) position increases with longer duration and greater interest rate volatility.

An interest-rate swap can produce the same interest-rate exposure as a short bond position. The hedge fund enters a swap as a fixed-rate payer. Should the swap rate rise, the fund manager then offsets the position with another swap, this time receiving fixed, locking in positive cash flow. The risk is a possible decline in interest rates. No borrowing of bonds is required, just collateral equal to a fraction of the swap's notional amount.

Forward Foreign Exchange Contracts

Market participants transact currencies for "regular" delivery. That is, the exchange rate is agreed upon, and then the currencies change hands, or "settle," two business days later. This is known as a "spot" transaction. Trades also take place for "forward" delivery. Here the counterparties agree to settle their obligations later than two days, say a week, a month, or longer.[7]

Forwards are particularly suited for speculating on FX. Suppose a hedge fund expects the euro to decline against the dollar. The trader can sell the euro in the spot market. But this means that the trader must borrow the euro and then deliver it to the buyer. When the trade is unwound, the euro is repurchased, sent to the trader's account, and then returned to the lender. This is transactionally expensive. We can accomplish the same thing easily with forwards. Assume the trader enters into a forward contract to sell euros at $1.25/€ in one month to a dealer. Nothing needs to be done for a month. Say in one week the euro falls to $1.24/€. Now the trader *buys* the euro forward from a dealer, but for a three-week settlement, so that the two contracts settle on the same day. The profit is locked in. On the settlement date, the trader sends $1.24 for each euro to the second FX dealer. The trader instructs that dealer to send the euros to the first dealer, who thereupon sends $1.25 to the hedge fund. Better yet, were both transactions arranged with the same dealer, nothing needs to be done on the settlement date other than the dealer sending the profit to the hedge fund.[8] But the key is that no borrowing of euros was required when the speculation was initiated.

Gold Futures Contracts

While we're on the subject of FX and forward contracts, let's make a slight turn to gold and futures contracts. Just as a forward contract, a futures contract represents an agreement between two parties to transact on a specific future date at a price agreed upon today for a particular underlying security or commodity. Indeed, a futures contract *is* a forward contract, but one with very special features. For one thing, after a futures contract is entered into, the futures exchange takes the other side of the contract, thus guaranteeing the performance of both counterparties. Second, the exchange sets the size of each contract, the range of possible settlement dates, and the underlying asset upon which the contract is based. Futures are an ideal vehicle for speculating on commodities. Even more so than foreign exchange, gold traders generally do not want to buy and sell physical gold with the storage costs and other headaches involved. A hedge fund expecting an increase in the price of gold "buys" a futures contract; that is, it agrees today (say, January 5) to buy gold at the agreed-upon price on the given future date (February 26 settlement). Conversely, if a gold price decrease is expected, the fund "sells" the contract today, or agrees to sell gold on the future date. Once the expected price change occurs (January 12), the fund simply does the opposite trade (same February 26 settlement). Since both contracts settle on the same day and the exchange is the counterparty to both the initial and terminal contracts, the profit (or loss) is immediately realized in the hedge fund's account. There was never any contract between the hedge fund and actual gold.[9]

Foreign Bonds

Hedge funds speculate on foreign interest-rate movements as they do on domestic rate movements. Suppose the fund manager is of the opinion that interest rates in Denmark are about to drop. He buys the benchmark ten-year Kingdom of Denmark bond, just as he would buy a U.S. Treasury bond in anticipation of a decline in U.S. interest rates. Simple enough? Too simple. Buying the Danish bond requires Danish kroner. A Kingdom of Denmark bond, therefore, presents currency-exchange-rate risk as well as interest-rate risk. The hedge fund is interested in the interest-rate exposure alone. To rid himself of currency-exchange-rate risk, the fund manager sells the kroner value of the bond forward via forward FX contracts, in the manner described above.[10]

Credit Default Swaps, Again

A credit default swap can be used as a market timing device as well. Prior to the creation of CDS contracts, it was difficult to speculate on pure credit risk. Suppose a hedge fund was confident that a particular corporate credit would improve, which would narrow the credit spread on the company's bonds, raising their price. Purchasing the bond would not be the right trade. For if the bond were purchased and, at the same time that the spread actually narrowed, the interest rate on government bonds rose, the yield on the corporate bond might possibly increase (the yield being the sum of the government bond rate and credit spread), depending on the relative magnitudes of the two effects.[11] The hedge fund would be right, but would lose money. That is not a good feeling. What happened? The trader wanted exposure to a company's credit risk, but the corporate bond position entailed interest-rate risk as well. Credit default swaps isolate the exposure. The hedge fund *sells* protection against default on the company thought to be improving. If and when the expected scenario plays out, the fund then *buys* protection on the same company. Why? Because after the improvement, the cost of protection is lower. The hedge fund has sold high and bought low. (See Chapter 23 for elaboration on both the mechanics and dynamics of this pair of trades.) Were the hedge fund to anticipate a credit deterioration, it would *buy* default protection via a CDS. Once expectations are realized, the cost of protection is higher, and the hedge fund sells.[12]

Margin Calls

Before proceeding to the final category of hedge fund activity, we need to define, and appreciate the implications of, a "margin call." It is important for all three types of hedge fund trades. Because market timing is so leverage-intensive, it is particularly appropriate here.

Hedge fund lenders demand margin, or equity. Hedge fund derivative counterparties require collateral. Suppose a security that the hedge fund purchased with borrowed money has declined in price. Since the amount borrowed has not changed, the difference between the security's value and the debt—the hedge fund's equity—has declined. The other side of this is that the amount borrowed as a percentage of the security's new market value—the leverage ratio— has effectively increased. In response, the lender will typically demand more equity. Otherwise, it will ask for some of the loan to be repaid— a "margin call." Similarly, a derivative position—selling protection via a credit default swap, for example—requires collateral. If the reference credit deteriorates, the net present value of the derivative contract ("mark-to-market"—see Chapter 23) to the hedge fund has turned negative. The counterparty demands more collateral—again, a margin call. Many, if not most, hedge funds are maxed out in terms of their equity. That is, their equity is fully employed, having reached the maximum leverage that lenders and counterparties permit. A margin call for more equity can then only be met by selling all or a portion of the security borrowed against (or unwinding part or all of the derivatives position). This, of course, is true of any investor utilizing leverage. What is special about hedge funds is that, in many cases, their holdings equal a significant fraction of the outstanding market amount of the security in question, or represent a large portion of the security's average daily trading volume. In this case, the very act of hedge funds selling their holdings in order to raise cash to meet the margin call will depress the security's (or derivative's) price. This forces a further margin call, which precipitates yet more selling and so on. This *forced* selling—remember, the hedge fund was willing to hold the position— precipitates a possible downward spiral which may well end with the hedge fund's equity wiped out, and defaults.[13]

Relative Value

Relative value trades are the most complicated of hedge fund strategies. Also known as "market neutral positions," they involve at least two securities (or derivatives), which together offset, or neutralize, risk. Instead of the trader expressing a view on the overall direction of a market or a security, in these strategies the trader establishes a position reflecting his or her view as to the *relationship* between two (and sometimes more, as we will learn) securities or markets. The examples will make this clearer.

Rich/Cheap

Government bonds of similar maturity cannot have significantly different yields. They all lack credit risk (or have equal doses of it), and time value of money considerations are reflected in their proximate yield curve positions. Suppose the benchmark Treasury five-year note, with a 3.5% coupon, trades at par and hence is yielding 3.5%. The previous five-year note, now with four years, nine months remaining to maturity, has a 3.75% coupon and is priced at $100.6496, for a yield of 3.6%. This 3.6% yield seems anomalous *relative* to the 3.5% yield of its benchmark counterpart. If anything, it should have a somewhat lower yield than the benchmark since the yield curve has a positive slope, and it has a shorter maturity.[14] The trader has no opinion regarding the absolute yield level of five-year Treasury notes, only that the yield *relationship* between two issues in the sector seems out of sync. A relative value trade is called for.

The older five-year note is termed "cheap to the curve" by virtue of its yield lying above the benchmark five-year.[15] Should the trader buy it simply because she or he considers it relatively cheap? Of course not. What if the day after the trade the benchmark's yield rises from 3.5% to 3.7% and the older note's yield rises from 3.6% to 3.7%. The trader was absolutely right—the two bonds should have had the same yield, and indeed their respective yields equalized in just one day. But the trader lost money! She or he purchased the bond at a 100.6496 price (3.6% yield) and now its price is 100.2160 (3.7% yield). What should she or he have done? Along with purchasing the relatively cheap note, she or he should have *sold* the benchmark note short to hedge (now you see where the name "hedge" fund comes from) against an overall increase in yield, which is what occurred.[16] At 3.7%, the benchmark's price is 99.0947. So she or he would have lost $100.6496 − $100.2160 = $0.4336 on the older five-year, but gained ($100 − $99.0947) = $0.9053 on the hedge. Selling the benchmark note "neutralizes" the impact of shifts in overall interest rates; hence the term *market neutral* position. At the same time it isolates the relative positions of the two bonds, which are the driver of the trade. Indeed, the trade made money because the yield differential narrowed, as anticipated.[17] The risk, of course, is that the differential will widen.

Yield Curve

As opposed to the view that two bonds on the same point of the yield curve should have similar, if not equal, yields, a yield curve trade expresses the view that two bonds on *different* points of the yield curve should present a particular yield *differential*. For example, the ten-year Treasury note may be yielding 4%, and the 20-year 4.5%. The trader may perceive this as too wide a spread. In yield curve terms, the curve's *slope* between the two points is *too steep*. Again, the fund manager has no view as to the absolute level of yields, only the *relationship* between the two bonds. He wants zero exposure to the market as a whole. A relative value trade is called for. The trader buys the 20-year bond and sells short the ten-year note. Conversely, if the trader feels that the slope is not steep enough, she sells the 20-year bond and buys the ten-year note.

Compared to the previous example, care must be taken here with respect to the hedge ratio. Since both their maturities and yields differ significantly, the bonds' reactions to yield changes will differ substantially—they have significantly different dollar-durations. The number of ten-year notes to sell short against each 20-year bond purchased is the ratio of the 20-year's dv01 to that of the ten-year's dv01.[18] Only in these proportions will the net position be market neutral. The ensuing dynamics are similar to the previous section. And the hedge fund's risk is that the slope changes in the opposite direction from that expected.

Butterflies

What a name for a bond strategy, huh? A butterfly is related to the yield curve trade just discussed. That trade focused on the relative yields of two *points* on the curve, that is, the slope. A butterfly trade focuses on two *sections* of the curve, that is, the *relative slopes*. Suppose the trader observes the following Treasury yield curve:

Five-year: 3.50%
Seven-year: 3.75%
Ten-year: 3.80%

Based on history or the implied forward rates, or her view of a "proper" yield curve, the trader believes that the slope between seven and ten years should not decelerate as much as it does from the five- to seven-year section. The *difference* in slopes is too sharp. In other words, the curve in the five- to ten-year neighborhood is, in her view, too "curvy." The seven- to ten-year section should steepen in slope compared to the five- to seven-year section or, equivalently, the five- to seven-year section should flatten in slope relative to the seven- to ten-year section. A quick reread of the previous yield curve trade leads immediately to the following conclusion: a *pair* of yield curve trades is in order here. The hedge fund should put on a yield curve steepening trade involving the seven-year and ten-year pair of bonds, and a yield curve flattening trade involving the five-year and seven-year pair of bonds.

The mechanics are easy now that we've already constructed single yield curve trades. Because there are so many numbers, let's summarize them, along with other information pertinent to structuring the trade. See Table 24.1.

The "steepener" trade calls for buying the seven-year note and selling short $0.0606/0.0817 = 0.74$ ten-year notes for each seven-year purchased. The "flattener" requires buying the seven-year note and selling $.0606/.0451 = 1.34$ five-year notes for each seven-year purchased. Instead of purchasing two seven-year notes, buy just one and then sell, proportionately, 0.67 five-year notes and 0.37 ten-year notes, producing the same exposure. The seven-year note is known as the "belly" of the butterfly note, the five-year note and ten-year note as the "wings." Each *pair* of trades is market neutral, as the proper hedge ratios force the dv01's—hence the interest-rate risk—to be equal and opposite at both ends. Furthermore, the *total* position is neutral with respect to an overall change in slope across the curve.[19] How? Since each pair of trades reflect opposite yield curve slope exposures and each employs exactly one seven-year note, they have equal and opposite curve exposure. The

TABLE 24.1 Data for Butterfly Trade

Years to Maturity	Yield to Maturity	Dv01
5	3.50%	.0451
7	3.75%	.0606
10	3.80%	.0817

question presents itself: If the position is neutral with respect to overall changes in interest rates and neutral with respect to an overall shift in slope across the curve, what is the position exposed to? A change in the contour of the curve. The hedge fund believes that the five-seven-year yield spread will narrow relative to the seven-year spread—a relative value trade.[20]

Bullets, Barbells, and Butterflies: The Reappearance of Convexity

Here's another way to look at a butterfly. Remember that the position was constructed so that each wing has the same dv01 as half of the belly. In other words, the interest-rate risk exposures of the five- and ten-year notes as a pair is equal to that of the seven-year note. In Chapter 13 we refer to a pair of bonds whose risk exposure is equivalent to that of a single bond as a "barbell." The single bond is sometimes referred to as a "bullet." A butterfly, therefore, can also be viewed as a combination of a bullet (the belly) and a barbell (the two wings). With respect to the butterfly position above, our hedge fund is long the bullet and short the barbell. And since the risk positions offset each other, the hedge fund is also market (and yield curve slope) neutral.

Now for something totally fascinating. We learned in Chapter 13 that a barbell with the same duration as a bullet (as the bullet's maturity lies between those of the two bonds in the barbell) will be more convex than the bullet. We also learned that convexity is priced into bonds, that is, the more convex, the more valuable a bond, all else the same. In turn, the value, hence price, of convexity is a positive function of interest-rate volatility. So here's the punch line: An increase in volatility, therefore, adds more to the price of a barbell than to that of a bullet. With the hedge fund short the barbell and long the bullet, a decrease in volatility produces a profit, an increase in volatility, and a loss. In other words, a butterfly can be considered a volatility trade!

What about the opposite position—a "short" butterfly? The hedge fund sells the seven-year note and purchases the five and ten combination in the proportions calculated above. In this case the hedge fund believes that the yield curve will become more "curvy" in the five- to ten-year neighborhood—the five- to seven-year section of the curve

388 • Advanced Topics

will become more positively sloped relative to the seven-ten-year section. Or the trader believes that interest-rate volatility in that maturity region is about to increase and therefore desires convexity. Either motivation calls for buying the barbell and shorting the bullet.

Employing Swaps

These yield curve trades, whether employing two bonds or two pairs of bonds, can be executed via interest-rate swaps. Remember, a swap presents market exposure similar to that of a bond. The fixed-rate receiver (payer) on a seven-year swap, for example, is faced with a dv01 essentially equal to that of the owner (short seller) of a seven-year government bond. This is an eminently sensible statement in the context of hedge funds. A hedge fund, as we learned above, buys (short sells) the seven-year note, financing (borrowing) it with a (reverse) repurchase agreement. As long as the trade is in place, the fund receives (pays) the fixed coupon on the bond and pays (receives) the repo rate which changes (that is, "floats") when it rolls over. Is this not similar to an interest-rate swap? Of course it is, as the swap position calls for receiving (paying) the fixed-swap rate and paying (receiving) the floating LIBOR rate. Now suppose the hedge fund trader perceives the difference between the ten-year and 20-year government bond yields as being too wide (that is, the slope between the two points is too steep). Instead of employing Treasuries in the yield curve trade as above, the trader does a parallel pair of trades with swaps: He enters into a ten-year swap as the fixed-rate payer and, at the same time, contracts to be the fixed-rate receiver on a 20-year swap, in the proportions as given above. The same for the butterfly, except the trade would require a trio of interest-rate swaps: receive fixed on the seven-year, pay fixed on both five-year and ten-year swaps, again with the weights as calculated previously.

Employing swaps in place of actual bonds presents equivalent interest-rate and yield-curve risk exposures. In terms of their respective net carry, however, the positions are not identical. Consider the yield curve trade using bonds. The hedge fund buys the 20-year Treasury bond and finances it with a repurchase agreement. She receives the bond's yield and pays the repo rate. The fund sells the ten-year Treasury short, acquiring it through a reverse repurchase agreement. For this she

TABLE 24.2 10-Year/20-Year Yield Curve Trade: Bonds versus Swaps

---

Bonds

Trade: Buy 20-year Treasury; short ten-year

Carry:

      Receive 20-year Treasury yield/pay repo rate

      Pay ten-year Treasury yield/receive reverse repo rate

Swaps

Trade: Contract to receive fixed on 20-year swap; pay fixed on
      ten-year

Carry:

      Receive 20-year Treasury yield + receive 20-year swap spread

      Pay ten-year Treasury yield + pay ten-year swap spread

---

pays the bond's yield and receives the (reverse) repo rate. The net carry on the swap position is a bit different. The hedge receives the 20-year swap rate and pays the ten-year rate; the two LIBORs cancel.[21] As this may be confusing, with the multiple cash flows involved, Table 24.2 provides a summary comparison.

There is another factor that differentiates the swap from the bond relative value trades. The fixed side of an interest-rate swap, as you know, equals the Treasury yield for that maturity plus a swap spread. Swap spreads are not the same across maturities. The trader structuring the ten- versus 20-year yield curve trade with interest-rate swaps will be receiving the 20-year Treasury yield plus the 20-year swap spread, and paying the ten-year Treasury yield plus the ten-year swap spread. Hence, the position does present the intended Treasury yield curve exposure, but it adds—presumably unintentionally—swap spread curve risk as well.

Corporate Relative Value Trades

The growth in the corporate bond market has spawned a new class of relative value trades. The size of typical corporate bond issues has increased dramatically, enhancing their liquidity, and thus reducing their bid-asked spreads, a precondition for active trading by hedge funds.[22] Many new types of corporate debt securities are now available with different types of risk exposure. And credit derivatives have been introduced which, besides affording a hedging vehicle, create new relative value trade possibilities. Here are just a few examples:

- *Capital structure trades.* These refer to different securities of the same issuer that lie on different points of the firm's "capital structure," or creditor hierarchy. A company's secured debt is senior to unsecured, for instance. It is less risky and hence should trade at a narrower spread to Treasury bonds (corrected for maturity). The hedge fund, recognizing that both bonds share the same likelihood of default—they only differ according to expected recovery value *in event* of default—may believe that their yields should be at a particular relationship to each other. Suppose the unsecured bond trades at too wide a spread to the secured in the hedge fund's view. Just as with the "rich cheap" trade discussed earlier, the fund manager will buy the cheap (in this case the unsecured) and short the rich (the secured), keeping the position duration, or dv01, neutral.

- *Credit default swap versus bond spread.* As explained in Chapter 23 on credit derivatives, the premium on a credit default swap (the CDS spread) should be close, but not necessarily equal, to the credit spread on a bond (bond yield less the Treasury yield) of the same issuer and similar maturity. Suppose the trader believes that the CDS spread is too high relative to the credit spread on a bond. He will sell protection on the corporate, receiving the CDS spread. At the same time, he will arrange to pay the bond spread, by shorting the corporate bond and buying the relevant Treasury bond.

- *Corporate versus other corporates.* Two companies in the same industry should trade at credit spreads that are not too far apart, unless their balance sheets differ significantly (see Chapter 9). The trader may believe that the companies' spreads are not where they should be. Similar to the Treasury bond pair example at the beginning of this section, the hedge fund will buy the corporate bond that is relatively cheap (too high a spread) and short the one relatively expensive (too narrow) in proportions that make the position duration neutral.

- *Corporate versus same corporate.* Some firms are large enough to issue bonds of different maturities. Credit spreads will not be constant for all maturities, even for bonds of the same issuer. Similar to a Treasury yield curve, a corporate spread curve relates credit spreads to maturity. The trader may view the slope of the curve as being too steep or too flat. A spread curve trade is in order, structured just as a yield curve trade above, but employing corporate rather than Treasury bonds.

Swaps Again

Earlier we saw how interest-rate swaps can be employed in place of bonds to express relative value views regarding interest rates. Hedge funds use swaps to create relative value trades focusing on the swap itself.

The fixed side of an interest-rate swap equals the yield on a Treasury bond of similar maturity plus the swap spread. We demonstrate in Chapter 17 that this swap rate is effectively a longer-term LIBOR yield.[23] Hence, the difference between the fixed-swap rate and the associated Treasury yield—the swap spread—reflects market participants' views as to the health of the banking system, whose borrowing cost is LIBOR based. Suppose the hedge fund has a view as to the swap spread, as opposed to the swap rate. If it believes the spread to be too wide (market participants being too pessimistic about banks as a whole), then agreeing to receive fixed on a swap is not the correct trade. Why not? Doing so subjects the trader to Treasury yield risk as well as swap spread risk. He needs to short a Treasury bond of maturity equal to the swap's term along with the swap position.

The spread on corporate bonds represents the market's view of the creditworthiness of the corporation. The hedge fund may form a view with respect to the *relative health* of the corporate and banking sectors. If the two spreads are at odds with this view, a relative value traded is in order. For example, suppose the spread on a high-grade, ten-year corporate issue is 2% while the ten-year swap spread is 1%. The trader is doubtful that this spread multiple is warranted. She buys the corporate bond and simultaneously agrees to pay fixed on a ten-year swap, believing that the difference in spreads will narrow. Since the yields on both the corporate bond and the swap equal the Treasury rate plus a spread, the pair of positions removes the exposure to interest rates overall and isolates the relative credit spreads.[24]

The swap spread curve relates, as you'd expect, the spread on interest-rate swaps to their terms. Earlier we examined how swaps are employed as an alternative way of placing a Treasury yield curve trade. In the present context the hedge fund trader may have a view as to the slope of the swap spread curve itself. Perhaps the ten-year swap spread is too wide compared to the five-year swap spread; that is, the swap spread curve is too steep. The trader enters a swap contract to receive ten-year fixed and another contract to pay five-year fixed. In addition, the trader shorts the ten-year Treasury note and buys the five-year, in order to isolate the swap spread curve exposure (and both pairs of trades are constructed to be duration-neutral).[25]

Convertible Arbitrage

Convertible bonds are usually the domain of equity traders. However, they technically are bonds and deserve a place on this list of relative value strategies. As explained in Chapter 10, a convertible bond may be exchanged by the investor for a fixed number of equity shares. This imparts to the instrument both bond and equity characteristics. Because the investor need not convert, but has the option to do so, the convertible is worth more than a bond that is otherwise equivalent but not convertible. It is this "more" that hedge funds focus on. If the fund manager is of the opinion that this excess amount, or "premium," is too low, he will purchase the convertible bonds and short that fixed number of shares. If too high, the reverse relative value position is created.[26]

International Relative Value Trades

Hedge funds are active in the international arena. We've already discussed how they take outright positions on currency exchange rate movements. Here are relative value trades.

Suppose interest rates in the United Kingdom are substantially above those in Continental Europe, specifically in countries employing the euro as their currency.[27] Given the structural links between the U.K. economy and those of Europe, particularly the vast trade in goods and movement of labor, the hedge fund believes that the difference in yields is too wide. Similar to a relative value trade with respect to two bonds in the same country, the trader would buy the

U.K. bond and short the European bond, making sure that the ratios are such that the net position is interest-rate neutral, as above. There is a problem, though. The U.K. bond is denominated in sterling; the European in euros. The position is exposed to currency fluctuations, which are not the focus of the trade. To eliminate the currency risk, the fund manager will use the forward foreign exchange (FX) contracts introduced earlier. He will *sell* forward sterling (to hedge the sterling owned by the hedge fund by virtue of the long bond position) in an amount equal to the market value of the sterling bond. Simultaneously he will *buy* forward euros (to hedge the euros shorted by virtue of the short bond position), equal to the value of the euro-denominated bond.[28]

Hedge funds also structure relative value trades with respect to exchange rates. Every currency trade, by definition, involves two currencies—this does not make it a relative value trade. Selling the euro, as shown in the market-timing section using FX forwards, *means* being short the euro and long the U.S. dollar—it is an *absolute* position. A *relative* value trade, from the perspective of a U.S.-dollar-based hedge fund, would be, for example, selling the euro and buying the yen, in equal dollar amounts. There is no exposure to the dollar's movement overall. With the first trade the fund is long dollars; with the second trade it is short the same amount of dollars. Hence, the hedge fund is "hedged." The exposure relates to the yen's and euro's *relative* positions with respect to the dollar. In this trade, the hedge fund believes that the yen will either appreciate more than the euro versus the dollar will, or depreciate less. (Or, equivalently, that the yen will appreciate versus the euro.)

Let's review. If a fund manager believes that the euro will depreciate against the dollar (absolute value trade), she sells the euro using dollars. The manager is, effectively, of the view that the dollar will appreciate (against the euro). If she believes that the euro will depreciate versus the yen, she sells euros (after borrowing them), which produces dollars, and simultaneously buys the yen using those dollars. She is, effectively, of the view that the yen will appreciate versus the euro. What if the manager believes that the euro will depreciate—period? She has no view of any particular currency appreciating—not yen, not dollars. In that case the manager sells euros, producing dollars as before, but buys gold with the dollars.

NOTES

1. These include Chapter 5, "How the Economy Works"; Chapter 6, "The Central Bank's Goals, Targets, and Operations"; Chapter 19, "Foreign Trade, Foreign Exchange, and Foreign Bonds" (sections on currency movements); and Chapter 20, "Emerging Markets" (sections on the unique economics of developing countries).
2. Indeed, the chapters on economic fundamentals (macroeconomics, the central bank, economics of foreign exchange, and emerging markets) comprise a minieconomics book on their own—"Everything an Investor Needs to Know about Macroeconomics in One Day!" My seminar students—bankers, traders, investors, and lawyers—have told me that they learned more useful economics in one session with me than in months spent in school. Truly.
3. I can't blame authors of other books for omitting descriptions of bond dealers. It's extremely difficult to really understand the business, let alone write about it, without having been one, as I have.

Part I

Chapter 1 (Pages 7–16)

1. Of course, the document you receive upon purchasing the bond will contain all these details.
2. In the market for U.S. Treasury bonds, traders actually use additional terminology. First, issues with maturities of ten years or

less are known as notes; longer ones are bonds. Second, the most recently issued note or bond in a maturity class—a "benchmark" issue—receives the prefix "the," and the other parameters are dropped. Our bond, if it were a benchmark, would be referred to as "the five-year note." It retains this appellation until it is replaced by the next five-year note issued by the Treasury.

3. Modern governments earn the bulk of their revenue from taxes. They also earn fees, such as tolls and customs duties.

4. Don't confuse debt with deficit. A country's debt (or a company's or an individual's, for that matter) represents the accumulation of past deficits.

5. Hence the term, "default-free" instruments.

6. Chapter 21 explains at length the reasons for this spread and the determinants of its size.

7. For those of you who enjoy algebra, let d = the ratio of government debt to GDP. Take the derivative of d (Δd) and you'll have: $\Delta d = b + (r - g)d$, where b is the budget deficit (relative to GDP), r is the government bond interest rate, and g is the macroeconomy's growth rate.

8. This is one of the "vicious circles" hounding developing countries (as we will see in Chapter 20).

9. This statement rings a bit hollow given the plethora of U.S. government "rescue packages" of 2008 and 2009. To be sure, they are meant to be temporary.

10. A debenture, technically, is an uncollateralized debt instrument.

11. Seismic changes in U.S. financial markets during 2008 led the Treasury to take over the mortgage finance agencies. This is not meant to be a permanent solution.

12. When market participants say that a yield curve "looks" different, they typically refer to the shape rather than the position (i.e., the slope as opposed to the level of rates). We discuss this more fully in Chapter 8, "The Yield Curve."

Chapter 2 (Pages 17–22)

1. Technically, it also needs to be noncallable in order to receive this designation.

2. For example, you'll almost always find this to be the case with residential mortgages.

3. The full coupon is paid in year seven because the full principal was outstanding the entire year.
4. The reason is simple. Suppose it's a four-year note. Investors may pay $82 for it (which is roughly a 5% yield). The Treasury raises $82, but the full $100 face value counts toward the government's debt total. Not a good idea politically!
5. We see in Chapter 4, on portfolio management, that if a bond has any sort of coupon, the return from holding it presents what is known as "reinvestment risk."
6. Zero coupon corporate bonds aren't a solution, as corporations haven't issued much of them, either (and some investors do not want to face credit risk).
7. Actually, in this role the investment banks are "underwriters." We investigate investment bankers again in the chapter (21) on bond dealers.
8. Sometimes the coupon rises in a number of steps; for example, 4% for the first two years, 6% for the next two, 8% next, and so on. To further complicate matters, many of these step-up coupon bonds are callable!

Chapter 3 (Pages 23–33)

1. We'll continue with this default-free assumption until we get to corporate bonds.
2. I know the chapter title says ". . . without the math." But this is so fundamental, that I'd be acting irresponsibly not showing it to you. Anyway, it's the only formula in the chapter, so you'll forgive me.
3. The term "yield" makes a lot of sense. It comes from farming (not the sign at the highway entrance!) A farmer toils, plants seeds, adds fertilizer, prays for rain, etc.. When the crop arrives, the farmer calculates the yield: How much came out given all the effort that was put in. It's the same with bonds. You "put in" the bond's cost, or price. In this case, less than $100. What do you "take out?" The coupon (relative to the price) plus the appreciation to par. What you took out relative to what you put in is the yield. Since the appreciation to par must happen at maturity (when the principal is repaid), the full name is "yield to maturity."
4. Here is where bonds fundamentally differ from stocks. If you know about stocks, I'm sure you've heard about price/earnings

(p/e) ratios. Given a p/e ratio that investors assign to an industry at any point in time, companies with greater earnings per share will have commensurately higher share prices. This is not so different from the effect of a bond's coupon on its price, as you learned in the previous section. However, there is no counterpart to the "time to maturity" concept with respect to stocks—stocks don't mature!

5. "Some?" Yes, "some" market professionals equate bond price reactions to market yield changes with risk. Not I. I'll hold off on using the term "risk" until the next chapter on portfolio management. You'll see why.

6. There could have been lots of fluctuations in the interim. The only thing we're assuming now is that five years later, rates are back to where they were at the beginning.

7. Why does it take three years of a 1% excess coupon (8% compared to a 7% yield) to make up for only two years of a 1.25% deficient coupon (5.75% coupon compared to 7% yield)? Because the excess 1% is paid later, while the 1.25% deficiency comes earlier—a simple time value of money idea. If you apply bond math, you'll see that at a 7% yield, the price of the note is par. Simply calculate the sum of the present values, discounted at 7%: Price $= 5.75/(1.07) + 5.75/(1.07)^2 + 8/(1.07)^3 + 8/(1.07)^4 + 108/(1.07)^5 = 100$.

8. The reason this happens is easy to see. Bond prices can't fall below zero (when you buy a bond, you pay money; you don't receive money!). But yields can rise, theoretically, to almost anything. And every time yields go up, prices must fall for fixed-coupon bonds. So it must be that every successive increase in yield has less of a negative effect on price.

9. In Chapter 9, we mention that firms at times will pay their bonds off early in order to be released from onerous "covenants" contained in the bond indenture.

Chapter 4 (Pages 35–47)

1. Another piece of investor information concerns his or her tolerance of risk (tolerance in the sense of how much compensation he or she needs in order to accept risk). We can proceed without

this for the purposes of this chapter. We must because before we introduce risk as a parameter, we need to define it in the context of bonds, which will have to await Chapter 12.

2. The math is straightforward: Investment = Proceeds/$(1 +$ ROR$)^h$, where h = horizon. Proceeds refer to all the money the investor receives on the horizon date. In this simple example, $100 = ($6 + $100)/$(1 +$ ROR$)^h$, and the ROR must be 0.06, or 6%, to solve the equation.

3. Use the bond price formula of Chapter 3 applied to a four-year, 6% coupon note with a yield to maturity of 6.25%. All the bond prices in this chapter are calculated using this fundamental formula.

4. When bonds are issued, they are typically priced at par, which means, as we learned in Chapter 3 on bond math, that its coupon is set equal to the yield to maturity the market demands of the bond on that date. Later, as the bond ages, market conditions may change, causing the yield to depart from the coupon rate.

5. Again we use the ROR formula of note 2. Note that in these simple examples, we can alternatively calculate ROR as (Proceeds − Investment)/Investment, or $(106 − 100.4224)/100.4224 − .0555 = 5.55\%$.

6. Be careful when applying the bond price formula. At the horizon date, the bond has only nine years to maturity, so you'll need to account for that in the formula.

7. Actually, this is not always true. We need to add the phrase, "all else equal." As we will see in Chapter 12, higher coupons tend to mitigate the price response to yield changes. It is possible, therefore, for a longer maturity bond to show less price sensitivity to yield changes than a shorter maturity bond, if the former's coupon is much higher.

8. It's also known as "market risk," a term I don't like because all risk emanates from the market.

9. On the other hand, if this investor purchases a three-month Treasury bill, he *will* face risk, as is explained in the next section.

10. If this were a corporate (or other nongovernment) bond, then the investor faces default risk regardless of the bond's maturity. And if the bond makes any coupon payments prior to the horizon date, there is risk even for government bonds, as is explained in the next section.

11. Some bond market participants—hedge funds, bond dealers—have no fixed horizon. They are prepared to buy or sell at any moment, or to do nothing at all. For these people, of course, every yield movement matters, since the horizon can occur at any moment.
12. Both these conclusions hold only when there are no intervening coupons. We deal with this possibility next.
13. Had we considered a scenario of an across the board *decline* in interest rates, the ROR would have exceeded 6.67%. Why? The positive impact on ROR from the higher bond price on the horizon, due to the lower yield, would have outweighed the negative ROR impact of lower reinvestment rate on the first coupon payment.

Part II

Chapter 5 (Pages 51–67)

1. Besides correcting for price changes, GDP *should* also correct for quality improvement or deterioration. The people in charge haven't really found an adequate way to account for quality changes yet.
2. Economists refer to this as the "nonaccelerating inflation rate of unemployment," or "NAIRU."
3. Another problem is measurement bias. A non-full day of work removes a person from the ranks of the unemployed. Yet, this person obviously is not working at his or her potential, hence a "gap" exists. Furthermore, unemployment rates are measured differently across countries. There are substantial differences as to how many hours of daily work constitute employment and how much searching for work is necessary for someone to be considered a member of the labor force. Therefore, care must be taken in making international labor market comparisons.
4. The Bank of England, the first central bank as we know it, has conducted central banking functions for only a few hundred years.
5. Of course, the weak economy may leave some households with little or no savings, because all their income is spent on necessities.
6. There is a fundamental, classical notion concerning the interactions between savings and the macroeconomy, and this is as good a place

as any to mention it. The source of funds for businesses to borrow and expand capacity—hence increase the country's potential GDP—is, ultimately, household savings. (Similarly, the excess of governments' expenditures building schools, bridges, etc., over tax receipts is met by borrowing from households.) In the long run, therefore, savings is certainly a positive thing. In the short run, however, savings means less consumption, and a wider gap, as the capacity built up from past savings is underutilized! This dichotomy, or disparity, between the secular and cyclical aspects of savings is known as one of the "paradoxes of savings."

7. The popular definition of *recession* is two consecutive quarters of real GDP decline. But that's not quite true, in terms of the calendar or in substance. However, it's a decent approximation of the National Bureau of Economic Research's official measure. Note that even if real GDP displays positive growth, yet is below the economy's potential growth rate, resources are not being fully employed. In particular, the unemployment rate increases. The economy is definitely weak, but it is not in "recession."

8. Should the economy rebound from recession, yet expand at a rate below potential for a number of quarters, job growth will be anemic and not much of a dent will be made in the unemployment rate. This is often characterized as a "jobless recovery."

9. Over time, though, the economy does adjust to the price increase—more fuel-efficient automobiles, utilities switching to other energy sources, industries investing in energy-saving equipment.

10. The federal government would probably like to stimulate aggregate demand by either reducing taxes and/or increasing its own spending. Politics surrounding budget deficits would be an impediment.

11. Witness the dramatic decline in the ratio of oil consumption to GDP in the United States over the past few decades—nearly 50% since the oil shocks of the 1970s.

Chapter 6 (Pages 69–82)

1. They are so termed because, unlike other paper assets, they can be used to pay for transactions. Stocks and bonds need to be sold—*liquidated*—in order to produce cash which can then be used for payments. Cash is already in a liquid state.

2. Fondly known to economists as the "nonaccelerating inflation rate of unemployment," or "NAIRU," expanded upon in the previous chapter.

3. Historically, the Federal Reserve's direct oversight was limited to banks, government securities dealers and, more recently, federal housing finance agencies. The extraordinary events of 2008 and carrying into 2009 have resulted in the Treasury and the Fed becoming involved—as owners, creditors, and/or guarantors—in a host of financial institutions. The text's explanations of central bank fundamentals and interactions with securities markets and the economy is as relevant today as it was prior to these market upheavals.

4. All central banks are restricted with respect to which securities they may purchase. The restrictions reflect the bank's low tolerance for credit risk and its need not to show favoritism to any private entity issuing securities. The Federal Reserve's universe of permitted securities has been greatly expanded as a consequence of the profound changes brought about by the upheavals of 2008.

5. The Fed will only deal with "primary" dealers, that is, bond dealers that satisfy the central bank's requirements as to, among other parameters, size, market share, and surveillance.

6. Repurchase agreements are described more fully in Chapter 22.

7. The short-term nature of repurchase agreements (repos) allows the Fed to be nimble in its supply of liquidity to the economy. The Fed, as anyone else, can never be sure its assessment of the economy is correct. As new data arrive, the Fed may need to adjust its liquidity provision, which short-term repos are perfectly suited to. Furthermore, a host of factors, not directly related to the macroeconomy, can affect liquidity, forcing movements in the federal funds rate without the Fed's intervention. Examples include seasonal needs for more cash and shifts in the public's asset holdings in and out of depository institutions. Even the weather matters! Clearly, these are temporary phenomena.

8. The Federal Reserve (with congressional approval) sets reserve requirements for banks. Although changes in these requirements would profoundly affect liquidity, hence interest rates, this is not a day-to-day policy tool of the central bank.

9. Recent events in the U.S. capital markets have precipitated new (or rehabilitation of unused) Federal Reserve tools and procedures. For

example, in 2008 the central bank created the so-called "Term Auction Facility" in order to make loans to banks without the bank being perceived as unable to access the interbank market. In addition, the Fed now makes direct loans to primary dealers (Primary Dealer Credit Facility), and it instituted a new Treasury bond lending program (Term Securities Lending Facility). Finally, the central bank is involved with the federal housing agencies and their activities in the mortgage market (see Chapter 1 on government-sponsored enterprises).

10. There are economists of the opinion that another channel exists through which central bank liquidity injections (and removals) influence aggregate demand and, thereby, economic activity. As a result of the Fed's purchases of bonds, for example, the public's mix of financial assets in its portfolio has shifted to some degree from bonds to cash. The more cash relative to interest-bearing assets, the more likely it is that households will use their cash balances to purchase goods and services. I am not a subscriber of this view, but to the extent that it holds, it is certainly a more direct link between the central bank's operations and aggregate demand than are interest rates.

11. There are a number of additional factors influencing the shape of the yield curve, as we explore in Chapter 8. This further vitiates the central bank's influence over the real economy.

12. The deep U.S. recession of 2008 and 2009 brought into sharp focus the realization that long-term interest rates did not follow short-term interest rates down after the Federal Reserve's massive injection of liquidity. This spurred the Fed to rethink its standard operating procedures. It reserved for itself the right to purchase long-term governments bonds (as opposed to lending to financial institutions and accepting those bonds as collateral via repurchase agreements). Doing so on a large scale, it was hoped, would raise the prices of these bonds, lowering their yields directly, hence circumventing the yield curve problem.

13. Corporate bond spread determinants are discussed at length in Chapter 9.

14. Collateral and covenants are discussed in Chapter 9.

15. This seems to have been the case, at least to some extent, in 2008 and 2009 at a number of major banking institutions.

16. We actually allude to this point toward the end of Chapter 5, in the section titled "Interest Rates."
17. Real interest rates reflect supply and demand for credit ("real" factors). The nominal, or measured, interest rate equals the real rate plus the inflation rate, given by the growth in liquidity.
18. The central bank's ability to target short-term rates and thereby influence economic activity can cause economic agents to alter their inflation expectations. In an inflationary environment, a serious reduction in liquidity, plus a conviction on the part of the bank to continue to do so (one that is trusted by market participants) will, over time, cause households and businesses to revise downward their inflation forecasts, thus relieving current price pressure. This speeds up the process of reducing inflation via actual liquidity reduction (and high real interest rates).

Part III

Chapter 7 (Pages 85–95)

1. Prices will not all increase to the same degree. In the short run, the cause of a general price increase is typically a tightening of the gap between actual and potential economywide output. In the long run, it is generally the result of an increase in the economy's liquidity. See Chapters 5 and 6 on macroeconomics.
2. "No frills" in that the bond is a "bullet," there are no minimum or maximum bounds surrounding the coupon, and, as explained in the text, the inflation rate is simply added to the annual cash flows to produce the actual coupon.
3. There are many ways to measure inflation, hence many inflation "rates." The inflation rate typically incorporated in inflation-protected securities is the percentage of change in the consumer price index (CPI) over the relevant period of time.
4. They do not differ based on default risk—they are both backed by the same government.
5. The U.K.'s inflation-protected bonds (known as "index-linked" bonds) use the structure of the previous section.
6. It is clear that as long as there is any inflation, the bond's principal grows over time. Each TIPS has a "factor" that reflects this ever-growing principal value. In our example, the bond's "factor" at

the end of the second year would be 1.0455. This means that the bond's "quoted" price in the marketplace needs to be multiplied by this factor in order to produce the total price.

7. This assumption implies that the nominal bond's yield one year from today remains 4.5% and that the IPB's real yield remains 3%.

8. I actually fudged a little bit here. The TIPS's coupon will be 3% × $101.50 = $3.045. But to be really honest, if inflation was expected to be 1.5%, the nominal bond's coupon would have been $1.03 × 1.015 − 1 = $4.545. Subtract 1.5% for inflation, and you get the same $3.045! So, I'll take the liberty of this approximation in the text.

9. These comparisons assume that the bonds began with equal real coupons and have the same maturity.

10. In fact, the TIPS will be somewhat *more* price sensitive than an ordinary bond to real rate changes. As explained in the text, the U.S. approach to inflation-protected bonds is to pay a fixed real coupon on an ever-growing nominal principal. Inflation, therefore, is reflected in the principal, not the coupon rate. Ordinary bonds add a fixed expected inflation rate to all the coupons. The lower coupon on the TIPS compared to the nominal bond of equal maturity results in a longer "duration" for the TIPS. As is explained in Chapter 12, longer duration bonds display greater price sensitivity to interest-rate changes.

11. The TIPS's factor (see note 5) does not change in this scenario; it reflects the accumulation of *past* inflation. So the bond's new quoted price will be $99.6292 multiplied by the factor.

Chapter 8 (Pages 97–114)

1. In Chapter 3 we learned that a bond's interest rate (in the form of coupon) is not necessarily the same as its yield to maturity. In this chapter we simplify and use the terms interest rate and yield interchangeably.

2. Recall from Chapter 1 that a benchmark bond is the Treasury bond most recently issued for a particular maturity class.

3. To be technically correct, this analysis applies perfectly only in the case of a zero coupon bond. The interest rate on such a bond is known as a "spot" rate. In Chapter 3 we learned that the yield on a

regular bond reflects the combination of the distance of the bond price from par and the coupon relative to the bond's price. In our example, the two-year yield would not be "locked in" by purchasing a two-year note, since the coupon needs to be reinvested. Still, if we substitute yield for spot rate, the analysis applies closely enough.

4. Believe it or not, we could have performed the same exercise for an investor with a one-year horizon, choosing between the one-year Treasury instrument and the two-year, which requires sitting after one year, and we would have arrived at the same conclusion—the average expectation is that the one-year rate next year will be 4%.

5. We're ignoring reinvestment of the coupon earned after the first year. See note 3.

6. When it comes to corporate bonds (or other securities with credit risk), we *can* say that the risk of default increases with the maturity of the instrument. See Chapter 9.

7. He can also choose to buy the two-year Treasury note at 3% and then reinvest for the third year at the then prevailing one-year rate, or invest today in the one-year rate at 2% and buy a two-year Treasury at the end of the year at whatever rate prevails then. Either way, the choice involves expectations of future rates and applying the text's analysis leads to the same conclusions.

8. This is good enough for now. By the end of the chapter, we'll see that forward rates are not necessarily equal to the market's expected future rates. But they're a decent proxy.

9. The Friday rate will count for three (Friday plus the weekend) in the averaging process. The day before a bank holiday counts for two (the day before the holiday plus the holiday).

10. Stronger or weaker than what? Than the economy's "potential" to grow, as explained in Chapter 5.

11. Actually, as is shown in the next section, the rise in forward rates through year 8 and their subsequent leveling off are not *necessarily* indicative of eight years of expected economic expansion followed by stagnation and recession (although they are certainly consistent with that view). Expected inflation plays an important role as well.

12. As we will soon see, a negative yield curve may also reflect market participants expecting declines in inflation, which is not necessarily

associated with a decline in economic activity. Finally, as we learned in Chapter 1, one outcome of a government reducing its budget deficit is a drop in (long-term) interest rates. Indeed, this often results from *expanding* economic activity triggering increasing tax revenues. I kept these issues out of the text because I did not want to belabor the point. The lesson to be learned here is that memorizing a so-called "rule" can be dangerous.

13. Real interest rates may well be negative in a recession. The central bank pushes short-term rates below the inflation rate, resulting in ultra-cheap financing costs in order to spur borrowing and spending.

14. As explained in Chapter 6, the central bank often accommodates the economy's need for more liquidity in the early stages of a macroeconomic rebound, holding short-term rates steady. For purposes of the example in the text, just assume that the downturn is not deep—that is, in the context of Chapter 5, the economy's gap is not wide—so the bank is willing to let rates rise after one year.

15. This is within the range of the average length of U.S. expansions since the end of World War II.

16. This example lays to rest the almost universally accepted notion that longer-term securities are unambiguously more risky than short-term securities. It depends on the investor's horizon. The longer the horizon, the more risky (in the sense of interest-rate risk) the short-term securities are.

17. We can't forget about the borrowers. Their distribution across maturities matters as well, but in the opposite direction. In order for a borrower to shift to a maturity different from the preferred maturity (which matches the term of the debt with the expected life of an asset to be funded with that debt), he or she needs to be paid. But the payment is in the form of a *lower* interest rate. Hence, the greater the concentration of borrowers at a particular maturity point, the higher the yield for that maturity relative to the simple average expected short-term rates to that maturity. For example, if the federal government decides to concentrate its funding of the deficit by issuing mostly 30-year bonds, that will raise the 30-year rate above the average 1-year rates expected over the next 30 years—the yield curve will slope more sharply upwards at the 30-year point than it otherwise would.

18. Speculating is not unique to hedge funds. Individuals and institutional investors speculate as well. Nor are hedge funds only for speculators. Some funds purchase bonds for their income and have longer term horizons. See Chapter 24.

19. Hedge funds, as do other speculators, also sell short. This would seem to mitigate the argument in the text, since a short must *pay* the yield on the bond, so a *lower* yield is compensation for more risk. Not so. Every newly created short position is balanced by a long—the short borrows the security to deliver to the buyer. The net balance of all the long positions in the market less the short positions must equal the supply of that security in the market. In other words, the marketplace is, of course, net long, and the long position holder must be compensated to accept the risk of holding that position.

20. There is a valid argument working in the other direction. Remember convexity from Chapter 3? The asymmetric tradeoff between yield and price changes benefits the investor, who pays for convexity by accepting a lower yield. Long-term bonds, all else the same, are more convex than are short-term bonds. This, to some extent, reduces the slope of the yield curve. And, just as volatility makes holding long-term bonds more risky for short-term horizon investors, volatility enhances the attractiveness of convexity, thus weakening somewhat the argument for a positive bias to the yield curve. More on this in Chapter 13.

Chapter 9 (Pages 115–130)

1. I use the terms "default risk" and "credit risk" interchangeably. Technically, though, they're not the same. A "credit event" is possible without a default.

2. So much for the saying, "Our employees are our most important asset."

3. If the company were to sell more shares to new investors or to existing equity holders, this would add to equity as well. If the company experiences a loss, the loss is "negative" retained earnings, which *subtracts* from equity.

4. Notice that we didn't subtract the company's tax bill from the $1,000 to arrive at the coverage ratio. Why? Because the government

takes their piece only *after* interest is paid to creditors. If there isn't enough money to pay interest, the government doesn't take anything. Taxes are paid out of *profit*, not out of revenue. Professional credit analysts refer to these available funds as "EBIT," or earnings (synonym for profits) before deductions of interest and taxes. These earnings represent the cash available to pay interest to creditors. So you can define this coverage ratio as EBIT/interest payments.

5. Equity holders might be happy. Whatever the level of net earnings (after interest and taxes), it is distributed over fewer shares of stock. Here you see the sharp difference between a stockholder's and bondholder's view of the balance sheet.

6. Product life cycles are shorter in technlogy. And demand for the products is more sensitive to the business cycle.

7. Creditors do not have to be lenders in the traditional sense. For example, they may be suppliers to the firm who have not been paid, or they may be the company's pension obligations.

8. Option-adjusted spread is really just an educated guess. But, then again, these people are highly educated.

9. The reason shifting the balance sheet from equity to debt adds potential return to shareholders while increasing risk to debt holders is as follows: If the risky project undertaken by the managers performs well, stockholders are entitled to the profits. Lenders, including the bondholders, don't share in the upside; their return is capped by the bond's coupon and principal. If, on the other hand, the project fails, the most shareholders can lose is their investment. And if it results in bankruptcy, the bondholders are left with the company's assets, the "leftovers." Unlimited upside, limited downside. Pretty strong incentive to take risk, isn't it? Now here's the punch line. This asymmetrical benefit to stockholders/ pain to debt holders is enhanced by substituting debt for equity. The greater the firm's leverage, the greater the potential rate of return to the remaining shareholders, as the winnings are divided among fewer holders. At the same time, there are more bondholders who need to be satisfied.

10. Of course, as the firm enters the open market to purchase its bonds, the price will rise to reflect the net excess demand. But this is as it should be. When all is said and done, the firm has less debt, hence its leverage, and default risk, is reduced. Even if this particular bond is now gone, having been repurchased by the company, any

remaining outstanding bonds should present a lower yield, hence a higher price.

11. This is known as a "noneconomic" call, since the call was exercised for a reason other than refinancing the bond at a lower interest rate. Since the bond was callable and not called to this point, the bond's coupon must be below interest rates in the market. Hence, when the firm calls, it will need to borrow at a higher rate than is on the existing coupon.

12. The three most prominent U.S. CRAs are Moody's Investors Services, Standard & Poor's, and Fitch. They also rate non-U.S. corporations as well as debt of sovereign nations (and U.S. municipalities).

13. An example is GNMA, the Government National Mortgage Association. It's the only agency with the word "government" in its name. Since it is actually part of the government, its debt (or the debt instruments it guarantees) has the same credit standing as Treasuries.

14. The takeover by the federal government in 2008 of the two housing finance agencies, FNMA (Fannie Mae) and FHLMC (Freddie Mac), when they were teetering on insolvency, assured investors of the government's commitment.

15. The grades get even finer than those shown in Figure 9.2. For example, BBB+ is superior to BBB, which in turn is a better credit rating than BBB−.

16. We revisit this concept of recovery value in Chapter 23, which covers credit derivatives.

17. The first part of the next chapter puts this idea into the context of interest rate movements over the business cycle.

18. "High grade" sounds much better than "low yield," even though the latter would be the more correct term. The proper pair should be "high grade" and "low grade," or "high yield" and "low yield." A marketing gimmick.

19. A leveraged buyout (LBO) involves investors issuing debt and using the proceeds to purchase a public firm. The company is now "out" of the public domain (that is, "privatized"), and the debt becomes an obligation of the firm. A recapitalization, in this context, involves a public company issuing debt to repurchase *part* of its outstanding equity. In both cases, the leverage ratio of the entity is markedly higher after the event.

20. Other members of this class are step-up coupon bonds, which are analyzed in Chapter 3, and zero coupon bonds, discussed in a number of contexts in this book (for example, Chapter 12).
21. To complicate matters further, PIK bonds are typically callable. Thus the issuer has a call option on the bond's principal and a PIK option on the series of coupons.

Chapter 10 *(Pages 131–142)*

1. This is subject to the caveat that in extreme situations investors do worry about government default, as discussed in Chapter 1.
2. Potential output growth equals, roughly, the rate of expansion in the country's labor force plus its productivity growth. In the United States it seems to be in the neighborhood of 3%.
3. We're being a little loose with the numbers because our focus is not so much the *level* of rates in each table entry but their co-movements (or lack thereof) across the business cycle.
4. There's a bit of "sleight of hand" here. High-grade bonds exhibit less yield volatility than those of high yield only as long as the bonds remain high grade. If a firm's creditworthiness deteriorates dramatically, possibly due to business cycle factors, it enters the speculative grade region and becomes high yield. Its resultant yield volatility won't show up in the statistic covering high-grade volatility, but it should.
5. A further implication of this conclusion concerns hedging. As explained at length in Chapters 12 and 21, hedging involves the "short" sale of a security (or derivative) to protect against a possible decline in price of a security owned in the portfolio. A hedge is successful to the extent that the instrument used as the hedge is correlated with the security being hedged against. This way a price decline in one is offset by that of the other. The analysis in this paragraph tells us that Treasury bonds are a poor hedge for high-yield corporates.
6. It is actually devastating for *all* corporate securities, including equities.
7. You will appreciate how crucial this concept of correlation is with respect to credit derivatives whose value is attached to more than one security or company (see Chapter 23).

8. In the event of default, if the value of the building exceeds the claim of the senior debt holders, the excess is used to partially pay off the subordinated claims. Our example makes the simplifying assumption that the building will not be worth more than the face amount of the senior debt. Hence, the subordinated debt holders do not look to the real estate for payment, as the senior debt holders do.

9. To be technically correct, correlation really measures the degree to which two variables together move away from their respective averages.

10. Sometimes there is a waiting period before the bond can be converted. In some cases a specific event needs to occur before the conversion feature is operative.

11. The correlation is not perfect; that is, it is not one for one. But it certainly is positive. The higher the stock price above the conversion price, in this case $33.33, the closer the correlation.

12. The conversion feature, in other words, is convex.

13. Callable bonds, and the effect of the call feature on the bond's yield, are discussed in Chapters 2 and 13.

14. The convertible feature—owned by the investor—is enhanced by stock-price volatility, as explained earlier. The call feature—owned by the issuer—is enhanced by interest-rate volatility.

15. Here's another interesting aspect of this rather complicated security. Calling the bond erases the investor's right to convert. If converting seems attractive, the investor may convert in anticipation of a call (known as "forced conversion").

Part IV

Chapter 11 (Pages 145–157)

1. You can review all of this in Chapter 4.

2. This number was arrived at by applying the standard pricing formula of Chapter 3 to a 7% (annual) coupon nine-year bond yielding 6.8%.

3. The concept of "roll" is found frequently in futures contracts, particularly for commodities. The contract whose settlement date is closest is termed the "nearby" contract. Speculators, hedgers, and other participants involved in futures often wish to keep their positions in the nearby contract (it is typically the most liquid). On the

settlement date, in order to maintain the desired risk exposure, the contract holder needs to reestablish the position by offsetting the existing contract and "rolling into" the new nearby contract.

4. All the rate-of-return calculations in this chapter follow the standard ROR formula presented in Chapter 4, namely: Investment = Proceeds/$(1 + \text{ROR})^{\text{horizon}}$. When the horizon is one year (and the coupons are paid annually), this simplifies to: ROR = (ending price + coupon − beginning price)/beginning price.

5. Why is the one-year rate—and not, perhaps, the shortest maturity (overnight)—the anchor? We're looking for an interest rate that reflects, as much as possible, the "pure" time-value-of-money factor, a change in which should, theoretically, affect all yields equally. The longer the maturity, the more the yield is influenced by additional factors, such as risk, as discussed in Chapter 8. So, we don't want to look further than one year. At the same time, interest rates for maturities of less than a year are "money market" rates (see Chapter 14). These are more reflective of the central bank's policies and the market's expectations of such, again biased away from the "pure" time value of money.

6. Or, to be technically precise, that interest rates in the future (forward rates) will be above the bond's yield today, the implications of which produce the same result.

7. In fact, it will rise by enough to bring the rate of return down to the one-year yield today! Why? Because you have a one-year holding period.

8. They're counting on essentially the same fallacy. If the interest rate on their loans exceeds that of their deposits, the positive slope points to rates increasing in the future. They will be rolling over their deposits at ever-increasing interest rates, eventually overtaking the rate on the loans and wiping out the spread (ignoring the extra yield they're getting for accepting credit risk).

9. The reason for the positive association between credit spreads and maturity is provided in Chapter 9. Essentially, the chances of a default event increase with time.

10. See note 4.

11. Using the formula repeated in note 4, with horizon = 1 in this case, the break-even calculation is then simply $98.2441 = (6.75 + horizon price)/(1 + .04).

12. The calculation is $98.2441 = (6.75 \times 1.07 + 6.75 +$ horizon price$) / (1 + .04)^2$.
13. In practice, recovery rates (for investment grade bonds) are more likely to be in the 50% to 60% neighborhood and, therefore, in this example would produce a negative return.
14. Proceeds equal $6.75 \times 1.07^3 + 6.75 \times 1.07^2 + 6.75 \times 1.07 + [100 + 6.75] \times$ recovery rate. The ROR calculation is $98.2441 =$ proceeds$/1.06^4$, which works out to a recovery rate of 94.44%.

Chapter 12 (Pages 159–173)

1. We could have made another observation from Table 12.1—one we've discussed before (see Chapter 3). This is the matter of *convexity*. For each of the bonds, the negative effect of the yield increase decelerates. Take the two-year note. In Table 12.1 the yield increase from 3% to 4% resulted in a 1.93% price decline. The next 1% increase in yield brought about only a 1.88% price decrease. Notice also how this convexity effect becomes more pronounced as the maturity gets longer. If this piques your interest, great. But you'll have to await the next chapter.
2. Why divide by 120? The total amount of cash the bond pays is $120 ($10 coupon the first year, $10 coupon, plus $100 the second). The first cash flow represents $10/$120 of the total; the second represents $110/$120.
3. Here's the exact calculation: Let's use the two-year, annual 10% coupon bond in the text, and compare duration to AWT. Let's assume that the bond is at par, which means that the yield is 10% as well. On a present value (or discounted) basis, the first cash flow is worth $10/1.10 = $9.0909. The second cash flow is worth $110/1.1^2 = $90.9091. All the cash flows, on a present discounted basis are worth $9.0909 + $90.9091 = $100 (of course, because the bond is par.) So, following the same approach as AWT, we calculate 9.0909/100 × 1 year + 90.9091/100 × 2 years = 1.9091 years.
4. If the bond's yield were to change, say, to 8%, then the averaging "weights" in the duration calculation would change, but not in AWT. Compared to the calculations in the previous note, the first cash flow's present value increases to $10/1.08 = $9.2593, and the

second to $110/1.08^2 = \$94.3073$. The sum is now $103.5665 (the new price), and duration becomes $9.2593/103.5665 \times 1$ year + $94.3073/103.5665 \times 2$ years $= 1.9106$ years.

5. Chapter 13 considers the duration of a callable bond, hence its price responsiveness to changes in yield.

6. Via basic time value of money (discounting) calculation: $\$100/(1.02)^2 = \$96.1169$; semiannual compounding of 4% per year is 2% per six months.

7. You might ask—and rightly so—why, then, does the two-year not decline in price by *exactly* 2%, and the five-year not by *exactly* 5%? That, my friend, is due to the convexity of fixed-income instruments, introduced in Chapter 1 and fully explained in Chapter 13.

8. Examine Table 12.2. Comparing the third to the second row (middle column) reveals that the 4 percent coupon five-year bond actually falls by less than 4.58% when its yield rises from 4% to 5%. Why? For the same reason that the zero coupon bond (second column) declines by less than 5%—convexity. See note 7.

9. Why? Once again it is a reflection of the convex characteristic of fixed-income securities.

10. The relationship becomes less exact the more the yield changes. The culprit—you guessed it—is convexity. Chapter 13 takes care of everything.

11. In fact, large financial institutions often speak in terms of "risk units." They may identify, say, the benchmark Treasury five-year note as "the numeraire," or the basic risk unit. That is, its dollar duration is equal to one risk unit. Every other bond's risk units are equal to the ratio of its dollar duration to that of the five-year note. The ten-year zero coupon bond in Table 12.5 contains $659.78/449.13 = 1.47$ risk units. Suppose the institution owns $20 million in face value of the five-year and $12 million of the ten-year. It would then aggregate its interest rate risk as $20 \times 1 + 12 \times 1.47 = 37.64$ risk units (per million dollars).

12. Because 1 basis point (bp) is a small change in yield, the dv01 is not an approximation; it is the *exact* price change caused by 1 bp change in yield.

13. The mechanics of selling a bond short—borrowing the bond via a reverse repurchase agreement and selling the bond—are

explained in Chapter 21 on dealers. Bond dealers sell short for precisely the reasons in our scenario.

14. There is another cost, also related to the liquidity factor. When the investor shorts the bond being used as the hedge, the investor pays the bond's coupon and receives the reverse repurchase agreement rate (see Chapter 22). The reverse repo rate is typically lower for less liquid bonds. Hence hedging with the five-year zero "costs" more than hedging with the ten-year benchmark.

15. Credit risk is discussed in Chapter 9.

16. The spread reflects credit risk. Credit risk can be hedged via credit default swaps, which are explained in Chapter 23. Alternatively, the investor can short a different corporate bond. But the bond used as the hedge must be correlated with the bond at risk. And its bid-asked spread will be wider than the Treasury's.

Chapter 13 (Pages 175–195)

1. One may argue that there may be a greater chance for yields to rise than decline. After all, the most they can fall is to 0%, whereas, at least theoretically, the sky's the limit on the upside. True. But the text's argument is still valid; it just needs to be restated: In order for the likelihood of gain to equal the likelihood of loss—for the bet to be "fair"—there must be a greater chance for yields to rise than to fall. (Alternatively, as long as yields are not too close to zero, the probability of a "normal size" change in yield is symmetric in either direction.)

2. Mathematically, the curve in Figure 13.2 is said to have a convex shape.

3. Technically, it's not the maturity that matters; it's the duration. As we observed in Chapter 12, a higher coupon reduces a bond's duration. It lowers convexity as well. Hence, a longer maturity does not necessarily make a bond convex, but a longer duration does.

4. This is not true of duration. As we observed in Chapter 12, duration actually *decelerates* with maturity. For example, the duration of the ten-year note is substantially less than twice the duration of the five-year note.

5. Just as in note 3, to be technically correct, we need to replace "maturity" with "duration" in this paragraph. It makes things a

little messy, but you'll get it in the "Barbells" section later in this chapter.

6. See Chapter 12 for the duration calculation.

7. Recall that modified duration equals duration/(1 + yield/2) for bonds that pay semiannually.

8. Why does duration move up as yields go down? Remember, duration measures the average waiting time for a bond's *present value* dollar. A yield decrease raises the present values of *all* future dollars. But its effect is greater the further into the future the dollar is scheduled to be paid. Hence, the yield decrease shifts the *average* waiting time toward the *later* dollar payments of the bond— longer duration. Conversely, a yield increase causes the further dollars to fall more in present value terms than the nearer dollars, thus reducing the average waiting time, hence duration.

9. As usual, durations are modified.

10. Chapter 21 provides an explanation of the relationship between liquidity and bid-asked spreads.

11. The 0.6311 for the ten-year is arrived at by solving the following simple equation for n (n = number of ten-year notes for each five-year note): five-year weight × five-year duration + ten-year weight × ten-year duration = target duration. In our case, the five-year duration is 4.4320 years, and the ten-year duration is is 7.8836 years. The "target" duration is that of the seven-year, 5.7191, as that is the duration we want to mimic via this pair of bonds. Each weight is the number of bonds multiplied by its price divided by the total portfolio value. The five-year's weight is (1 × 100)/(1 × 100 + n × 94.2225); the ten-year's weight is (n × 94.2225)/(1 × 100 + n × 94.2225).

12. The barbell does not have the same dv01 as the seven-year note because it costs more money—$159.7276 rather than $106.7573. This is easy to fix. Just scale down the five- and ten-year amounts by $106.7573/$159.7276 = 0.6684. That is, instead of 1 five-year, purchase 0.6684 units. And instead of 0.6311 ten-year notes, invest in 0.6684/0.6311 = 0.4218. This preserves the barbell's duration of 5.7191 years, since the percentage allocations to the two bonds have not changed.

13. If you're checking the calculations—which is not a bad idea— realize that the weights in the barbell change. The components

are always 1 five-year note and 0.6311 ten-year notes. But their respective prices change as yields go up and down, as does the price of the barbell, so their weights are not constant.

14. An explanation is in order here. A ten-year bond callable in five years must yield more than a ten-year noncallable of the same issuer and seniority (because the issuer will call when rates fall enough, to the investor's disadvantage), and must also yield more than a five-year noncallable (because the issuer will decline to call when rates rise, to the investor's disadvantage). The rows in Table 13.3 are not meant to imply that all three bonds have the same yield. They are meant to illustrate how differently the bonds react to yield changes from an equal starting point. (A high coupon/yield was chosen as it better highlights the special nature of callability and its interaction with interest-rate risk.)

15. Although not mathematically sophisticated, this approach succeeds at getting to the heart of the matter, provides the correct intuition and, in a crude way, does conform to the approach of the quantitative analysts.

16. I would have termed this "concavity," but market participants are enamored of words containing the letter x (to say nothing of their fear of dental work). Another reason may be that "negative convexity" highlights the fact that investors need to be compensated for accepting something negative, whereas they pay for something positive.

17. We don't analyze options much in this book. Suffice it to say that option values respond positively to increases in volatility, offsetting the negative effect on the callable bond's price.

18. As in note 17, we do not analyze putable bonds in the text. If it makes you feel better, callables are much more common than putables, by a wide margin.

Part V

Chapter 14 (Pages 199–206)

1. Actually, 4-, 13-, and 26-week maturities. Unlike most other money market instruments, U.S. T-bills follow a weekly calendar.
2. Technically, the market quotes this bill as trading at a 4% "discount." A newly issued three-month Treasury bill has 91 days to

maturity (see note 1). So you're really earning $(1/99) \times (365/91) = 4.0515\%$.

3. Money market mutual funds are an example of institutional investors that purchase large denomination bank deposits. Fund investments are limited to maximum 13-month maturities.

4. Caps place a maximum interest rate; floors set a minimum. They are analyzed in Chapter 16.

5. Yen denominated deposits between banks are effected onshore in Japan. Offshore interbank transactions would be known as Euroyen with an associated yen LIBOR. The same applies to other currencies.

6. To avoid confusion, the exchange rate should better be written euro/dollar. Radio reports, though, cannot make this distinction.

7. The SEC oversees the functioning of much of the capital markets in the United States. Registration is a process that includes providing a host of information (such as audited income statements over a number of years, affiliations of key corporate officers, etc.) to potential investors.

8. A *letter* of credit, on the other hand, is indeed a *credit* provision (compared to the *liquidity* provision of a line of credit). In this case, the bank steps in precisely when the firm's credit condition deteriorates. In fact, because the bank is the ultimate guarantor of the commercial paper in this case, the interest rate on the paper reflects the bank's creditworthiness more so than the issuing firm's.

9. This is technically incorrect. As explained in Chapter 22, a repo consists of a sale of securities plus an agreement to repurchase the securities at a specified later date.

Chapter 15 (Pages 207–213)

1. Other possible reference rates include a Treasury bill interest rate or the "prime" interest rate of banks.

2. Actually, if the FRN issuer has no default risk, the note should pay the Treasury bill rate, which is below LIBOR.

3. Well, not exactly. If the yield curve is positively sloped, we learned in Chapter 8 that this implies market expectations of increasing rates. In turn, this means that the rate on longer-term

fixed-coupon instruments will reflect the higher future (or forward) interest rate. So, to be really correct, the sentence in the text needs to be reworded: FRNs are suitable for investors expecting interest rates to rise *more* than the market expects, as implied by the yield curve. Otherwise, a fixed-coupon bond would be preferable.

4. Is there an actual formula to price a floating-rate note, similar to that in Chapter 3 for fixed-coupon bonds? At first glance it would seem impossible to have a formula, since the future cash flows are unknown. If we don't know what LIBOR will be in the future, we don't know what the note will pay, so how can we price it? Hence it seems that we can't value the note using the basic principle of finance, that the price of an asset equals the present value of future cash flows. But professionals do use a formula—they just insert the word "expected" into the end of the previous sentence. How do they calculate expected LIBOR? They use the implied forward interest rates from actual LIBOR rates of various maturities, just as was done in analyzing the yield curve in Chapter 8. Once these are calculated (and the FRN's spread is added to each forward rate), the formula simply adds up the discounted *expected* future cash flows, similar to the approach that led to the fixed-coupon bond price in Chapter 3.

5. The entries in Table 15.1 abstract from the difference between LIBOR and Treasury yields. They are not equal; the assumption is simply that they move together (i.e., that the risk of the banking sector is constant).

6. I would be remiss if I did not mention another risk factor concerning floaters, at least in a note. It's empirically relatively small, so keeping it here is okay. Table 15.1 states that changes in LIBOR, the base rate of FRNs, does not affect the price of floaters. This is technically true only if the note is at par. This section showed that a change in the issuer's credit condition can cause its FRN to move away from par. Suppose it is trading at a premium to par. Then an increase (decrease) in LIBOR will cause the price to decline (rise), similar to the reaction of a fixed-coupon bond. But if it is trading at a discount to par, an increase (decrease) in LIBOR causes its price to rise (decline)!

Chapter 16 *(Pages 215–226)*

1. The name of the note, you see, should truly be "negative" floater, not "inverse." Negative words, however, don't appeal to investors, so Wall Street avoids them!

2. The method for deriving forward rates from observed market rates is discussed in Chapter 8.

3. In fact, this is how the market establishes the fixed portion of the inverse floating-rate note's coupon in the first place. Given the yield curve in the second column of Table 16.1, the fixed component of the inverse floater must pay 8% so that it "breaks even" with its plain vanilla floating-rate note (and fixed-coupon bond) counterpart. It is just another version of the basic NFL (no free lunch) rule of finance: securities of the same issuer and maturity must produce the same return to maturity if market expectations are realized.

4. This is an approximation because it ignores reinvestment of the coupons until the notes mature. (See Chapter 4 on reinvestment risk.)

5. We've come across this idea in callable bonds (Chapter 3 and later in Chapter 13), in the convexity feature of fixed-coupon bonds (Chapter 13), and in convertible securities (Chapter 10).

6. Or, if the issuer has credit risk, the note would pay less than the full credit spread.

7. Now you're ready to appreciate the "built-in" floor in an inverse floating-rate note. Although LIBOR can rise above the fixed spread in the inverse floater's coupon, the rate can never fall below 0%. This has two implications. First, the implicit floor benefits the investor. Hence, the coupon is somewhat reduced to pay for it. Second, an increase in LIBOR volatility (for an unchanged LIBOR *level*) enhances the value of the floor, raising the price of an inverse floater.

8. Caps and floors are also sold as stand-alone products (by banks, dealers, hedge funds). For example, a borrower has an outstanding floating-rate note, paying LIBOR plus 2%, with five years remaining. Fearing a sharp increase in rates, the borrower can buy a 6% cap. By doing so he or she receives from the cap seller the difference between LIBOR and 6% whenever LIBOR is greater

than 6% on the coupon reset dates. The FRN borrower/cap buyer makes a regular (e.g., semiannual) payment to the cap seller of, say, 1.5%, or makes one large up-front payment. Similarly, an investor with a plain vanilla FRN can separately purchase a 2% floor, which would pay the difference between 2% and LIBOR whenever LIBOR is below 2%.

9. The note will specify the grade of oil (e.g., West Texas Intermediate) and whether the relevant oil price is taken from the spot (cash) market or from futures contracts.

10. The options embedded in range floaters are actually different from those embedded in the other examples. They are structured as "digital options" (which make a fixed payoff once a threshold—in this case the range bounds—is breached).

Chapter 17 (Pages 227–248)

1. This is actually the *maximum* length of time the swap contract is to be in effect, although it may terminate earlier. With a corporate bond, a default by the borrower ends the bond's life (and forces early repayment of the principal). Similarly, a default by either of the parties to a swap results in early termination of the contract.

2. Semiannual frequency calls for payments every six months, plus resetting the floating rate on each of those dates. Quarterly frequency is also quite common. A bit confusing, but typical, is an interest-rate swap in which the fixed payment is semiannual and the floating payment is quarterly. In any case, since the payments are not for a complete year, the day-count conventions mentioned in Chapter 1 apply here.

3. Yes, I know that the popular press uses these words (and some market participants do as well). This doesn't mean that they're right.

4. Not exactly. This implication is technically true only if the counterparties have entered the swap on a stand-alone basis. As we see in Chapter 18, investors (and others) use swaps in conjunction with bonds and a variety of cash instruments. They do not necessarily have a view on the direction of interest rates.

5. Why has the fixed rate changed? Market participants have revised upward their expectations for LIBOR over the next five years.

6. Of course, a bank's risk is crucially related to the quality of its loan portfolio (plus its equity cushion and, where relevant, government support). Thus, there is a large degree of commonality between swap spreads and corporate bond yield spreads.

7. Or half those amounts every six months if the periodicity is semiannual.

8. The reason for the word "essentially" in the first sentence of this paragraph is that the dv01s of the two alternative strategies—buy and then sell the bond versus enter a five-year swap to receive fixed then offset by paying fixed—are not exactly the same. Recall from Chapter 12 that duration, hence dv01, is also a function of yield. Since the interest-rate swap's fixed rate is the five-year Treasury yield plus the swap spread, it effectively has a higher yield than the Treasury, modestly reducing its dv01.

9. This is not as restrictive as it might seem. Empirically, the swap spread shows much less volatility than U.S. Treasury interest rates. This implies that, on average, a swap position can substitute for a Treasury bond position, but because of swap spread volatility, the net profit/loss will not be perfectly duplicated (but will be in the same direction).

10. Let me clear up possible ambiguity in some of the middle column entries. With the Treasury yield unchanged, the swap spread widening more *or* less than the Treasury yield means an increase in the spread. Symmetrically, with the Treasury yield unchanged, the swap spread narrowing more *or* less than the Treasury yield means a decrease in the spread.

11. This number is arrived at by discounting the product of 0.15% × 100 by 1.056 (because the new five-year swap rate is 5.6%), compounded, for five years.

12. In the language of the marketplace, "the net present value of a pure derivative is zero."

13. Think about purchasing a 5.75% coupon five-year bond, at par. A few days later, the market is such that the yield on the bond drops to 5.6%. Is the bond worth more than par? Sure. How do you know? Because you can sell it at a price above par due to its coupon now being above the required yield to maturity.

14. Indeed, this observation explains the choice of the word "derivative" for these financial contracts. In mathematics, derivative refers to the

effect a change in one variable has on another related variable. If there is no change, the derivative equals zero. Just like swaps!

15. We would have arrived at the same conclusions concerning counterparty risk had we considered the case of a speculator *paying* a fixed rate on a swap in order to profit from an interest-rate increase. If the swap rate increases, it presents a positive present value to the speculator. A dealer default erases this. Conversely, should swap rates decline, the dealer has positive value, and the speculator's default wipes it out.

16. It is interesting, and sensible, that a greater degree of credit risk is more likely to be reflected in increased collateral rather than a wider spread in the swap rate. This is certainly not the case with corporate bonds. Any factor raising the risk of default and/or the likely loss in the event of default will result in a widening of the credit spread (see Chapter 9). This cannot be the case with swaps. Say the risk of default increases for both counterparties. The fixed-rate receiver demands a wider spread, and the fixed-rate payer demands a narrower spread. Obviously, both cannot happen. But they both can post additional collateral.

17. The counterparties may agree at the outset to mark-to-market and adjust collateral only upon a minimum move in swap rates, or swap value.

18. Note that a five-year swap (receive fixed, pay floating), for example, can be hedged with, say, an opposite ten-year swap (pay floating, receive fixed) position. This is parallel to the discussion in Chapter 12 of hedging a five-year Treasury note by shorting a ten-year note. And, just as we explain there, the five-year/ten-year swap hedge ratio is calculated by the ratio of the dv01s, and is subject to yield curve risk.

19. Bid-offer spreads are discussed at length in Chapter 21.

20. Exactly how "happy" is A? Were A to offset the swap now, he'd need to receive 5% and pay LIBOR. This would result in a negative cash flow of 1% on $1 million for the next seven years (pay 6%, receive LIBOR on the first swap; receive 5%, pay LIBOR on the second). As explained above, the present value of this cash flow is the (negative) value of the swap to A. So canceling it amounts to negating this negative value, which quantifies how happy A is. And this is exactly how sad B is, since offsetting it would have produced this exact positive value.

21. There is no one "inflation rate." The counterparties will choose the index from which the inflation rate is to be calculated. The most common is the consumer price index, as compiled by the U.S. Bureau of Labor Statistics. Recall from Chapter 7 that this is the index used in the U.S. Treasury's inflation-protected securities.

22. These swaps actually have a zero coupon structure, with the cumulative cash flows exchanged between the counterparties only at the contract's end, making them similar to the cash flow structure of U.S. style TIPS (see Chapter 7).

Chapter 18 (Pages 249–262)

1. Notice the similarity between this choice and that between the two sides of an interest rate swap, as analyzed at the beginning of the previous chapter. Indeed, it is more than similar; it is parallel.

2. Of course, unlike the five-year note, the ten-year will need to be sold prior to its maturity, with the attendant price risk. Furthermore, the five-year presents reinvestment risk on the coupons, so the yield is not totally locked in. Nevertheless, with respect to the risk parameters under consideration in this chapter, the five-year Treasury is a proper contrast to the Treasury bill.

3. The expected increase must be substantial enough so that the average floating interest rate over the five years meets or exceeds the fixed rate that could have been locked in.

4. Commercial paper and LIBOR, as do most (investment grade) money market instruments, display a very high positive correlation, which allows us to characterize commercial paper as paying LIBOR plus a spread.

5. Chapter 15 explains the structure of a floating-rate note, and it shows that it presents floating interest-rate and fixed credit exposure.

6. We understand clearly the underlying economic expectations that would drive an investor to strategy 5 or 6. What about strategy 3 or 4? An investor may believe that rates are set to rise but is worried about credit deterioration (stagflation, perhaps). This calls for strategy 3. Anticipation of credit improvement together with interest-rates declining (the economy exiting from stagflation) point to strategy 4. Strategies 1 and 2 target investors who take no credit risk.

7. Remember from Chapter 3 that a bond's price rises above par in response to lower market yields because an above-market coupon is to be paid until the bond's maturity. If the bond is maturing now, then the premium vanishes.

8. Actually, investors with the ability to leverage their portfolios, such as a hedge fund, could theoretically borrow funds to purchase credit risky instruments, with the maturity of the borrowing equal to that of the asset. This cancels the interest-rate exposure. A hedge fund could alternatively short a government bond with maturity matching that of the risky asset. The text's focus is on "long only," nonleveraged investors, who do not generally have these alternatives available to them.

9. Note that the *expected* inflation premium (not the actual) floats.

10. The other entries in Table 18.4 do not solve this problem, either.

11. The actual mechanics for U.S. TIPS are somewhat different. The inflation rate, calculated over a six-month period, precipitates an upward adjustment to the nominal principal on which the fixed real coupon is calculated. But the basic idea is preferred.

12. Technically, these swaps have a zero coupon structure, with the cumulative cash flows exchanged between the counterparties only at the contract's end. The depiction in Figure 18.5 nonetheless retains the essence of the arrangement and is simpler without any loss of generality.

Part VI

Chapter 19 (Pages 265–288)

1. The foreign exchange rates typically quoted in the market and in the financial news media are for "spot" transactions, that is, currency trades for normal settlement. Market participants also transact for "forward" settlement. The currency amounts and rates of exchange are set during the trade, but the counterparties deliver the respective currencies at an agreed-upon date in the future. Forwards are discussed in Chapter 24 in the context of currency speculation.

2. The convention to quote all currencies, including U.S. dollars, per British pound developed naturally. That is, for hundreds of years until relatively recently, the United Kingdom was acknowledged as the foremost global economic power. The United States took

over that position, and hence its currency is now quoted as the pound is, except when it's versus the pound itself. The euro is a different story. The convention for quoting $ per € did not *evolve* because of economic reality; it was *imposed* upon the market.

3. Here's an analogy that you may find useful. Investors, speculators, and the like buy and sell equities. A strong desire by market participants to buy a particular stock raises its price until it elicits enough sellers to make supply and demand equal. But there is no direct effect on the company whose name is on the shares; in particular, its balance sheet is unchanged. However, were the company to buy back its shares using cash it has, the net number of shares in the marketplace would now be lower. Furthermore, the company's balance sheet now shows less cash on the asset side and less equity on the liability side. Conversely, a strong desire by market participants to *sell* reduces the price of shares. The company is not involved. But the company's balance sheet changes if the company itself issues new shares. The central bank is like the company; its name is on the paper called currency.

4. From a definitional standpoint, a foreign bond need not involve currency risk. Many foreign governments, companies, and other entities issue bonds denominated in U.S. dollars. These would qualify as "foreign" solely because of the issuer's location. Since they are dollar denominated, they present no (direct) foreign exchange risk. In fact, their price risk depends heavily on the movements in *U.S.* interest rates. We do deal with these types of bonds in Chapter 20 on emerging markets (where you will see that the emerging market's currency will present *indirect* FX risk).

5. "Spot," as in note 1, refers to the exchange rate in the market for "regular" delivery (as opposed to a "forward" transaction). This is the rate you see quoted in the newspapers.

6. To be precise, the coupon paid in yen needs to be translated to dollars at the ending exchange rate just as the principal is. Since the coupon is so low, it will not make a material difference to the rate of return. Nevertheless, we do account for this effect in the next example.

7. This price is arrived at using the standard yield-price formula presented in Chapter 3 (though the Japanese convention is just slightly different) assuming annual coupons and no accrued interest.

8. Empirically, from the perspective of a U.S.-dollar–based investor, exchange rate volatility has historically accounted for a greater proportion of the return variability in a foreign bond portfolio than has bond yield volatility. This is particularly true for emerging markets.

9. As we will see in the next chapter, governments default as well, though the fear of such is usually relegated to governments of developing countries. We will also see that in such an event recovery of investments is problematic.

10. Lots of people are good at explaining what happened yesterday. I'd like to hear them explain what will happen *today*.

11. "Wait a second," you say. "Didn't you tell me back in the macro-economics chapter that inflation arises when the economy grows faster than its potential growth rate?" Yes, I did. In the short run, that is, over business cycles, inflation is driven by that differential known as the "gap." In the long-run, inflation must be a monetary phenomenon, since spending must be accomplished with liquidity in some form (see the very end of Chapter 6).

12. How this "introduction" is effected is explained in Chapter 6.

13. In the short run, the relationship between liquidity and economic activity is via interest rates (Chapter 6). If a central bank on the gold standard adds too much liquidity, interest rates fall. Aggregate economic activity is stimulated, prices rise (unless the economy is operating well below potential), precipitating the gold/dollar dynamics in the text and the ensuing correction. Conversely, tight liquidity raises interest rates, likely reducing economic activity (relative to potential), with the reverse gold/dollar adjustment process.

14. I said "reflects," not "equals." First, in the short run the level of economic activity relative to potential affects the inflation rate (notes 11 and 13). Second, in the long run, with the economy operating at its potential, inflation equals the growth in liquidity minus the growth in GDP.

15. You might argue that the prices of the computers in the two countries should adjust until their respective prices, recognizing the exchange rate factor, are equal, rather than the exchange rate adjusting. True. But the upcoming analysis in the text will follow equivalently, as you will see. (In fact, the actual price adjustments in the world will likely be some combination of these two.)

16. Market participants refer to this as a "no arbitrage" argument. It goes like this: Suppose the exchange rate were ¥114/$. Under our assumption of zero transportation costs, an American would buy a boatload of Japanese computers, pay ¥67/200/114 = $589 for each, then turn around and sell those computers in the United States for $600 each. Free money is impossible. Everyone would rush to buy the yen, bidding up the exchange rate until it reached ¥112/$. Were the rate to break through ¥112/$, the arbitrage would go the other way, forcing it back to ¥112/$.

17. You might have heard (or read) an analyst (not a currency trader) remark that a particular currency is "over-" or "undervalued." Very likely, the statement is meant relative to "purchasing power parity." For example, say inflation in the United Kingdom was measured as 3% over a particular period and in continental Europe as 2.5%. If the pound depreciated by less than a 0.50% against the euro from the start of that measurement period (and certainly if it appreciated), then the pound would be said to be overvalued against the euro. If it depreciated by more than a 0.50%, it would be described as undervalued.

18. Some academic theoreticians (and institutional investors who subscribe to the "real yield approach") take this a step further. Since all investors look for the highest (risk-adjusted) return, they would all be drawn to the currency offering the highest real interest rate among investable countries. This attraction of capital would drive that rate down and all the others up. In equilibrium, risk-adjusted real interest rates should be equal all over the world!

19. See note 17.

20. Exceptions are the most basic of commodities, such as wheat or iron ore.

21. It doesn't matter who does the currency conversion. If the foreign exporter to the United States receives the dollars, he or she will need to sell those dollars to get the home currency. Either way, this puts downward pressure on U.S. currency.

22. This effect is not the result of oil's dollar denomination. Similar downward pressure on the dollar would occur even if oil were denominated in the currency of the oil exporter. Say Saudi Arabia or Norway raises the price of its oil. The United States would have to give up more dollars in exchange for riyals and krones to pay for the same number of barrels imported.

23. Some qualification is in order when it is the central bank of an emerging economy, as we will see in Chapter 20.

24. When a central bank buys foreign currency, not only does it add to the supply of its own currency in the market but it removes the foreign currency. However, this is only temporary. The bank will likely use the FX to purchase interest-bearing assets denominated in the currencies, thus returning the supply to the market.

25. So what is to be done? There is no easy answer. Obviously, policy makers face a trade-off, and the choice often is as much political as it is macroeconomic.

26. Some countries peg their currency to a weighted average of foreign currencies, which is known as a "basket peg."

27. A regime that allows some movement of the currency within a relatively tight "band" around a peg is quite common. Also common is a "crawling" peg, which adjusts the peg periodically according to a disciplined formula (often reflecting inflation differentials, as per the PPP discussion above).

28. Because Mexico shares a border with the United States, many of the impediments to PPP listed earlier vanish.

Chapter 20 (Pages 289–297)

1. On the other hand, when international institutions offer aid to "less developed countries," just watch them line up.

2. This is not to say that industrialized countries cannot default. Indeed, the global macroeconomic and market turmoils of 2008 and 2009 revealed the possibility—at least in the minds of market participants—of default by some of the hitherto strongest economies. In "normal" times this possibility is considered remote enough for their government debt to be considered credit risk-free.

3. In U.S. dollar terms, per capita GDP of industrialized countries run in the tens of thousands, while in developing countries the figure is thousands on the high end, hundreds on the low end.

4. Another implication is the sparseness of a middle class. In examining the history of industrialized countries, it seems that members of the lower class find their escape to the middle class through hard work, if and when available. Members of the middle class, in turn, look to rise out via entrepreneurship. Entrepreneurship is an

integral component of long-term potential GDP expansion. It is responsible, for example, for much of the growth spurts in the United States since its establishment and is a vital part of any rebound from recession. The interaction in developing countries between poverty and the paucity of a middle class, and indeed their mutual reinforcement, is a major barrier to growth.

5. Often a "band" around a central rate is chosen as opposed to one exact number. This gives the currency some room and relieves the central bank from intervening in the market at every slight exchange rate movement.

6. Indeed, this is what happened to Mexico in 1994. A recession forced the hand of the central bank. It lowered interest rates, but the peg, of course, collapsed. Foreign capital fled, and the recession deepened markedly until the Bank of Mexico was bailed out by the U.S. Federal Reserve.

7. This was an important aspect of the unstable situation in Southeast Asia in the second half of the 1990s. Low interest rates also resulted in easy money, which ultimately found its way to bad loans and default.

8. This seems to have been China's policy in the decade of the 2000s.

9. Indeed, this is why the debt rating agencies tend to assign a higher grade to own currency-denominated debt of developing countries than to debt denominated in the currencies of the major industrialized economies.

10. The CDS product is explained in detail in Chapter 23.

11. Corporate credit analysts would refer to this as a "mixed" ratio, since the numerator is extracted from the central bank's (that is, the "country's") balance sheet, whereas the denominator comes from the trade account (that is, the country's "income statement" vis-à-vis the rest of the world).

Part VII

Chapter 21 (Pages 301–320)

1. This is not to say that a financial intermediary cannot perform both functions—dealer and broker. Most large entities do. A grocery store can employ a butcher as well as sell you the meat. But these are separate functions.

2. Note that this is *not* because the dealer is holding the bond in order to speculate on a price increase. Rather, it simply takes time to locate a buyer.

3. Notice that the credit risk of the corporate bond is not what causes the wider bid-offer spread (it causes a wider *credit* spread in the bond's yield—Chapter 9). Rather, the existence of the credit risk reduces the number of clientele, in turn forcing a wider spread.

4. As we will shortly see, dealers require capital, and its scarcity (and cost) can be a significant barrier to becoming a dealer.

5. If the dealer already owns the security, then we're back to the previous situation (where the dealer purchases the bond and must search for a buyer), aren't we?

6. Another reason the dealer may be anxious to sell is that holding onto securities requires paying for them, hence borrowing funds and incurring financing charges. Additionally, it requires capital, which is scarce and costly. We'll see this later in our discussion of dealer financing arrangements.

7. A dealer may be concerned about making another dealer aware that he has bonds that need to be sold. As a result, the dealer may employ a broker to find another dealer and identify himself (if at all) only after the trade is agreed to. These intermediaries are known as "interdealer brokers."

8. We'll learn the mechanics or how this is done later in the chapter.

9. This is not a perfect hedge, as it leaves the dealer with what is known as "basis risk," as explained in Chapter 12.

10. If the dealer already owned the bond, we'd be back in the situation we just examined, wouldn't we?

11. There's a timing issue here. Government bonds normally are settled the day after the transaction. That is, if the dealer purchases the bond on Monday, payment needs to be made (and the bonds delivered) on Tuesday. The financing can be arranged on Tuesday, as long as the funds are available that day (which is the case with repurchase agreements, as we are about to see). Other bonds can have a longer delay between the trade date and settlement date. A corporate bond purchased Monday does not require payment until Thursday. The dealer can wait until Thursday to get the funds, as long as those funds are available that same day. If borrowed

funds arrive the next day (as can be the case with commercial paper, for example), the dealer must arrange to issue the paper Wednesday so that the funding can arrive in time. The point is that financing vehicles have shorter settlement delays than bond transactions, sometimes none at all. Hence the dealer can buy a bond today and worry about paying for it tomorrow or later.

12. The dealer is entitled to the interest that has accrued over the days of his or her ownership of the bond. It equals the bond's coupon multiplied by the fraction of the year the bond was held by the dealer.

13. Actually, the relevant measure is the "current yield" (see Chapter 3)—the coupon divided by the bond's price, since the dealer did not necessarily pay par for the bond.

14. Of course, the dealer hopes the bid-offer spread will more than make up for the negative net carry.

15. Another reason may be that, as Chapter 22 explains, some bond dealers run a "matched book." This typically involves longer-term financing.

16. The events of 2008 have opened a new avenue of financing for dealers. If part of a qualifying investment bank, the dealer may borrow directly from the Federal Reserve. (See Chapter 6 for an explanation of the "discount window" and how it affects liquidity in the macroeconomy.)

17. This would very likely be another dealer who has purchased the bond and not sold it as yet, hence is looking for financing. (The same situation our dealer confronted in the previous case.) Another likely candidate is a hedge fund, purchasing bonds with leverage (see Chapter 24), or an investor looking to add yield to a portfolio by lending the bond and acquiring more cash to invest (Chapter 22).

18. Remember, "actively traded" translates into "liquid" which, in turn, means a narrow bid-offer spread.

19. It is unlikely to be drastically different since the economy, hence interest rates, does not usually experience major shifts within three months.

20. Basis risk can go the other way, too. The yield on the bond purchased can rise, say, by 2 bps, and that of the hedge by 7 bps. Since the dealer is short the hedging bond, he or she will make

more money on its price decline than lose on the original bond. Indeed, the yield changes on the two bonds can even go in opposite directions. It is unlikely, but it is possible.

21. There is a "carry" consideration in all these cases for the dealer. When the dealer owns the bond and finances it, the dealer earns the bond's yield and pays the repo rate. The difference, as we've seen above, is the net carry. The dealer is also short the hedging bond. With respect to this position, the dealer *pays* the bond's yield, and *receives* the (reverse) repo rate. There is net carry here as well, as we've seen. Putting both sets together, the dealer earns (or pays, if negative) the "net, net carry!"

22. Should yields go down while the corporate bonds are held in inventory so that the bonds are ultimately sold at a higher price, the Treasures will need to be purchased to cover the short at a higher price as well, thus offsetting the gains. But that's what hedging means—it works both ways.

23. The first was that yields on benchmark Treasury issues and others of similar maturity do not move perfectly in tandem. We might term this a form of liquidity risk.

24. When this does occur, it is known as a "parallel shift in the yield curve."

25. Another way to describe this risk is by noting that the swap with A has a negative value to the dealer now that swap rates are 7%. Had B still been around, that swap would have had a positive value, offsetting the negative of the first. With B gone, the dealer has no offset.

26. After all, the fixed swap rate equals the Treasury yield plus a swap spread. We go through a number of such scenarios in Chapter 17.

Chapter 22 (Pages 321–340)

1. U.S. government bonds are typically quoted in thirty-seconds (e.g., 100:1 means 100 plus 1/32). The text uses decimals for simplicity.

2. For instance, suppose the bond is at par. By adding accrued interest (next section) the bond is worth, say, $100.5. If the repo rate is 2%, then the repurchase price would be $100.5 + .02 \times (1/360) \times \$100.5 = \$100.5056$ (money market interest rates generally assume a 360-day year).

3. In a market sense (though perhaps not in a legal sense since MM has "purchased" the bond) the dealer "owns" the bond between Tuesday and Wednesday. As the owner, the dealer is entitled to the bond's interest for that day.

4. It is actually the bond's "current yield." If the bond is not far from par, current yield and yield to maturity are nearly equivalent (see Chapter 3).

5. Notice the impact of correlation. If the creditworthiness of the dealer and the market price of the bond are perfectly negatively correlated—the bond's price rises when the dealer is closer to default and vice versa—then MM has zero risk. MM is at risk solely to the extent that there is less than perfect negative correlation. Said the other way, the repo lender faces more risk the more correlated the borrower's fortunes are with the price of the bond. This is exactly the same point made in the discussion of secured corporate bonds in Chapter 10 (and the senior tranche of a CDO forthcoming in Chapter 23). There, the lender's only risk lies in the possible positive correlation between the corporate issuer and the collateral.

6. A later section discusses repos that span longer than one day. Haircuts on these repos will generally be deeper, since a longer period increases the possibility of the dealer defaulting and/or the bond price declining.

7. If it were held in inventory, we'd be in the long position discussed earlier.

8. A second dealer would, in fact, be the most likely candidate as counterparty. Why? By their very nature, dealers borrow money to hold inventory, as our dealer did in the previous example. This is particularly true if the bond in question is a benchmark Treasury, as dealers own much of the issue during its distribution from the government to ultimate investors. If it is an older issue, dealers are less likely to own it (and be in need for financing). That situation is covered later in this chapter.

9. Got it? If not, you can read all about it in Chapter 24 as an example of a "yield enhancement" strategy.

10. Chapter 21 on dealers goes through this process more carefully.

11. Corporates (and mortgages) also present credit risk. Selling short Treasuries, therefore, leaves the dealer with basis risk, as discussed Chapter 21. This can be hedged through various credit derivatives

(see Chapter 23). Note that selling Treasuries short to hedge securities in position is done in a way that makes the net exposure "duration neutral," as explained in Chapter 12.

12. Note 11 applies here as well but, of course, in the reverse direction.

13. Dealers do these trades as well, as part of their proprietary trading activities (Chapter 21).

14. Relative value trades can also involve derivatives, if they are available for those securities. In such cases, no financing with repo or borrowing with reverse repo is necessary. See Chapter 24.

15. This is compounded by the fact that some investors have a policy of not lending their bonds.

16. The more technical term for this situation is that the bond in question is being financed at a "special collateral" rate as opposed to the general collateral rate.

17. Also known as "weighted-average maturity," this recognizes the phenomenon that mortgages can be repaid prior to their stated maturity, which is somewhat similar to an amortizing bond (Chapter 2).

18. Market participants refer to this as "when issued" ("w.i.") trading.

19. Assuming the three months to the next auction contains the typical 91 days.

20. The calculation is simple, though perhaps not obvious. We calculate the dv01 of the bond to be 0.077983. We know that a yield change produces a price change according to the "bond price sensitivity equation" in Chapter 12: the change in price of a bond equals the bond's dv01 multiplied by the change in its yield, given in basis points. Since we know the change in price to be 0.6319, we solve this equation in reverse and find the yield change to be 0.08%.

21. This choice is not unlike that of the corporate or other institutional borrower in Chapter 8 choosing between short- and long-term debt instruments. The slope of the bond yield curve reflects the choices of these market participants. The repo desk's choice, along with those of other dealers doing the same thing, helps determine the shape of the repo yield curve.

Chapter 23 (Pages 341–369)

1. Don't confuse a credit derivative with the credit *risk* inherent in any derivative. Credit risk (also known as "performance risk") refers to

the possibility that a counterparty to any derivative contract will not perform according to the contract's terms, whether it is an interest-rate, foreign exchange, or, indeed, a credit derivative contract.

2. Not all bond reference securities begin at par. Had the starting price been 101, the change would be $(101 - 99)/101 = 1.98\%$, and this would have been subtracted from the bond's coupon.

3. Replacing bond BBB with a group, or portfolio, of bonds turns the swap into a "basket" TRS. If the basket comprises an entire bond index, it is an index-linked swap. The applications in the text apply similarly to these products.

4. These spread savings may well be priced into the swap's spread over LIBOR.

5. Indeed, investors can also use the TRS as a hedging instrument. Worried abut a decline in price for bond BBB, the investor contracts to *pay* the bond's total return and receive LIBOR plus a spread. Should bond BBB's price actually fall before the swap's term ends, the investor is *paid* the drop in price, thus offsetting the actual bond's price decline.

6. This is rather complicated. An arbitrageur can borrow funds (through a repurchase agreement—see Chapter 22) to buy the corporate bond plus purchase protection on it with a CDS. At the same time, he or she shorts a Treasury bond (through a reverse repo). This being riskless, it forces the CDS premium to reflect the relationship between the corporate spread and the difference between the repo and reverse repo rates.

7. People like to say this. But it's not exactly true. Speculating on default *was* possible before the advent of credit default swaps—by selling short the bonds of a company thought to be on the verge of defaulting. Say the bond was borrowed (through a reverse repo) and sold short by the speculator at $90. It subsequently defaults with a recovery value of $60. The speculator then purchases the bond in the distressed debt market for $60 and returns it to the bond lender for a profit of $30. So this sort of speculation, while possible, required the ability to borrow corporate bonds. Furthermore, while the trader is short, he or she would need to purchase Treasury bonds (financed with repo) to hedge the interest-rate risk in the short corporate position. All this is unnecessary when employing a CDS.

8. The exact nature of this discounting process is discussed below.

9. Unless the original contracts stipulated otherwise, the two dealers have the right to refuse the assignment. They can argue that they had agreed to accept the performance risk of the investor as counterparty, not the other dealer. One way to convince the dealers to accept assignment is by adjusting the terms of the swap or reducing the lump sum payment (or promising future business!).

10. Here's how I arrived at this figure. The net value of the contract is $100,000 (1% − the difference between the original 4% protection cost and the 5% current cost—multiplied by the notional $10 million) over each of the next four years. Now we need to get the present discounted value of that stream of payments. So discount each year's payment by 1 + 0.085, compounded according to the year. Why 8.5%? Because it equals the current 5% Xerox credit spread, plus the 3.5% U.S. Treasury rate which we assume to be unchanged.

11. In order to more regularize CDS collateral (hence reduce counterparty risk), market participants in 2009 agreed to "fix" the CDS premium. This will make the CDS structure and its mark to market similar to that of a corporate bond. CDS contracts on investment grade bonds, for example, might trade with a 1% spread. This means that if a CDS is entered into on company X, whose market spread is 3%, there will be an up-front payment by the protection buyer of the present value of 2% times the notional amount, discounted over the term of the swap (as in the previous note). If the market spread for X is 0.75%, the protection *seller* makes an up-front payment equal to the present value of 0.25%, etc. Only if the market spread equals the fixed spread of 1% will there be no payment at inception. This would be considered a "par" situation.

12. There is, however, a collateral requirement, as we have seen, and this may require funds to be set aside. The next section shows how this is handled.

13. Some may argue that the events of 2008 were both the result of, and contributed to, a "bust" in these very same structured products. Whether or not that is true, this class of derivatives is here to stay, albeit perhaps in evolving form.

14. You can call this leverage—the same $100 million is exposed twice.

15. Although "CDO" technically refers to the bonds issued by the special purpose entity, market participants (and financial news writers) often use the term CDO to refer to the entire deal structure, even when they really mean SPE.
16. For ease of exposition, we are assuming that the SPV holds only fixed-rate bonds and issues fixed-rate liabilities. In practice, it will also (sometimes exclusively) hold loans, which typically pay a floating rate, and issue floating-rate notes. As well, just for simplicity, we assume the commercial paper pays 4%, even though commercial paper rates vary as they are rolled over.
17. For simplicity, the value of the assets purchased by the SPE equals the funds raised from selling the debt tranches. Normally some of the funds are used to pay investment banks, underwriters, legal fees, rating agency charges, and other expenses.
18. Or, to the extent there is recovery value, more than $100 million need to default in order to hurt the seniors.
19. PIK bonds are discussed at length in Chapter 9.
20. It is in the SPE's interest to receive an AAA rating for the senior tranche, because this greatly reduces the interest expense. Moody's Investors Service requires calculation of the portfolio's "diversity score" as one of the factors upon which its rating is based.
21. Notice that the inverse of this ratio parallels the leverage ratio of Chapter 9 (and Chapter 24 to follow), the key measure of credit risk for a corporation (and hedge fund).
22. The dynamics of the cash distribution are known as the "waterfall." Following a rain, each cliff along the waterfall's route accumulates water only if the cliff above it is saturated. You'll see the analogy directly.
23. Note that even if they were floating rate notes, their prices would decline, since the credit spreads on floaters are fixed (see Chapter 15).
24. This is an important point, lost on many investors and observers during the "collapse" of the structured securities market in 2008 and 2009. A decline in price of a bond reflects deterioration, which does not necessarily become default. Historically, most (reasonably) deteriorated corporate bonds are good for their money at maturity.

25. How did I get this number? Easy. The portfolio manager needs to sell enough bonds so that the ending O/C ratio is at least 1.3. Before he sells anything, the assets have been reduced to $350 million due to the defaults in group Z. The senior tranche is down to $291 million, having already received $9 million from the asset's interest payments to the SPE. The manager sells Y^* from group Y, using the proceeds to pay off more of the senior tranche, so that ($350 million $- Y^*$)/($291 million $- Y^*$) = $1.3 million. Solving this for Y^* gives us the requisite number in the text.

26. Actually, the loss would have been slightly less since the bonds in group Z have higher coupons, so their survival would have provided more income to the SPE.

Chapter 24 (Pages 371–393)

1. If this is not clear, think of it this way. The hedge fund manager participates in the upside of an investment's performance. On the downside (unless the fund manager's own money is in the pool), losses are absorbed by the clients. Not so different from the equity position in a company compared to debt.

2. Mechanics of repurchase agreements are presented in Chapter 22.

3. The purpose of the haircut, of course, is to provide a cushion to the lender. Should the hedge fund default, the security can decline in value and still cover the fund's debt obligation. For this reason, the size of haircuts increases with the volatility of the security being financed. These ideas are covered more completely in Chapter 21 on dealers and Chapter 22, which is devoted to repurchase agreements.

4. Repos are generally overnight. Long-term repo typically extends just a few months, if that. Bonds have long maturities. Thus the net carry depends on the steepness of the yield curve. (Now it is clear why it is said that the steeper the yield curve, the greater the profits for financial institutions such as banks, dealers, and hedge funds.)

5. We haven't covered options in this book. Had we, another example would be a hedge fund purchasing a bond and *selling* options on the bond. This would be an explicit form of yield enhancement via options, compared to the similar, but implicit, form explained in the text. Now you can understand how hedge funds *hedge* the

options embedded in the callable, PIK, and other such bonds—they *purchase* explicit options.

6. Interest rates for different maturities display different volatilities. Furthermore, if the hedge fund owns corporate bonds, then the volatility of the bond's credit spread needs to be recognized along with the pure yield volatility. Once we become more careful in this manner, we need to incorporate the correlations of the different components of volatility relevant to the fund's portfolio, and we arrive at the industry standard risk measure, known as VAR, or "value at risk."

7. Forwards are technically a type of derivative instrument. The counterparties agree to all the terms of their trade today—currency pair, exchange rate, size of transaction, settlement date—but do not carry out their obligations until the future date. Indeed, the full name of this agreement is a *forward contract*.

8. In case you're wondering, there is an arbitrage mechanism that ensures that developments in the currency spot market are mirrored in the forward markets.

9. I chose to discuss gold in this foreign exchange context because I believe gold functions more as a currency—a global one, that is—than as a commodity (see Chapter 19 on foreign exchange for elaboration).

10. An alternative to purchasing the bond would be to enter a kroner interest-rate swap as the fixed-rate receiver. This produces the desired interest-rate exposure without (except for the collateral marking to market) the exchange rate exposure.

11. There is something the hedge fund could have done, even in the old days. Simultaneously with purchasing the corporate bond, the trader would short the benchmark government bond of similar maturity. This hedges the interest rate risk and retains the pure credit exposure. But this would require financing the corporate bond as well as engaging in a reverse repurchase agreement for the government bond, with the transactions costs plus net carry considerations this set of trades would entail. Credit default swaps obviate all of this.

12. Fund managers are not limited to speculating on individual names. Credit default swap contracts are available on *portfolios* of bonds, also known as bond *indices*. These contracts are termed CDX.

13. The dynamics described in this paragraph go a long way to explaining (at least the first wave of) the huge defaults by hedge funds and dissolutions of major financial institutions in 2008. Indeed, one more step can be added. Upon default of the hedge fund, the lending institution takes ownership of the collateral, the security in question. Having no desire to hold the security, the lender sells into the falling market and exacerbates the price decline.

14. Granted, as a nonbenchmark ("off-the-run" in market lingo), the bond should yield more. But 10 bps more than the benchmark ("on-the-run") is too high a cost for reduced liquidity, in the trader's opinion.

15. "The curve" refers to the yield curve formed from benchmark" government bonds.

16. Actually, the number of benchmark bonds to sell against the older bond purchased in order to hedge the overall market exposure is not one for one. As we learned in Chapter 12 (and as we will need to recognize in the following sections), the proper hedge ratio is the ratio of the dv01s of the two bonds. However, as their maturities are close and both bonds are not too far from par, a one-for-one trade is approximately correct.

17. Professionals consider another factor before instituting a relative value trade—the "net carry." The hedge fund will likely borrow funds (net of the haircut—see earlier in the chapter) to purchase the older bond. Hence, the trader will earn the yield on the bond and pay the repo, or financing, rate. As part of the short, she or he will *pay* the yield on the benchmark and *receive* the (reverse) repo rate (Chapter 22 on repos). The net figure may be positive, enhancing the attractiveness of the trade, or negative, imposing a cost on the trade.

18. The hedge must be "managed." That is, if yields shift and the position is maintained, the hedge ratio will not necessarily be constant as durations are sensitive to significant yield changes. Finally, net carry, as explained in note 17, is a consideration as well.

19. This statement means the following. If both the five–seven-year section of the curve and the seven–ten-year section increase or decrease in slope equally, there will be no net gain or loss. Each pair of trades is a yield curve trade on its own, but in opposite

directions. Hence, an equal yield curve shift results in the two trades canceling each other out. The position is exposed only to *relative* yield curve shifts.

20. This trade, reflecting a view as to the relative slopes of two sections of the yield curve, does not necessarily require the sections to be contiguous, as in the text's example. An alternative could have been the five-seven-year pair versus the ten-twenty-year pair. Butterfly trades are typically constructed contiguously. For if the trader believes that the ten–twenty-year section of the curve is out of line with the five–seven-year, then the trader must logically believe that the seven–ten-year section is out of line with either the five–seven-year and/or the ten–twenty-year.

21. The LIBOR payments cancel only if both floating rates on the two swaps are of the same maturity, say three-month LIBOR. The trader could have structured one of the swaps to be against one-month LIBOR, leaving some risk with respect to movements in the short-term LIBOR curve. Similarly, using bonds, the trader could finance one of the bonds with overnight repo and lock in a term repo for the other, thus creating repo curve risk.

22. Until the 1990s, $250 million would have been considered a "large" corporate bond deal. Today, over a billion dollars is quite common.

23. Chapter 14 provides a discussion of LIBOR, the London interbank offered rate, and Chapter 17 demonstrates why the fixed swap payment must reflect market expectations of LIBOR over the term of the swap.

24. For this trade, instead of an individual corporate issuer, the hedge fund's view of credit risk more likely relates to a corporate sector as a whole; for example, the high-grade sector or, perhaps more specifically, the BBB sector. To reflect this view, the hedge fund trader would either purchase a portfolio of bonds reflecting the sector or buy a dealer-created security linked to these bonds. Alternatively, the fund manager can enter into a total return swap referencing an index of corporate bonds, as shown in Chapter 23.

25. Another well-known relative value trade employed by hedged funds involving swaps is known as "strips versus swaps." A "strip" is a series of futures contracts, in this case for interbank deposits known as Eurodollars (*not* the euro currency against the

dollar), for successive settlement dates. Since interest-rate swaps call for LIBOR payments on the floating side, and Eurodollar futures are marked to LIBOR rates, the combined yield for a strip should be similar to the fixed side of a swap. If the respective yields are far apart, the hedge fund will buy the strip and sell the swap, or vice versa, depending on which is cheap and which is rich.

26. Short or long positions in the convertible bond present the hedge fund with interest-rate risk. Hedge funds, as said many times, isolate their risk exposure. The trader will employ Treasury bonds (or interest rate derivatives) to neutralize this exposure in order to concentrate on the conversion relationship. Be aware as well that the "premium" explained in the text and elaborated upon in Chapter 10 is in essence an option. Hedge funds may, therefore, approach this trade from an options perspective, which changes the hedge ratio. And they may utilize call options on the issuer's stock relative to the convertible bond. But we do not cover options in this book so, unfortunately, I must leave it at that.

27. As explained in Chapter 19 on foreign exchange, the focus of this trade should be on *real* interest rates, that is, observed rates less the (expected) inflation rate in the country. This is the implicit assumption of the text.

28. An alternative would be to employ foreign currency-denominated interest-rate swaps in place of actual bonds in the trade. The hedge fund would contract to receive the fixed rate on a sterling interest-rate swap and simultaneously contract to pay fixed on a euro-denominated interest-rate swap. This pair of trades preserves the relative interest-rate exposure desired by the hedge fund. And, because swaps are used in place of actual securities, there is little cash involved (except for the initial collateral and possible mark to market) so that the currency risk is essentially absent.

INDEX

ABOUT THE AUTHOR

Steven I. Dym is a strategist at Marine Capital Partners, a UK-based hedge fund. During his career, he has held positions at Washington Square Capital, the Bankers Trust Company, and the Federal Reserve Bank of New York, and has taught finance and economics at the New York University Graduate School of Business and the University of Minnesota Carlson School of Management.

Printed in the USA
CPSIA information can be obtained
at www.ICGtesting.com
CBHW071924150524
8581CB00008B/85